The

Broken
Mirror

The
Broken
Mirror

UNDERSTANDING AND TREATING BODY DYSMORPHIC DISORDER

Revised and Expanded Edition

Katharine A. Phillips, M.D.

OXFORD
UNIVERSITY PRESS
2005

For my patients and for everyone who has participated in BDD research;

your courage, trust, and generosity have immeasurably increased

understanding of BDD and have made this book possible

———

OXFORD
UNIVERSITY PRESS

Oxford University Press, Inc., publishes works that further
Oxford University's objective of excellence
in research, scholarship, and education.

Oxford   New York
Auckland   Bangkok   Buenos Aires   Cape Town   Chennai
Dar es Salaam   Delhi   Hong Kong   Istanbul   Karachi   Kolkata
Kuala Lumpur   Madrid   Melbourne   Mexico City   Mumbai   Nairobi
São Paulo   Shanghai   Taipei   Tokyo   Toronto

Library of Congress Cataloging-in-Publication Data
Phillips, Katharine A., M.D.
The broken mirror: understanding and treating body dysmorphic disorder /
Katharine A. Phillips, M.D.
p.   cm. Includes index.

ISBN 978-0-19-516719-1

Printed in the United States of America
on acid-free paper

CONTENTS

ACKNOWLEDGMENTS

I want to thank many people and organizations for helping to make this book possible.

I thank my many researcher colleagues for collaborating on the research discussed in this book. While it isn't possible to mention all of them, I'd like to give special thanks to some of my early collaborators, who were very helpful in getting my BDD research off the ground while I was still receiving psychiatry training at McLean Hospital/Harvard Medical School in the late 1980s and early 1990s. They include Drs. Susan McElroy, Harrison Pope, Jim Hudson, and John Gunderson. I'd also like to thank my colleagues at Butler Hospital and Brown Medical School, including Drs. Steven Rasmussen, Jane Eisen, Ray Dufresne, and Lawrence Price, as well as my department chairman, Dr. Martin Keller, and the President/CEO of Butler Hospital, Dr. Patricia Ryan Recupero. Thank you also to Drs. Eric Hollander, Andrew Nierenberg, Scott Rauch, James Kennedy, and David Castle. Drs. Sabine Wilhelm of Massachusetts General Hospital/Harvard Medical School and Rocco Crino of the University of New South Wales in Sydney, Australia, deserve special thanks. They have contributed immeasurably to my knowledge of cognitive-behavioral therapy (CBT) and have offered many wise and valuable insights about treating BDD with CBT. They also kindly reviewed the CBT chapter in this book. I would also like to express my gratitude to Dr. Roberto Olivardia, who also reviewed this chapter, and to Dr. David Veale, who contributed significantly to the CBT chapter in the book's first edition. Thank you also to Barbara van Noppen and Leslie Shapiro, whose input contributed to the chapter for family members and friends. I'd also like to acknowledge and thank my research staff and volunteers over the years for all of the hard work they've done, especially William Menard and Christina Fay, who are interviewing participants in one of my studies.

Without the support of the following organizations, my research and this book would not have been possible. Most of all, I would like to thank the National Institute of Mental Health, which has provided invaluable support over the years for my BDD research, including treatment studies. Thank you also to The National Alliance for Research on Schizophrenia and Depression (NARSAD), Butler Hospital and Brown Medical School, and McLean Hospital and Harvard Medical School. Forest Pharmaceuticals, Solvay Pharmaceuticals, and Eli Lilly and Company have provided unrestricted educational grants that supported greatly needed treatment studies.

I'd also like to thank members of the media for their role in bringing BDD to the attention of the public. Many journalists, producers, television show hosts, and others have produced compelling, accurate, and helpful stories and shows about this disorder. Through these critically important efforts, BDD has come out of the shadows; millions of people have learned about it, and many have gotten effective treatment. This work has made a tremendous difference in people's lives.

And most of all, I'd like to thank my patients and everyone with BDD who has participated in my research and other BDD researchers' studies over the years. It's only through your generous participation that we've learned so much about this devastating illness and how to treat it. By participating in research, you've helped diminish the suffering of countless people, and you've made this book possible.

WHY I'M UPDATING THIS BOOK

Since I wrote the first edition of this book, we've made tremendous strides in understanding the relatively common and devastating illness called BDD. When the first edition of *The Broken Mirror* was published in 1996, very few people—the public or professionals alike—had even heard of BDD. Now, even though it's still underrecognized, the word has gotten out. Many people have heard of BDD, know what it is, and are seeking effective treatment. Because BDD has been hidden for so long, yet causes so much suffering, this progress is enormously gratifying.

When I recently reread this book's first edition, I was struck by how far we've come and that it was time to update it. We still need a lot more research on BDD, so we can understand it even better, but a wealth of very informative BDD research has been done in recent years. We know much more about BDD now than when I wrote the first edition nearly a decade ago, which has enabled me to significantly expand and update this book. This revised edition includes a recommended approach to medication treatment that's much more specific than I could include in the first edition, because more treatment research has been done, and promising new medications have become available. We've also learned a lot about cognitive-behavioral therapy (CBT), so this edition has much more specific information and advice about this treatment. I've also included some CBT treatment forms that may be useful in your own treatment. I've updated many other sections of the book, reflecting the tremendous strides we've made in understanding BDD in recent years.

I'm able to write this revised version largely because of the research that's been done during the past decade. Research allows us to ask questions and systematically seek answers, while minimizing personal biases and expectations. Because of the generous support of funding agencies such as the National Institute of Mental Health, I've been able to focus my research and clinical work on BDD. I've seen and treated many more patients than when I wrote the first edition, and I've conducted much more research, including treatment studies.

Much of what I say in this revised edition comes from two series of people with BDD who participated in my research studies—a total of more than 500 people. This is, to my knowledge, the largest series of people with BDD ever studied. The first series, which I described in the book's first edition, is much larger now. It contains more than 300 individuals who I systematically interviewed in detail. These individuals were seeking an evaluation or treatment from me, and some participated in one of my medication treatment studies. In addition, a newer ongoing study supported by the National Institute of Mental Health has allowed me to obtain information about 200 additional people with BDD. This study, in which people are interviewed once a year for 5 years, is the first to investigate how people with BDD do over time. These participants had the same interview as the first series of people and also answered additional questions. The second study has the advantage of containing what is to my knowledge the broadest, most diverse sample of people with BDD ever studied. Many of the study participants were not seeking or receiving mental health treatment at the time of their first interview (unlike many of the people in my first series), and they're probably therefore more representative of people in the community with BDD. (The demographic characteristics of these two series are shown in Appendix A.) In most ways, these two series of people have very similar BDD features. So to keep things simple, when I describe results from these studies in the book, most of them are for the two groups combined. I've also evaluated and treated hundreds of additional people with BDD who didn't participate in a research study, which has also enriched this edition of the book.

Many other researchers from around the world are also increasingly studying BDD. Their work, which has made extremely important contributions to our understanding of BDD, is also included in this revised edition. For the four-year period 1990 through 1993, PubMed (the National Library of Medicine's listing of peer-reviewed articles published in professional journals) listed only 17 articles on BDD. For the four-year period 1999 through 2002, that number had jumped to 95. Many of these publications are listed in Chapter 18. This important work has been possible only because BDD sufferers have generously participated in these research studies. Because of their generosity, our knowledge of BDD, and clinicians' ability to help people with BDD, has grown enormously.

I hope you find this edition of *The Broken Mirror* informative and helpful, even if you've read the first edition. The purpose of this revision is to help BDD sufferers—as well as family and friends—better understand and overcome this distressing and often-devastating illness. I focus on providing a comprehensive picture of what we know about BDD, as well as practical and useful treatment advice. Based on what we've learned over the years and now know, most people with BDD can overcome this very painful disorder.

The
Broken
Mirror

·· one ··

Why BDD Matters

Millions of people have a secret obsession. They're obsessed with how they look, with a perceived flaw in their appearance. They worry that their nose is too big, their breasts are too small, their skin is blemished, their hair is thinning, their body build is too small—any body part can be the focus of this obsession. It's easy for us to discount these concerns. How can she worry so much about her looks when she's so pretty? Why is he so upset about his hair—it looks fine! But people with these body obsessions suffer greatly, some are severely tormented, some consider suicide.

Most of us care about how we look—we think about our appearance and try to improve it. A recent survey of 30,000 people in the U.S. found that 93% of women and 82% of men care about their appearance and work to improve it. And other surveys have shown that many of us are *dissatisfied* with some aspect of how we look. We're not pretty enough or sufficiently handsome. Who wouldn't like a leaner body, smoother skin, more attractive eyes, a flatter stomach? If we could look better, most of us would. Indeed, most of us try. We wear makeup, buy flattering clothes, check our reflection in mirrors, carefully shave, and curl or straighten our hair, hoping to look okay. But when do normal concerns become an obsession?

The concerns of body dysmorphic disorder (BDD) echo these normal concerns but are more extreme. People who have BDD not only dislike some aspect of how they look, they're *preoccupied* with it. They worry too much. They'd like to worry less, but they can't. Many say they're obsessed.

They also suffer. Their worries about their looks cause them emotional pain and interfere with their life. Some BDD sufferers function fairly well despite their distress—no one would ever know how unhappy they are. Carrie, who worried about slight facial blemishes and her "small" breasts, was sometimes late for work because she got stuck in the mirror checking her face. And she missed parties because she thought she looked so bad she didn't want people to see her. Yet she had many friends and did her job well. Because of his supposedly thinning hair, David had problems concentrating on his school work and missed the prom, but he still got good grades.

But when BDD is severe, friendships, intimate relationships, and work disintegrate. Jane was so tormented by her "huge" nose, "crooked" lip, "big" jaw, "fat and round" buttocks, and "tiny" breasts that she dropped out of school and couldn't keep a job. She stopped dating and seeing her friends. Because she thought she looked so monstrously ugly, she locked herself up in her house for five years, finally even trying to kill herself.

What's so intriguing about BDD is that people who have it focus on defects that others don't see or consider minimal. Ironically, Jane was actually an attractive woman who had none of the defects she abhorred. David's hair looked fine, and Carrie's breasts were somewhat small, but not noticeably so. But to the BDD sufferer, the problem looks hideous and repulsive, magnified by the mind's eye.

BDD concerns don't make sense to others. How can she worry so much about her hair when it's so nice? How could he be so upset about a few pimples? He should just stop thinking about it. "I'm always telling my wife she looks fine," a high school teacher told me. "Why can't she just stop worrying? Wrinkles aren't that important! I tell her this all the time, but it doesn't seem to help." BDD is a problem because these people *can't stop worrying;* reassurance doesn't put an end to their concern.

Of the many patients I've seen over the years, those with BDD have been among the most tormented. As a 21-year-old man said to me, "This obsession is the perfect torture. I'd rather be blind or have my arms cut off. I'd be happy to have cancer, because it wouldn't isolate me the way this does, and people would believe that something was wrong with me. They wouldn't trivialize it. I could talk to people about it, and they'd understand."

Since treating Carrie, David, and Jane, I've met and treated many people with BDD. They have all suffered. Families and friends, girlfriends and boy-friends suffer as well. They worry about their loved one and may endlessly reassure them, hold mirrors, or apply hair tonics—to no avail. They may care for them, pay for surgery, try to find help—for a problem that makes little sense to them. Sometimes they don't even know what the problem is. They know that their loved one is depressed or won't go out, but they don't know why. People with BDD may be too embarrassed to reveal their concern to anyone, even their closest friend or spouse.

After hearing about Carrie's, David's, and Jane's concerns, I decided to learn more about this fascinating and little-known disorder. I hadn't even heard of it during medical school or in the lectures of my psychiatric training. I hadn't noticed any articles about it in scientific journals. I did, however, remember seeing BDD in the psychiatric profession's diagnostic manual. The description there was brief but enough to make me think that Carrie, David, and Jane had this mysterious disorder. I started my search to learn more about it.

I am a physician, a psychiatrist, a clinician, and a researcher. I've been studying BDD and working with people who have this disorder for 15 years. BDD sufferers have come out of hiding; I haven't had to search for them. They've thought that their face is too wide, their stomach is too fat, or their eyes look ugly. Or that their facial muscles are sagging, their skin has marks or scars, their penis is too small, that. . . . The list goes on. Some search endlessly for an elusive physical cure for what actually is a psychiatric disorder. Many go to doctor after doctor—dermatologists, surgeons, and others—without obtaining relief. Some have surgery after surgery without ever being satisfied with how they look.

Many suffer in silence. People with BDD often feel as though they're harboring a burdensome secret no one will ever understand. Many haven't ever told *a single soul* about their appearance concerns—not even relatives, spouses, or close friends. They feel too embarrassed and ashamed. "I feel foolish talking about my concern," one man told me. "The usual reaction is 'What?!'" Or they fear others will think they're vain. And when they finally divulge their secret, and the people they confide in can't see the "defects" or consider them minimal, they feel miserable, isolated, and misunderstood.

One woman hadn't told her husband about her appearance concerns, even though they'd been married 50 years. "It's a barrier between us," she said. "It's something I think about a lot, and that I get upset about, but I've never been able to share it with my husband. Even though he's a very understanding person, I'm afraid he wouldn't understand. This is my one secret."

As Cassandra said, "If only I could tell someone what this is about!" Her words reflected what so many people with BDD feel: "I feel so incredibly ridiculous and vain! I also have a feeling of humiliation and shame. I'm miserable, but I can't explain it. It's such a secret. It's as painful as cancer, but I can't tell anyone and get support."

BDD isn't rare. Secrecy and shame are part of the reason BDD is underrecognized and underdiagnosed. Researchers have found that about 1% of people in the general population have BDD, although studies of students report far higher rates (as high as 13%). BDD is also fairly common in people who receive dermatologic treatment or cosmetic surgery. Taken together, these studies indicate that BDD affects millions of people in the United States alone, and that it's at least as common as many other well-known psychiatric disorders, such as schizophrenia, manic depressive illness, panic disorder, and anorexia nervosa. BDD affects people of all socioeconomic strata and from all walks of life. BDD also occurs around the world—in Japan and other Asian countries, the Middle East, South America, Europe, Canada, Africa, Australia and other countries and continents.

When I started my research, BDD was virtually unknown, even though it's been described for more than 100 years. I myself knew very little about it until some of my patients were courageous enough to reveal their concerns. To learn more about BDD, I've conducted lengthy interviews with hundreds of people with the disorder, the largest sample of this kind. I've also treated hundreds of people with BDD. With other researchers, I've done many additional studies of BDD, which provide the basis for much of the information in this book.

I wrote this book because BDD causes so much suffering, isn't rare, and yet is still very underrecognized. It's a serious and often devastating illness that can even lead to suicide. We all need to know that it exists, how to identify it, and what treatments work. Many of my patients have struggled for years with their obsession, having no idea that it's a known disorder with a name and available treatment. Many are relieved to learn they have an identifiable disorder and that they aren't alone in their suffering. And many have significantly benefited from the treatments I'll describe—medications known as serotonin-reuptake inhibitors (SRIs, or SSRIs) and a type of therapy known as cognitive-behavioral therapy (CBT). With these treatments, some people improve partially; others describe their response as miraculous.

This is a new frontier: we still have much to learn about BDD. Research on BDD is perhaps 30 to 40 years behind that of other major psychiatric disorders, such as depression. But even though our knowledge is incomplete, there's a great deal we already know. I'll describe what's known about BDD—what patients experience, what I and other researchers have learned about it, what treatments are helpful, and how you can help someone with BDD. I will also grapple with some complex questions that have no clear answers but which people often ask: What causes it? Is it related to other psychiatric disorders? How does it compare to the "normal" appearance concerns most of us have? I hope I convey what my patients would want you to know. I also hope that BDD sufferers and their family members will use this book to identify and understand their symptoms and seek effective treatment, for there is hope for BDD sufferers. As Jane said to me, "I can't imagine any suffering greater than this. If I had a choice, I'd rather have cancer. You need to tell people about BDD. Tell them this is a serious disorder."

·· two ··

Patients Speak

*"I'm surprised to hear other people have this problem. I thought
I was the only one."*   **Alex**

Jennifer's Story

*T*his is incredibly embarrassing," Jennifer began. "It's really hard for me to talk
about this. I don't want to be here." She fidgeted anxiously in her chair and
looked at the floor. Her hands shook, and she seemed close to tears. Jennifer
had in fact canceled her first two appointments with me, and she'd finally agreed
to come in only at her mother's insistence. I had spoken briefly with her mother
on the phone, who said she was feeling desperate—her daughter had a serious
problem that neither of them could cope with any longer.

I asked Jennifer if she could explain what was so embarrassing. "I don't like
talking about my problem," she said. "You'll probably think I'm silly or vain.
But I'm not," she said with tears in her eyes. "This is a very serious problem.
I can't even tell you how bad it is." She sat silently for a minute, looking down
anxiously, as if trying to decide what to say and how to express it. "Well, I guess
I should tell you what it is. I think I'm really ugly. In fact, I think I'm one of
the ugliest people in the whole world."

Jennifer was by anyone's standards attractive. She was a 22-year-old woman
with long strawberry-blond hair, large green eyes, and a beautiful complexion.
She reminded me of the captain of my high school cheerleading squad, a pretty
and vivacious young woman. How could Jennifer think she was ugly? What
could she possibly believe was wrong with how she looked? I wondered what it
could be. I couldn't see any flaws anywhere.

At first, Jennifer was reluctant to discuss the details. "Well, I just think I'm
not pretty," she said. "I've felt this way for a long time, and I can't seem to
convince myself I'm wrong. I know what you're going to say. You're probably
going to tell me I look fine—everyone does—but I know it's not true. I look
terrible!"

"What upsets you so much about how you look?" I asked. "My skin," she replied, after some hesitation. "See all these pimples and scars and marks?" I really couldn't see what she was describing. From where I was sitting, her skin looked clear. Jennifer stood up and walked over toward me. "See these marks?" she asked again, jabbing her finger at her cheek and nose. In some of the places she pointed to I could discern some small whiteheads, but I had to be within a foot of her to see them. Even then I had to look closely.

Jennifer sat down again and went on to describe how since her early teenage years she'd been preoccupied with the "acne" and "marks" she'd just pointed out. She also thought her skin was too pale. "I look like a ghost. Everyone else looks really good; I stick out like a sore thumb. I'm the one who looks ugly," she said.

"When did the problem start?" I asked her. "When I was around 11," she replied. "It started with my nose. One of my nostrils stuck out more than the other. I remember catching a view of myself in the mirror one day and panicking. I thought, 'Is that what you look like? You look terrible, like a freak!'

"My nostrils don't really bother me anymore. My skin took over for them. Now all I think about is how bad my skin looks. I think about it for most of the day. People can see it from 50 feet away!" Jennifer cried as she said this— she truly believed that she was ugly and that her ugliness was visible to the entire world.

At this point Jennifer wasn't sure she wanted to continue. It was too upsetting to talk about her problem. But, with encouragement, she managed to go on. "I try not to think about it, but I have to," she said. "I think about it for most of the day. It's the first thing I think of when I wake up in the morning. I rush to the mirror, wondering 'How does it look?' How my skin looks in the morning totally determines how my day goes. Unfortunately, 80% of the time it looks horrible."

In high school Jennifer thought so much about her supposed ugliness that she couldn't concentrate in class. Her preoccupations crowded her mind and sapped her energy. "I dressed up a lot, I got really tan, wore blue eye shadow, and did a lot of things with my hair to distract people from my skin. But it didn't work. I couldn't concentrate on my school work, and I didn't want to be seen. It was too hard for me to stay in school," she said. "I started calling my mother in the middle of the day to pick me up. She didn't want to get me because I was supposed to be in class, but I was so upset and cried so much she'd come and take me home."

While doing her homework, Jennifer spent so much time examining her face in a mirror she kept on her desk that she couldn't complete her assignments. When she started reading, she felt compelled to check the mirror. "I had to see how my skin looked," she explained. "I had to see if it was any worse. Sometimes I'd get stuck there for hours, examining it for imperfections.

"I'd pick at it, too," she added, "which just made it worse. Sometimes I'd pick and pick with pins dipped in alcohol trying to get rid of the pimples and get the pus out. I'd pick at all kinds of things—little bumps, blackheads, any mark or imperfection. Sometimes I'd be up doing this at 1:00 or 2:00 in the morning, and then I'd fall asleep in class the next day, if I even went. Sometimes it would even bleed. I always felt terrible afterward. I'd make such a mess of my skin that I'd get totally hysterical."

As a result of her skin concerns, Jennifer's grades slipped from As and Bs to Ds, and she was put in a class for students with academic difficulties, even though she was bright. After missing many days of school, she dropped out of the ninth grade, even though she'd wanted to go to college. "I really tried to stay in school," she said. "But I couldn't do it. It was too much."

Jennifer also missed parties because, as she explained it, "No one would want to hang out with me because I'm so ugly." When her friends encouraged her to go, telling her how pretty she was, Jennifer didn't believe them. "They were just feeling sorry for me and trying to be nice. How could I go when I looked so horrendous?"

She did date one boy after she'd dropped out of school but saw him largely in her own house. "I hardly ever went out with him because I didn't want anyone to see my skin. I'd have him come over to my house. When he came over, I pulled all the shades down and turned down the lights so he couldn't see how bad my skin looked. But I stopped seeing him because I figured he'd just leave me anyway when he found out how bad I looked."

After dropping out of high school Jennifer tried waitressing three different times, but each time she quit or was fired because she missed so much work. "I wouldn't go if I had even one pimple. Sometimes I left in the middle of the day because I thought the customers were making fun of my skin behind my back." A job as a filing clerk was more tolerable, since she didn't have to be around other people as much, but she had trouble with that job, too. She thought about her skin for most of the day and secretly checked it in a pocket mirror over and over. "I tried not to," she explained, "because it took me away from my work. But I couldn't resist. *I couldn't stop thinking about my face, and I had to check it. I had* to make sure I looked okay, but I usually thought it looked bad. When I looked in the mirror I felt totally panicked seeing all those pimples and marks. Sometimes I even had to leave work and go to bed for the rest of the day. It was just like when I was in school."

When Jennifer had to work in a room with several other people and sit under fluorescent lights, she quit her job. "Sitting that close to other people was really hard because they could see how bad my skin was," she explained. "And the fluorescent lights were the last straw. I remember the day I quit. I was doing some filing, and all I could think of was that those awful lights showed up all the marks and pimples and holes in my face. I looked like a monster. I couldn't stop thinking that everyone in the room was looking at me! I tried to calm myself down and focus on what I was doing, but I couldn't. I had a panic attack. I ran out of that room and never went back."

Jennifer went on medical disability because she couldn't work, and continued to live with her parents even though she wanted to live on her own. Her parents bought her most of what she needed, and she rarely went out. "I do go out sometimes, but mostly at night when no one can see me," she said. "Sometimes

I go to a 24-hour grocery store at midnight, when I know no one else will be there. For a long time I've bought most of my clothes through catalogs. I'm too scared to go out—everyone will see how ugly I am," she explained. When she did venture out she first spent at least two hours putting on makeup. "I look as though I'm wearing a mask, but at least I sort of cover up the pimples and scars," she said. She also painstakingly covered herself from head to toe with a bronzer to make her skin less white and to look "less like a ghost." She couldn't go out if there was any chance of rain because her bronzer would streak and run.

"It's getting worse," she said. "Last week, I got up my courage and decided to go out in the daylight, which I hardly ever do. I started driving to the store, and, just my luck, I got stuck in a major traffic jam. I was sitting there, in four lanes of traffic, waiting for the traffic to move, but it wasn't moving, and these people in the other cars were looking at me. All I could think was that they were looking at my face, thinking 'That poor girl; look how ugly she is. How can she go out in public when her skin looks so bad?' I tried to convince myself that it wasn't true, but my heart started racing, and I was sweating and shaking. I couldn't stop thinking that they were laughing at me. I got so panicked I had to leave. So I left my car in the middle of the traffic jam, and I ran until I found a phone booth. I called my mother and I stayed there hiding until she got me. That's how bad it got—I left my car sitting in the middle of the highway!"

Jennifer thought her problem was physical, not psychiatric, so she'd seen at least 15 different dermatologists. Some gave her antibiotics and other medications, but most said she didn't need treatment. "I'm every dermatologist's nightmare," Jennifer said. "I keep going back to see them, asking them over and over if my skin looks okay. I didn't believe them when they said my skin was fine. I wouldn't go away. I asked and asked them about my skin, and I begged them for treatment. A lot of them refused to see me anymore. They're probably all seeing therapists because of me!"

One of the dermatologists had in fact called to refer Jennifer to me for treatment. He told me that Jennifer had beautiful skin but was so obsessed with it that she might benefit from seeing a psychiatrist. But, at that time, Jennifer preferred to see dermatologists.

She finally did see a dermatologist whom she convinced to do a dermabrasion, a painful face peel usually reserved for treating severe acne. "The dermatologist really didn't want to do it," Jennifer said, "but I was so desperate that she gave in." After the dermabrasion Jennifer felt better about her skin for several months, even though her friends asked her what had happened to it. "They all thought it looked worse because it was red for a while," she said. "But I was thrilled. I didn't care if it was red because at least the pimples and marks went away." But within several months Jennifer's preoccupation returned and was even worse. She then had another dermabrasion, even though her parents implored her not to and the dermatologist was reluctant to repeat it. But Jennifer felt desperate. That procedure didn't help her feel any better either. She was so depressed over this, over the fact that her "last hope" didn't help, that she considered suicide.

When she first saw me, Jennifer still believed her problem was physical, not psychiatric, and she really wanted to see another dermatologist, not a psychiatrist. But her mother had insisted. "All my daughter does is ask me if she looks okay, over and over again, all day long," she told me. "She looks through magazines, asking me if her skin looks as good as the models'. No matter what I say, she can't be reassured. She's a pretty girl—I don't know what to do!" She had even told Jennifer that she'd have to move out of the house if she didn't stop her questioning, but Jennifer couldn't stop. "I *have* to ask her," Jennifer said. "I ask her at least a hundred times a day. I try not to, but I can't stop."

Jennifer also insisted that her mother hold magnifying glasses and shine light on her face from different angles when she inspected herself in the mirror so she could get a better look at her skin. Her mother reluctantly did it because Jennifer was so upset if she refused, but this took more than an hour a day and never really helped. "If it helped I might be willing to keep doing it," her mother said, "but she just keeps asking me if her skin looks okay and if she has scars, and she just keeps looking in the mirror. It might be hard for you to believe this, Doctor, but this problem is ruining our family—the constant questioning, the constant tears. She won't go out. We've tried to be patient, but nothing we do seems to help. We love our daughter and want to help her, but we can't take it anymore!"

Jennifer's story isn't unusual. Although her body dysmorphic disorder was severe, her long struggle is typical of what many people experience. So many people have told me, after reading the first edition of this book, "I'm just like Jennifer!" Body dysmorphic disorder, or BDD, is a painful yet underrecognized psychiatric disorder—one in which normal-looking or even attractive people are preoccupied with one or more defects or flaws in their appearance. What's unusual about the defect is that it isn't visible—or is hardly visible—to others. People with this disorder may, for example, think that their hair is too curly, too straight, or too thin. Or that they have "veins" on their cheeks, scars on their nose, or skin that's too red or too pale. Or that their nose is too big, their lips too thin, their hips too big, or their breasts too small. Any body part can be the focus of concern. In reality they look fine. Often they have no defect at all. If they do have a flaw, it's generally minimal—something other people don't particularly notice. When I meet someone with BDD, I can't figure out what the supposed defect is by looking at them. Other people can't either. The "defects" are more in their minds than their bodies.

People with BDD not only focus on a defect that others don't notice—they think about it excessively. They worry. They obsess. It causes them emotional pain. And it interferes with their life.

BDD is an intriguing disorder. How can someone with no perceptible flaw, or only a minimal flaw, in his or her appearance focus so excessively on something others don't notice? How can an attractive young woman like Jennifer think she looks monstrously ugly—that she's "one of the ugliest people in the whole world"?

The good news is that BDD is becoming better known—by professionals and the public alike. The bad news is that so many people are still unfamiliar with BDD and are unaware that it's a common and treatable disorder. Many people with BDD have gone from doctor to doctor—dermatologists, plastic surgeons, ophthalmologists, psychiatrists—without ever finding out that BDD was their problem. Many professionals and laypersons still haven't heard of BDD. Even though this is changing, BDD is still underrecognized.

Chris's, Keith's, and Andrew's Stories

One of my first patients with BDD was a shy, articulate young man named Chris, who made an appointment with me to be evaluated for depression. When I first met with him, he told me that depression was his problem—that he'd been feeling down, unmotivated, uninterested in things he usually enjoyed. He was having trouble sleeping, and found it difficult to concentrate on his job. His girlfriend had recently left him.

Chris indeed sounded depressed, and it seemed as though he had a fairly straightforward case of depression. But when I asked him if he was bothered by anything else, Chris seemed unusually hesitant and uncomfortable. He was silent for several minutes and seemed to be struggling to decide whether to tell me something. "There *is* something else bothering me. I wasn't sure I'd be able to tell you about it, but I should because it's why I'm here. It's my main problem. I'm depressed because of my hair."

Chris struggled to explain. "This is really embarrassing for me to talk about, but I'm devastated over my hair. I think it's falling out and that I look terrible. I realize I'm probably distorting—that I really don't look so bad—but I can't stop worrying about it." Chris had recently joined a hair club and had tried many hair tonics, which cost him $300 a month—a significant financial burden. But none of these remedies had diminished his preoccupation. Now he was considering getting a hair weave and was saving his money to pay for it.

Chris also worried about his nose—that it didn't look right. He was reluctant to describe this concern, too, but explained that he thought his nose was too wide and too long. "I'm so worried about my nose, and especially my hair, that I can't concentrate at work. I had a big assignment last month, and I had a hard time getting it done because I thought my hair looked especially bad. I thought more was falling out than usual. This probably sounds ridiculous to you, but I was so distracted by these thoughts and by the fear that I was going to be bald that I was a week late with the assignment. That was a big blow for me because I'm a perfectionist. I do a good job at work, and I pride myself on getting my assignments done on time. What was really hard was that my boss called me in to talk about my lateness and to ask me what the problem was. Of course I couldn't tell him what it was. I'd be totally mortified. I made up an excuse about a close friend being sick, even though I hate to lie." Chris worked as an accountant and had deadlines to meet. "It probably sounds ridiculous that I can't meet my deadlines because of my hair. It really shouldn't matter what my hair looks like. But I can't help it!"

Chris was also very nervous going out to parties and bars with his girlfriend. "Before my hair problem began, I didn't have much trouble talking to people when I went out. I was never the life of the party, but I'd go out. I liked to see people, and I never avoided social events that I wanted to go to. But it's really hard for me now because of how I look. When I do go out, it's hard for me to talk with people—I can't concentrate on the conversation. All I can think about is whether my hair looks okay and whether they're noticing how thin it is. I constantly check out their hair and compare it to mine. Then I usually feel worse because I think their hair looks better. That's why my girlfriend left me. She likes to go out and said she can't stay with me if I stay home or leave parties early because of my hair. She thinks I look fine, and she can't understand why I can't just forget about it.

"The final straw for her came last month," he continued. "Last month was a really bad time for me—I'm not sure why. I was supposed to be in her brother's wedding. I went to the dress rehearsal, but on the morning of the wedding I panicked. I looked in the mirror and I thought 'Where's your hair?' I thought I looked balder than ever. I spent about an hour frantically putting gel in it, combing it, and blow drying it, trying to make it look fuller. I even had my girlfriend help me with it, even though she was really frustrated and angry with me. But no matter what we did to it, it didn't look right. I kept trying to convince myself that it really didn't matter—that people would be looking at the bride and groom, not at my hair. But I just couldn't go. I felt so demoralized and desperate."

Chris's problems intrigued me. How could his hair and nose have caused him such difficulties? His hair was a little thin, but not so thin that I'd noticed it when I met him. And his nose looked fine. Why was he so worried? How could these worries interfere with his job when he'd always been such a high achiever? Why couldn't he go out to parties? How had it gotten so bad that he'd missed the wedding and his girlfriend had left him?

Soon after I saw Chris, another patient, Keith, called me. He said he was calling about something important, and sounded very anxious and agitated over the phone. "Dr. Phillips," he began, "I'm calling about something that's making me feel really panicked. It's been a problem for a while, but I haven't been able to tell you about it." I asked him what it was. "Well, I couldn't tell you about it in person because it's too embarrassing. But maybe I can over the phone. . . . I'm . . . I'm upset about my hair." I was puzzled. Why would he be so upset over his hair? His hair had always seemed fine. And two men with hair problems in the same month? This seemed like an unusual coincidence.

Keith went on to explain that he was very worried that his hair was too thin. "I keep worrying about it," he explained. "I try to stop thinking about it, but I can't." I wondered whether Keith might actually be losing his hair for some reason—perhaps he had an undiagnosed medical illness that can cause hair loss.

But I was wrong. Keith continued to explain. "It's actually not my overall hair—it's my bangs. My bangs aren't right. They're too thin and the shape is wrong. I don't think my hair is falling out. I just think my bangs look *really bad*."

Keith was extremely embarrassed about this. "I'm afraid you're thinking I'm silly to be worried so much about my hair, but I can't help it. I think I look like a dork!" Keith was concerned I wouldn't take him seriously. I thought about my recent meeting with Chris and wondered whether Keith, too, might have BDD. He did.

When I next met with Keith I was surprised to learn that he had many worries about his appearance. He thought that his ears were "too pointy—like Mr. Spock's," that he had "lines" on his face, and that his eyes were "small and beady." His most embarrassing concern was that certain parts of his body—his chest and buttocks—were "shaped like a woman's." I'd known Keith for more than two years and had worked closely with him during that time. He'd told me about many of his problems and had gotten fairly comfortable talking about embarrassing topics. But this problem had been too embarrassing for him to discuss. In fact, it had taken him more than two years to get up the courage to tell me about it! And he could initially raise it only over the phone, not in person. I commented that he'd seemed comfortable talking about other personal matters—what made this one so hard to discuss? He replied that it was somehow much easier to talk about his depression or his mania—even his sexual problems. For reasons he found difficult to articulate, he was particularly ashamed of his appearance concerns. He was afraid I'd think he was superficial and vain. He also feared that by talking about his "ugly" body parts, I'd notice them even more than he thought I already did. He finally summed it up: "I just didn't have the guts to tell you. It's almost taboo to discuss it. I can't believe I brought it up."

Soon after that, I met Andrew. Like Chris, he came in to be evaluated for depression, not BDD, because he was too embarrassed to divulge his BDD. I wouldn't have found out about Andrew's BDD if I hadn't asked him if he had any ideas about why he was depressed. His answer: "I've had five nose and chin operations, and I don't look any better."

Andrew had BDD for more than 20 years. It started after he had minor nose surgery for a deviated septum, during which he thought the surgeon changed the shape of his nose. In desperation, Andrew had five more operations to improve its appearance. But with each operation, he believed his deformities worsened. To make matters worse, when he had the second operation the surgeon suggested that Andrew also have a chin implant, which triggered a new obsession that his chin was too small. "My life stopped every year or so to have another operation," Andrew said. He dropped out of college and quit jobs to have the procedures. "Each time, right after the surgery I was ecstatic, because I thought this time I'd finally look right. But when the bandages were removed I was heartbroken. I thought I looked even worse, and I became more deeply depressed."

His family and friends tried to talk Andrew out of the operations, reassuring him that he was a good-looking man with no observable defects. The surgeons also didn't want to operate. "You might wonder why they kept doing more operations," Andrew said. "But they couldn't turn me down because I was so miserable. I *had* to have more surgery. I kept hoping that the operations would help—that I'd look better and that people would like me more and accept me more if I looked better." But with each procedure Andrew became more withdrawn, to the point where he rarely went out and never dated. "A few years ago I got very close to suicide," he said. "I gave my things away and made out a will. I had it all planned—the day, the time, the place—but I chickened out. Sometimes I think I should have gone through with it."

BDD from the Past and Around the World

Before I started seeing patients with BDD in the late 1980s, I wanted to learn what was known about it. So I searched through all the articles I could find that had been published in professional journals, and I had many articles translated from other languages, such as Russian, Japanese, German, Italian, and French. My search uncovered few research studies but many case reports of BDD—descriptions of a single person or a few people with the disorder. The reports came from a surprisingly wide variety of countries—England, Italy, France, Germany, Russia, Japan, the former Czechoslovakia, and others. I read about a young man from Germany who thought his cheeks were too "rosy and round" and who, to try to make them thinner, severely starved himself. I read about a young woman from England who worried that her breasts were too small and who'd been refused breast augmentation surgery. Another young woman from England was so concerned about "lines" under her eyes that she wanted to kill herself. "I am constantly thinking about them, about my face and how I have changed," the author wrote of her preoccupation. "Makeup is just a waste of time. Life is not worth living."

A report from Japan described several people with BDD. One was a 25-year-old man who was preoccupied with his "flaccid" nose and thought his eyebrows had "declined." Another was a 28-year-old woman who was also preoccupied with a supposed nose deformity, which she thought had been caused by being hit in the nose with a brush. Six nose operations didn't diminish her concern. The third patient, a 25-year-old woman, complained that her eyelid was drooping, her nose was deformed, and the whites of her eyes were yellow. Four surgical procedures hadn't helped. In fact, she believed that one of the operations had given her a snoring problem.

I found descriptions of BDD from more than 100 years ago. I was struck by how descriptions from more than a century ago were just like the patients I was seeing. William Stekel, wrote in 1949 about "the peculiar group of compulsive ideas which concern the body. There are people," he wrote, "who occupy themselves continuously with a specific part of the body. In one case it is the nose; in another it is the bald head; in a third case the ear, the eyes, or (in women) the bosom, the genitalia, etc. These obsessive thoughts are very tormenting."

One of psychiatry's most famous patients—known by the pseudonym "the

Wolf Man"—probably had BDD. The legendary Sigmund Freud, the Wolf Man's first psychoanalyst, didn't even mention BDD symptoms in his description of his patient, even though they were a significant problem. Why not? Had the Wolf Man mentioned it to Freud, or had he kept it a secret? Was he too embarrassed to bring it up? Perhaps he wasn't yet worried about his appearance, although BDD usually begins during adolescence. Ruth Brunswick, the Wolf Man's second psychoanalyst, did describe her patient's preoccupation. In 1928 she wrote that "(he) neglected his daily life and work because he was engrossed, to the exclusion of all else, in the state of his nose" (its supposed scars, holes, and swelling). "His life was centered on the little mirror in his pocket, and his fate depended on what it revealed or was about to reveal."

This quote describes many of the patients I've seen. Jennifer, too, neglected her daily life and work because she was so engrossed with supposed defects in her appearance. And her life was also centered on the little mirror in her pocket. Without realizing it, when Jennifer repeatedly checked her pocket mirror at work, she was doing what the Wolf Man had done more than half a century before.

Body dysmorphic disorder is a relatively new name for this disorder, having been used only since 1987, when it first formally entered psychiatry's classification manual of psychiatric disorders. For the previous 100 years, BDD was more commonly known as *dysmorphophobia*, a term coined in the 1880s by Enrico Morselli, a brilliant and prolific Italian psychiatrist, who saw many patients with BDD. Dysmorphophobia comes from *dysmorfia*, a Greek word meaning ugliness, specifically of the face, which first appeared in the Histories of Herodotus. It refers to the myth of the "ugliest girl in Sparta," who, upon being stroked by the hand of a goddess, became the "fairest of all Spartan ladies" and later married the Spartan king. Herodotus writes, "Thither the Nurse would bear the child every day to the Shrine and set her by the Statue and pray the Goddess to deliver her from her ill looks."

In the late 1800s, Morselli saw many patients with BDD, which he described as an "idea of deformity." "The dysmorphophobic patient," he wrote, "is really miserable; in the middle of his daily routines, conversations, while reading, during meals, in fact everywhere and at any time, is overcome by the fear of deformity ... which may reach a very painful intensity, even to the point of weeping and desperation." Subsequently, BDD was described by some of Europe's most prominent turn-of-the-century psychiatrists, such as Emil Kraepelin and Pierre Janet. Janet considered BDD to be relatively common. In 1903, he described a 27-year-old woman he called Nadia, the gifted and intelligent daughter of a distinguished French family. Nadia worried about many aspects of her appearance, including her red and spotted skin, her feet and supposed tallness, and her "long and ridiculous" hands. Nadia worried that no one would ever love her because she was "ugly and ridiculous," and for five years she confined herself to a tiny apartment that she rarely left. "If they saw me in plain light, people would be disgusted," Janet wrote of Nadia's concern.

"Beauty hypochondria" ("*Schönheitshypochondrie,*" in German) and "one who is worried about being ugly" (*"Hässlichkeitskümmerer,"* in German) are other colorful labels used in the 1930s to describe a BDD-like preoccupation with imagined ugliness. "Dermatologic hypochondriasis" depicted a BDD-like syndrome that focused on supposed defects of the skin and hair.

The vivid case descriptions written during the past century bear testimony to BDD's long history and to the fact that people from a variety of cultures have suffered from it. Indeed, BDD is well known and recognized in certain countries—Japan, for example—but has escaped adequate recognition in many others, including, until very recently, the United States.

While it's not entirely clear why BDD has been largely unknown in the United States and certain other countries, a likely reason is that it's often kept secret. Keith wasn't my only patient to take several years to reveal his concerns. Some people, like Jennifer, tell family members and friends about their worries and may even describe them to doctor after doctor, but many others keep them secret.

Some have finally mustered up the courage to mention their concern to someone they trust, but when they're reassured that they look fine, they feel misunderstood. They may interpret reassurance to mean that the person they've told doesn't take them seriously and doesn't understand their suffering. So they may never mention it again.

Others don't realize their problem is psychiatric. They go to surgeon after surgeon, dermatologist after dermatologist, hair club after hair club seeking a nonpsychiatric cure for a psychiatric problem. This, too, has contributed to BDD's underrecognition. If people with BDD do see a psychiatrist, they may be too ashamed to bring it up. They may muster up only enough courage to talk about the depression and anxiety that people with BDD often experience, keeping the reason for their suffering a secret even from those who can help them.

"No One Takes Me Seriously":
Letters from BDD Sufferers and Their Families

BDD isn't rare. While we have only limited data on its prevalence, these data suggest that it's far more common than is generally recognized. Preliminary data from a growing number of researchers suggest that BDD may affect about 1% of adults in the general population, from more than 2% to 13% of students, and 13% of people hospitalized in a psychiatric hospital. It's been found that 9% to 12% of people seeking treatment from a dermatologist, and 6% to 20% of people who receive cosmetic surgery, have BDD.

These numbers translate into many millions of people in the United States alone. While these findings need to be confirmed in larger-scale studies, I and other researchers have been surprised by the relatively high rates of BDD we've found in the groups we've studied. When stories about BDD have run in newspapers and magazines, I've been deluged with calls and letters. I hear from people who wonder if they have BDD and want treatment, from family members who think a loved one may be suffering from the disorder, from professionals asking for information and sometimes for help for their own family members. One woman, who read about BDD in her local newspaper, wrote the following:

> I am 45 years old—and I don't ever remember not feeling this way. It is very difficult to discuss with anyone, as no one seems to take me seriously or can relate to the amount of pain I feel. Therapy has helped me work on many of my other issues, but I seemed to skirt around this more serious problem, which didn't get addressed . . . The hardest part for me in this is that no one takes me seriously and so I never feel heard. It is very distressing and has affected many areas of my life.

The sense of isolation and aloneness implied in this letter is more directly conveyed in the following letter, which a woman wrote to me after seeing a story about BDD on *Dateline NBC* in 1993:

> I am 29 and never knew that there was anyone else out there who thought the same way I do about themselves.

Another woman wrote me about her brother's long struggle with severe BDD:

> My 49-year-old brother has suffered from body dysmorphic disorder his entire adult life. He has been hospitalized, had shock treatment, taken drugs, and received psychotherapy on and off for years as he imagines people are making fun of his looks. Nothing has helped him. Now, thank God, this disorder is finally being recognized and hopefully can be successfully treated.

The following letter conveys that this disorder can indeed be treated successfully. The young woman who wrote it had responded to psychiatric treatment after several years of suffering:

> My history of BDD is relatively short, but very painful! I had what would probably be a mild case of it years ago in regards to my eyelids. I chose to have cosmetic surgery done and instead of remedying the situation, I became obsessed—I was sure that my eyelids looked even worse and terribly abnormal. It consumed me. I consulted six more cosmetic surgeons, mirrors began to be a terrible problem, I became reclusive, and I thought about it from the minute I woke up until I fell asleep. It was a nightmare. I'm sure you're familiar with the story. Anyhow, this went on for two years before I got help. . . . I'd have to say I'm about 85% recovered from the BDD and that is a *big* relief!

In contrast to this hopeful letter, I received an extremely sad one sent to me by a woman whose son had been preoccupied with the shape of his head. She had just read about BDD in her local paper and realized that this was the disorder with which he had suffered for so long. She started her letter with the following:

> "I read the enclosed article nearly a month after my dear son hanged himself in sheer desperation. Until we read the reporter's words, none of us had any perception of my son's suffering and feeling that no one could help him . . . My son had been telling us for many years how he felt and that he wanted to die.

The last letter shocked and haunted me for a long time. I spoke with the woman, who told me about her family's and her son's suffering and of her long and unsuccessful quest for a diagnosis and effective treatment. No one could tell her what his problem was. And she felt that no one had truly understood the depth of his suffering. She blamed herself for this. She felt she should have understood. In retrospect, her son's suffering and hopelessness couldn't have been clearer, but at the time it *had* been hard to understand—he was a handsome young man whose head looked completely normal. Her self-blame made his death all the more painful.

The tragedy of this young man's death and other stories I heard spurred my resolve to learn more about this serious and underrecognized disorder—to start doing research so we could understand who gets it, how to identify it, and how to treat it.

Hope for People with BDD

In many ways, we're only beginning to understand BDD, and much more research is greatly needed. At this time, there are still many questions. What causes BDD? Is it rooted in a person's genes, life experience, or societal pressures? Is it a disorder of the brain, the mind, or society? Why do some people get it but others don't? Is it related to eating disorders, like bulimia and anorexia nervosa—disorders that also involve distorted body image? Or is it related to obsessive compulsive disorder, a disorder characterized by obsessive thoughts—for example, about contamination or harm—and compulsive behaviors that, like those of BDD, often involve checking and reassurance seeking?

How is BDD related to koro, a disorder in which men fear that their penis is disappearing into their abdomen and will kill them? And where exactly should we draw the line between BDD and the normal concern with appearance that so many people have? Is BDD simply an exaggerated version of this normal, common concern—a more intense, problematic variant of it? Or is it something different?

While continued research is essential, we aren't totally in the dark. There's a lot that we *do* know—what people with BDD experience, what other problems and disorders they commonly have in addition to BDD, how BDD affects peoples' lives. We know that this disorder often responds to certain psychiatric treatments. The suffering of many people with BDD—including Jennifer, Chris, and Keith—has been significantly alleviated by these treatments. Some are completely free of their tormenting concern.

Jennifer's symptoms were alleviated by clomipramine (Anafranil), a certain type of antidepressant medication known as a serotonin-reuptake inhibitor. After several months on this medication, she began to notice that she thought about her skin much less often—only an hour a day instead of most of the day. It became much easier to resist extra peeks in the mirror. Her preoccupation no longer tormented her. She also felt better about how she looked. She still thought that she had "some pimples," but she realized they weren't particularly noticeable. They were no longer devastating. As she explained, "This is more of a normal dislike—it isn't taking over my life anymore. I've put this problem in perspective. I don't love my skin, but I can accept it. It no longer ruins me." She stopped asking her mother about her appearance, and she's been able to leave her house, go into stores to shop, and look for a job.

Keith responded to a combination of a serotonin-reuptake inhibitor known as fluoxetine (Prozac) and a type of therapy known as cognitive-behavioral therapy. He stopped worrying about his appearance almost entirely. Like Jennifer, it's now much easier to go out in public because he no longer thinks that everyone is staring at him. The serotonin-reuptake inhibitors, which are antidepressant medications with antiobsessional properties, appear particularly effective for BDD. Those currently marketed in the United States are citalopram (Celexa), escitalopram (Lexapro), fluoxetine (Prozac), fluvoxamine (Luvox), clomipramine (Anafranil), paroxetine (Paxil), and sertraline (Zoloft). Cognitive-behavioral treatment also appears effective for BDD. This treatment helps patients stop their compulsive behaviors, face the situations they fear, and develop more accurate and helpful appearance-related beliefs.

The field of psychiatry is rapidly advancing; some of the things we now know about the workings of the brain were barely imaginable even a decade ago. Many advances—such as those in brain imaging and genetics—will be applied to BDD and are likely to exponentially increase our knowledge. A statement made by Eric Kandel, a famous neuroscientist and Nobel Prize winner, about his area of research struck me as particularly applicable to BDD: "We are at the foothills of an enormous mountain range."

·· *three* ··

What Is Body Dysmorphic Disorder?

"One day I saw my face in a certain light, and I panicked. I thought, 'Is this what you've looked like all along? How awful! How can you live with this?'"   **Lauren**

"My Problem Isn't Very Severe": Do I Even Have Body Dysmorphic Disorder?

Sarah, a 24-year-old medical student, called me after she'd seen *Dateline NBC's* 1993 piece on BDD. "My problem isn't very severe; I'm not sure I have body dysmorphic disorder," she told me over the phone. "My concern with my appearance isn't that extreme, but it probably *is* excessive. It's a problem for me."

I looked forward to meeting with Sarah. At this point I'd seen many people with severe BDD—people like Jennifer and Andrew—but fewer people with mild BDD, and I was interested in what she'd have to say. Did she have mild BDD? Did she even have BDD? I also hoped I could be helpful. She *had* said her concern was a problem.

When I first saw Sarah I had no idea of what her concern could be. She was very appealing—quiet yet also animated—with a lovely smile. She did have a few small pimples on her chin, but only a few, and to my eye they were barely noticeable. Nonetheless, this is a concern of many people with BDD—perhaps it was hers.

But it wasn't. We started off talking about medical school and the hospital rotation she was on. She was sleep deprived but loved her work and what she was learning. She was trying to decide what her specialty would be—perhaps pediatrics. "My work is going well," she said. "But I'm having problems with my social life. It's hard for me to get into relationships. I isolate myself because of my appearance worries."

Sarah went on to describe what bothered her. "I don't like my thighs," she said. "They're flabby. They have this rippling look, and the skin isn't taut. I also worry a lot about varicose veins on my legs and ankles. I think they look *really* bad. They're dark purple, and some of them bulge out of my legs. They bother me a lot. I get very upset when I think about these things—very nervous and anxious. It causes me a lot of emotional turmoil. It's worse on some days than on other days; some days aren't so bad, but it can be very upsetting."

I asked her if there was anything else that bothered her. "Well, my hair too," she replied. "It's just not right. Sometimes it's too flat; sometimes it looks asymmetric. I can spend a lot of time combing it. And I've never been very happy with my weight. I'm always on a diet. In fact, I've gained a few pounds in the past month because there's always candy on the ward where I'm working now. But my weight doesn't stop me from doing things the way my other concerns do. I don't like it, and I'm trying to change it, but I don't really consider it a big problem."

"Do your other concerns cause you problems?" I asked. "Yes, they do," she answered. "I avoid the beach even though I love it. If I go, I worry about my thighs and my veins the entire time, and I can't have fun. And I wear pants even on really hot summer days—even if it's 90 degrees out. It's pretty uncomfortable, and it probably looks pretty strange. It also makes my feel phony— why can't I just be myself? Why do I care so much about how I look? I don't have an answer to that question, which is very frustrating. I try to talk myself out of my concerns, but I can't, and that adds to my frustration.

"I've seriously considered moving to a colder climate," she added. "I probably will when I begin my residency. The summers in New England aren't that long, but they're much too long for me! In a colder climate I won't seem so strange wearing pants all the time, and I won't have to turn down invitations to the beach. I think I'll feel less self-conscious.

"But the bigger problem is that I've avoided dating because of these things. I finally got up the courage to go out with someone I'm seeing now. I like him a lot, and I want the relationship to continue. But my appearance is interfering. It sounds stupid, but I'm afraid he'll reject me when he sees my veins and my thighs! This worry is a burden and a hindrance. I'm afraid I'll never be able to get married because of it."

Sarah stopped at that point, and she looked upset. "I'd really like to get married sometime," she said. "I don't want this to get in the way. The big problem right now is that I haven't told my boyfriend about these things. It's hard to be intimate. I try to hide my legs, but that's pretty hard to do when you spend a lot of time with someone and are romantically involved with them."

I asked Sarah if there were factors other than her appearance that might be contributing to her relationship problems. She responded by saying that she had often asked herself this question. "I've always been somewhat shy and reserved," she said. "But I've always wanted to go out with men, and I've always strongly felt that I wanted to get married someday. But maybe there *are* other reasons for my intimacy problems. My parents didn't have a good marriage, so maybe I'm unconsciously afraid of getting seriously involved with someone. I've always been somewhat sensitive to rejection, so I do think I hold back to some degree before getting involved with men. But at the same time, I'm also pretty trusting. I really don't know how to answer your question. Perhaps the best I can do is say that my appearance concerns are a *big part* of my relationship problems. I think if I didn't worry about how I look, I'd risk more in relationships.

"People tell me I'm attractive and that men find me attractive, but I find it hard to believe them. I can't be reassured. Actually, *overall* I think I look fine. But the things I told you about are very upsetting. My sister has seen my thighs and thinks they look fine. She keeps asking me to go to the beach with her because she loves to go too. But I rarely go. I feel much too self-conscious."

It did sound as though Sarah had BDD. She was very distressed over her concerns, and her relationships had suffered because of them. I wondered how bad the defects that she described really were. Were they slight or nonexistent, or were they as grotesquely unsightly as she thought? I couldn't see her legs because she was wearing pants, but presumably the defects were less severe than she believed—her sister, at any rate, thought she looked fine.

I also wondered about her hair. She had mentioned that this was a problem. I couldn't see anything wrong with it. It was a beautiful deep auburn and was cut fashionably short. I asked her to tell me about it. "Yes, my hair's a problem, too," she said. "It really bugs me because it never looks right. First it's too flat, then one side sticks out more than the other." She pointed to demonstrate. "But it's more than a bad hair day. It's upsetting."

Sarah went on to describe how she sometimes got stuck in the mirror trying to get her hair right. "I comb it and recomb it, style it and restyle it. I apply mousse, then hair spray, then I use a curling iron. When it doesn't look right, I wet it and start all over again. Sometimes I do this literally for hours."

I wondered how she managed to function as a third-year medical student. These students spend their time on the wards with patients and usually are very busy. How could she be doing her work if she was spending hours a day in the mirror? "Has this gotten in the way of your work at all?" I asked her. "Well I try really hard not to let it," Sarah replied. She seemed anxious, and her voice was starting to quaver. "I try not to ever look in the mirror when I'm at work, because when I do I can get stuck there. If my hair looks bad, I can't resist fiddling with it and then the whole routine can start. Once I start, I have to complete it. I've actually been late for rounds and lectures because I got stuck. My friends have even come looking for me in the bathroom when I've been late for rounds and the whole team was waiting for me. That was really embarrassing! I know I told you at first it wasn't really a problem at work. But I guess sometimes it is a little bit because sometimes I'm late."

Many people with BDD don't like to admit the problems their symptoms cause them. Many try to ignore them and go on with their job, with raising children, with their lives. Some make a valiant effort to keep a stiff upper lip. But it's usually a struggle, even when the BDD is relatively mild.

"A big problem is that the patients' rooms have mirrors in them. If I can prevent myself from glancing in them when I enter their rooms I do much better. My preoccupation stays under better control, and I don't get stuck there. The mirror acts like a switch. When I look in, the obsession turns on, and it can get pretty out of control."

Despite her useful strategy of not checking mirrors, Sarah still encountered a problem when she got up each morning. "I need to look in the mirror to get myself ready for the day," she explained. "And that's a problem because I can get stuck there, and I've been late for work." A few months earlier, however, she had come up with an idea that worked—getting ready after her shower and before putting in her contact lenses. "Then the mirror's steamed up, and without my contacts in I'm practically blind. So I really can't see myself very well, but that's actually good. I just comb my hair and walk out without really seeing it. It's very anxiety provoking for me to do that because I'm petrified that my hair looks terrible. But I tell myself it probably looks fine and that the anxiety is nothing compared to what I feel when I get caught up in the grooming."

Sarah also avoided shopping malls with lots of mirrors in them and kept her distance from mirrors when buying clothes. "Getting my hair cut is especially hard—I *hate* getting it done," she said. "I keep my eyes glued to a newspaper or magazine the whole time so I don't get too upset. I *want* to look in the mirror, but I don't."

Like Sarah, most people with BDD have a special and torturous relationship with mirrors. Most check excessively, and some get stuck in them for hours each day, caught between a desire to flee the unattractive image they see and a compelling desire to examine and fix it. But fixing it isn't simple and is usually unattainable. Because excessively looking in mirrors can generate such intolerable anxiety, people who've found ways to stop this usually say they're better off. "But resisting that huge urge to take a peek isn't easy," Sarah added. "I feel I'm almost physically pulled to them when I go near them—as if there's a magnet in them. It takes a lot of willpower not to look in."

Sarah returned to talking about how her symptoms affected her work. "My legs cause less of a problem at work because I can cover them, and I don't see them in mirrors. But they still bother me. When I see patients' legs I think of my own and how ugly they are. Sometimes it really upsets me. But I'm very serious about my work, and I just try to get my mind back on what I'm doing. I usually manage."

Sarah was in fact doing very well in school, and her patients liked her a lot. She was especially commended for her sensitivity to her patients' suffering. "Maybe it's because I myself suffer with this problem," she said. "You may think that sounds really bad—in fact, incredibly insensitive!" she said with a nervous laugh. "How can I compare my appearance problems to the suffering of my patients who have cancer or are amputees? I realize how ludicrous that sounds, and I feel very guilty even saying it. It makes me feel spoiled and vain. But, you know, even though I think I have a pretty mild case of BDD, it still causes me a lot of pain. I try to tell myself that it's silly—that it shouldn't bother me so much—but it still bothers me a lot. I worry that I'll always be alone in life because of this problem."

A Spectrum of Severity:
From Mild to Life-Threatening

Milder BDD, like Sarah's, can be distressing and can interfere to some extent with living. But it isn't devastating. However, when BDD is very severe, it can destroy virtually every aspect of one's life. Some people, like Jennifer, stop working and stay in their homes, sometimes for years. Some adolescents drop out of high school or college. Parents may stop caring for their children because they're so preoccupied with their appearance that they can't focus on their children's needs. Some people with BDD think they look so ugly that they never date or marry. Some don't even buy food because they can't leave their home. Others, in an attempt to look better, lose dangerous amounts of weight.

Some even get into life-threatening accidents. Jennifer ran through red lights because she was convinced people were laughing at her while she was waiting for the light to change. One man stared so intently at his reflection while washing windows that he fell off a three-story ladder. Others are so intent on examining their face in the rearview mirror while driving that they get into car accidents. One man, who thought he looked like an "alien," *planned* to get into a car accident. He felt so hopeless over his facial "defects" that he planned to crash his car so he could destroy his face and have it completely surgically reconstructed. He explained that the car accident was necessary because 15 surgeons had refused to do the procedures he requested; even if he could find a surgeon willing to operate, his insurance company wouldn't pay for it, so the accident was necessary. That way the surgery would be paid for—and it would *have* to be done. Another woman was equally desperate; she was so distressed by the shape of her breasts that she repeatedly slashed them with a knife. Some suffer so intolerably that they attempt suicide. Some people kill themselves.

But most people with BDD don't get into serious accidents or act in self-destructive ways. Like Sarah, those with milder BDD live relatively normal lives. They work, see friends, date, and raise families. I treat college students who get good grades and graduate, homemakers who successfully juggle raising children and running a home, accountants who meet their deadlines, and doctors who give their patients superb care. Many people with this disorder are productive; some are very high achievers. All of them suffer, but they manage, sometimes well.

A psychiatrist colleague of mine wondered if one of her patients had BDD but thought it unlikely because he was functioning so well. This colleague had treated several other people with BDD whose symptoms had severely impaired their functioning and she consequently thought that *all* people with BDD had extreme difficulties with work, socializing, and other aspects of life. But it turned out that the patient in question, who was a college professor, did in fact have BDD. He managed to perform well at work because of the effort he made to stay focused on his work and to keep his symptoms from interfering. The professor, however, viewed his functioning as less than optimal. He hadn't applied for a job he'd wanted because he feared he'd be turned down because of his "awful" appearance. And he'd refused a promotion that would require more work because his preoccupations were so taxing. "Even though I'm very high functioning and successful," he explained, "I'm not working up to my capacity, although no one would ever know it."

So BDD's severity spans a spectrum, ranging from relatively mild to life-threatening. In this way, BDD is like other medical problems. Severe diabetes can lead to hospitalization and serious medical complications, such as blindness, whereas people with a milder form can remain active and productive. Heart disease, too, spans a spectrum from severe to mild; it can seriously limit one person's ability to work and engage in leisure activities but impose few limitations on another person's activities and enjoyment of life.

Psychiatric problems are no different. Depression can be severe and life-threatening: a severely depressed person may be unable to eat, sleep, or get out of bed, and may even commit suicide. But depression can be milder: many depressed people, despite their suffering, manage, with effort, to function adequately. No one would ever know they were depressed. One person with a severe phobia may not be able to leave her house, whereas someone with a milder case may go out despite her fear. BDD is similar. When it's severe, it's as crippling as any serious psychiatric or medical illness. At the milder end of the spectrum, it's more manageable and even shades into normality.

Some people I've seen, who had heard or read about a particularly severe case of BDD, told me they thought they didn't have the disorder because their symptoms "weren't that bad." Others, with severe BDD, thought they might not have the disorder because their symptoms were *so severe* there couldn't possibly be other people who had the same problem, who suffered as much as they had. But they all had BDD.

BDD varies from person to person in other ways. Some people are preoccupied with their hair, others with their buttocks, others with their legs, testicles, or eyebrows. Any body part can be the focus of concern. Even among people concerned with the same body part, exactly what they dislike can differ. One person might think her hair is too flat, whereas another believes his sticks out too much. One person may think his skin is too red, whereas another feels hers is too white.

Although no one with BDD has exactly the same experience as anyone else with BDD, all people with BDD have important things in common. The severity may differ, the body areas may differ, the behaviors may differ somewhat from person to person, but there are many things they share. Everyone with BDD is concerned with some aspect of their appearance that they consider ugly, unattractive, or "not right" in some way. Everyone is distressed or doesn't function as well as they might because of their preoccupation. The details differ from person to person, but these basic themes are shared by all.

How Is BDD Defined?

The basic features of BDD—what *everyone* with the disorder experiences—are described by BDD's diagnostic criteria. These criteria, on the next page, are from DSM-IV (the *Diagnostic and Statistical Manual, Fourth Edition*). DSM-IV is the manual used in the United States and many countries around the world by health professionals to make psychiatric diagnoses. Although the criteria may seem skeletal, they are useful because they provide guidelines for identifying who does and does not have BDD. What these diagnostic criteria indicate, in a nutshell, is that people with BDD look normal, but they're preoccupied with the idea that their appearance is defective in some way. This preoccupation causes them significant distress or interferes with their functioning.

I'll now go through BDD's diagnostic criteria, shown in Table 1, one by one. This may help you figure out if you or someone you know has BDD.

Criterion 1: Preoccupation

Criterion 1 describes the preoccupation that occurs in BDD. People with BDD worry that some aspect of their appearance looks defective in some way. They may describe the body area or areas as ugly, unattractive, flawed, "not right," deformed, disfigured, or even as grotesque, hideous, repulsive, or monstrous. People with BDD have more than an occasional thought that they don't look right—they're preoccupied. They think excessively about their supposed appearance problem; some people in fact find it hard *not* to think about it. They say such things as "I think about it a lot," "It's always on my mind," "It's like a second reel that's always going," or "I'm obsessed." People with BDD generally spend at least an hour a day thinking about the supposed defect. On average, they spend somewhere between 3 and 8 hours a day.

The definition then states that the defect is imagined or slight. Some people with BDD "imagine" their defects, in the sense that they're preoccupied with something that others don't perceive at all. Other people with BDD actually have a physical defect, such as mild acne, a small scar, or slightly thinning hair, but by definition the flaw is slight. Nonetheless, they're preoccupied with it and consider it ugly and clearly visible to others. A study from England, which used an objective measure of facial appearance known as morphoanalysis, found that

---

Table 1.   Definition of Body Dysmorphic Disorder

1. Preoccupation with some imagined defect in appearance. If a slight physical anomaly is present, the person's concern is markedly excessive.

2. The preoccupation causes clinically significant distress or impairment in social, occupational, or other important areas of functioning.

3. The preoccupation is not better accounted for by another mental disorder (e.g., dissatisfaction with body shape and size in anorexia nervosa).

in BDD the disliked body area usually looks normal. I've found that about a third of people with BDD have a defect that's slight, whereas in about two thirds the body part of concern looks completely normal. Considering their overall appearance, in my experience, nearly everyone with BDD is of average or above average attractiveness.

But the word "imagined" is complicated and can be problematic. While some people with BDD realize that they imagine their defect—that it really looks okay and they're blowing it out of proportion—many are certain—or nearly certain—their view is correct. They think they *really do* look terrible, and they balk at the word "imagined." They worry that if they're imagining their defect, they may be labeled as "crazy." Some insist that because they're not imagining the defect, they must not have BDD, even though they really do. One person asked me, "My problem is really there; it's true. Do you deal with true things or only imaginary things?" He thought that if I dealt only with "imaginary things," then I wasn't the doctor he should be seeing.

It isn't known why people with BDD see themselves differently than other people do. Do they see what other people see but *interpret* it differently, considering the body part unattractive when others don't? Or do they actually *see* the body part differently? The question isn't so much whether the defect is "real" versus "imagined," but rather why it is that people with BDD perceive their appearance differently than other people do.

Yet another knotty issue is how to determine whether a defect, if present, is "slight," which the definition requires. If the defect is very obvious to others—if it's immediately noticeable—then by definition the person doesn't have BDD. But what if the defect is more subtle? Who's to judge whether it's slight or not? These questions take us into a subjective realm where reality and distortion can't always be clearly differentiated. To some extent, just as beauty is in the eye of the beholder, so is ugliness. If someone with BDD thinks her legs are huge, but I think they're only "slightly" big, who is right? Should a woman who's 5'11" and preoccupied with her height be considered "slightly" or obviously tall? In some cases, I don't notice the defect when I meet someone, but when it's pointed out I can see that it's actually there. Is such a defect "slight" or "nonslight"?

It's helpful to consider what *most people* observe. I often have corroboration from others—clinicians, family members, or friends—who agree that the defect is nonexistent or slight. The most common reason people with BDD are turned down for surgery or other medical treatment is that the physician can't perceive the defect or considers it too minimal to treat. One patient was referred to me by a dermatologist who described her as "a woman with beautiful skin." Many patients have been brought to me by family members who recognize that their loved one has an inaccurate view of how bad the defect is. I and several dermatologists did a study in which we independently rated the severity of skin defects and found that in general we closely agreed about which defects were slight and which were clearly noticeable. This suggests that such judgments can be made with reasonably good agreement and objectivity.

Occasional BDD sufferers themselves agree that the defect is really only slight and that they have a distorted view of how bad it is. They're more likely to recognize this after they've had psychiatric treatment. As one young man told me, "My view of my appearance is illogical—I know I really look okay. I'm making a mountain out of a molehill."

If the defect is slight, then BDD's definition requires that the person's concern is "markedly excessive"—that is, they must be preoccupied. In addition, they overreact to the minor defect in terms of how it affects their life. Charles, a college student, left his dorm room only once during a two-week period when his mild acne worsened. He missed his classes and avoided all social activities. He even didn't visit a close friend who just learned he had cancer. True, Charles had some pimples, but hardly enough to warrant such extreme avoidance. Charles qualified for BDD because his defect, while present, wasn't particularly noticeable, and his reaction was excessive.

What if I can't assess the severity of the defect because of its location? This is another challenge in diagnosing BDD. Many people with an "unassessable" defect have another supposed defect that's visible and can be assessed, which allows the diagnosis to be given. For example, although I didn't evaluate one patient's buttocks, I could see that his concern with his "crooked" eyes was unfounded. In other cases, an "unassessable" defect has been assessed by someone else who thinks it's fine; men with penis concerns often say that spouses and doctors alike have told them the size is normal. This information also allows a presumptive diagnosis of BDD to be made. Making the diagnosis can also be complicated if skin picking (a common symptom of BDD) has caused noticeable scarring. If it can be ascertained that the acne or scarring was fairly mild before the picking began, the person is a candidate for the BDD diagnosis.

I should emphasize, however, that in my experience the need to make difficult judgment calls is the exception rather than the rule. Of the patients I've seen, only 3% have had an unassessable defect in the absence of others I could assess. Only about one-third have had an actual defect, and in only a minority of cases was it difficult to determine whether it was "slight" (therefore qualifying for BDD) or clearly present. Most people I've seen had what I considered a *nonexistent defect. In some cases, the disliked body part is actually very attractive.* One woman who was obsessed with her "ugly" hair actually had beautiful hair. While she despaired because she thought it was "frizzy and ugly," other women asked her who her hairdresser was so they could have theirs done in a similar style. Another young woman had been asked to work as a model, and as a child she'd been told that she would someday be Miss America; however she believed that such requests and statements were motivated by pity for her ugliness.

It's worth considering whether people with more noticeable, "clearly present" defects (who don't qualify for a BDD diagnosis because of the obvious nature of their deformities) might nonetheless have features of BDD. Do people with birth defects, accident victims, or others with very noticeable physical flaws have experiences similar to those of people with BDD? Are they preoccupied with their flaw? Do they suffer as a result? Does it interfere with their functioning? Do they feel very self-conscious in social situations?

I've met some individuals with obvious defects for whom the answers to these questions are "yes." And research findings suggest that, for some individuals, the answers are "yes." Although by definition they don't have BDD because their defect is very obvious, they're preoccupied, distressed, and sometimes impaired by their appearance concerns. It's possible that much of what I'll be describing in this book applies to them as well. And what about people with physical features that, strictly speaking, aren't defects or flaws—for example, tattoos they no longer like? Do some of them have features of BDD? Some appear to. This is another important question that needs to be studied.

Criterion 2: Distress or Impairment in Functioning

To return to BDD's definition, I've already briefly discussed criterion 2 in Table 1 (distress or impairment), noting that the degree of distress and impairment in functioning varies considerably. This criterion is very helpful; requiring significant distress or impaired functioning for the diagnosis helps guard against overdiagnosis of BDD. Not everyone who dislikes his or her appearance has BDD. After all, concern with appearance is very common, especially during adolescence. Studies have shown that most of us dislike at least some aspect of how we look. And this concern is no doubt amplified by the messages that bombard us in fashion magazines, clothing advertisements, and makeup commercials. Magazines, television, billboards, and movies are filled with beautiful and glamorous people who, intended or not, set a certain standard for how we should look.

So criterion 2 (along with the requirement for preoccupation in criterion 1) draws a line between normal and excessive concern, and it indicates that people with normal appearance concerns shouldn't be considered to have a psychiatric disorder. A problem with this criterion, however, is that it isn't clear exactly where to draw this line. How much distress is required for the diagnosis? And how much impairment? While this issue of how to distinguish between "normal" and "abnormal" also applies to other psychiatric and medical disorders, it's particularly complicated with regard to BDD, because BDD echoes the very common concern so many of us have with how we look. Where normal concern leaves off and BDD begins is sometimes a difficult judgment call.

Nonetheless, if a person experiences at least moderate distress because of their perceived defect (as opposed to none or only mild distress), this is compatible with a diagnosis of BDD. More severe distress—or extreme and disabling distress—is clearly indicative of BDD. Regarding impairment in functioning, if a person avoids anything—for example, dating, school, or any social situations—that's consistent with having BDD. Even if the person doesn't avoid anything, they may still qualify for BDD if their appearance concerns interfere with their functioning in other ways—for example, if their work or school performance are impaired to at least a moderate degree. This might occur because their concentration is poor, their work or schoolwork is interrupted by BDD thoughts or behaviors, they're late for things, etc. And in cases of moderately severe or severe BDD—like Jennifer's, Chris's, and Andrew's—it's crystal clear that the impairment is significant and, therefore, the diagnosis applies.

People with BDD commonly experience interference in areas such as the following. They may avoid these situations partially or completely, or they may experience other types of interference in these areas:

- Spending time with friends
- Dating
- Intimate relationships
- Attending social functions and events
- Doing things with their family inside and outside of home
- Going to school or work each day
- Being on time for school or work
- Missing school or work
- Focusing on school or work
- Productivity at school or work
- Doing homework or maintaining grades
- Daily activities
- Maintaining a household, doing errands, going shopping

Criterion 3: Differentiating BDD from Other Disorders

The purpose of criterion 3 (the preoccupation isn't better accounted for by another disorder) is to ascertain that people with anorexia nervosa and certain other psychiatric disorders don't get misdiagnosed with BDD. Anorexia nervosa is a disorder in which people—usually young women—think they're fat and lose excessive amounts of weight to avoid being fat; in reality, they're terribly underweight. Sometimes they become skeletal but still fear they are, or will become, fat. According to DSM-IV definitions, someone whose only concern is that she's too fat and who is significantly (about 15% or more) underweight (and who meets certain other criteria for anorexia) should be diagnosed with anorexia nervosa, not BDD.

But the relationship between BDD and anorexia gets complicated when we consider the following: some researchers suggest that the core disturbance in anorexia nervosa isn't a problem with eating or food, but with body image. Indeed, people with anorexia fulfill criterion 1 for BDD in that they're preoccupied with a defect in their appearance (being fat) that others don't perceive. This view raises the very interesting and even heretical question of whether anorexia might be a form of BDD. If so, we would need to delete BDD's criterion 3. The interesting relationship between eating disorders and BDD is one that I'll return to in Chapter 16. For the time being, however, if a person's only significant appearance concern is that she's too fat, and she otherwise meets all diagnostic criteria for an eating disorder (see Appendix B), she should be diagnosed with an eating disorder, not BDD. However, a person can have *both* an eating disorder *and* BDD. A woman who thinks she's too fat *and* her nose is too bumpy has both disorders. In fact, many women with an eating disorder also have BDD. In other words, they have additional problematic body image concerns unrelated to being fat or overweight.

"A Sign on the Road"

The DSM-IV criteria for BDD provide a useful common language for BDD sufferers, clinicians, and researchers alike. They help researchers ascertain that they are all studying the same phenomenon. It's important that what I call BDD is what a researcher elsewhere calls BDD; this allows a coherent body of knowledge about the disorder to be developed. The criteria also allow clinicians to make the diagnosis, which, in turn, guides treatment. They can also be helpful to patients. As a man with BDD said to me, "I read DSM to find out what was wrong with me. It was a relief to know what I had. Finally, I'd found the road and a sign on the road telling me where I was."

While the criteria are useful guidelines, they do have the limitations I've discussed. In addition, they don't fully convey the experience of people with BDD. They don't tell us about their lives—the private torment, the fears, the isolation. Nor do they reflect what's unique about each person's experience.

Patients' experiences tell us far more than diagnostic criteria ever could. Jennifer and Sarah had certain things in common with Jane, whose story follows. They all fulfilled the diagnostic criteria for BDD: each was preoccupied with physical defects that were nonexistent or minimal and went unnoticed by others. Each was significantly distressed or impaired by her concerns. But in some ways, their experiences were quite different. Sarah's symptoms were relatively mild, and she functioned well despite them. Jane's symptoms, in contrast, were very severe. Because of them, she couldn't work and had been hospitalized. She thought she was so ugly that people stared at her through binoculars. And she even believed that people driving by her were so distracted by her "ugliness" that they got into car crashes when they saw her.

"My Biggest Wish Is to Be Invisible"

I clearly remember meeting Jane. As she rose from her chair in the waiting room I was struck by her long dark hair, soft features, and deep blue eyes. She was in her mid-thirties, fashionably dressed, tall, thin, and stately. She looked kind and earnest—but very timid and anxious. As she entered my office she explained that a friend had driven her to her appointment because she was too afraid to drive alone—which had everything to do with why she had come to see me.

"My biggest wish is to be invisible," she began. Despite her severe anxiety, she had the courage to get straight to the heart of the matter. Many people who see me are far too anxious to talk about their appearance right away. "Why do you want to be invisible?" I asked. "So no one will laugh at me and think I'm ugly," she replied. "That's my biggest fear." On the one hand, Jane's statements were hard to understand. She seemed a lovely woman, both her demeanor and her appearance. At the same time, I thought I understood. By now I had seen scores of people with BDD and knew this was how many of them feel.

"I think I have this disorder you're studying," she continued. "And I'm *totally* paralyzed by it. I think I have a really bad case. I haven't worked in ages. And you may not believe this, but I've hardly left my house in six years. This is one of the few times. That's why I couldn't come alone—I was much too scared." I had heard many people say they couldn't leave their house because they thought they were too ugly—but six years?

Jane wanted to start at the beginning. "My hatred of my appearance began when I was 12," she began. "I became obsessed with my nose; I thought it was too big and shiny. It started when I heard a boy in my class make a comment about Jimmy Durante. I can't even remember what he said, but he was snickering, and I was sure it was a mean comment. I thought he might be making fun of *me*—of *my* nose. I couldn't be sure, but I kept worrying that maybe there *was* something wrong with my nose, even though I'd never worried about it before. After that I started lifting up my lips to raise my nose so it wouldn't look so big. After a while, I couldn't concentrate in school because all I could think of was my nose. I didn't do my final eighth-grade project because I couldn't stand up in front of the class and have people see my nose. I skipped school that day and got an F. All my grades dropped—I went from straight As to Ds and Fs. I got very withdrawn, and I stopped seeing my friends."

"What were you like before then?" I asked. "I really wasn't very concerned with how I looked," she replied. "I was very active, a good student, and I had lots of confidence. But I was always very sensitive. And I wasn't very interested in boys and thought I should have been, so I wondered if something was wrong with me. But basically I was fine. Then the nose problem started, and my life went downhill. I've thought about it every day since."

"When I was 16 things got even worse," she continued. "When I was much younger I'd fallen against a table and got a slight scar on the top of my lip, but it never really bothered me until I was 16, when I got it surgically revised. Now I realize that was a mistake. Obviously, I got the revision to make the scar less noticeable, even though it was pretty faint, but it just made it worse. After the operation, I noticed a funny irregularity in a certain light, and it's been a disaster ever since. I think about it all the time—24 hours a day. I even have dreams about it. In my dreams people ask me things like, 'What's that thing on your lip?' and then they make nasty comments about it."

Jane's concern with her faint scar started at the time she was having problems with her boyfriend. "Maybe it was the stress," she said. "But I don't want you to misunderstand," she added. "Some of my therapists have tried to convince me that my appearance concerns are just a symptom of other problems—that they aren't my real problem. After years and years of trying to figure this out, I've finally come to the conclusion that they're wrong. *My obsessions have a life of their own.* They're a problem in their own right! They're not just a symptom of other problems." Jane started crying as she said this.

"I've been incredibly frustrated when I've been told that this isn't my real problem and that I had to figure out what my real problem is," she said. "*This* is a real problem. I do have other problems. I don't want you to think this is my only one. I've had problems with my parents, and I don't get along with my brother. Our family has had some serious financial problems. But this obsession is the biggest problem in my life. *This* is the problem that's kept me in my house for six years. I don't know if it's related to my childhood. Sometimes it feels *chemical*, totally out of my control, as if there's something biological driving it." Jane had fortunately found a therapist and a psychiatrist who took her concerns seriously and who treated her BDD as a legitimate disorder. That attitude alone had helped her greatly.

Jane returned to her story. But first she pulled her suede jacket up over her chin and mouth so I couldn't see her face from the nose down. She smiled slightly through her tears. "I have to hide my face before I tell you about this one," she said. Then she became completely serious. "It started when I was in my early twenties. I started worrying about my jaw when a surgeon I'd seen for a nose job said my nose was fine but my jaw was too big. I was totally devastated by that comment, and I've been haunted ever since. How could a simple comment like that trigger such a strong obsession that I've had ever since?"

Over the years, Jane had also worried about other things—that her breasts were too small and her buttocks too "big and round." "I tried to go to school to become a fashion designer—I was told I had a lot of talent—but I had to drop out. I couldn't go. I couldn't let people see how bad I looked. So many of my body parts were totally unpresentable. Then I tried working, but I stayed only a few weeks at each place. I felt I was really ugly and really unlikable. I just couldn't let people see me. It got worse and worse. I stopped dating, and then I stopped going out at all. I'm sure I'll never get married because of this. How can I? I never meet anyone. I'm totally isolated.

"My sister and grandmother started buying my clothes and food. I started spending my entire day in my parents' house. Sometimes I watch television, but mostly I walk back and forth between the bedrooms on the third floor, thinking about how ugly I look. When relatives come over, I hide upstairs and don't see them. I don't even see them on holidays like Thanksgiving. I feel overwhelmed and hopeless and out of control. Sometimes I panic, and I think 'I can't tolerate this. I'm going to die. I have to kill myself. I wish I could be put to sleep.'"

Jane started crying again. Her pain seemed too much to bear. "The hardest part of this is the isolation. I didn't see my own mother for two years, even though she lived in the same house with me. I was so ashamed of my appearance and that I'd dropped out of school and wasn't working that I completely avoided her. My family has no idea that I have this problem. I've kept it a secret. It's immature for me to be so concerned with how I look. I've been too ashamed to tell them."

Jane then described the one time she'd left her house in six years. "I got sick," she explained. "I tried putting off going to the doctor, but the pain got pretty intense. My grandmother convinced me to see him. When I finally went, I covered my face with bandages, so no one could see how I looked."

I thought of someone I'd seen several times in the town where I live. His face was notably disfigured—reddened and deeply scarred—and his nose and lips were misshapen. He looked as though he had birth defects and had suffered third-degree burns. This is what Jane *felt* she looked like—so deformed that when she left her house she covered her entire face with bandages.

"So coming here today was a big event. I haven't been out in so long that I was afraid to drive by myself. Sometimes when I drive I get especially freaked out because I think everyone is looking at me as they drive by and that they're thinking how ugly I am. Sometimes I think my face will frighten them so much that they'll crash their cars."

Jane had received a lot of treatment, both surgical and psychiatric. A nose job didn't help her feel any better about her nose, so she had it redone. The second procedure didn't help either. The revision of the scar on her lip actually triggered a new obsession. She continued to seek surgical treatment but finally stopped after four surgeons refused to do any further procedures.

"Later, when I realized my problem was psychiatric, not physical, it was still really hard for me," Jane said. "The first time I was hospitalized, the doctors and nurses on the psychiatry ward hadn't heard of BDD, so it was hard for them to understand me or take me seriously. I think they tried, but they didn't really get it. No one knew my inner torment. They tried to reassure me and talk me out of my concern, telling me I looked fine. The reassurance just made me feel pathetic. It felt patronizing. If I'd had any other problem, they would never have taken that approach. They would have realized it doesn't work."

Jane had received cognitive-behavioral therapy, a type of therapy that focuses on helping patients resist compulsive behaviors, such as mirror checking, and face feared situations, such as social situations. It also helps people develop more accurate and helpful appearance–related beliefs. She had also been treated with many psychiatric medications, including antipsychotics, lithium, tranquilizers, antidepressants, and others. A type of antidepressant known as a monoamine-oxidase inhibitor had been very helpful for several years but then stopped working. Because she then became so severely depressed over her appearance, Jane received electroconvulsive therapy (ECT), also known as shock therapy. This treatment, which is often extremely effective for severe depression, did temporarily help her depression somewhat but not her BDD. "It's still on my mind all the time," she said, "and I still consider suicide because of it."

Jane had also been in several support groups for people with a variety of psychiatric difficulties such as anxiety and depression. "Everyone else was pretty open about their problems, and I was to a certain extent. I talked about my depression and my family problems. But I couldn't discuss my appearance. I told them there was a big thing I was worried about, but I couldn't tell them what it was, even though I was in the group for four years. It was too humiliating, and I was afraid they wouldn't understand. I was afraid they'd focus on my defects more and notice how horrendous they looked. And I was afraid of their reaction, which I'd hear negatively, no matter what. That's what *always* happens. If someone says I look nice, I think that means I must have looked bad some other time. Or if someone says I have nice eyes, that must mean that something else about me is ugly. Or what if they didn't say something positive about my appearance the next time they saw me? I'd assume that meant I looked terrible! My *biggest* fear was that they'd *validate* my concern. I couldn't take the risk. So my isolation continued."

At the time she saw me, Jane was considering a consultation for a cingulotomy, a type of brain surgery that patients with severe psychiatric disorders sometimes undergo when other treatments haven't worked. Its effectiveness in BDD isn't known because it hasn't been studied. "I really don't want to have brain surgery," she said, "but I can't go on suffering like this."

I didn't treat Jane, but I spoke with her several times after I'd seen her. I'd recommended to her and her doctor that she postpone the surgery consultation and try a new combination of medications. With her new medications (a higher dose of fluoxetine [Prozac] than she'd taken in the past plus a medication called buspirone [Buspar]), she gradually felt better. Four months after I'd seen her she gave me a call. "You won't believe this," she said. "The medications have helped immensely. I can get out of the house, and I'm doing volunteer work as a receptionist." It was hard to believe that she had made such progress— even harder to believe that she was doing something that required her to interact so closely with people. "I still have BDD feelings," she said, "but I can view it more rationally. I can tell myself that people aren't looking at me. It's a real triumph to allow people to get so close to my face."

I heard from Jane again about six months later. Although her BDD wasn't entirely gone, she was still feeling much better and was still successfully volunteering. But about a year later, she called to tell me that she'd been feeling tired and more depressed. She decided to stop her medications, and her BDD symptoms gradually came back. But then I talked with her again, and this time she had good news: she had tried another medication (sertraline [Zoloft]) and had restarted therapy—and she was feeling great.

I hope that these stories, and others throughout this book, will convey *both* the common themes of BDD—what all people with this disorder share—*and* the uniqueness of each person's experience. Everyone with the disorder has much in common, yet each person's experience is his or her own. And even though BDD is quite different in some ways from normal appearance concerns, it also echoes them—it is an amplified, exaggerated, and sometimes quite distorted version of what most of us experience.

$$\cdot\cdot four \cdot\cdot$$

How Do I Know If I Have BDD?

BDD is Common But Underdiagnosed

BDD isn't rare. In fact, the numbers shown on the next page indicate it's fairly common. Research studies have found that about 1% of adults in the general population in the U.S. and Italy have BDD. These studies used DSM criteria and diagnosed BDD with face-to-face interviews, so the percentages may be fairly accurate. Studies of students have found far higher rates of BDD—from more than 2% of high school students to as many as 13% of college students. Some of the student studies used self-report questionnaires rather than face-to-face interviews to diagnose BDD, so they may have overdiagnosed it to some extent. We need much larger and more scientifically rigorous studies to more precisely determine how common BDD is in the general population and in students. But in the meantime, these study results indicate that millions of people in the U.S. alone have BDD.

Studies in clinical settings also suggest that BDD is fairly common. A study of 122 people in Minnesota who were hospitalized on a psychiatric inpatient unit found that a surprisingly high percentage (13%) had BDD. BDD was more common than schizophrenia, obsessive compulsive disorder, social phobia, eating disorders, and many other disorders. Rates of BDD among people receiving mental health treatment as an outpatient have found varying but often high rates, depending on the group being assessed. A study of patients with anorexia nervosa, for example, found that 39% also had BDD. Several studies of depressed outpatients found that BDD is more common than a host of other psychiatric disorders in people with depression (See Appendix D for a summary of these studies).

BDD also appears fairly common in other patient groups. In a research study I and my colleagues did of people who were seeing a dermatologist, 12% had probable BDD. Studies of people seeking cosmetic surgery have found that from 6% to 20% have BDD.

Some of my patients are convinced that these rates of BDD are falsely low. "Those are the ones who confess," one man told me. "If someone did a survey and asked me if I had BDD, I'd deny it. I'd be too embarrassed and ashamed.

**Table 1.   Studies have found that BDD occurs
in approximately. . . .**

- I in 100 adults in the general population (0.7%–1.1%)

- I in 50 to I in 8 students (2.3%–13%)

- I in 8 patients who are psychiatrically hospitalized (13%)

- I in 7 to nearly half of outpatients with atypical major depression*
  (14%–42%)

- I in 8 to 9 outpatients with social phobia* (11%–12%)

- I in 100 to I in 3 (average of I in 6) people with obsessive compulsive
  disorder* (OCD) (3%–37%)

- 4 of 10 hospitalized patients with anorexia nervosa* (39%)

- I in 8 to 11 patients seeking treatment from a dermatologist (9%–12%)

- I in 5 to 15 patients seeking cosmetic surgery (6%–20%)

*See Appendix B for a definition of these disorders; outpatients are people who seek treatment
without being hospitalized.

Also, if I was stuck in my house, how would I be in a survey? I wouldn't answer
the door."

It is clear, however, that health care professionals usually miss BDD. As a
result, BDD sufferers may not find out that they have BDD, and treatment may
not succeed because it doesn't target BDD. Five research studies have looked at
this important question. In these studies, the researchers asked a series of people
about BDD; they detected and diagnosed it in people who had it, because they
systematically asked everyone in the study about BDD symptoms. Then the
researchers looked at the patients' medical records to see whether their clinician
had correctly diagnosed BDD. The dismaying finding was that in all five studies,
the doctor or therapist hadn't diagnosed a single person with BDD. This was
the case in the Minnesota inpatient study; in that study, all of the patients with
BDD said that BDD was their most important problem or a major problem.
And in my study of 200 people with BDD, half of those treated with psychiatric
medication never revealed their BDD symptoms to their doctor.

These research results are very consistent with what I've heard for more than
a decade from my patients and people participating in my research studies. A
staggeringly high proportion of them have suffered with BDD for many years,
even decades, but were never diagnosed, even though they'd seen plenty of
doctors and therapists.

So why is BDD so underrecognized and underdiagnosed? Here are some
likely reasons.

Why BDD is Underdiagnosed

Secrecy and Shame

BDD is often a secret disorder. The BDD sufferer doesn't reveal their appearance concerns, and the health professional doesn't ask. Many people I've seen have never mentioned their appearance concerns to others. Many who've been in treatment with a mental health professional have never discussed their BDD symptoms, even though they were a serious problem. In the Minnesota inpatient study, all of the patients with BDD wanted their doctor to know about it but said they wouldn't raise it with their doctor unless they were specifically asked, because they felt too ashamed. In a study of patients with anorexia nervosa, of whom 39% also had BDD, all of those who also had BDD said they wouldn't reveal their BDD to their treater unless they were specifically asked because they were too ashamed. It takes courage to mention the concerns and discuss them. *If they aren't asked about, they may not be revealed.*

Reasons for secrecy and shame include the following:

- Worry about being considered superficial, silly, or vain;
- Worry that once the perceived defect is mentioned, others will notice it and focus on it more, causing even more embarrassment and shame;
- Fear that disclosure of the worry will be met with reassurance that the BDD sufferer looks fine. Many people with BDD interpret this response, although honest and well-meaning, to mean that they were foolish to have mentioned it, or that their emotional pain isn't being taken seriously or understood. If they get this response, they may not mention it again.

Lack of Familiarity with BDD

Many, including health professionals, still aren't aware that BDD is a known disorder that often responds to psychiatric treatment. Despite its long history, BDD entered psychiatry's diagnostic manual, DSM, only recently. When I began my research in the late 1980s, most of the mental health professionals I asked had never even heard of BDD. Fortunately, this is changing, but BDD is still among the lesser-known psychiatric disorders.

BDD Can Be Trivialized

BDD can be easily trivialized. Why should he care so much about a few pimples? How could she be so worried about her face when she's so pretty? The fact that BDD sufferers generally look fine, combined with the fact that appearance concerns are so common in the general population, contribute to its trivialization. BDD can be mistaken for vanity. But anyone who knows someone like Jennifer or Jane is only too aware of how serious—even life-threatening—the disorder can be.

Misdiagnosis

People with BDD may also have depression, social anxiety, or other symptoms that are often less embarrassing to discuss. Thus, they may receive the diagnosis of depression or social phobia, but not BDD. In addition, patients who reveal their BDD symptoms are sometimes told the symptoms aren't their "real problem"—that their real problem is low self-esteem, a relationship problem, or another issue. Although these problems may coexist with BDD, the BDD itself should also be diagnosed and treated if present. Sometimes, these problems— such as depression, social anxiety, or low self-esteem—are actually due to BDD. In these cases, it's even more critically important to diagnose BDD.

Pursuit of Nonpsychiatric Medical and Surgical Treatment

Many people with BDD see dermatologists, plastic surgeons, and other physicians rather than mental health professionals. They search, usually unsuccessfully, for a cosmetic solution to a body-image problem. Many people are unaware that BDD is a known psychiatric disorder for which psychiatric treatment is often effective. Although surgeons and dermatologists are increasingly aware of BDD, many are not. A 2001 survey of 265 members of the American Society for Aesthetic Plastic Surgery found that the surgeons thought that only 2% of patients seen for an initial cosmetic surgery consultation have BDD, whereas research studies indicate the rate is actually 7%–20%.

Screening Questions for BDD

How do you know whether you or someone you know has BDD? For the time being, psychiatric diagnoses—including BDD—are made primarily by asking questions that ascertain that DSM-IV criteria for the disorder are fulfilled. There are as yet no blood tests, brain-scanning techniques, or other tools sufficient to diagnose psychiatric disorders, although such tools are being developed.

I've developed several "diagnostic instruments" for BDD, which consist of questions useful in making the diagnosis. The questions (the BDDQ) on the next page are in a self-report format; that is, the BDDQ is a questionnaire that the patient fills out. The other set of questions, which is included in Appendix C (the BDD Diagnostic Module), is asked by a clinician. Both mirror the DSM-IV diagnostic criteria for BDD discussed in the last chapter and shown in Table 1, and they ascertain whether these criteria are fulfilled.

You're likely to have BDD if you give the following answers on the BDDQ (shown on the next page):

Body Dysmorphic Disorder Questionnaire (BDDQ)

Name _____

This questionnaire assesses concerns about physical appearance.
Please read each question carefully and circle the answer that
best describes your experience. Also write in answers where
indicated.

1. Are you very concerned about the appearance of some
   part(s) of your body that you consider especially
   unattractive?   Yes   No

   If yes: Do these concerns preoccupy you? That is,
   you think about them a lot and wish you could think
   about them less?   Yes   No

   If yes: What are they? _____

   Examples of areas of concern include: your skin
   (e.g., acne, scars, wrinkles, paleness, redness); hair
   (e.g., hair loss or thinning); the shape or size of
   your nose, mouth, jaw, lips, stomach, hips, etc.; or
   defects of your hands, genitals, breasts, or any
   other body part.

   If yes: What specifically bothers you about the
   appearance of these body part(s)? (Explain in detail):

   _____

   _____

**(NOTE: If you answered "No" to either of the above questions,
you are finished with this questionnaire. Otherwise please
continue.)**

2. Is your main concern with your appearance that you
   aren't thin enough or that you might become too fat?   Yes   No

3. What effect has your preoccupation with your appearance had on your life?

   • Has your defect(s) caused you a lot of distress or
     emotional pain?   Yes   No

   • Has it significantly interfered with your social life?   Yes   No

   If yes: How? _____

   _____

   _____

(continued)

• Has your defect(s) significantly interfered with your
school work, your job, or your ability to function in
your role (e.g., as a homemaker)?   Yes   No

If yes: How? _____

_____

• Are there things you avoid because of your defect(s)? Yes   No

If yes: What are they? _____

_____

_____

• Have the lives or normal routines of your family or
friends been affected by your appearance concerns?   Yes   No

If yes: How? _____

_____

_____

4. How much time do you spend thinking about your defect(s) per day
on average? (add up all the time you spend) (circle one)

(a) Less than 1 hour a day
(b) 1–3 hours a day
(c) More than 3 hours a day

• Question 1: Yes to both parts
• Question 3: Yes to any of the questions
• Question 4: Answer b or c

Question 1 establishes whether preoccupation is present, and question 3 establishes whether the preoccupation causes significant distress or impairment. Regarding question 4, while the BDD criteria don't require that the defect be thought about for a specified amount of time a day, it's useful to ask this question. If you spend at least one hour a day thinking about it, I'm more likely to diagnose BDD. In fact, I have significant reservations about diagnosing BDD in anyone who spends less than an hour a day in total thinking about their perceived defect, because I'd generally consider them insufficiently preoccupied to fulfill criterion 1 for the diagnosis. Everyone I've given the diagnosis to has at some point spent at least this much time focused on their concern.

A note of caution about the BDDQ: it's intended as a screening instrument, not a diagnostic one. What this means is that the BDDQ can suggest that BDD is present but can't necessarily give a definitive diagnosis. The diagnosis is ideally determined by a trained clinician in a face-to-face interview. There are several reasons for this. First, in general, clinical judgment should be used to confirm that answers on a self-report questionnaire indicate the presence of a disorder;

for example, is any distress or impairment that's reported on the questionnaire problematic enough to warrant a psychiatric diagnosis? In addition, for BDD to be diagnosed, it must be determined that the physical defect is nonexistent or slight. Finally, as required by DSM-IV criterion 3, a clinician should ascertain that appearance concerns aren't better accounted for by an eating disorder. A "yes" answer to question 2 raises the question of whether an eating disorder is a more accurate diagnosis. This issue is complicated, however, because weight concerns could indicate the presence of either an eating disorder or BDD (see chapter 16).

Additional information about the BDDQ, including its psychometric (measurement) properties, is included in Appendix C. That appendix also includes the clinician-administered counterpart of the BDDQ (the BDD Diagnostic Module), a brief set of questions that determines the presence of BDD. In addition, Appendix C includes a clinician-administered instrument that assesses the severity of BDD symptoms (the Yale-Brown Obsessive Compulsive Scale modified for BDD).

Clues: Mirror Checking, Grooming, Skin Picking, and Others

The BDDQ questions ask about the core definitional features of BDD—what's required for the diagnosis. But BDD has some features that, while not necessary for the diagnosis, can provide clues to its presence. These include frequent mirror checking, excessive grooming, face picking, reassurance seeking and other behaviors.

I've sometimes observed strangers doing things that have made me wonder if they have BDD. I once saw a young man in a parking lot who stood outside his car repeatedly checking his hair in a side-view mirror, frantically combing and recombing it. He wasn't simply taking a quick glance, as some people might—instead, he seemed "stuck" there, and appeared extremely agitated and distressed over the state of his hair. I once drove behind a woman on a busy highway for about 20 miles who spent most of the time looking in her rearview mirror fixing her hair, rather than looking at the road. And what about the young woman I saw at a baseball game who seemed to have normal body hair everywhere except her arms, which had none? Had she removed it through excessive "grooming," trying to improve "excessively" hairy arms? Did any of these people have BDD? Without talking with them, I couldn't make the diagnosis. But their behaviors were clues to the diagnosis that made me wonder.

Some of the more common clues to BDD are in Table 2. Many of the questions in Table 2 ask about behaviors, such as mirror checking and reassurance seeking, that many people with BDD perform (these are described in Chapter 7). Other questions ask about consequences of BDD—for example, being housebound (these are described in Chapter 8). If you answered "yes" to any of the questions in Table 2, this doesn't necessarily mean that you have BDD. But "yes" answers—especially many "yes" answers—suggest that BDD may very

Table 2.   Clues to the Presence of BDD

1. Do you often check your appearance in mirrors or other reflecting surfaces, such as windows? Or do you frequently check your appearance without using a mirror, by looking directly at the disliked body part?

2. Do you avoid mirrors because you dislike how you look?

3. Do you frequently compare yourself to others and often think that you look worse than they do?

4. Do you often ask—or want to ask—others whether you look okay, or whether you look as good as other people?

5. Do you try to convince other people that there's something wrong with how you look, but they consider the problem nonexistent or minimal?

6. Do you spend a lot of time grooming—for example, combing or arranging your hair, tweezing or cutting your hair, applying makeup, or shaving? Do you spend too much time getting ready in the morning, or do you groom yourself frequently during the day? Do others complain that you spend too much time in the bathroom?

7. Do you pick your skin, popping pimples or trying to get rid of blackheads or blemishes, because you're trying to make it look better?

8. Do you try to cover or hide parts of your body with a hat, clothing, makeup, sunglasses, your hair, your hand, or other things? Is it hard to be around other people when you haven't done these things?

9. Do you often change your clothes, trying to find an outfit that covers or improves disliked aspects of your appearance? Do you take a long time selecting your outfit for the day, trying to find one that makes you look better?

10. Do you try to hide certain aspects of your appearance by maintaining a certain body position—for example, turning your face away from others? Do you feel uncomfortable if you can't be in your preferred positions?

11. Do you think that other people take special notice of you in a negative way because of how you look? For example, when you walk down the street, do you think others are noticing what's unattractive about you?

12. Do you think that other people are thinking negative thoughts about you or making fun of you because of how you look? Are you "paranoid" because of this?

(continued)

13. It is hard for you to leave your house, or have you actually been housebound, because of how you look?

14. Do you frequently measure parts of your body, hoping to find they're as small as, as large as, or as symmetrical as you'd like?

15. Do you spend a lot of time looking for information or reading about your appearance problems in the hope that you'll reassure yourself about how you look or find a solution to your problem?

16. Have you wanted to get cosmetic surgery, dermatologic treatment, or other medical treatment to fix your appearance when other people (for example, friends or doctors) have told you such treatment isn't necessary? Have surgeons been reluctant to do cosmetic surgery, saying the defect is too minor or they're afraid you won't be pleased with the results?

17. Have you had cosmetic surgery or dermatologic treatment and been disappointed with the results? Or have you had multiple surgeries, hoping that with the next procedure your appearance problems will finally be fixed?

18. Do you work out excessively to improve your appearance?

19. Do you diet, even though others tell you it isn't necessary?

20. Do you avoid having your picture taken because you think you look so bad?

21. Are you late for things because you worry you don't look okay or because you're trying to fix an appearance problem?

22. Do you get depressed or anxious because of how you look?

23. Have you felt that life wasn't worth living because of your appearance?

24. Do you get very frustrated or angry because of how you look?

25. Does it take you longer to do things because you're distracted by appearance worries or related behaviors such as mirror checking?

26. Do you feel more comfortable going out at night, or sitting in a dark part of a room, because your defects will be less visible?

27. Do you have panic attacks or get very anxious when you look in the mirror because of how you look?

well be present. In this case, it's a good idea to get an evaluation from a professional who's knowledgeable about BDD.

Additional Clues: Depression, Social Anxiety, and Other Symptoms

Many people with BDD are depressed. Others have problems with alcohol or drugs. Many are anxious, and some have panic attacks. Indeed, BDD often coexists with or causes other psychiatric symptoms and disorders, which can provide additional clues to its presence.

I and other researchers have carefully assessed the frequency of other psychiatric disorders (e.g., depression) in people with BDD. Conversely, we have studied BDD in patients with other psychiatric disorders. Appendix D shows these findings in greater detail. These study results indicate that major depression is the most common disorder in people with BDD. Major depression is characterized by depressed mood, decreased interest and pleasure, and other symptoms, such as sleep and appetite disturbance. (See Appendix B for a further description of this and other psychiatric disorders.) While major depression is fairly common, affecting 10 to 20% of the general population at some point in their lifetime, more than 80% of people with BDD have major depression at some point in their life. For many, the depression is quite severe. In some cases, the depression and the BDD seem to be somewhat "separate," whereas in many cases, the depression appears largely due to BDD.

In a study that my colleagues (Dr. Andrew Nierenberg of Harvard Medical School) and I did, BDD was more than twice as common as OCD in people with depression. In a research study of depressed people in Italy, BDD was more common than many other disorders, including OCD, social phobia, simple phobia, generalized anxiety disorder, bulimia nervosa, and substance abuse or dependence. These results are striking because, as a little-known disorder, BDD generally isn't looked for in people with depression. In addition, Dr. Nierenberg and I found that depressed people who also had BDD had onset of depression at a relatively young age and unusually persistent depression. These findings suggest that depressed people—especially those with long-standing depression—should be asked whether they have BDD symptoms.

Certain other disorders also commonly co-occur with BDD and may be a clue to its presence. One of these is social phobia (also known as social anxiety disorder), an excessive fear of social or performance situations due to a fear of doing something embarrassing or humiliating. Another is obsessive compulsive disorder (OCD), characterized by obsessions (intrusive, recurrent, unwanted thoughts that are difficult to dismiss despite their disturbing nature) and compulsions (repetitive behaviors that are intended to reduce the anxiety caused by obsessions). A high percentage of people with BDD have had problems with alcohol or drugs. The only study I know of that's assessed how common BDD is in this group was the Minnesota inpatient study I mentioned earlier. This study found that a surprisingly high percentage—26%—of inpatients with a substance use disorder (drugs or alcohol) also had BDD.

So it's important to ask people with these disorders whether they have symptoms of BDD. It's important to inquire, because BDD sufferers may be too embarrassed and ashamed to volunteer their symptoms. In the depression study and the substance abuse study I just described, not a single person revealed his or her BDD symptoms to their doctor or therapist until specifically asked about them, reflecting BDD's often secretive nature.

How to Avoid Misdiagnosing BDD

In addition to being *under*diagnosed, BDD can easily be *mis*diagnosed as another psychiatric disorder. This occurs because BDD can produce symptoms that mimic another disorder, such as social phobia. Table 3 lists some of the disorders that are most commonly confused with BDD.

It's important to note that all of the disorders in this table can *co-exist* with BDD. In other words, a person with BDD can have other disorders *in addition to* BDD. In fact, people with BDD often have depression, social phobia, or OCD as well as BDD. (See Appendix D for more detailed information). If a person with BDD also has other psychiatric disorders, both those disorders and BDD should be diagnosed and targeted in treatment.

BDD is usually easy to recognize if you keep in mind the reasons for misdiagnosis and underdiagnosis, as well as the clues in this chapter. But what's most important is taking your own concerns or those of someone else seriously. If you simply reassure someone with BDD that they look fine (even though they do), they may take this to mean that you aren't really listening to or don't understand their problem. Asking about and listening to the concerns—and taking them seriously—is the best approach to take.

Table 3. Misdiagnosis and How To Avoid This

Disorder That's Diagnosed Instead of BDD	Brief Definition*	Why BDD May Be Misdiagnosed As Another Disorder	How To Avoid Misdiagnosing BDD
Major depression	Depressed mood, decreased interest, and other symptoms such as sleep and appetite disturbance for at least several weeks in a row	Depressive symptoms that coexist with BDD are diagnosed, but BDD is missed; or BDD symptoms are considered a symptom of depression, and BDD isn't diagnosed. In my clinical experience, this is the most common diagnostic error.	• Look for BDD in people with depression • Don't assume that appearance concerns are simply a symptom of depression • Diagnose BDD if it's present
Social phobia (Social anxiety disorder)	An excessive fear of social or performance situations due to a fear of doing something embarrassing or humiliating	BDD often causes social anxiety, withdrawal, and avoidance; the social anxiety may be quite noticeable, but the BDD may be kept secret. This can lead to misdiagnosis of BDD as social phobia or avoidant personality disorder.	• Don't assume that social anxiety or avoidance is just due to social phobia. • If social anxiety or avoidance are largely due to BDD, BDD rather than social phobia should be diagnosed • Some people have *both* BDD and social phobia, in which case both diagnoses should be given.

Agoraphobia	Anxiety about being in places or situations from which escape might be difficult or embarrassing, or in which help might not be available, in the event of having a panic attack or panic-like symptoms	Because some people with BDD think they're too ugly to leave their house, or because they fear that others are taking special notice of their perceived defect, they may feel anxious in and avoid a variety of situations.	• People with features of agoraphobia should be asked whether they're anxious in and avoid situations because of how they look. If the avoidance is largely because of BDD, BDD should be diagnosed instead of agoraphobia.
Obsessive compulsive disorder (OCD)	Obsessions and/or compulsions that are time-consuming, distressing, or impairing	Because BDD and OCD are both characterized by obsessions and repetitive behaviors, BDD can be misdiagnosed as OCD.	• If the obsessions (preoccupations) and behaviors focus on physical appearance, BDD is the more accurate diagnosis.
Panic disorder	Recurrent panic attacks that come out of the blue followed by concern about having more attacks, worry about the consequences of the attacks, or a significant change in behavior related to the attacks	People with BDD can have panic attacks as a result of BDD. They may feel intensely uncomfortable and fearful—and experience physical symptoms, such as a pounding heart, sweating, or trouble breathing—because they're so upset by how they look. These attacks of extreme anxiety can be triggered by the mirror or thinking someone is staring at the person or mocking their looks.	• To receive a diagnosis of panic disorder, the panic attacks must come "out of the blue"—not triggered by BDD or another disorder. • If BDD is the cause of panic attacks, BDD should be diagnosed. Panic attacks may be the initial clue that leads to the diagnosis of BDD.

(continued)

Table 3. Misdiagnosis and How To Avoid This *(continued)*

Disorder That's Diagnosed Instead of BDD	Brief Definition*	Why BDD May Be Misdiagnosed As Another Disorder	How To Avoid Misdiagnosing BDD
Trichotillomania	Recurrent hair pulling, resulting in noticeable hair loss	Some people with BDD remove their hair (body, head, or facial hair) to try to improve their appearance.	• If the purpose of the hair pulling is to improve a perceived "defect" in appearance, BDD should be diagnosed rather than trichotillomania.
Schizophrenia	Symptoms such as delusions, hallucinations, disorganized speech, behavior that is grossly disorganized or abnormal	BDD beliefs are often delusional, and many people with BDD believe other people take special notice of them (referential thinking)	If the delusional beliefs and referential thinking are limited to appearance, and there are no other symptoms of schizophrenia, BDD is the more accurate diagnosis.

*See Appendix B for a more detailed definition of these disorders.

·· five ··

BDD Comes in Many Forms

*"I'm the ugliest thing in the world. I hate my skin and my hair,
and my hips are too fat. I hate how I look. I feel repulsive. It's
the first thing I think of in the morning: how am I going to look
today?"* **Janice**

Overview of Body Parts and Behaviors

*E*very time I meet someone with BDD and listen to their story, I hear familiar themes. In some ways, it's similar to that of other people with BDD. But each person's experience is also in some ways unique.

This is shown by Table 4 on the following pages, where I've listed 15 examples of body areas of concern, along with accompanying behaviors and consequences. People with BDD can dislike any part of their body and can perform an unlimited variety of behaviors to cope. But although each person's experience is unique, certain patterns and themes are evident.

The first description in the table refers to Carol, a young woman who thought that her thighs were too flabby and her nose misshapen. In reality, her thighs were taut; on close inspection, her nose was slightly misshapen, but not noticeably so. She nonetheless believed these defects were clearly visible to other people and that others even took special notice of them. Because she was so upset by her reflection, she avoided mirrors. She also avoided swimming, many social events, and dating.

Which Body Parts Are Disliked?

It's interesting that William Stekel's observation from half a century ago—in which he noted concerns with the nose, balding, ears, eyes, breasts, and genitals—are supported by recent research findings. My data, as well as that of other researchers, show that people with BDD are usually concerned with specific parts of the body, often the areas he mentioned.

Table 4.   Examples of Preoccupations, Behaviors and Consequences*

Appearance Concerns	Associated Behaviors and Consequences

1. Thighs too flabby
   Nose misshapen
	1. Believes others take special
	      notice
	   Avoids mirrors
	   Avoids swimming, social activities,
	      and dating
	   Had nose surgery
	   Diets

2. Thinning hair	2. Excessive hair combing
	   Checks mirrors excessively
	   Problems with girlfriend
	   Social avoidance
	   Consulted a dermatologist

3. Hair "never right"
   Body shape abnormal (hips too
      wide, shoulders too nar-
      row, waist too high and
      wide)
	3. Checks mirrors and windows
	      excessively
	   Buys excessive hair products
	   Gets lots of haircuts and perms
	   Questions others about
	      appearance
	   Wears baggy clothing
	   Avoids gym class, swimming, and
	      social activities

4. Beard growth asymmetric
   Eyes too small
   "Blotchy" skin
	4. Believes others take special
	      notice
	   Checks mirrors excessively
	   Compares self with others
	   Shaves excessively
	   Picks skin
	   Wears tinted glasses to hide eyes
	   Grew long hair to cover face
	   Avoids magazines, social activi-
	      ties, dating
	   Housebound

5. Lines around mouth
   Hair loss
   Chin too prominent and
      asymmetric
   Teeth crooked, curved, and
      too large
   Cheeks sunken
   Nose too large
	5. Believes others take special
	      notice
	   Excessively checks and avoids
	      mirrors
	   Compares self with others
	   Seeks reassurance
	   Avoids social activities and dating
	   Difficulty working
	   Had braces several times

Table 4.   (*continued*)

Appearance Concerns	Associated Behaviors and Consequences
6. Facial skin and muscle tone flabby Hair too curly Dark circles under eyes Acne	6. Checks mirrors and other reflecting surfaces excessively Frequent hair perms and straightening Frequent makeup application Compares self with others Avoids shopping, school, social situations, dating, and sex
7. Nose bumpy and too small at tip after surgery Facial and body hair excessive and dark One tooth longer than another Body too fat	7. Believes others take special notice Excessively checks mirrors Avoids dating Had teeth filed Saw an endocrinologist to evaluate body hair Had electrolysis Diets Excessively exercises
8. Thinning hair Shrunken and sagging facial muscles Facial skin too loose Lips too thin Cheekbones asymmetric Penis too small Body build too small	8. Avoids mirrors Repeatedly touches doorknobs to tighten skin Excessively lifts weights Wears a hat Stuffs shorts and wears shirts down to knees to cover crotch Grew a beard to cover face Missed school Avoids shopping and social activities Leaves the house only at night Uses numerous hair tonics
9. Ugly face Facial scar	9. Checks mirrors, car bumpers, and windows excessively Camouflages scar Late for school Difficulty interviewing for jobs
10. Penis too small Wrists and body build too small	10. Believes others take special notice Checks mirrors excessively

(*continued*)

Appearance Concerns	Associated Behaviors and Consequences
Pot belly	Compares self with others
	Avoids showers in gym class
	Covers crotch with long clothes and wears bulky clothes
	Lifts weights excessively
	Avoids dating and sex
	Consulted a urologist for penis surgery
11. Nose too large Hair too curly Forehead too high Face too long and thin Breasts too small	11. Believes others take special notice
	Checks nose, brushes hair, and applies makeup excessively
	Asks others for reassurance
	Wears padded bras
	Holds head in certain positions so nose looks smaller
	Covers forehead with bangs
	Spends large sums of money on hair products
	Unable to go to school, work, swim, or socialize
12. Waist fat Nose too wide Chest hair asymmetric Pubic, underarm, and leg hair ugly Skin too white	12. Believes others take special notice
	Checks mirrors and store and car windows
	Changes clothes frequently
	Sits and stands only in certain positions so waist isn't visible under clothing
	Shaves body hair
	Wears bronzer
	Avoids commercials and ads with "gorgeous people"
	Avoids dating, sex, swimming, shopping, and public transportation
	Had several nose jobs and liposuction
13. Circles and puffiness under eyes	13. Believes others take special notice

Table 4.   (*continued*)

Appearance Concerns	*Associated Behaviors and Consequences*
Lines on face Stomach too fat Buttocks misshapen	Checks mirrors and other re- flecting surfaces excessively Seeks reassurance Compares self with others Avoids salty foods Takes diuretics (water pills) Camouflages with makeup Avoids swimming Had liposuction
14. Thinning hair Hips too slim Acne scarring Large pores on face Shoulders too broad	14. Believes others take special notice Compares self to others Avoids haircuts Got a hair weave Picks skin
15. Nose unattractive Chin and neck too large and wide Facial rash and acne Body too fat	15. Believes others take special notice Avoids mirrors Worries nose will break or oth- erwise be damaged Compares with others Covers face with hands Seeks reassurance Picks skin Sleeps and uses alcohol to avoid thinking about appearance Avoids restaurants, other public places, and dating Housebound

*The descriptions are examples of what people with BDD experience; they don't provide a comprehensive list of all BDD concerns.

Table 5, which reflects data from more than 500 people who have participated in my research studies, illustrates that BDD can strike virtually anywhere. The skin, hair, or nose are most often disliked. On average, people are concerned with five body parts over the course of the disorder. But the number can range from only one to virtually every body part. It's likely that people under-report

Table 5. Location of Perceived Defects in BDD

Body Part	Percent (%) of Patients with Concern*
Skin	73
Hair	56
Nose	37
Weight	22
Stomach	22
Breasts/chest/nipples	21
Eyes	20
Thighs	20
Teeth	20
Legs (overall)	18
Body build/bone structure	16
Ugly face (general)	14
Face size/shape	12
Lips	12
Buttocks	12
Chin	11
Eyebrows	11
Hips	11
Ears	9
Arms/wrists	9
Waist	9
Genitals	8
Cheeks/cheekbones	8
Calves	8
Height	7
Head size/shape	6
Forehead	6
Feet	6
Hands	6
Jaw	6
Mouth	6
Back	6
Fingers	5
Neck	5
Shoulders	3
Knees	3
Toes	3
Ankles	2
Facial muscles	1

*The percentages add up to more than 100% because people are usually concerned with more than one aspect of their appearance.

worries about certain body areas—for example, the breasts and genitals—because they're embarrassed, and that the true percentages for certain areas are higher than those listed here.

Some people with BDD also have "subclinical" concerns with certain body areas; that is, in addition to the body parts they're preoccupied with, they dislike others, but not to the point where they're preoccupied with them or experience distress or impairment as a result. Heather, for example, disliked her "wide" nose and her weight, but her weight wasn't a significant concern and didn't preoccupy her. "It's much less severe than my nose," she said. "I don't like it, but it's not really a problem." In my research, I've made an effort to identify the body parts that are the focus of preoccupation, and have listed only excessive and problematic concerns in Table 5. If I had identified all the body parts which people had any dissatisfaction with whatsoever, the percentages for each body area would be much higher.

Some people with BDD think they sometimes look okay. As one woman said, "When my hair looks okay, I think I look attractive. But when it's bad, which it often is, I think I'm really ugly." People who are worried about minor acne may think they look fine when their skin is better—but when it's "broken out," it's a disaster.

I've found that skin concerns are most frequent. Two thirds of people with skin concerns obsess about perceived acne or scarring, followed by concerns with marks (one third) and skin color (one quarter), typically thinking it's too red or too white. But virtually any aspect of the skin can be disliked—facial pores that are considered unusually large, veins, capillaries, or other skin flaws. Some people think their skin is the wrong color—typically too red or too white. Others obsess about wrinkles, lines, sagging, shriveling, or stretch marks, which they may consider a sign of aging.

Like Jennifer, who was preoccupied with pimples, scars, and facial marks, as well as her "ghost-like" skin color, some people have multiple skin concerns. Ellen was obsessed with supposed facial acne and scars, as well as veins, which were barely discernible to other people. Like Jennifer, she excessively checked mirrors and repeatedly asked her mother for reassurance—for example, "Do you think this pimple will go away? Will I have a scar?" To improve her skin, Ellen spent lots of time applying makeup and picking, sometimes using pins. She also compulsively washed her hands to avoid causing pimples while she picked. Dermatologic treatment temporarily diminished Ellen's preoccupation, but, as she described it, she became "more sensitive to smaller imperfections," resulting in no overall improvement in her concern.

Hair concerns are also very common. The most common worries focus on hair loss, thinning, or balding (a concern of one third of people who dislike their hair) and excessive facial or body hair (also present in one third of people with hair concerns). But hair obsessions may focus on virtually any aspect of the hair: it's too curly, too straight, too full, not full enough, uneven, messy, or dirty. James, a teacher, thought his hair "never looked right." He feared that it was thinning and that other people laughed at him because he was going bald.

Each day he applied hair potions that cost him hundreds of dollars a month. Although his friends said his hair looked fine, he was so upset over it that he bought a thousand-dollar hairpiece. But this didn't help. As he stated, "I was never satisfied; I still battled myself and wanted to get rid of it." In fact, James was so unhappy with his hairpiece that he destroyed it in a fit of rage.

While men are more likely than women to worry about thinning hair, women have this concern as well. One woman said her mother had very thin hair, and she feared she would eventually look even worse than her mother, becoming completely bald. It was hard to come in to see me because she feared she became "balder and balder" with each visit.

Getting a haircut is usually a very distressing—even traumatic—event for people with hair concerns. "I'm terrified of getting my hair cut," Jon told me. "Getting the right haircut is *crucial*. There's very little stability in my life because of the BDD. How I feel and function depends on how I happen to look and the quality of my haircut."

Hair concerns may also involve other body hair. Men may be preoccupied with supposedly uneven, light, or heavy beard growth. Men or women may think they have too much or too little body hair. Marie, an attractive 24-year-old nursing student, worried that she had "excessive" and "dark" hair on her nose and arms. She thought about her hair nearly "all day every day," and she repeatedly looked at her arms, tweezed her hair at work, and, using special lights, checked her facial hair in mirrors for an hour a day. She tried to hide her hair with makeup, had electrolysis, wore long sleeves in the summer, and covered her face with her hands. Marie described her preoccupation as "severely upsetting," saying that she felt "masculine" and "like a freak" whom no one would ever love.

Nose concerns are also very common. About 60% of people with nose concerns worry that their nose is too large. More than a quarter worry it's bumpy or misshapen. Less commonly—sometimes after nose surgery—they think it's too small. One woman thought her nose was "bumpy and swollen"; a middle-aged man thought his was "puffy." People with nose concerns are especially likely to have surgery—often repeated surgeries. One woman I treated first thought her nose was too large, and then, after surgery, felt it was too small. A college student first believed his nose was too long, but then, after surgery, thought his nostrils were too wide.

I once had an interesting conversation with a psychiatrist from Japan who was familiar with BDD. He was surprised to learn that I'd found that people in the U.S. usually worry that the nose is too large; in his experience, in Japan the concern is often that the nose is too small. In addition, he said that concerns with hair loss are uncommon in Japan. These observations raise the interesting question of whether cultural factors may influence the exact worry that people have.

BDD can also involve larger body areas. Many men are preoccupied with their overall body build, thinking they look too small or inadequately muscular. This form of BDD is called "muscle dysmorphia." They may wear many layers of clothing to enhance their size, excessively lift weights, or use potentially dangerous anabolic steroids to bulk up. Others—often women—are concerned that they're too large or overweight. Of the people in my studies, 22% were excessively concerned with their weight.

While people with BDD are concerned with, on average, about five different body parts over time, some are preoccupied with virtually every body area. Sometimes concerns with different body areas are present simultaneously, and sometimes sequentially. I've identified three common patterns:

1. About 30% are concerned with one body part—or one set of body parts—over time. One man was concerned with his receding chin and never developed another concern. Another became concerned simultaneously with his "sunken" eyes and "swollen" nipples; he remained concerned only with these two things, without developing new concerns.
2. About 40% are concerned with one body part and then add new parts over time, with continuation of their previous concerns. At age 13, Ted worried that his ears stuck out, then at 18 he also became concerned with his crooked lip, and at age 25 he started to worry about a scar on his neck. At 25, he had all three concerns.
3. The third pattern is more complex, and occurs in about 30%. Over time, concerns with one or more body parts disappear and other concerns emerge. Jane, whom I described in chapter 3, fit this pattern. She first worried about her nose and then a scar on her lip. Later, she became preoccupied with her jaw, breasts, and buttocks, but stopped worrying about her buttocks. One concern can begin when another ends. One man stated after nose surgery that his nose looked more acceptable, but his "stomach took over for (his) nose."

While some people with BDD want to be unusually attractive or look "perfect" overall, in my experience most don't—they simply want to look normal. They might not *mind* looking like Elvis Presley or Marilyn Monroe, but this isn't what they're obsessed with. What they're obsessed with is getting rid of the perceived defect and looking normal. They want to no longer look like the Elephant Man; they want to no longer stand out in a crowd. They say things like, "I don't want to look tanned like George Hamilton; I just want to look *not pale*." "Being average looking is okay. My goal is to be acceptable." As one man said, "I don't care whether I'm attractive. I just want to look normal. I wouldn't mind looking like Beetle Bailey; I just don't want things on my face."

People with BDD describe their perceived appearance problem in various ways. They may say that the defect, or their appearance more generally, is ugly, unattractive or abnormal. Or they may say that it looks defective, flawed, wrong, odd, not right, or off. Some people use words like "deformed," "monstrous" or "hideous." They describe themselves as the Elephant Man or the wife of Frankenstein. One man said he looked like a cartoon character, and a woman said that she resembled a distorted figure from a Salvador Dali painting.

For simplicity's sake, I'll generally use the term "defect" or "flaw" to refer to these various appearance concerns. I'll also use this term to refer to more than one concern and to more general excessive concerns with appearance that aren't so easily pinpointed or confined to a specific body part or parts.

"My Face Is Falling"

Most people with BDD describe the perceived flaw in quite specific and understandable terms—for example, "My ears are pointed," "I have a scar right here on my neck," "My hairline is receding," or "My waist is too wide." But others express it in ways that are vague and hard to understand. One man was preoccupied with his "inadequately firm eyes." A woman described in a published case report complained of "a funny and crinkly nose," and another stated, "the skin under my eyes joins my nose in a funny way." A woman I interviewed was extremely distressed because her face was falling. I tried very hard to understand what she meant. After much discussion, it seemed that she thought that her facial muscles were wasting away and her facial skin was sagging. But she thought "my face is falling" best described her concern.

"I Hate Everything About My Looks!"

A common misconception about BDD is that it has to involve one, or just a few, specific body areas. But some people dislike so many areas that they hate most of their body. One man intensely disliked and was preoccupied with 33 "abnormal" body areas! Other people dislike so many body parts that they don't break down their concern into individual areas. They say things like, "My entire body is ugly," or "I hate everything about how I look."

Some people, however, discuss their appearance concerns in more general terms because they're too embarrassed to reveal and discuss the specific areas they dislike. Or they're afraid that describing the problem more specifically will draw more attention to it. After all, it's much easier to say, "There's something wrong with how I look" than "I think my penis is too small." As one woman said, "I told my doctor about my aging fears, but not about the wrinkles or hair. It's easier to talk in generalities."

The first two times I saw Larry, he told me, "I just don't like my face; I don't like how it looks. It feels different from everyone else's." "Is there anything in particular that you don't like?" I asked him. "No, nothing specific—I just don't like it," he replied. It wasn't until the third time I saw him that he felt comfortable enough to reveal the specifics: that his nose was too wide, his forehead too small, and his eyes too beady. "I was much too embarrassed to tell you these things before," he said. "I feel ashamed."

"I Look Like a Gorilla"

Some people find it easier and more accurate to describe their appearance concerns in terms of animals, other people, or even food. One of the first people with BDD whom I saw had many appearance concerns, one of which was his "egg-shaped head." Another person said he looked like a chicken. This was, in his view, the best description of his appearance and was as important as his specific concerns—wrinkles on his face, a large nose, a thin face, and sunken cheekbones. In a published report a person complained of "chipmunk cheeks." A woman concerned about excessive facial hair described herself as a gorilla. Such unflattering descriptions reflect how the person *thinks* he or she looks. They help us see how people with BDD see themselves and how they think others see them.

Some people compare themselves to other people, stating that they look like a burn victim, the Hunchback of Notre Dame, Gomer Pyle, or the Elephant Man. One man who disliked his hair said he looked like Kramer on the TV show *Seinfeld.* His hair actually looked nothing like Kramer's. Other people associate their perceived defect with a family member or relative. "My looks remind me of my father, who I dislike," a 40-year-old woman told me. "He was ugly emotionally and physically." Some men who are concerned with thinning hair fear that they look like a bald uncle or will end up looking like their bald father. Others say that they've always been told that they look like a particular relative, and their worry focuses on what they consider a prominent and unattractive aspect of that relative's appearance.

"I'm Not Feminine Enough"

Some people link their perceived defect with other characteristics they consider negative, such as aging or a lack of masculinity or femininity. In the same breath, they may, for example, mention their worry about wrinkles and aging. While they're concerned with the perceived ugliness of the wrinkles per se, they're also upset because they consider them a sign that they're getting old. One young woman I saw had been hospitalized because she was so desperate over the belief that her appearance had changed, and that new lines on her face made her look 10 years older than she actually was.

Some women are concerned about not being feminine enough. Often, they're worried that their breasts are too small. Or they may be upset about excessive facial hair, which they think makes them look masculine. The concern that they're not feminine enough can be as distressing as the perceived defect itself. One young woman who worried that her breasts were too small said that she felt she "really wasn't a woman, because breasts symbolize femininity." Even though men frequently asked her out on dates and told her she was quite feminine, she didn't believe them.

Marie, the nursing student preoccupied with facial hair, told me, "The hair makes me masculine looking. When I was young, I had short hair, and people sometimes mistook me for a boy. Maybe that has something to do with it. The hair makes me feel masculine and like a freak."

Similarly, men who are concerned that their penis is too small often say that they feel unmasculine and that women don't find them desirable. "It makes me feel unmanly, like I'm not masculine enough," one young man told me. "It's embarrassing and something I feel I need to hide. What I obsess about is I'm half of a man." Another said, "My penis doesn't look ugly, but it looks unattractive and unmanly. All of my concerns are related to maleness. I have shame about being a man."

A quiet young man told me, "It's not so much that I'm ugly but that I look nerdy. I've always done very well in school, but I'm not good in sports. When I was younger I was skinny and I wore thick glasses. I want my nose to look more masculine—I look like a little nerd with my long nose."

Fear of the Future: "Soon I'll Be Totally Bald!"

Fear of the future is a prominent theme for some people with BDD. They worry that their perceived defect will become worse and uglier with time. "I always fear the future," a pretty young woman told me. "I fear my skin will get worse and worse."

"I get very depressed over my appearance because I truly believe it will get worse as I get older," Carmella said. "I don't think I can live with myself if my hair keeps getting thinner and my wrinkles get worse. How can I go on? My problems that won't get worse—like my teeth—don't cause me such horrible panic." Olivia feared that she wouldn't be able to work in the future because she'd look worse as she aged. "No one will want to hire me when I'm older and even uglier," she said. Eric feared that his hair would get thinner and thinner and that he would soon be completely bald. "Bald guys are total rejects," he told me. "My life will be over when I lose all my hair."

Fear of the future sometimes focuses on a belief that the person used to look fine but now their looks have been ruined and will continue to deteriorate. "Sometimes when I look in the mirror I get an image of how I used to look," Ed said. "It only lasts for a minute. Then I see how I look now, and I worry about next week and next year. Will I get even uglier?"

"My Face Is Asymmetrical"

Symmetry concerns are common: one third of the people in my studies had this concern about at least one area of their body. They worry that one side of their body doesn't perfectly match the other, or that certain features are uneven or off balance. Symmetry worries most often involve the hair, breasts, and nose. One woman was preoccupied with having more freckles on one side of her face than the other. A 25-year-old man worried that one side of his face was different from the other—that his bone structure was asymmetrical. Another man obsessed about the supposed asymmetry of his eyebrows—that one was a little higher. A teenager was concerned that one eyelid hung over one of his eyes more than the other one.

Some people worry that their hair is uneven and may spend hours a day cutting it to make it perfectly even. A college student told me, "I'm obsessed with having my hair an even length. It *has* to be even. I compulsively cut it to even it up. I cut it every morning, and then I carry scissors with me and cut it throughout the day. I try to resist—I've thrown away a lot of scissors—but I can't. I've even hit my hands with a hammer and slammed them in a car door so I'd stop cutting. But that didn't work either. I *have* to make my hair even so it will look better!"

"I'm Not Big Enough"

A variation on the BDD theme that affects primarily men is the fear that their body build is too small and not muscular enough. Mark, a muscular man in his twenties, believed his upper body was too thin and that he wasn't big, strong, and masculine enough. He thought he looked "dwarfed and wimpy." To build himself up, he drank protein drinks every day and lifted weights for hours daily, which he called an "obsession." At least 20 times a day he asked his father, "Do I look okay? Am I getting bigger?"

Mark always wore long-sleeved shirts to hide his "skinny" arms and avoided going to the beach, where his body would be more exposed. He avoided being around other people because he was so embarrassed by his supposed smallness. When I met Mark, he was wearing five layers of T-shirts and sweatshirts to look bigger.

Mark has muscle dysmorphia (previously referred to as reverse anorexia). Men with this form of BDD obsess about their body size and perform typical BDD behaviors, such as camouflaging with clothing (to hide their body or make it look bigger), mirror checking, and reassurance seeking. They also use food supplements and compulsively work out, sometimes to the point of injuring themselves. To bulk up, some men even use illegal and potentially dangerous anabolic steroids.

"I Look Depressed"

Jacob's and Max's experiences were a less common variation on the BDD theme. "I look depressed," Jacob told me. "I feel my mouth is unattractive and that I'm not likable because I look depressed. Looking depressed equals looking like something people don't want to see, which is distasteful." Jacob thought he looked depressed because his mouth was turned down, and he'd considered surgery to straighten it.

In addition to thinking his mouth was too small, Max felt he didn't have the right expression on his face. "I keep trying to get the right expression on my mouth, like the popular kids," he said. "I get caught up in the mirror thinking 'Which way does my mouth look the best? Most natural, most attractive?' My mouth feels ugly and wrong. I'm afraid of offending other people with my appearance."

"My Fingers Are Getting Shorter"

"Sometimes my hand gets fat, and all of my fingers get shorter," Jim told me. "I actually *see* them change—it's a process I perceive. They aren't fat and short all the time. It happens two or three times a day. It can happen when I'm around other people, especially good-looking people, or when I'm feeling nervous. Some of my doctors thought maybe I had a seizure disorder or another neurological problem, but I don't. I know it's impossible for this to happen, but it's what I see."

Occasional people have an experience like Jim's—their body parts sometimes change shape or size and become unattractive in the process. Jim also saw his eyes come closer together at times, and his cheeks changed from thin to fat and back to thin again. "My cheeks look bad when they're fatter," he said, "and my eyes look strange when they're closer together."

While it's unusual for people with BDD to say that their body parts frequently change size or shape in such a dramatic way, and experiences like these raise the question of whether a neurological disorder is present, they echo what some people with BDD say—that they sometimes look worse than at other times, or that their perception of the defect can change. For example, facial scars can look darker, and moles can look bigger, at some times than at others. Reports such as these raise the interesting question of whether people with BDD actually see something different from other people that is, whether they experience a visual illusion. Another possible explanation is that by focusing in on the body area more closely at some times than at others, the perceived flaw may look somewhat different at different times (see Chapters 10 and 11).

"I'm Afraid My Nose Will Break!"

There are still other bodily concerns. About 15% of people with BDD think that the unattractive body part—for example, their nose—is fragile and in danger of breaking, or that the body part doesn't work correctly. They believe, for example, that their legs are too skinny *and* that they can't walk correctly. Or that their lip is misshapen *and* their speech is slurred. Or that their nose is crooked *and* they make whistling noises when they breathe. And occasionally people believe that they have an underlying illness, such as cancer, that's responsible for their appearance problem.

Julie had one of these variations on the BDD theme. "I have a nose problem; I hope you're an expert on noses," she began when I first met her. I assumed that she, like most of the people I'd seen, was concerned with how it looked. Indeed, in the past Julie had worried that her nose was too big and bumpy. But now her concern was different. "This is very humiliating because it sounds so silly. My concern is irrational, and I'm afraid you'll think I'm crazy," she told me. "No one understands my problem. The problem is I'm totally obsessed that my nose is fragile and is going to break. It's tormenting me!

"I worry all day long that I've damaged it. Whenever I bump it or brush against something, I panic. I think I've ruined it. If I blow my nose and see blood, I think I've damaged it. Sometimes I even think that I've hurt it by crinkling it up or letting cigarette smoke get near it! I constantly look in the mirror for evidence of damage. If I see any little problem—a spot or a pimple or a tiny vein—I think it's evidence I've ruined my nose. It can be anything. Sometimes it's a blackhead or a broken blood vessel. Other times it's a pore. Sometimes I feel tingling and aching in my nose, which means I must have broken it. I try to talk myself out of it, saying things like 'You'd have to hit it with a sledge hammer to damage it.' But that doesn't really help." Julie also developed what she called a "sniffing obsession." "When I was wondering if I'd hurt my nose, my nose felt funny when I sniffed, so I had to keep sniffing to see if it was OK. It was a way to check on whether I'd damaged it."

The problem had started when Julie had had nose surgery 20 years earlier to remove a small bump. After surgery, the surgeon commented, "I worked really hard on your nose, so take care of it and don't damage it." Julie took this to mean that her nose was fragile, and it triggered her obsession. For the next eight years, she secretly visited her surgeon as often as twice a week. "I never told anyone I was doing this, not even my husband. I was much too ashamed. I kept going to the surgeon to ask about my nose—I wanted reassurance that it wasn't broken. It was a compulsion to run for reassurance. I even dragged my three kids with me, and sometimes I'd wait for two hours. The office staff thought I was crazy, and they tried to keep me from the doctor. When he reassured me, I felt a little better, but only for a few minutes."

When she first saw me, Julie was more worried about her nose than usual, because she'd just seen a television show on "botched" nose jobs. "I've been so preoccupied that I haven't been able to keep up the house or keep a job," she said. "And it's hard for me to enjoy social activities. I don't even bother going a lot of the time. I'm so focused on my nose that I can't think of anything else. I don't plan social events because I'm afraid my nose problem will flare up and I won't be able to go.

"It's a huge problem in my marriage, too," she added. "My first husband left me because of it. I drove him nuts! I asked him all day long about my nose and whether I'd damaged it, and I'd have him hold magnifying glasses and special lights to check it for damage."

During childbirth, Julie was so petrified that her nose would be damaged that she hadn't even felt labor pains. While having dental work, she was terrified the dentist would damage her nose by bumping it while she was anesthetized and that she'd be unaware of the damage. As a result, she refused Novocain. She preferred the intense physical pain of unanesthetized dental work to the emotional pain of unrecognized nose damage.

"The Walking Concept Was Erased"

Occasional people with BDD worry that their supposedly ugly body part doesn't work correctly. Ben was concerned not only that his legs "looked funny" but also that he couldn't walk normally. As a teenager he'd been preoccupied with his supposedly thin upper lip, but several years later, as he put it, "my legs replaced my lip." His problem began with pain in his right foot, for which he consulted a physician, who diagnosed a fallen arch. This diagnosis frightened

Ben, and he incorrectly assumed that he'd never be able to walk again. He then worried about his walking "all day long," wondering whether his walking would become abnormal.

Eventually, Ben began to think that he really couldn't walk normally. "The walking concept was erased," he said. "It was as if I'd had a lobotomy." He also started worrying that the muscles in his legs "were becoming thin like toothpicks and disappearing." Although several doctors tried to reassure him that his walking, as well as his legs' appearance, were normal, Ben couldn't be reassured. "I felt crippled," he said. "The damage was already done."

Concerns such as these—as well as those involving bodily fragility—resemble typical BDD beliefs in that they are distressing preoccupations about one's body. But they differ from typical BDD concerns in that they don't focus on appearance per se. Most of the patients I've seen with such concerns also had a more typical BDD concern that involved the same body part; that is, they worried that the fragile or malfunctioning body part was also unattractive or deformed looking. Whether less typical concerns such as these should be considered to constitute BDD, or a separate disorder such as hypochondriasis or obsessive compulsive disorder (see Appendix B for definitions), is unclear, although the similarities between them and BDD concerns are striking.

"I'm Shrinking Because I Have Cancer"

A few patients I've seen attributed the perceived defect in their appearance to an underlying medical illness. A woman who believed that her shoulders and upper body were shrinking attributed this to cancer. Because she feared she was "shriveling up," she'd seen countless physicians and had had numerous tests, all of which were normal. Ben, the young man I just described who worried that his legs were becoming thin and atrophied, worried that these changes were due to multiple sclerosis.

Robert attributed his appearance problems to hypothyroidism. He had initially worried that his hair was falling out, for which he'd seen several dermatologists. Most reassured him that his hair was normal, but one prescribed a steroid, later discontinued by another physician. He then saw a nutritionist, who prescribed vitamins and iodine. As a result of excessive iodine intake, Robert developed hyperthyroidism, and the iodine was discontinued. Even though his thyroid tests normalized, Robert became convinced that he was now hypothyroid. He became preoccupied with the thought that his eyes were sunken and that his skin had "lost its firmness and tone," which he attributed to the supposed hypothyroidism. Eventually, he became immersed in the concern that his "whole appearance had changed," thinking about it all day long and berating himself because he believed that he had ruined his appearance by making himself hypothyroid.

In addition to BDD, all three of these people received a diagnosis of hypochondriasis—a preoccupation with the idea that one has a serious disease. It's interesting that in the International Classification of Diseases (ICD-10), the international counterpart of DSM-IV, BDD is considered a type of hypochondriasis. However, as I'll discuss in chapter 16, BDD and hypochondriasis have some important differences and are probably distinct rather than the same disorder. Only a few of the hundreds of people with BDD I've seen have attributed their appearance concerns to a bodily illness.

"My Daughter's Ugly!"

I once got a call from a woman who was frantic over her daughter's nose. "I worry that it doesn't look right, that it's crooked," she told me, "even though everyone else says it looks fine. *She* doesn't worry about it, but *I* do! I know I'm too upset about it, and it's causing my daughter problems. I keep pushing on it to make it straight, and I'm afraid I'm ruining her self-esteem."

Like this woman, some people don't worry about their *own* appearance— they worry about someone else's. They obsess that their son's ears are sticking out or their boyfriend's hair looks wrong, when in fact these body areas look okay. They may insist that their loved one get surgery, even when it isn't necessary. I call this phenomenon "BDD by proxy"—that is, excessive worry about someone else's appearance, which may or may not cause the person to worry about it themselves.

I'm aware of a very sad case in which a man in his 50s was convinced his daughter was going bald and that he was the cause. He was in such despair over this that he killed himself. This brings home how serious this form of BDD can be.

"I Feel More Air Where My Hair Used to Be"

Some people have subtle tactile sensations in the area of the perceived defect. About a quarter of people with BDD experience sensations such as itching in the area of perceived blood vessel markings, tightness where they see acne, "gritting where fat rubs together," or "too much air" where they think their hair is thinning. Usually, these sensations are fairly mild and not problematic.

But in some instances, the sensations are troubling because they're a reminder of the defect's presence or because they're painful. Some people who think their lips look abnormal feel they're dry and cracked, which can be irritating and unpleasant. The woman who thought cancer was causing her shoulders and upper body to shrink also had prominent and constant shoulder pain. The pain was in and of itself a troubling problem.

"I'm Just One Big Pimple...."

People with BDD generally think that other aspects of their appearance look okay. But they're so focused on the perceived defect that they consider these other aspects less important. They believe the defect is the most obvious and important part of how they look. They tend to view themselves not as an attractive person with a small bump on their nose, but as one whose most obvious and prominent feature is a grotesque nose. Thus, many consider themselves to be unattractive overall. (See Chapter 11.)

Some people with BDD are so intensely and exclusively preoccupied with the supposed defect that they're oblivious to other aspects of their appearance. Matthew had been so focused on his mild acne, it was all he could "see." He told me, "Before I got better with the medication, I was just one big pimple, without any feet or even any toes!"

Some people with BDD don't seem to notice or be bothered by aspects of their appearance that would probably concern most people. Instead, they're preoccupied with a defect that others consider nonexistent or slight. Jeremy, who was in his early thirties, was nearly bald. But this didn't bother him. What troubled him were tiny bumps on his nose that were barely visible. He explained that he wasn't concerned about his hair because hair loss was natural, whereas his acne should have resolved 10 years ago. Similarly, a young woman I saw had large, deep, red ulcers on her legs caused by a medical illness. But they didn't particularly bother her, and she often wore shorts, even on cool days. Instead, she was preoccupied with her supposedly wide nose and her "sunken and dull" eyes, which other people considered attractive. Another woman concerned with her breasts told me, "My husband tells me that if I'm going to be upset about my appearance, I should worry about my stretch marks. But I can't do anything about them, so why should I care?"

These observations raise some fascinating questions about BDD, which I'll discuss later. Why do some people with BDD focus on one area whereas others focus on others; in other words, how does the body part get "selected"? What do people with BDD actually see? Do they see what other people see, or do they see something different? And how can some people with BDD become so intensely focused on a defect that others can't see, or consider minimal, while ignoring aspects of their appearance, such as leg ulcers, that are obvious to others?

·· six ··

Painful Obsessions

"It's constantly on my mind. And it's unbelievably painful. People don't understand. If you told someone, they'd think you were off the wall."   **Matt**

"I Can't Get It Out of My Mind"

I'm obsessed about my appearance," a 50-year-old secretary told me. "I think about it all the time. It's a crazy way of thinking. It's torturing me. . . . It's always in the back of my mind. I can't push it away. It's like a clock ticking. It's always there, taunting and haunting me." Another woman said of her preoccupation: "It feels like a magnet. I can't get my mind away from it. I constantly fight with it."

Most people with BDD actively think about their appearance problem for at least an hour a day. Of the people in my studies, about a third think about it for 1 to 3 hours a day, nearly 40% for 3 to 8 hours a day, and about a quarter think about it for more than 8 hours a day. The remaining 10% think about the defect for less than an hour a day, but for a substantial period in the past they'd thought about it for at least an hour a day.

Some people think about their perceived defect "all day, every day"—it's always on their mind, making it difficult to focus on anything else. One woman said, "My BDD is a shadow—it's always with me. I can't get rid of it." Others say that they "actively" think about it for only part of the day, but they're always "aware" of their concern; it's always in the back of their mind. Some say they always have "two reels going." With one reel, they focus on the matter at hand; with the other, they're thinking about how they look.

One man described his preoccupation with his "small" head as follows: "It's constantly there. I can't get it out of my mind. It's like a monkey on my back. I never stop thinking about it, not even for a day or an hour. I even obsess in my sleep." Another said, "It's always there. Even if I'm focusing on other things, it's still there. It's like a radio that's *always on*. You may not hear it for a while, but if you stop and think about it, you know it's there." Ray told me, "I was very preoccupied. It was all I could think of. My mind would go back and forth from the hair to the chest and from the chest to the hair, back and forth like a yo-yo."

Susan described her thoughts about her facial freckles as "invasive." "They force themselves into my mind." Other people, however, experience their thoughts not as invasive but as something that's "always there," to the point where they seem a part of themselves.

Most people with BDD realize that they spend too much time thinking about their appearance. But others don't. The thoughts are so much a part of their life that they don't realize they worry too much. They think that everyone worries about their appearance for hours a day.

What do the thoughts consist of? They vary, but they're usually quite negative—for example: "There's a pimple on your face; everyone's going to see it and think you're ugly" or "I'm disfigured. It's ugly. I deviate." One person thought, "You stick out in a crowd; you look ridiculous. People are looking at you funny because of your ears." Jane told me, "I have two tapes playing in my head at all times: one of them says not to worry and another says I'm ugly."

Some people focus on surgery they think was botched. "I *constantly* think about the operation I had on my nose," Greg said, "and I think, 'It's not me. Now it's too short and too thin. It looks like a woman's nose, not a man's nose.' And I obsess about how angry I am at the doctor and how I shouldn't have had the surgery. I also think a lot about what all the different surgeons have told me. Things like 'You could have something done, but it's not a good idea,' or 'Don't do anything to it; it could get worse.'"

Some people have nightmares about their concerns—they're haunted, even while they're sleeping. In their dreams, their worst fears come true. One woman described the following dream: "I have nightmares of getting my hair cut. All of my hair is getting cut off the front. I wake up in a panic." Another woman told me, "I dreamt I was walking down the street and suddenly I had a lot of hair on my face. People were pointing at me and laughing at the gobs of hair on my face." A woman who disliked her hair described this dream: "I dreamt a friend of mine with beautiful long hair was getting married. All of the brides-maids except me also had beautiful hair. The bride told me I couldn't be in the wedding unless I wore a wig. I couldn't even be in the church because of my hair, and I had to leave."

One reason preoccupations with the defect take up so much time is that they're difficult to resist and control. Many people do try to resist them by pushing them aside and trying to focus on something else. But others find their preoccupations so powerful that they don't even try to divert their attention away from them. I've found that about a quarter of people with BDD usually try to resist the thoughts, and a third make some effort to resist them. But a quarter rarely try to resist them, and 15% make no effort whatsoever to resist them—they simply let them enter their mind. Degree of resistance can fluctuate, however, with more of an effort made to resist the thoughts at some times than at others.

Most people have only limited control over the thoughts. Virtually no one with BDD who hasn't been treated says they have complete control over them. Nearly 50% have little control, and nearly a quarter no control. This is a particularly difficult aspect of BDD. "I try to ignore them, but I can't," one man told me. "They won't leave me alone. It's like trying to will away a headache; you can't just make them stop." The woman who was concerned about her supposedly shrunken shoulders said, "My concern about this takes over—it's controlling me. It's very scary. I can't stop it." Another woman told me, "One of the hardest things about this disorder is that I can't control my own thoughts! They have a life of their own. I feel powerless over them. I try to resist them and distract myself from them. Sometimes I can, even though it's difficult. But often I can't. It seems so silly—I should be able to stop thinking them. But I usually can't."

Sometimes people with BDD are told to just stop worrying about how they look. If only it were this simple! BDD's core features are lack of control over the preoccupation and thinking about it too much. People with BDD would love to have their problem disappear and simply forget about it; after all, they, more than anyone else, would like to end their suffering. But they can't—*this is what BDD is all about.*

This was very true for Cassandra. "I'm so agonized by my body dysmorphic symptoms," she said. "I feel a complete lack of freedom, like I'm a caged animal. It cuts you off from the freedoms of life. I can't get out of it. I can't escape from the thoughts. I wish there was a way of reaching greater freedom."

"It's Like an Arrow through My Heart"

When I met Bill, a 40-year-old landscaper, he was so profoundly distressed over his appearance that he couldn't put his pain into words. I first met him in a darkened room in the hospital. He was wearing a baseball cap that he pulled down over his forehead to partially cover his eyes. His head was down in his knees.

While looking down at the floor, he started to tell me about his problems. He was anxious and very hesitant to discuss them. He had no friends, and he'd just been fired from his job. He felt that life wasn't worth living. When I asked him what he thought the cause of his difficulties was, he replied, "It's really hard to talk about this, Doctor. I don't know if I can. It's too embarrassing, and it hurts too much."

Eventually, Bill told me what had happened and why he was in the hospital. He was worried about his nose, which he thought was covered with huge pockmarks and pores. Except for the pores, he thought he looked fine. But he believed the pores made him grotesque and ugly, like the Elephant Man. He'd thought about them for hours a day for the past 15 years. He wore the hat to hide them. And he'd insisted on meeting with me in a dark room so I couldn't see them.

"I can't begin to describe this to you," he said. "It's humiliating and very embarrassing. Who am I to complain, when so many people are worse off than me? To lose control over your life because of marks on your face—it's embarrassing, and it seems ridiculous! But every morning when I get up, I want to die. I rush to the mirror and see the marks. I can't face it anymore. Every day, the holes look like they're getting bigger. I go back and forth between the mirror and my bed, feeling hopeless. I feel a pain and terror. I think 'How can I face this? How can I go on living if I look like this?' " He tried to conceive of other equally painful experiences. "Maybe it's how a woman feels after she's been raped. Maybe it's how cancer victims feel. It's like an arrow through my heart.

"It ruined my life. I got very depressed. I stopped seeing people. I was so obsessed I couldn't work and I got fired. It crushed me. Before I came into the hospital, I went to a hotel room to kill myself. I kept looking at myself in the mirror, thinking I couldn't live with the marks. I was scared, because I wanted to die, and I hated myself. I paced around the room, arguing with myself, telling myself it was stupid to be so worried about the marks. But everyone could see them—I couldn't hide them! I decided I couldn't go on living like this, and I tried to suffocate myself."

Many people with BDD describe their pain in similar ways. A young man told me, "The pain is unbearable, unremitting. My life is a devastation. It's so painful it's hard to put it into words. Every day is hell."

Descriptions such as these may sound extreme, even melodramatic. But these people weren't being melodramatic. Many of them understated rather than overstated their suffering. Most were very embarrassed and hesitant to describe their emotional pain and even apologized for it, thinking they were selfish or silly for suffering as much as they did.

But their pain is very real and profound. Of all the patients with various psychiatric problems whom I've worked with over the years, my patients with BDD have been among the most severely distressed and tormented.

The distress and emotional pain may be less severe than Bill's; it spans a spectrum of severity. I've found that 6% say their preoccupations cause mild distress; 40%, moderate distress; 44%, severe distress; and 10%, extreme and disabling distress.

I've tried to understand the reasons for the pain. One is that the thoughts are so often present and hard to control. It's awful to spend so much time thinking unbidden thoughts that interfere with focusing on other things and rob time from enjoyable or important activities. In addition, the content of the thoughts—believing that you're unattractive, defective, ugly, or disfigured—is very distressing. One man tried to explain: "Think about how you'd feel if someone cut your nose off. That's how I feel about how I look."

In fact, many people with BDD wish they were worried about some other body part instead, because they think it would be less painful. A young woman who thought she was losing her hair said, "I wish I worried about something else, like my skin. At least I could cover it with makeup. But I can't change my hair." But a young woman who hated her skin said, "I wish I worried about something else, like my hair because I could wear a wig. But I can't change my skin. The scars are there forever."

Another woman similarly said, "I'd rather worry about a big nose because you could just get a nose job—and your nose is supposed to be there anyway. Scars aren't supposed to be there, so it's worse." The source of this pain is a belief that another body part could be more easily covered or fixed, whereas the disliked body part is unchangeable. This creates feelings of helplessness and despair.

Another source of emotional pain is that people with BDD think other people view them as disfigured, even repulsive. Furthermore, they believe they can't easily hide their flaw from others. People who worry about their facial features—the most common location of BDD concerns—point out that a facial flaw is particularly painful because it's on their face, where other people generally focus and fix their gaze, so it's hard to hide it.

In addition, BDD symptoms are often accompanied by feelings of low self-esteem, inadequacy, embarrassment, humiliation, and shame. Although not universal, these feelings are very common. Many people with BDD feel badly about who they are. They feel rejected by others, and assume that others will judge them negatively.

"I've always disliked myself so much I can't imagine people liking me or how I look," Sonya told me. "My appearance concerns are all tied up in feelings of inferiority. They make sense to me, because they're related to low self-esteem, feeling like damaged goods." A man with BDD said, "When I go into a store I feel like the lowest thing in the store. Maybe people and women would like me more and accept me more if I looked better." "My face is the source of all the pain in my life," a 35-year-old artist said. "I feel hopeless about it. It's a feeling I'll never belong anywhere or be happy. It's a feeling that I'm unacceptable. I feel the outside world sees me as unlovable, rejected, unacceptable, ugly."

Shame is very common in BDD and appears to be a core aspect of the disorder. Pierre Janet, one of the greatest psychopathologists of all time, underscored the importance of shame in BDD. In fact, he referred to BDD as an obsession with shame of the body. In his 1903 description of Nadia, a 27-year-old woman, he noted her embarrassment and shame over many aspects of her "ugly body," including her skin, hands, legs, and feet, and a fear that no one would ever love her because of her "ugliness."

Feelings of deep shame make sense because BDD preoccupations involve strongly negative feelings about oneself—thoughts of being unappealing and defective. This view of the supposedly defective body part often extends to the person more generally. One woman said, "Whenever I see myself, I see something very inadequate. The one word I associate with my body is shame." A high school teacher said, "Shame is central to my appearance concerns. BDD equals ridicule." Men may be ashamed because they consider it unmasculine to worry so much about how they look.

Another source of suffering is feeling selfish and vain for being so preoccupied with such "trivial" concerns. Like Sarah, some people with BDD feel it's wrong—even immoral—to be so focused on how they look. This is what I call the "double whammy" of BDD: not only do BDD sufferers have painful thoughts they can't stop thinking, they also berate themselves for having those thoughts. Many feel guilty and consider themselves morally weak and defective because they're so preoccupied with something they feel is so trivial. They feel ashamed of being ashamed.

As one woman told me, "I shouldn't be so worried about this. I get down on myself because I am. It's hard for me to talk about it, because appearance shouldn't matter. I don't want to be the kind of person who cares so much about something so superficial. I can't even talk about my problem because I'm so ashamed of it. I refer to it as 'you know what.'" Another woman had similar feelings, "It sounds very superficial, but it isn't. I feel ridiculous thinking about it. I feel spoiled and shallow. I feel guilty because I could be blind or crippled. I *try* not to think about it, but I can't."

But other people with BDD don't consider their appearance concerns trivial. They point out that attractiveness is important and highly valued in our society. Thus, their concerns seem justified. But more common are feelings like the following: "I feel like a horrible, terrible person because I'm so concerned with my breasts. How could I be so vain, so concerned with my appearance? It shouldn't be that important to me." This woman berated herself even more when she learned that her best friend had breast cancer. "I felt even more strongly that I was a bad person—here I was obsessing about how big my breasts were when my best friend had breast cancer and had to have a mastectomy. I feel like this is a very selfish disease that I can't control. I'm the one who deserved the mastectomy!"

Rather than a problem of excessive vanity, BDD should be viewed as an illness like depression or anorexia nervosa or heart disease. It has a life of its own and doesn't reflect moral weakness. If people could stop thinking about their appearance, they would. If they could put an end to their suffering by simply willing their symptoms away, they would. The self-blame only adds to their pain.

Others feel guilty because they think they should be able to fix the problem—for example, by dieting or working out enough. Still others are self-critical because they feel responsible for creating the defect; they believe that something they did ruined their appearance—something that might have been prevented. "I look in the mirror, and I say 'What did I do!?'" Tina said. "I get really down on myself because I destroyed my looks by picking at my skin."

Tom thought he ruined his appearance by using Accutane, a medication for severe acne. The Accutane got rid of the few pimples he had, but it also dried Tom's skin, which, in his view, was catastrophic. He blamed his dermatologist but mostly blamed himself. "I ruined my skin," he told me. "I ruined my looks. I can't believe I did this to myself!" Tom's guilt and self-blame became obsessional and extreme and magnified his suffering.

Many people with BDD are isolated from other people. This is one of the hardest things about BDD. Such feelings often stem from the belief that other people consider the BDD sufferer defective and unlikable. A college student didn't go home for the holidays because she thought her family would be repulsed by her skin and wouldn't love her. As she said, "I fear being an outcast." Another student said, "I'm afraid I won't be able to lead a normal life—date, have sex, have friends. I feel like a freak because I have a defect. No one could ever love me."

A young man told me, "Maybe people, especially women, would like me more and accept me more if I were better looking. I often ruminate about my ugliness and think I can't survive because people choose their friends and partners on the basis of looks. I'm disgusting and repulsive. I'm overwhelmingly lonely."

Contributing to the isolation is the feeling that other people don't seem to understand or take their concerns seriously. After all, people with BDD look fine to others, who are usually incredulous or reassuring. "I feel foolish talking about my concern," one man said. "The usual reaction is 'What?!'" When someone has a medical problem, they usually have observable and "understandable" symptoms, like a rash, or test results, like an X-ray, that confirm that the illness is real and justify the person's distress and limitations. The same is true for many psychiatric disorders. An adult with anorexia nervosa who weighs only 70 pounds is clearly ill. A panic attack, too, is observable and obviously not under the person's control; the physiologic arousal of the attack—for example, rapid breathing or sweating—is dramatically obvious and "real" to anyone who might witness it. Even though others may not fully understand the symptoms, they know that something is wrong and that the person is suffering and needs treatment.

But BDD is different. Because the BDD sufferer looks fine, it's hard for others to understand the preoccupation and pain it causes. How can someone be so obsessed with something that, in the eyes of others, doesn't exist? Or if a slight defect is present, how can it interfere so much with their life? Why can't they just forget about it? It generally makes little sense to others. So people with BDD often feel misunderstood and alone.

"I've been very isolated with my concern because people thought I was crazy," one man told me. "They didn't understand, so I've kept it largely to myself. It's an extremely private inner turmoil. I feel alone." "The pain is as bad as when my dog who I'd had for 15 years was put to sleep," a college student told me, "but that was easier because people can understand your grieving. People can't understand BDD."

"Everyone is Staring at Me!"

One reason BDD is so painful and embarrassing for many BDD sufferers is they think other people take special notice of—and even mock—their defect. If someone glances in their direction, they think they're being looked at in horror or with disgust—that the glance reflects the fact that their defect is repulsive. One man concerned about a minimal scar on his neck said, "I know people are smirking at me when they see me. When I cross at a crosswalk I think people in cars are thinking, 'I wonder what happened to him. Look how

ugly he is.' " Another man worried about mild acne said, "When I go out, I
think everyone's noticing it. I think they're thinking 'What's that ugly thing on
his face?' It would be like if you painted big red marks all over your face and
then walked down the street. Everywhere I go I feel like a neon sign is pointing
at my face!"

People with BDD usually think that others can see the defect, but what I'm
discussing here goes beyond this. The phenomenon I'm describing—known in
psychiatric terms as *referential thinking*—is that others take *special notice* of the
defect. Benign events in the environment unrelated to the person—or events
that are related to them but have nothing to do with the supposed defect—are
interpreted as referring to the flaw in a negative way. About 60 percent of the
people in my studies have had such experiences—for example, thinking that
others are staring at, talking about, or making fun of how they look. About half
of them think that other people *probably* are taking special notice of them, and
about half are *completely convinced* of this. Some use the term "paranoia" to
describe their experience.

This was a serious problem for Jennifer, who left her car in the middle of a
traffic jam because she thought other people were horrified by her skin. When
she walked down the street, she believed that people stared at her skin and
thought, "That poor girl—look at her skin. It looks terrible!" When she entered
a restaurant she believed the acne and marks distracted people from their meals,
and she could eat out only if she hid in a booth in the restaurant's darkest
corner. Even then, she had to look down at the menu while ordering her food
so the waitress couldn't see her face. At work she thought co-workers were
laughing at her behind her back. Because of this, she often left work in the
middle of the day and eventually quit her job.

Conversations may be erroneously interpreted to refer to the person with
BDD. "Whenever people talk about shaving or beards, I think they might be
referring to *my* beard," Bart told me. "They're really mean." Some BDD sufferers think others can see the defect from impossibly long distances. One man
thought that other people could see his minimal acne from 20 feet away, and
Jennifer believed hers was visible from 50 feet. A man who sang in a choir
thought the entire audience could see a small scar on his neck.

These experiences are similar in some ways to what we all experience. We've
all noticed that someone is looking at us, and we may wonder why. Do we
remind them of someone they know? Are they interested in the book we're
reading? Are they noticing our glasses because they're considering buying a
similar pair? It's possible that they're observing our appearance—perhaps something negative. But it's also possible that they're noticing something positive
about how we look. Are they even noticing us at all? Perhaps they're looking
in our direction but thinking about something else, like what they need to buy
at the supermarket. The possible explanations are myriad and endless. But most
people with BDD don't seriously consider, or even think about, these various
possibilities. They assume the person is scrutinizing the defect and thinking
about it in a negative way.

This way of thinking isn't limited to BDD. Some people with very obvious and noticeable physical deformities think in a similar way, assuming the behavior of others is a negative reaction to their physical deformity, even when it isn't. And studies show that physically normal individuals may also think in this way. In a very interesting experiment by Robert Kleck and A. Christopher Strenta, normal-appearing young adults were told that a noticeable and authentic-looking facial scar was being applied to their face with cosmetics, but it was then removed without their knowledge. These study participants subsequently believed that the "scar" had a strongly negative impact on how other people behaved toward them and that others rejected them because of it. In other words, the participants erroneously found plenty of "evidence" that others were reacting negatively to their "physical defect" (which they didn't actually have). This misattribution is surprisingly similar how people with BDD think. Importantly, the researchers noted that misattributing social outcomes to one's supposed physical deformity can lead to low self-esteem and social withdrawal, which may in turn negatively influence interactions with others. This is what happens in BDD. And it's one of the things that cognitive-behavioral therapy (which I'll discuss in Chapter 14) aims to change.

I've tried to present other possible explanations to patients. Perhaps the other person wasn't actually looking at you. Perhaps they were thinking about something else. Perhaps they were looking at you but not in terms of your appearance. Perhaps they thought you seemed to have an appealing personality. But most people with BDD find it hard—if not impossible—to believe such explanations. They *see themselves* in terms of their imperfect appearance and assume that others must be doing the same. Often, it's only after they respond to psychiatric treatment that they can consider other explanations and actually believe them.

Sometimes this referential thinking is more unusual. Jane thought that other people stared at her nose through binoculars. Another thought that as she walked by other people, they said "She's ugly," or muttered "Dog!" under their breath. When Alex was a child, he thought his mother left the table during meals because he was so ugly. "This happened more often as I got older and uglier," he said.

Steven's experience was a particularly poignant example of referential thinking. He was often pursued by women who found him very attractive, but he was convinced that he was ugly—in particular, that his facial structure "wasn't sophisticated or full enough." When he was around others, especially young women, he thought that they took special notice of him—but in a negative, not a positive, way. He was sure they were snickering and laughing at the shape of his face, and he felt mortified, deeply shamed, and sometimes angry. I would guess that, most of the time, any laughing Steven observed had nothing to do with him. But I wouldn't be surprised if other people, especially young women, sometimes *did* notice Steven—in a positive way.

Some BDD sufferers describe a no-win variation on this theme. "If people look at me I think it's because I'm ugly," one woman told me. "If they *don't* look at me, it's because I must be ugly. And if they look at me and then look away, they must be thinking that I'm not worth looking at. I feel shut out and rejected."

These types of experiences reflect important aspects of BDD. One is that many, if not most, people with BDD erroneously believe that other people view the perceived defect negatively. Second, people with BDD generally experience interactions with other people in terms of their appearance. They look at the world through "appearance-tinted glasses," viewing themselves through this lens and assuming the rest of the world does too. They find it difficult to believe that other people don't focus on the defect that the BDD sufferer perceives. One study found that people with BDD are more likely than healthy control subjects to misinterpret facial expressions as angry. This finding fits with referential thinking in BDD—in particular, that other people are being mocking or mean.

One component of BDD treatment is to help patients understand that most people value many different aspects of the people they know and love, such as their warmth, kindness, and personality. And when others do notice how the BDD sufferer looks, they're unlikely to focus on the perceived flaw.

Experiences such as these can be as problematic and painful as the core BDD preoccupation itself. When people feel mocked and rejected, they feel even more ashamed, defective, and isolated. "People always stare at me," Joyce said. "I feel transparent. Whenever I hear people whispering I think they're saying mean things about me and how I look. It's very painful, and I avoid people because of it."

Different Degrees of Certainty

Stephanie realized her view of her appearance wasn't accurate. "I have X-ray vision," she said. "No one else would see the marks on my face. My mind is playing tricks on me. *It magnifies every crazy little thing!* I look in the mirror, and a mark *jumps out* at me. I see it a mile away, but I know that's stupid."

Hal also realized that he had an inaccurate view of his skin. Sometimes the acne was actually there, but it was slight and not anything other people noticed unless he pointed it out. But, in his mind, it would grow to hideous proportions, so it was all he saw when he looked at his face. "My imagination goes haywire," Hal said. "In my mind, this little pimple becomes a massive ugly thing that everyone is staring at. It's as if you drew huge red circles around any tiny imperfection on your face. That's how it seems to me, but I know I'm distorting how bad it is." Another man similarly said, "This is irrational. It's a very small detail that no one else would notice. I'm like an anorexic. I'm distorting but I can't stop thinking about it."

These people had good insight—they recognized that their view of their appearance was inaccurate. Even though they couldn't stop thinking about it, they realized that they really weren't ugly. As one man said, "I have a foggy pair of glasses on my brain."

But most people with BDD don't recognize that they see themselves differently than other people do. They think their view is *probably* accurate. Still other people think their view is *definitely* accurate; they're *completely convinced* that it's right and undistorted. Those who think the defect *probably* is as bad as they think it is, but who can acknowledge that their view might be distorted, have *overvalued ideation*; that is, their *insight is poor*. They say things like, "It's *probably* as bad as I think it is. I don't *think* I'm distorting, but it's a possibility." Or "I'm *pretty* sure my skin looks as bad as I think it does, but I'm not convinced." There's a small element of doubt. Often, they're not sure what to believe. "I think I look atrocious," one person said, "but maybe I don't. I probably do, but there's a question mark in my head. Your mind doesn't know how to tell the truth from the nontruth."

Some people with BDD don't have good insight or even poor insight. Instead, they're *completely convinced* that their view of the defect is accurate and undistorted. They can't be persuaded by others that it's inaccurate. There is no element of doubt. They say things like, "I'm 100% convinced that I'm right. I'm not exaggerating how bad it is. Everyone else is wrong. No one can talk me out of this. There's no question mark." Or "If you said you didn't see it, I wouldn't believe you, because *I* see it." Or "I see it in pictures. I know what I see." One man said, "I'm as certain of what I see in the mirror as you are that the box on this table is rectangular, not round."

Frustrated friends and family members often bear testament to the tenacity and fixity of the beliefs, which they've vainly tried to argue the person out of. In psychiatric terms, such thinking is considered *delusional*; that is, the individual firmly holds on to a belief that others don't share. People with absent insight (delusional thinking) may try very hard to convince others of how terrible the defect looks. Some, with great agitation, present photographs to document supposed changes in their appearance, or produce "evidence" that they're right—for example, hair on a towel or in the drain may be considered irrefutable evidence that hair loss is excessive.

One possible explanation for this view is that they actually *see* something different from other people; that is, they have a different perceptual experience. Another possible explanation is that they see what we see but consider it very unattractive, perhaps because they have high standards. Yet another possibility involves excessive focusing on a minimal defect, which might lead to a distorted view of the importance, or even the appearance, of the supposed defect. I'll discuss these possible explanations further in Chapters 10 and 11.

Thus, insight in BDD ranges from excellent to good, to fair, to poor (or overvalued ideation), to absent (or delusional thinking), as shown in the diagram below. Fewer than 1% of the people I've seen currently had excellent insight, only 3% had good insight, 12% had fair insight, 31% had poor insight, and 53% had absent insight (delusional thinking). However, virtually all of these individuals were currently symptomatic with BDD; after successful treatment, insight often improves. (See Chapters 13 and 14.)

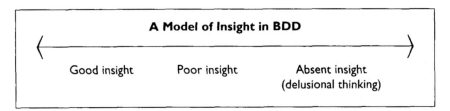

So on average, people with BDD are fairly convinced that their view of the defect is accurate. They also tend to think that most other people share their view. It's usually hard to talk people with BDD out of their view, and they only occasionally try to talk themselves out of it. While some realize that their appearance beliefs have a psychological or psychiatric cause, many don't, thinking that they're simply true.

For some people, insight can fluctuate between the different categories shown in the diagram, rather than always remaining the same. A sales clerk told me, "Some days I think my skin's not so bad, but other days I'm convinced." Marie often had fairly good insight that her facial hair wasn't excessive, stating "Most of the time I know it's not real or that bad; my view is very distorted." But at other times she thought her concerns made some sense—that "maybe it's really there." Some people who think that they may not look so bad become convinced that they look terrible when they examine themselves in the mirror. They lose the insight they had. Cassandra recognized that she had a distorted view of her freckles. "Yes, they're there. But they're not so bad. I know that no one else thinks they're hideous, and I know I'm blowing them out of proportion. But sometimes, they seem really bad. I look in the mirror and I panic. I think, 'They really *are* that bad!'"

Sometimes insight gets poorer when the BDD sufferer is around other people. One man told me, "Sometimes I distort, and sometimes I don't. When I don't go out, I think I imagine the acne. I know I'm making a mountain out of a molehill. But when I go out, I can become 100% certain that it's awful and hideous. I think other people definitely see it. I can change between these points of view within an hour." Sometimes, other kinds of stressors, and anxiety, also seem to temporarily decrease insight. And insight may improve with psychiatric treatment. Hannah, who had been concerned with acne and red and white facial discoloration, realized after treatment with fluvoxamine (Luvox, a serotonin-reuptake inhibitor) that her view had been distorted. She now recognized that her skin looked fine. She was so certain of this that she even went swimming, without makeup—something she'd never done before.

So BDD appears to span a broad spectrum of insight, including delusional and non-delusional thinking. The delusional form, however, is more severe.*

---

*I have found that patients with the delusional form of BDD are similar to those with the nondelusional form in nearly all ways (such as demographic features, BDD symptoms, and treatment response), although those with delusional thinking tend to have more severe BDD—they're more preoccupied, distressed, and impaired by their symptoms, and they tend to feel more stressed and have poorer quality of life.

Research findings suggest that people with the delusional and nondelusional forms of BDD respond to the same medication—the serotonin-reuptake inhibitors, also known as SRIs or SSRIs. These medications are antidepressants with antiobsessional properties. What's important about this is that the SRIs aren't typically thought to effectively treat people with delusional thinking—but they are effective for delusional BDD. (I'll say more about this in Chapter 13). These findings are intriguing and also offer hope for people with delusional BDD.

·· *seven* ··

Mirror Checking, Grooming, Camouflaging, Dieting, and Other BDD Behaviors

"His life was centered on the little mirror in his pocket, and his fate depended on what it revealed or was about to reveal."

Ruth Brunswick, 1928

"I Have This Ritual Every Morning...."

Amanda grew up in a family where appearance didn't really matter. "So I don't know why I worry so much about it," she said "It's ridiculous—I shouldn't really care. But I do." Amanda thought that overall she looked acceptable, but disliked her hair, which she thought stuck out and "looked bizarre." She was also overly concerned about a faint scar on her face and thought her neck was too large.

To look better, Amanda spent hours a day arranging and combing her hair. "I don't do it all at once," she said, "but if I added up all the time I spend, it would be a lot. I have this ritual every morning where I take a shower, and then I take at least an hour in front of the mirror getting ready to go to work. I stay in the bathroom looking in the mirror, combing and recombing my hair. I blow dry it and put gel on it, and then I comb it again. I try arranging it in different ways so it doesn't stick out in the wrong places. I go through the whole process at least five to ten times so I can look decent enough to leave the house. I try to make it look better, but it never really works."

During her morning ritual, Amanda also applied and reapplied makeup to cover her slight scar. Sometimes, she picked at it. She also checked mirrors at work. "When I'm at work, I go into the bathroom to see if I look okay and to check my makeup and my hair. I'm drawn to the mirror. Sometimes I get stuck there, combing my hair. It's a problem because it makes it hard for me to do my job. I'm supposed to be waiting on people, but I'm in the mirror instead."

Amanda worked as a sales clerk in a clothing store and sometimes kept her customers waiting too long. "My boss isn't exactly pleased with my job performance because sometimes I'm not waiting on people, and he's wondering where I am," she said. "I think he knows I'm in the bathroom, which is kind of embarrassing. I'm surprised he hasn't fired me yet. I'm actually thinking of leaving, because it's not the right job for me. I meet new people all day long, and they all get too close to my face. I'm wondering what they're thinking about my hair and the scar—I'm sure they're thinking I look bad. I feel nervous all day, and I can't look people straight in the eye because I feel so self-conscious about how I look."

Amanda considered moving to a colder climate so she could more often cover her neck with a turtleneck. "I don't know whether I'll go that far, but it's a little ridiculous to be wearing a turtleneck when it's 60 or 70 degrees out, which is what I do sometimes. My neck looks huge, and I need to cover it," she explained. "In a colder climate, I wouldn't look so strange wearing turtlenecks all the time. And working in a clothing store, I'm supposed to dress well. During the summer I can look pretty weird."

Amanda performed several behaviors characteristic of BDD: mirror checking, excessive grooming, skin picking, and camouflaging. Jennifer, Jane, and Sarah also did some of these things, as do most BDD sufferers. These behaviors are done to examine, hide, or improve the supposed defect, or to be reassured that it doesn't look so bad. Most people check their perceived defect in mirrors or other reflecting surfaces. Others compulsively pick at their skin. Most BDD sufferers frequently and secretly compare themselves with others. Others question family members or friends, sometimes over and over again: Do I look okay? Can other people see the problem? Sometimes they try to convince others that the defect looks really bad, asking such questions as "Can't you see this on my face?"

Camouflaging the perceived defect with clothes, makeup, or a hat is also common, as is seeking plastic surgery, dermatologic treatment, or other medical treatment. People with BDD may go to doctor after doctor, asking for blood tests, medications, or surgical procedures. Sometimes they have treatment after treatment, without finding the cure they're hoping for.

The table on the next page summarizes common BDD behaviors. I've found that more than 90% of people with BDD does at least one of them. The average number performed is 6, and some people do as many as 13. Although the behaviors in table 6 are particularly common, there are others, such as repeatedly measuring the "defective" body part (e.g., one's waist), reading about the problem area (e.g., books on hair growth), and scouring the internet for solutions. These behaviors, too, are generally intended to obtain reassurance, fix the defect, or hide it from others.

Some behaviors are more unusual and creative. Rob, a 30-year-old factory worker, was preoccupied with his supposedly loose facial skin, receding hairline, and small penis. To tighten his skin, he did something unusual: repeatedly touching doorknobs. While he realized that this behavior didn't really make

Table 6. Common BDD Behaviors

Behavior	Percent (%) of People with Behavior
Camouflaging	91%
• with body position/posture	65%
• with clothing	63%
• with makeup	55%
• with hand	49%
• with hair	49%
• with hat	29%
Comparing body part with others/scrutinizing the appearance of others	88%
Checking appearance in mirrors and other reflecting surfaces	87%
Seeking surgery, dermatologic, or other medical treatment	72%
Excessive grooming (combing hair, applying makeup, shaving, removing hair, etc.)	59%
Questioning: seeking reassurance or attempting to convince others that the supposed defect is unattractive	54%
Touching the defect	52%
Clothes changing	46%
Dieting	39%
Skin picking	38%
Mirror avoidance*	24%
Excessive tanning	22%
Excessive exercise	21%
Excessive weight lifting	18%

*Avoidance of all mirrors for at least several days in a row.

sense—touching a doorknob wouldn't actually tighten his skin—Rob nonetheless did it, *hoping* he might look better. For his hair, he used a fairly conventional camouflaging technique—wearing a hat. But to assuage his worries about his penis size, he tried a more unconventional approach: sewing an extra pocket in his underwear so he could stuff it and make his penis look bigger. A teenage boy kept candy balls or wads of paper in the side of his mouth to widen his supposedly thin face.

Questioning and reassurance seeking can also take unusual forms. While most reassurance seekers ask family members or friends, one woman questioned total strangers, in the ladies' room and even in elevators in busy public buildings. "I asked them, 'Would you tell me—do I look okay?' I knew I looked bad," she told me, "but I couldn't face it, so I tried to get people to tell me I looked okay."

A man tied up his calves with rope while he slept to try to make them smaller. A teenage boy who thought his facial features were asymmetric tried to "straighten them out" by tightly tying socks around his head. He reasoned that this technique might stretch his skin and somehow fix his problem. These were their ingenious—yet ineffective—attempts to cope with their painful preoccupation.

Some behaviors are more avoidant than compulsive; they involve *not doing* rather than excessive doing. Some people avoid having their picture taken—they're missing from their family photo albums and high school yearbook. Or they destroy all photos ever taken of them. One man avoided doing chores around the house because he feared any activity would make his calves larger. Some people avoid showering or washing or brushing their hair because they fear more hair will fall out. A teenage boy refused to eat foods like ice cream, which would wet his lips and make them redder and more noticeable. The strategies that people devise to decrease their discomfort with their appearance are limited only by their ingenuity.

Compulsive Behaviors: "I Can't Resist"

Most BDD behaviors have certain things in common. They're usually time consuming and hard to resist or control (for this reason, they're often called "compulsive"). They sometimes decrease emotional distress but may increase it. They require enormous mental effort. And they typically interfere with day-to-day functioning.

Typically, behaviors are performed over and over again. This is because there's doubt or dissatisfaction about what was seen or done. Did my nose *really* look okay? Maybe I didn't get a good enough look. . . . My hair *still* isn't right! I can't go out until it is! . . . I don't *really* believe that I look okay; she just said that to be nice. I have to ask again! Another reason people perform these behaviors is to prevent a feared catastrophe (for example, camouflaging pimples with makeup to avoid scrutiny by others). Thus, BDD behaviors are sometimes referred to as "safety behaviors."

People with BDD can spend hours a day doing things—such as grooming—that many people without BDD do in minutes. Or they frequently do things, like seeking reassurance, that most people do rarely if at all. In more extreme cases, people spend up to 10 hours a day in front of the mirror, or 12 hours a day picking their skin. Table 7 on the next page shows the amount of time people with BDD say they spend each day on BDD behaviors.

There's usually a strong drive to perform the behaviors, and they're difficult to resist or control. Some people try to resist, but others don't—they "give in," or simply do them "automatically." As Jennifer said of her mirror checking: "I couldn't resist: I *had* to check my face. I *had* to make sure I looked okay." This is one reason behaviors may be done over and over or for long periods of time. As one woman said, "My rituals are like an itch that I have to scratch."

How much control do people with BDD have over their behaviors? When they try to resist doing them, how successful are they? The most common response to this question is little control, with 44% giving this response. Almost no one reports having complete control.

The degree of resistance or control may vary depending on the activity. Many people with BDD resist asking for reassurance. They may feel a very strong urge to ask, but they worry that people will think they're vain or consider their question strange, and they successfully resist the urge. In contrast, people with BDD typically don't resist camouflaging. They simply do it. They put on their hat or their baggy clothes, without trying to stop. This may be because camouflaging doesn't necessarily take much time—sometimes it's done just once at the beginning of the day, so it feels less necessary to resist it. Or it may be that people don't usually feel worse after covering up. They often feel worse after mirror checking or skin picking, which may contribute to a desire to resist and control these behaviors.

The behaviors are usually preceded by an upsetting thought, such as "How does it look?" "Do I look okay?" Or "I know I look terrible and I have to fix it!" Feelings of worry, anxiety, and tension drive the desire to perform the behaviors. In response to the question, "How anxious do you think you'd get if you *didn't* perform your behavior?," 26% report that they would experience extreme and disabling distress (see Table 7). Thirty-nine percent would experience severe distress, and 24% moderate distress. Only 9% said they would experience mild distress, and 2% no distress. Thus, many people do the behaviors before their anxiety becomes unmanageable, to ward off and avoid what they fear will be an even more painful emotional state.

Do the behaviors diminish tension and anxiety? Sometimes. Many people *sometimes* feel less anxious after mirror checking, if they think they look a little better than usual, or at least not as bad as they feared. They may also feel less anxious if they checked themselves in a "good" mirror, in "good" light, or on a "good" day. But they sometimes feel *more* anxious—if they think they look as bad as, or worse than, they feared. In fact, many people with BDD *usually* feel worse after mirror checking—more anxious, tense, and worried. They check to reassure themselves that they look okay, but often their worst fear is con-

Table 7.   BDD Behaviors: Time Spent, Resistance, Control, Anxiety, and Interference*

TIME SPENT ON BEHAVIORS
- None — 0%
- Less than 1 hour a day — 10%
- 1 to 3 hours a day — 42%
- More than 3 and up to 8 hours a day — 39%
- More than 8 hours a day — 10%

ATTEMPT TO RESIST BEHAVIORS
- Always try to resist — 2%
- Try to resist most of the time — 14%
- Try to resist some of the time — 27%
- Rarely try to resist — 29%
- Never try to resist — 29%

CONTROL OVER BEHAVIORS
- Complete control — 1%
- Much control — 5%
- Moderate control — 23%
- Little control — 44%
- No control — 27%

DISTRESS EXPERIENCED IF BEHAVIOR ISN'T PERFORMED
- No distress — 2%
- Mild distress — 9%
- Moderate distress — 24%
- Severe distress — 39%
- Extreme and disabling distress — 26%

INTERFERENCE IN FUNCTIONING DUE TO BEHAVIORS
- None — 4%
- Mild — 19%
- Moderate — 49%
- Severe — 24%
- Extreme and disabling distress — 5%

*From the Yale-Brown Obsessive-Compulsive Scale for BDD (BDD-YBOCS), which rates severity of BDD thoughts and behaviors. See Appendix C for a more detailed description of this scale.

firmed. The distress can be so unbearable that it fuels hopelessness and thoughts of suicide.

Why would someone who usually feels *more* anxious after mirror checking keep checking? The usual explanation is that they *sometimes* feel less anxious after checking, and they hope this will be one of those times. One man told me, "I check in the *hope* that I'll look better this time—that *this* will be one of the times that my fear and anxiety decrease. There's a small chance, a hope."

Sometimes, anxiety and distress diminish temporarily after the behavior is done, but then, after some time has passed, the unpleasant feelings return. People who pick their skin, for example, may feel better immediately after picking, but then, several hours later or the next morning, they feel much worse, after surveying the damage they've caused. Similarly, reassurance seekers may feel better temporarily—for a few minutes or hours—after being told they look fine, but, with the passage of time, their anxiety returns as they begin to doubt the veracity of what they were told. The temporary decrease in anxiety and distress may actually reinforce the behavior, impelling the BDD sufferer to perform the behavior once again.

For some people, the behaviors are minimal enough so they don't interfere with functioning or quality of life. But, for most, the behaviors are unmanageable and a major problem in and of themselves. More than three quarters report that their behaviors interfere with their functioning to a moderate, severe, or extreme extent.

A homemaker who spends two hours a day checking mirrors doesn't have as much time for her children and running the household. A teenager may spend his date alone in his bathroom because he can't tear himself away from the mirror. A salesperson may miss work because she was up picking at tiny pimples until the early hours of the morning, and can't bear to have the resulting disfigurement seen the next day. Wearing a hat can make it hard to go outside on a windy day, eat in certain restaurants, or interview for certain jobs.

BDD behaviors can create problems for family members and other loved ones, and strain even close relationships. Reassurance seeking is particularly likely to do this—the questioning can be so incessant that friends and family can't tolerate it. Requesting others to join in rituals, and avoiding daily activities or special occasions so rituals can be done, can also be very hard on loved ones. Occasionally, the strain ends friendships and causes divorce. Fortunately the treatments I describe in Chapters 12–14 can greatly diminish these behaviors.

The Mirror Trap

If there's any behavior that's prototypic of BDD—that reflects its essential nature—it's mirror checking. Most people with BDD have a special and torturous relationship with mirrors. The mirror reflects their greatest hope—that they look okay—and their deepest fear—that there's something hopelessly wrong with how they look, that they're defective and flawed in a very noticeable and profound way.

Nearly ninety percent of people with BDD excessively check mirrors, spending a long time at one sitting, or checking repeatedly during the day. Most do both. Some who don't check excessively instead avoid mirrors, generally to escape the disappointment, anxiety, and frustration their reflection brings them.

Some people alternate between excessive checking and mirror avoidance. This leaves very few people with BDD who have a normal relationship with mirrors.

While checking is often done in a bathroom or bedroom mirror, virtually any reflecting surface will do; mirror substitutes often become an important part of the BDD sufferer's life. Store windows, car bumpers, toasters, watch and clock faces, TV and computer screens, one's shadow, tweezers, and the backs of spoons all become vehicles of hope and great disappointment.

Before I started my research, the importance of mirrors in the lives of BDD sufferers escaped me. In much of what had been written about the disorder, mirrors weren't even mentioned. But when I started talking with patients and learning about their experience, the importance of mirrors became increasingly clear. One of the first patients I saw brought this home to me when she described her panic attacks, which were triggered by the mirror.

This is what she told me. "At least 10 times a day I have the urge to look in the mirror, but I don't. I try to avoid mirrors, because I worry that if I look and don't like what I see, I'll panic and be debilitated. But there are many times when I just can't resist, and I go running—I just hope that what I see won't be exaggerated. About 50% of the time, I don't feel so bad. I even feel somewhat relieved. I don't look that bad, and the problem doesn't seem to be getting worse. I can go about my business. But about half the time, I look worse. Or I think something like 'You look okay today, but you won't next year.' Thoughts like these overwhelm me with anxiety, and I have a panic attack. I have trouble breathing, I get sweaty, and sometimes I feel dizzy. Sometimes I feel so bad I go to bed for the day. Sometimes I don't go to work."

I've heard similar stories from countless others. While most people don't have full-fledged panic attacks, most feel anxious and fearful around mirrors. What they see affects their mood and even their functioning. As Jennifer said of her skin, "It's the first thing I think of when I wake up in the morning. I immediately rush to the mirror, wondering 'How does it look?' How my skin looks in the morning completely determines how my day goes."

Many people check mirrors in the hope that they don't look as bad as they fear or that they'll look different. They look to reassure themselves. Is my hair okay? Are my legs too fat? Is my makeup smeared? As one woman told me, "I check because I'm hoping to find a miracle—that I look okay." Others check to make sure they know what they look like or that their view of the defect is correct. As one man said, "I check to see that I'm right, and that the scar is still there. It always is—I'm not stupid." Many check so they can camouflage the perceived defect or otherwise try to improve their looks.

After checking, many people sometimes feel better but often feel worse. How they feel depends on whether they like what they see, which may hinge on such things as lighting, whether the mirror is a "good" one, how well they've applied their makeup, or how their clothes look. Many others nearly always feel worse after looking. The mirror confirms their worst fear—that they really are ugly, the perceived defect really is hideous. Very few usually feel better. Jennifer's experience was fairly typical: "Unfortunately, 80% of the time I think I look terrible."

When the mirror reflects an acceptable image, the relief is usually only temporary. Doubts return, along with the urge to check again. Do I *really* look
okay? Maybe I really don't. I need to check again to be sure. As one person
told me, "When I look in the mirror I can be reassured for a few minutes. But
then I usually feel worse. The more I look, the crazier I get. Overall I feel worse
and my anxiety increases. And sometimes I get stuck there inspecting myself
and worrying. I can't leave. It's like I'm superglued."

Jay became more obsessed, anxious, and depressed after looking in the mirror. "I get very caught up in the mirror," he told me. "I think 'Which way do
my lips look the best? Which position is most natural, most attractive?' The
mirror definitely contributes to my problem—it takes it to another level of
obsession."

A study by Drs. David Veale and Susan Riley compared mirror gazing in
people with BDD and people without BDD. They found that people with BDD
spend much more time in the mirror, and are driven to look in the mirror by
the hope that they'll look different, the desire to know exactly how they look,
a belief that they'll feel worse if they don't look, and a desire to camouflage
themselves. They're more likely to focus on specific parts of their appearance,
practice the best position to show in public, and to use "mental cosmetic surgery" to change their body image. People with BDD were also more likely than
the control group to look in non-mirror reflecting surfaces (e.g., the TV screen)
and to feel worse after mirror gazing.

Indeed, other research findings indicate that increased body awareness and
body focus tend to lower self-esteem. The more people concentrate on their
bodies, the more critical they become. Feedback on one's body, such as that
provided by mirrors, increases body awareness, which can intensify dissatisfaction with one's appearance.

People with BDD also typically get extremely close to mirrors, often within
an inch or two of their reflection. They zero in on the despised body areas to
get an even more microscopic look. Try holding your hand an inch or two away
from your face. What do you see? Lines jump out at you, the color looks uneven
and splotchy, all kinds of tiny imperfections become magnified. This is what
happens when BDD sufferers stare in the mirror: they get a very distorted view
of how they look—a view that's very different from what other people see.
Looking in non-mirror reflecting surfaces, such as car bumpers, also seriously
distorts their image.

Like many other BDD behaviors, mirror checking can feel very "compulsive";
it's something that *has* to be done. "I can't resist checking," Amanda said. "I
have an overwhelming urge to do it. I *have* to look to see if I look normal."
The urge, or compulsion, is often preceded by a thought, such as "How do I
look? Do I look okay? Has it gotten any worse?" But mirror checking can also
be "automatic"—something that's "just done" while walking past a window
or store mirror. Many people check mirrors both "compulsively" and
"automatically."

What do people do when they check? Typically they inspect the supposed
defect, often in excruciating detail. A college student told me, "I examine the

front of my hairline to see if the density is decreasing. My hair used to be a half an inch further down. Even on a daily basis I could see the changes." The inspection may be done from different angles or with different lights to get as good a look as possible. "I look at myself a lot at special angles," Eliza told me. "I have three mirrors in my bathroom so I can get a better look." Some people try to fix the perceived defect while inspecting themselves. They comb their hair, reapply their makeup, rearrange their hat, pick their skin, or pull on their nose. One woman tilted her head, squinted her eyes, and covered the lower part of her face. "It made me look more like my old self," she said, "the way I want to look." A 22-year-old man said, "I make funny faces in the mirror to change my face."

Other people don't need mirrors to check. They simply look at the body part directly. A librarian repeatedly inspected her arms during the day to see how hairy they were, hoping to reassure herself that they were okay. A young man checked his calves over and over to see whether they were too thin, especially while showering, resulting in very long showers. Some people frequently analyze their appearance in photographs or videos. One man told me, "I'm constantly analyzing my face in pictures. I'm thinking 'How do I look?' or 'Is my hairline going up?'"

Checking takes time needed for other things. A business executive stayed up most of the night, staring at a small scar on his cheek, and was always exhausted at work the next day. A physicist who spent two to three hours a day checking mirrors performed her job well but had to stay late each night to complete her work. A man who checked mirrors 40 times a day for 15 minutes each time couldn't work at all because of this behavior. Mirror checking can also interfere with relationships and social activities. Many people get stuck in the mirror and don't go out because they feel too ugly to be seen.

It can be especially hard to eat out. One person asked me if I'd ever noticed how many restaurants have mirrors in them. "A lot do," he told me. "Or they have pictures with reflecting glass on them. It's easy to get distracted by checking out how I look." Going to museums can also be hard. "When I go to museums," he said, "I count my freckles in the reflections of the paintings instead of looking at the pictures."

Occasionally, mirror checking triggers a suicide attempt. Seeing the defect reflected back can be too much to bear. The mirror itself can become the vehicle, with broken shards of glass used to inflict self-harm.

One man didn't look in any mirrors for 11 years because seeing his skin was so frightening. He combed his hair and shaved in his mirrorless basement for all those years. "Looking at myself in the mirror is like looking at a scary picture," he told me. "Now I look in them, but I still try to avoid them as much as I can. Especially in restaurants. It helps to some degree. Looking is very painful and makes me angry. I think 'I can't believe this—how I look.' The mirror is the enemy. I curse the person who invented the mirror."

Grooming: Cutting, Combing, Teasing, Tweezing, and Washing

Each day, during his girlfriend Angela's lunch break, Daniel met her in the parking lot of the textile company where they worked. Then they drove to a nearby park. While sitting in her car, he had Angela comb and style his hair so it would look fuller. She also applied expensive tonics that were supposed to stimulate hair growth.

"I had her do it at least once a day because I couldn't see my hair well enough in the back. She followed the directions better than I did. And looking in the mirror is really traumatic for me. This way I'd be sure it got done at least once a day. I'd also ask her if she saw any changes."

Daniel felt badly about asking Angela to do this for him, but thought it was necessary. He had severe BDD and suffered tremendously. "Having her do it kept me going," he explained. His insistence that she groom his hair every day strained their relationship. "She wanted to leave me because I was so obsessed with my hair and because I insisted that she work on it every day. I talked about my hair all the time, for hours at a time. We constantly fought over it. The relationship eventually deteriorated to where I wanted to end it, too. But I tried to hold on to her because I needed her to do my hair. The main reason I was still with her was so she could do my hair and monitor me for hair loss."

Daniel wasn't alone in having someone important to him participate in his grooming rituals. Daniel also combed and styled his hair himself, and applied hair thickener and hair spray "to create an optical illusion" of having more hair.

Nearly 60% of people with BDD groom excessively. Often they do it in front of the mirror. They may do it at home, in the car, at work, at school, or in other people's homes. As one woman said, "I do it wherever I can." Some people excessively groom only before going out, whereas others do it regardless of their plans.

One woman spent at least four hours on her hair every morning—washing, setting, combing, and teasing it—so her family couldn't use the bathroom. She continued to comb and tease it repeatedly throughout the day. She told me, "My hair looks horrendous if I don't do my hair ritual. It's too flat and not full enough." Todd performed a similar ritual. "I fix my hair many times a day while I'm looking in the mirror. I comb it, brush it, and spray it, thinking 'Please just look normal.' I do it with my real hair and with my hairpiece. I'd look like a monster if I didn't do these things." A college student washed his hair three to four times a day, trying to get it to look better. Another man, who thought his hair was too curly, first straightened it, then permed it, then straightened it, and finally shaved it all off. Laura spent so much time parting her hair with a comb, trying to get it right, that she made her scalp bleed.

William had a particularly complicated grooming ritual he felt driven to perform each morning. "First I wash my face and remove the dead skin. Then I wash my hair with shampoo and hair thickener, and then I brush it a lot to remove the frizz. Then I style it so it's a certain way. Then I do my beard: I brush it, style it, and dry it. Then I do my hair again—the whole routine. Then I do my skin again, then I put on hair spray, and then I trim my beard. I have to do it in a certain order. If I get out of order, sometimes I have to start it over again. My day is determined by the outcome of this routine. . . . I don't want to do it—I try to shorten it. I've tried for 30 years, but I can't. I *have* to finish it."

Some people cut and recut their hair, trying to get it exactly even or just the right shape. Some carry scissors with them and cut at work or school. Others have haircutting "binges," cutting in a frenzied burst of compulsive activity. Some people end up with extremely short hair.

Suzanne thought her hair was too flat, so she spent hours a day trying to cut it exactly right, hoping to improve the shape. She couldn't trust hairdressers, but she also acknowledged that by cutting it herself, she "butchered" it. Then for a time she wore what she called "strange hairdos," which was yet another effort to get her hair "just right." She then went through a period of curling and recurling her hair to give it bounce and shape. "I had to do it over and over again to get it just right, and I wouldn't stop. I wouldn't let anyone see me do it, because it was embarrassing. It made sense to me at the time, but I still realized that other people would think it was strange for me to spend so much time on my hair. It seems silly now, but at the time it was agony."

Diane compulsively cut her hair for up to eight hours a day. "I couldn't stop cutting it," she told me, "even though I had to take care of my children. I had to get it looking exactly even and right. I cut minuscule amounts so it wouldn't get too short, but it did get really short because of the time I was spending. I bought wigs because I was so embarrassed about how short it was—I was prac- tically bald—but I cut the wigs too, and I spent all of my money on them. To tell you how bad it got, once I cut myself by accident with the scissors, and I was bleeding. I was so caught up in the cutting that I couldn't even stop to take care of the bleeding." When I asked her how she'd feel if she couldn't cut her hair, she answered, "I'd get so extremely upset that I'd have to be hospitalized. When I'm in a bad period, I wouldn't be able to stop even if the house was burning down."

Like Suzanne and Diane, some people with hair concerns avoid hair salons and barbers because they feel so anxious looking in mirrors, or they fear their hair will be wrecked. Or they're too embarrassed about their hair to allow anyone to focus on it so closely. But some people frequently go to the beauty parlor, even several times a week, desperate for a solution to their hair problem. One woman who did this said, "Every time I go I drastically change my hair style—I don't just get a trim."

Some people with BDD spend lots of time getting rid of their hair. Those concerned about excessive body hair may spend hours a day tweezing it, re- moving it from their face, arms, or other parts of their body. Others have frequent electrolysis. Eyebrows may be repeatedly plucked or shaved to create the right shape. Some men shave for long periods of time, or shave many times a day, to get their beard to look the way they want. Josh, who worried about supposedly asymmetric beard growth, couldn't leave his house without shaving again. Another man shaved many times a day to get rid of his supposedly uneven shadow, to the point where he bled.

Other people apply and reapply makeup. "I use a lot of makeup, and I take a long time to put on my eyeliner and lipstick," Emma said. "I'm in agony if I can't do this. I need my fix! After I do it I feel a little less ugly. But then I worry that I've smeared it, and I keep checking mirrors to see if I have to fix it. I'd guess that I reapply my makeup as often as 30 times a day."

Many people have complex and time-consuming skin routines. They may wash their face ten times a day, or spend a half hour each time they wash it. Many use special soaps, cleansers, and acne products. Shiela tried to prevent acne by washing her face for hours a day, which damaged her skin. "The washing is a lot like the picking," she said. "I do them both to decrease my skin obsessions, but they actually create skin problems. A dermatologist told me to stop washing, but I couldn't. For about three years I was in a vicious cycle: I washed to get my face really clean to prevent acne and to get rid of the effects of picking, like the blood, and then I picked some more. Sometimes I stayed up all night doing this."

People have varying degrees of resistance and control over these behaviors. A teenager who spent two hours a day fixing her hair, combing her eyelashes, and reapplying her eyeliner told me, "I can't resist this behavior, even though it drives my parents crazy. I've tried but I can't."

Although people who groom sometimes feel they improve their appearance, this often isn't the case. The teenager I just described said that she sometimes felt better—when she got her hair to curl the way she wanted it to—but usually she felt worse. If anxiety is diminished, the relief is usually only temporary.

Grooming rituals are especially problematic when staying at other people's homes. Some people with BDD in fact avoid traveling or staying with friends or family because it's so difficult to cart their beauty products with them or fully enact their grooming routine in private. "I won't stay overnight places because I need my special makeup light," Anne Marie said. "I don't go away on weekends because of it." Others describe the embarrassment they'd feel spending hours at a time in someone else's bathroom. "I never visited my in-laws or my family because of my combing," one man told me. "I couldn't take up the bathroom for that long, and I needed to keep my problem a secret from them. I think it's one of the reasons my wife left me—we could never visit her family."

The Batman Mask and
Other Forms of Camouflage

John was a 34-year-old electrician who thought he was good looking except for his skin. "I like to blend in with the crowd," he said. "But I can't with white skin." He'd had this concern since he was 12, when he dreaded going to gym class and the beach because people would see his skin. Over the years, his preoccupation became increasingly painful. To decrease his self-consciousness, he always wore long sleeves and pants. "But that isn't enough," he told me. "Other parts of my skin are still exposed."

John's solution was to use a skin bronzer. "I put it on all the exposed areas of my body. I *never* go out without it," he said. In fact, he was wearing the bronzer during his interview with me. "I spend at least an hour a day trying to paint a perfect picture, so no one knows it's makeup. I look jaundiced, but that's better than pale. It helps me get to work, and it makes my life bearable."

But it also created some problems. "First of all, it's much too much of an effort to paint this perfect picture every day," he said. "And it's very expensive. I'm too embarrassed to buy it in a drug store, so I order it through a catalog. But the hardest part of it is how it affects my girlfriend." This part was hard for John to talk about. It was clearly a very painful subject.

"I couldn't be spontaneous with her, because I had to put the stuff on first, and it always took a long time. We couldn't just go out and do something. I didn't even tell her about it for a few years. The hardest thing I ever did was tell my girlfriend about it. . . . It's why I never moved in with her. It would be too degrading to put it on in front of her.

"It's especially hard wearing the stuff in the summer, because it runs," he continued. "I'd love to go to a baseball game or the beach . . . but I can't. What put me into the deepest, darkest depression of my life was when I was outside in the summer watering the lawn with my girlfriend, and the hose split. I got covered with water, and the bronzing stuff ran. I've never been so humiliated in my entire life. I got very depressed, and I had to go into the hospital for my depression.

"It must be hard for you to understand how desperate I felt," he said. "Maybe this will help. After the hose accident happened, I realized I needed a better solution for my problem. So I decided to take some tanning pills. I knew it was a dangerous thing to do, because I was told they can damage your liver and gallbladder. But I was so desperate, I took them anyway. I had terrible stomach pain, but I kept taking them. A month later, I had to have my gallbladder taken out. I'm convinced it was because of the tanning pills. Before I had the operation, I made sure I put my bronzer on. Before the operation, all I could think about was how I'd look on the table, not that I could die!"

Ninety-one percent of the people in my studies have, like John, used camouflaging. I use "camouflaging" to refer to attempts to minimize or conceal a perceived appearance flaw so it's less visible and noticeable to other people. Some people use bronzers or other methods to change their skin color. More commonly, they camouflage with hats, clothing, their hair, or makeup. Some wear wigs; others adopt a certain body posture, such as constantly jutting out a supposedly small jaw, or turning the "bad side" of their body away from others. Camouflaging methods are numerous and varied.

You may recall Bill, the man who wore a baseball cap pulled down over his forehead to cover "pockmarks" on his nose. He removed his hat only when he was alone in his own room. Bill had considered using makeup to cover the pores but didn't because looking in the mirror to apply it made him much too anxious. He also used his body position to hide the pores. "I hold my head in a certain way," he said, "turned to the right, so the bad side of my nose is turned away from people. And I always keep the lights turned down so the pores aren't so visible. But the only time I feel really good is on Halloween. When I give out candy to the neighborhood kids, I wear a Batman mask, which completely covers the pores. It's the only time I feel okay being around other people."

A 65-year-old man, who'd had severe BDD for nearly 50 years, told me the same thing: "If I wore a mask my problems would be over, but I can't do it in this world. I love Halloween, because I'm free for a fleeting moment."

Hats are used to cover thinning hair or other hair problems, the forehead, eyes, eyebrows, skin, nose, or some other feature. Joe had worn a hat for the past 15 years. "Just about the only time I take it off is when I sleep," he said. "I've taken it off in front of my girlfriend only a couple of times. I felt so nervous about the thinning I couldn't keep it off for very long."

The hat had its advantages and disadvantages. On the one hand, it alleviated Joe's anxiety enough so he could work part time as a truck driver. Wearing it at work wasn't a problem. But wearing it in certain social situations was. "My girlfriend likes to go to a nice restaurant every once in a while," he said. "She's always asking me to take my hat off so we can go. She gets really dressed up, and I look stupid wearing this hat. But I can't do it. I feel so ashamed of my hair that I can't take it off, and I always back out at the last minute. Once I did go without it, and I ended up leaving in the middle of the meal, which was really embarrassing. I was so nervous, I was sweating in the restaurant over how my hair looked, and I couldn't stay. We've gotten into some big fights over this. I realize how strange it must look in certain places," he continued. "People probably even talk about it sometimes. But it's better for them to think I'm eccentric than ugly."

"I always wore this blue beanie in high school," a 27-year-old graduate student said. "A friend asked me why I was wearing it. I was wearing it to flatten my hair and put it in a certain shape. I was also trying to hide it. I recently tried wearing it again, and I looked like a bag lady."

Like hats, wigs are used to cover hair that's considered thin or unattractive in some other way. Some men with BDD join hair clubs and buy expensive hairpieces, which they usually don't like. Some buy hairpiece after hairpiece, trying to find the right look.

Camouflaging with clothing is also common. Luisa hated her legs—especially her thighs. She thought they were "flabby, misshapen, and dimpling." To hide them, she wore "big, shapeless clothes." She almost never wore shorts or a bathing suit. "I'm so embarrassed by how my legs look, I can't bear to let other people see them," she said. "I always keep them covered." Another woman was very preoccupied with her "fat" stomach and only wore clothing that made it look flatter. Pleated skirts were completely taboo, because she thought they made her stomach look big.

Jessica hated her "flat-chestedness." She was once teased about her breasts in junior high school and had been mortified ever since. She wouldn't wear certain bathing suits, and always used padded bras to look bigger. She kept searching for the perfect bra, one that enhanced her breast size but also looked natural.

Men do similar things, trying to appear larger, smaller, or taller. Some wear long shirts to cover their crotch; others wear shoes with lifts. Some wear only long-sleeved shirts or pants, even in the heat of summer, to cover "thin" wrists or arms or "misshapen" knees. One man told me, "I've never gone out of the house in a short-sleeved shirt in my entire life, not even in the summer." And men with muscle dysmorphia, who think their body build is too small, often wear bulky clothing or several layers of clothes to look larger. One man I interviewed was wearing six shirts. But clothing solutions, too, are often unsatisfactory, because they can lead to frequent clothes changing and endless shopping for the perfect cover.

Body parts are sometimes used to camouflage other body parts. Hair is combed over to cover an area that seems particularly thin. Bangs are pulled down to conceal a supposedly short or misshapen forehead. Men may grow a mustache or beard to hide a supposedly uneven lip or a scar. One person's camouflage can be another's BDD: what one person considers excessively thick bangs, another might consider the perfect cover for forehead scarring.

Many people use their hands or body posture to conceal the disliked area. One man sat and stood only in certain positions so his shirt wouldn't rest against and reveal his "love handles." An unusually attractive woman stood in a certain way at her wedding so the congregation wouldn't see her face.

Camouflaging methods are virtually limitless. Makeup, dark glasses, and tinted car windows are other forms of cover. Lights may be kept low or turned off. Some people never sit near a window because they fear the light will illuminate their flaw. Some prefer winter, because they can cover themselves with clothes and because there are fewer hours of daylight during which the defect can be seen.

The intent of camouflaging is to decrease anxiety and emotional distress, especially when around others. In fact, camouflaging is a type of "safety behavior"—a behavior that's intended to increase comfort in certain situations. Many people feel this approach is somewhat successful. Even though applying makeup, for example, may take too much time and can be expensive, some people have told me they'll never give it up.

But camouflaging has its limits. It can be very time consuming, and it's often only partially successful. Men who wear makeup worry that others will detect it. Men and women alike may feel "fraudulent" because of their camouflaging techniques. "I don't like wearing all this heavy makeup," a young woman told me. "I feel like a fraud. And my breast implants make me feel unnatural and fake." Another problem is that when they cover up, people don't have the opportunity to learn that nothing terrible will happen if they don't and that they really look okay.

Yet another problem is that camouflaging may appear unusual, or even strange. A young man who thought his nostrils were too wide, even after having three nose surgeries to narrow them, camouflaged them with his hair, completely covering his face with long bangs. The problem was, he had trouble seeing. Another man wouldn't leave his house without covering his entire head with a black hood, which terrified other people. Bill's Batman mask wasn't an adequate long-term solution to his problem, either. And John's experience with his bronzer and tanning pills is a poignant example of camouflaging's limitations.

Buying Beauty Products and Clothes: "I Have to Find Something That Works!"

The cosmetics industry fuels our economy and promises us sex appeal, youth, and eternal beauty. What would we do without these products? We all need such things as soap and shampoo, and many of us feel we couldn't possibly survive without makeup, hair gel, and conditioners. Purchasing such products is a necessary part of our lives—a ritual as routine as buying our groceries or drinking our morning coffee. It's not only women who buy such products. In 1997 in the United States alone, it was estimated that men spent a shocking $3.5 billion on men's toiletries (hair color, skin moisturizers, tooth whiteners, etc.)

But while much of this behavior is normal, for some people with BDD, it gets carried to an extreme. They spend lots of time and money buying products for grooming and camouflaging. One woman spent more than $100 a week on shampoos and conditioners. "I go out many times a week to buy beauty products—mostly hair products," she said. "I can't walk out of a drug store without one. I keep looking for the perfect product."

Others buy expensive makeup from mail-order catalogs or the internet. Sandy got hers from California. "It costs me an arm and a leg, but I have to cover the white area on my face. I've tried every product that's sold in drug stores and cosmetic counters. None of them work. They wear off, and they come off in the rain. I have to have something that will stay on. And it got too embarrassing to keep buying all those things. The salespeople in the drug store must have thought I'm nuts!"

Ken went to the drug store every day, searching for an acne cure. He spent hours each time examining the different products, and sometimes spent more than $100 a week on them, even though he couldn't afford it. He described his behavior as compulsive—he couldn't resist doing it, and felt extremely anxious if he didn't go. Several times, when his funds were low, he was so desperate to find a solution that he shoplifted skin products.

Clothes shopping, too, can be expensive and time consuming. While some people avoid shopping because mirrors or trying on clothes makes them so anxious, others shop excessively, trying to find something that will improve their looks, distract others from their flaws, or provide the perfect cover. "I spent so much time shopping, and I was so concerned with clothes," Maureen said. "It was like an addiction. It was a way to cope with my ugliness. I needed clothes to make me look good."

In fact, some people with BDD are diagnosed with "compulsive shopping." This problem consists of a powerful urge to shop that's very difficult to resist or control. In some cases, BDD causes the shopping problem. A waitress I treated had bought so much makeup that she was $9,000 in debt; even though she was nearly broke, she traveled hundreds of miles to buy more special makeup that cost her another $1,000. I've seen other people who were $40,000 in debt from BDD-related purchases, such as clothes, makeup, and other beauty products.

The urge to buy—the hope that *this* product or outfit will solve the problem—overpowers the rational argument that nothing else ever has, and this won't either. Ken said of his acne soaps and medicines, "Some are better than others, but I haven't found any miracles." Nonetheless, he felt compelled to keep buying them, desperate for a solution to his painful problem.

Clothes Changing

Nearly half of people with BDD compulsively change their clothes, frantically trying to find an outfit that will minimize their perceived flaws and help them feel presentable. One woman told me: "I change them 4 or 5 times a day because they don't look right. They don't hang right. They make my legs look too fat and my shoulders look too broad. I get very anxious and I think that people are analyzing my appearance, so I have to change them. Sometimes I change them even when I'm home alone. I keep checking my body in the mirror and changing until I look right. It can take up a lot of time."

It can in fact take hours a day. Tiffany spent 3 hours each morning picking out clothes, putting them on, appraising herself in the mirror, then ripping them off and flinging them on her bed in disgust. "I *can't* leave the house without doing this," she told me. "It's horrible. I *try* to stop, but I can't. It wastes so much time, and my bedroom is a mess! My husband keeps accusing me of having an affair, because I'm so obsessed with picking the right outfit! But I'm not! I tell him that I'm just trying to find a way to stand my awful body."

Skin Picking: "I Can't Stop Destroying My Looks"

When Pamela came to see me, she began by saying, "I'm a picker." Pamela considered her skin picking the most troubling part of her BDD. "I can't stop destroying my looks," she said. "I have this compulsion of picking at my face at any tiny blemish. I try to remove any ugly things on my face. . . . I feel addicted to this compulsion."

Pamela was a 25-year-old music student with no obvious skin lesions. She'd picked at her skin for the past eight years, trying to remove small blemishes and imperfections that to her were "hideously ugly." To decrease her chance of getting pimples, she also picked to remove any dirt that she feared might be under the surface of her skin. Pamela usually picked for several hours a day but sometimes for up to 12 hours at a time. Occasionally, she stayed up all night picking.

I asked Pamela to describe her picking. "The way it usually goes is that first I check a mirror," she said. "I check in school with a pocket mirror, I check in store mirrors, or I check in my bathroom mirror at home. I hope to find a miracle when I check, but I never do—there's always something wrong with my skin. I see a tiny blemish, and I start obsessing that my skin looks ugly and that other people will notice it. I think, 'I see a bump there! People are going to notice it! I have to get rid of it!' I get very self-conscious and I start. The worst time for me is the morning, when I'm getting ready for the day, and at night before I go to bed. Sometimes I get totally caught up in it, and I don't even think of anything else.

"When I can't pick, I get shaky and anxious—I *have* to do it! I'm drawn by the mirror—I *have* to look and see how I look, and then I *have* to start picking when I see anything wrong, even though I know no one else will probably see it. I can't resist. Then, afterward, I check to see how I look. Usually, I look so terrible that I isolate myself. . . . I pick hoping to make my skin look better, but I usually make it worse."

Pamela's picking caused notable lesions that required dermatologic treatment. "The treatment helped my skin heal, but it didn't help me stop the picking," she said. "One dermatologist told me to just stop doing it. If only it was that simple! I've tried to stop a hundred times, but I can't. I've tried cutting my fingernails, and then I wore artificial fingernails and bandaids to avoid doing more damage to my face. It really didn't work."

Pamela's boyfriend had recently broken up with her because of her picking. "I could no longer hide my need for privacy to pick—I was much too embarrassed to tell him about what I was doing. And the picking took a lot of time—I ran out of excuses about where I was and why I couldn't do things with him."

More than one third of people with BDD pick their skin. This relatively high frequency isn't surprising, given that skin concerns are so common in BDD. People with BDD who pick are usually concerned about minimal acne, scars, or scabs, or such things as "large" pores, "bumps," "small black dots," "white spots," "ugly things," or other supposed imperfections. They pick to make their skin look better—to make it smoother, clearer, more attractive. They pop pimples, dig at white heads or blackheads, or smooth bumps. Some try to remove dirt, pus, or "impurities" from under the skin. While many use their hands to pick, pinch, or squeeze, others use tweezers, needles, pins, razor blades, staple removers, or knives.

Picking with implements like these for hours a day can cause major skin damage. One woman picked an actual hole through her nose. Some people have go to the emergency room, because they pick through their facial skin into major blood vessels and need stitches. A colleague told me about a patient who picked so deeply at a pimple on her neck with tweezers that she ruptured her carotid artery, the major blood vessel to the head. She required immediate emergency surgery; the surgeon said that the picking nearly killed her.

Even though skin picking can cause extensive skin damage, it's important to realize that people with BDD don't intend to mutilate themselves. Rather, they're trying to improve how their skin looks. The problem is that the behavior is so compulsive that they can't stop, which is what causes the damage.

For some people, picking is a relatively inconsequential aspect of their BDD. But for most, the picking is in and of itself a serious problem; some consider it their major problem. One woman attributed her suicide attempt and psychiatric hospitalization to her belief that she had "ruined (her) face because of picking." Two woman I know of needed psychiatric hospitalization largely because of their picking and eventually committed suicide.

Skin picking has been described in the professional literature, particularly the dermatology literature, for many years, but it's been little researched. Traditionally, this behavior has been considered a type of "neurotic excoriation," a broad and antiquated term used for more than 100 years that doesn't specify the cause of the picking or indicate treatment approaches. Not all people who pick their skin have BDD. Skin picking can occur as a symptom of other psychiatric disorders. In some cases, it's simply a habit rather than a symptom of a disorder.

To determine whether picking is a symptom of BDD, ask the person why they pick. Do they pick to remove or minimize supposed defects or imperfections in their appearance, such as pimples, bumps, acne, or scars? If so, and if the other criteria for BDD are met, the picking behavior is a symptom of BDD. It's often a clue to the diagnosis.

But often the picking is kept secret. Many people are very ashamed of this behavior and reluctant to reveal it to others. One adolescent who was referred to me because of his picking talked at length about other, more minor problems and didn't mention his picking at all. When I finally asked him about it, he acknowledged that it was his major problem but that he'd been too embarrassed to bring it up.

But some people talk about it quite openly. One young woman I saw not only talked about it with others—she even picked her friends' skin. "I can't stand to see anyone with things on their face," she explained. "I have to make their face smooth! When I see them, I pick off the little imperfections. They're my friends, so they let me do it." Another woman told me, "I look for anything to pick. I want to pick my friends' skin because I pick my own and there's nothing left. I especially like to peel other peoples' backs when they're sunburned." She also liked to peel paint off walls, paper off jars, and dried glue off her hands.

People with BDD who pick are similar in many ways to those with BDD who don't pick. But there are some interesting differences. Although skin concerns are common in both groups, those who pick are more likely than those who don't to be concerned with their skin (close to 100% versus about 50%).

They're also more likely to excessively groom and camouflage, perhaps because they sometimes do create actual skin defects that they feel they need to cover. People with BDD who pick their skin are also more likely than those who don't pick to have actual skin defects, as opposed to none. Sometimes the minimal defects lead to the picking, and often they result from the picking. A vicious cycle can occur in which a minimal defect leads to picking behavior, which then creates more defects and more picking. Sometimes, skin defects caused by the picking are clearly present and noticeable.

People who pick their skin are also more likely to be treated by a dermatologist: approximately two-thirds versus fewer than one-third. Although dermatologic treatment is sometimes needed to treat the skin damage or infections that the picking can cause, it usually doesn't decrease BDD symptoms (the skin-related preoccupations and associated picking). As I'll discuss further in Chapters 13 and 14, picking behavior often diminishes with serotonin-reuptake inhibitors or with a type of behavior therapy called habit reversal. Because the picking can be so time consuming, distressing, and damaging, it's important to focus on it in treatment.

Reassurance Seeking: "Do I Look Okay?"

Many people with BDD never breathe a word to others about their appearance concerns—largely because they'd be much too embarrassed to mention them. As a college student said about her face, "People must notice it's long, but I haven't asked. I'd be *much* too embarrassed! And if people said they didn't notice it, I wouldn't believe them anyway. I'd think they were just trying to be nice."

But about half of people with BDD question others about how they look. Often, this consists of requests for reassurance: "Do I look okay?" "Is the problem noticeable?" The purpose is to allay anxiety and be reassured that the supposed defect isn't as bad or as noticeable as feared.

Some BDD sufferers instead try to convince others of the reality or ugliness of the defect. A question isn't asked; rather, a statement is made. "Can't you see this on my face?" "Can't you see I'm ugly?" A third variation on the theme is repeated requests for help in improving the defect—for example, questions about how to straighten "excessively curly" hair, or repeated requests for cosmetic surgery.

Kevin, who was preoccupied with his "large" lips, "small" legs, and "sparse" body hair, asked his mother 5 to 10 times a day whether he looked okay. "I need to know I look decent, so I ask my mother, 'How do you think I look?' I call my friends and ask them too, and I have huge phone bills because of it. They always say I look fine. Sometimes I feel better, and sometimes I don't. When I'm feeling really bad, I think they're just trying to be nice."

A 44-year-old homemaker who worried about a small scar on her face realized her worries were irrational, but questioned others because it was comforting. "I want the reassurance," she told me. "It's a reality check." She repeatedly asked her husband, "Do you see it? How bad is it?" She also sought reassurance at cosmetic counters to "get an objective view." As she explained, "My husband loves me, so he might have a biased view of how bad it is."

A young man who feared he was losing his hair and that his body build was too small repeatedly asked his father, "Dad, do you think I'm losing my hair? Do I look big enough?" He was also concerned that his penis was too small, and he frequently asked his father whether the chart of penis sizes he'd gotten from a book was accurate.

Many people confine their questioning to family members or close friends. But others ask doctors or even strangers. One woman who'd been in therapy for several years spent most of her therapy sessions asking her therapist if her nose looked all right. "It's just about all she talked about," her therapist told me. "I'd try to steer her away from the subject, but it was useless. She was so obsessed—and so upset—that she couldn't stop talking about it. No matter what I said, she couldn't be reassured that she looked fine. She thought I was just being nice."

Sometimes people with BDD don't directly question others because they're afraid people will think they're vain or that their question is strange. So instead of directly asking, they bring up the topic in a more indirect way. A man concerned with his body build explained, "I wanted to ask other people how I looked, but I didn't want them to know I cared so much about it. I thought it would seem like a sign of weakness that I was bothered by it. Instead, I hinted around the subject, talking about appearance or body size in a more general way, hoping to get them to say 'You look big.'"

A teacher directly asked her husband about her "sagging" eyes, saying "Do you see it? How bad is it?" "But when I'm around friends or at social events, I can't directly ask," she said. "It would be too embarrassing. So I switch into philosophizing. I talk about things like how society overvalues appearance, and all the cosmetic surgery that's done. I'm somehow hoping I'll be told I look okay."

Sometimes, the intent is to get others to confirm that the defect is bad. One woman tried to get her husband to comment positively on other women's breasts, which was a way of affirming that hers were unattractive. "The point was to get him to agree with me because I'm right." Another woman, in great desperation, dragged her three young children to the mirror each day, pointing to invisible marks on her face and insisting that they agree that they saw them and how awful they looked. She told me "I'd harangue them and harangue them, and they'd just cry."

Some people use photos to convince others of how much they've changed and how bad they now look. One of the first people with BDD whom I met handed me a several-year-old photo within a few minutes of my meeting her. "Can't you see how much I've changed?" she asked jabbing the photograph with her finger. She implored me to agree with her, pointing out how much hair had fallen out, how much fuller her cheeks used to be, and how different her eyes were—how lifeless and dull they'd become. She described at length how the photograph clearly demonstrated these changes, although I couldn't see them. A young man showed me a year-old photo of himself, pleading with me. "Can't you see how I've changed? Physically, I've changed *drastically* in the past few years. My whole face is different! Can't you see that?!" He seemed desperate for me to agree with him. At the same time, I sensed he feared I might.

Some patients have tried to convince me that their view is accurate by holding their face at different angles or changing the lighting in the room. "Can't you see they're flat?" a young woman asked me about her cheekbones, turning her head and holding it at different angles.

Other variations of questioning behavior are asking others how to fix the problem—the best way to curl hair or how to pay for liposuction—or a discussion of the defect and the problems it's caused. Virtually all one man talked about was his hair—his belief that it was thinning, how his life would be different if it weren't, and how to fix it. These discussions dominated his conversations with his girlfriend.

Reassurance seeking typically causes problems. It can take up a lot of time and be very difficult for family members and friends. Whereas mirror checking, grooming, and picking can be done in private, questioning always involves someone else. If it's limited to once or twice a day, it's generally tolerable. But if it's more frequent, it can dominate and ruin relationships.

I've been told by many people with BDD that their spouse, girlfriend, or boyfriend left them because they spent so much time talking about, or asking about, their appearance. Other aspects of the disorder—such as avoidance of social situations—often contribute to relationship problems as well. But it's surprising how often the questioning is considered a major part of the problem.

Peter, a 40-year-old unemployed carpenter who hated his ears, jaw, and eyes, discussed his appearance and questioned his wife so often that she left him. "All I did was complain about how I looked and talk about how I wanted plastic surgery," he said. "I didn't accept her reassurances. She considered it mental abuse. She ended up hating me because of my obsession and because I talked about my looks all the time. Once I drove her so crazy talking to her about it that she pulled a knife on me. She threatened me, 'If you think you need surgery, now you'll *really* need it!'"

One parent told me something that's been echoed by many other family members: "The most frustrating part of it is that no matter what I say, it doesn't really help." Indeed, responding to requests for reassurance is a no-win situation. Saying the person looks fine doesn't help, but neither does telling them that something is wrong. If you say they look fine, they usually don't believe you. They think you're just trying to be nice or that you didn't get a good enough look at the problem. Or maybe you need new glasses. A handsome young man told me that he could "just tell" that his parents think he's ugly, even though they tell him he's handsome, because it's "their moral obligation." Another told me that "reassurance doesn't really help, because why did everyone laugh at me at camp and in the locker room?" And a very attractive woman said, "When people say I look fine and I get complimented, they overdo it, so I must be really ugly."

If the person with BDD does believe you, the relief is usually only temporary. The doubts soon return. Maybe the reassurance giver didn't get a good enough look. Maybe they're just trying to be nice because they're your friend. And the questioning starts again. As Julie said, "When my surgeon reassured me, I felt a little better, but only for a few minutes. It never lasted very long." And she'd go back to ask again. A young woman told me, "When people say I'm pretty, I like it. I need the feedback. But I feel good for only a few minutes. I see how I look, and I feel terrible. I know what I see." When reassuring words temporarily decrease anxiety, they may actually increase the questioning behavior because the fleeting relief of anxiety reinforces and fuels more questioning. The BDD sufferer asks once again, looking for relief, even if only temporary.

Responding by agreeing with the questioner and saying that the defect is there and looks bad is usually even worse. This response is often given in desperation because reassurance hasn't worked. On the one hand, BDD sufferers may welcome the agreement because someone is finally telling them they're right; at the same time, their worst fear has been confirmed.

Another response that doesn't work is something like the following: "Well, now that you point it out I can see it, but it's really not that bad. Before you showed it to me I didn't even notice it." The person with BDD usually hears it differently. The "really not that bad" and "didn't even notice it" parts go unheard or are considered untrue. Responses such as these can plunge the BDD sufferer into a serious depression. To summarize, the bind is this: no matter how you respond, it usually doesn't help.

As I'll discuss further in Chapter 17, the best approach is not to comment on the perceived defect. I have my patients and their loved ones agree together that, overall, responding isn't helpful. When others don't respond with reassurance, over time the questioning may diminish.

Comparing: "She Looks Better Than I Do!"

"I always look at other peoples' noses—mostly their pores—comparing myself to them to reassure myself," Bill said. "I see other people have pores and they're doing okay, so I should. But I can't reassure myself. I just get more down on myself." Another man compared himself with others and thought, "Why can't I have regular skin like that? Why can't I have normal skin?" "I compare to reassure myself by seeing someone else with the same problems," he said, "but I never see anyone else with the same problems."

Comparing is the most common BDD behavior of all. More than ninety percent of people with BDD do this. They frequently and silently compare their "ugly" body part with the same body part on others, thinking such things as "Do I look okay compared to her?" They seem to have built-in radar for the body part of concern, quickly focusing on it. As Mike described it, "I zero in on other peoples' ears and compare them to mine."

One woman frequently compared herself to other women and also contrasted young people with old people to see if they had lines on their face. "I know *every line and wrinkle on every person's face*," she said. She usually felt that she looked worse than other people, which triggered panic attacks. "I say to myself, 'I wish I could have that baby-smooth skin.' I think how lucky any older woman is who has no wrinkles." Another woman, who thought her breasts were too small, compared her breasts with those of every woman she saw. She said, "I panic when I see cleavage!"

BDD sufferers generally don't feel much better when they compare. In fact, they often feel worse. Aaron, who worried about his slightly receding hairline, told me, "I check out everyone's hair. And everyone looks better than me, even bald guys. At least other bald guys have a little hair left that looks good. Mine looks terrible—thin and stringy. I'm the one guy who can't lose his hair and keep any of his looks." He then added, "It's okay if other people are bald. They can look handsome, but I don't because I have a long face."

Aaron experienced the typical no-win situation. People with BDD generally think that other people look better than they do, which reinforces their feelings of defectiveness. A handsome young man told me, "I constantly stare at other people's noses and compare their's to mine—I'm an expert on noses. I think how bad I look and how good they look. I'm envious of good-looking people." "Do you ever see anyone who looks as bad as you think you do?" I asked him. "Occasionally I see people who look as bad as me, and I feel sorry for them," he replied. "I don't want people to feel sorry for me."

If people with BDD see someone who looks as bad as they do, they still don't feel much better about themselves. Somehow they interpret the situation negatively, thinking such things as "He doesn't have much hair, but he's laughing and seems to be enjoying himself. Why can't I?" Or "She looks as bad as I do, but she has a boyfriend. What's wrong with me?" A 40-year-old man said, "I stare at peoples' faces thinking 'He has freckles and he's talking to people. Why can't I do that?' " The situation is interpreted in terms of—and usually ends up reinforcing—the BDD sufferer's own perceived shortcomings.

"When I'm standing in line at the drug store or the grocery store, I talk to myself, trying to reassure myself that I don't look so bad and that I should stay in line instead of leaving," Jason said. "I look at other people and think they're uglier and worse off than me. But then my thinking takes a negative turn: I think things like 'It's true, he's really ugly, but he doesn't seem to care. He seems to be doing fine! What's wrong with me?' Or I check out all the successful people on TV—a lot of them aren't attractive, but they're smiling and seem happy, so I think maybe I can be happy too. But then I get down on myself because I'm not."

It's common to compare with people on TV or in magazines. "The models have thicker hair than I do," Jordan told me. "As I look through magazines I think 'Why can't I look like that?' Then I feel even worse." "I have to buy *Cosmo* every month," Laura told me, "because I have to compare my body with the models'. I always feel worse when I do it, because they always look better than me, but I can't resist doing it. It's a monthly ritual; it's something compulsive that I have to do."

Comparing can take lots of time and make it difficult to focus and concentrate. It's hard to focus on a conversation, or instructions your boss is giving you, if your attention is on the other person's physical attributes. One socially active woman couldn't really converse at social gatherings because she was so intent on analyzing other people's skin.

The comparing is done so surreptitiously that others don't realize how closely they're being scrutinized. I've never been aware that this behavior was occurring except in those rare instances when the person commented that I looked better than them. To my surprise, one person I saw told me that I had "a real cute nose." Never having received such a compliment before, I wondered what had motivated this remark. It was only after I'd seen more people with BDD that I realized how often comparing occurs, and that this woman believed that nearly *everyone's* nose looked better than hers.

Some people assume that other important people in their life are also comparing them to others and finding them less attractive. This can wreak havoc in relationships. Linda compared her breasts with those of every woman she saw, and she assumed her husband was doing the same. "It was a terrible problem in our relationship, because I'd think he was constantly looking at other women and thinking they were more attractive than me. I'd get insanely jealous and make all kinds of accusations. We even had to go into couples' therapy because it was such a problem. Now I realize that I was projecting my own behavior onto him. He wasn't comparing me with other women; I was!"

Doctor Shopping: The Never-Ending Quest

I got a call one morning from a psychiatrist in Boston who needed some advice about a patient. "He's seeing all the ophthalmologists in Boston," he told me. "He thinks his eyes look cross-eyed, and he can't be reassured that they're not. He's seeing doctor after doctor. They all tell him he looks fine, but he won't stop doctor shopping. He wants to get his eyes fixed."

This story isn't unusual. Many people with BDD seek nonpsychiatric treatment, often dermatologic or surgical. They see dermatologists for slight or nonexistent hair loss or skin problems, requesting various types of treatment. They see surgeons to have their lips thickened, jaws widened, ears pinned, or breasts enlarged. They see endocrinologists for supposedly excessive or insufficient body hair, dentists for braces, orthopedic surgeons for a supposedly crooked spine, podiatrists for "bent" toes, and urologists for penis enlargement. They may see doctor after doctor, trying to find one who will provide the desired treatment. Others visit nonprofessionals, seeking electrolysis, a hairpiece, or hair-growth tonics. There's no limit to the types of treatment requested.

"Seeing doctors is an obsession for me," Victoria told me. "I'm looking for something from them. I want to keep going until I find out the answer. I've seen all types—general practitioners, orthopedists, and podiatrists. I'm trying to find someone who can tell me why my feet are so misshapen. They all tell me that nothing's wrong with my feet. One doctor said my problem was that I had an obsession with body image. I agree that I have a body-image problem because I'm so obsessed, but I also need to find out what's wrong with my feet."

Doctors are seen for various reasons: to diagnose a perceived appearance problem, do testing to determine the cause of the perceived problem, obtain reassurance that it looks okay, or give treatment. They may be asked to provide treatment after treatment, or to redo a disappointing procedure done by themselves or another physician.

Jennifer had seen at least 15 different dermatologists. She visited each of them repeatedly, asking them over and over if her skin looked okay. "I saw some of them several times a week," she said. "I couldn't be reassured that my skin was fine. I wouldn't go away. I asked and asked them about my skin, and I begged and begged them for treatment. A lot of them refused to see me anymore."

Usually, the person wants reassurance from the doctor, but if he or she isn't available, the office staff may be asked instead. One person was certain all the staff in her surgeon's office thought she was "crazy." "I go there all the time to ask if I look okay. They look the other way when they see me coming. I know I'm driving them out of their minds."

Dwayne had seen 5 dentists, 4 dermatologists, and 16 plastic surgeons. He disliked "everything" about his appearance, which he described in the following way: "I must be an alien from another planet because I look so strange. I was totally obsessed with getting surgery. It's all I talked about. My girlfriend threatened to leave me if I got it. None of the doctors wanted to treat me. The dentists said braces wouldn't help me. One of the dermatologists said I should just wash my hair more. Fifteen surgeons refused to treat me because they said I looked fine. One of the surgeons said it was a good thing I didn't have much money, because I'd be mutilated if I did. I finally got a nose job from one surgeon, but it didn't make me look any better."

Dwayne was so desperate for more surgery that he was thinking of going to another country where it would be easier to get it, or threatening suicide if a surgeon didn't agree to do it. He was also considering getting into a car accident so he could destroy his face and have it completely reconstructed. "That way," he said, "insurance would pay for it."

Mac had been turned down for surgery many times because the surgeons said he looked fine. "But I kept going back to them, and going to new surgeons, trying to find one who would do it. I know when they saw me, they said, 'Oh no, it's him again!'" Finally, in desperation, Mac tried to break his nose with a hammer so a surgeon would agree to operate. As he explained, "That way, something would have to be done."

A Japanese psychiatrist has referred to people with BDD who obtain repeated surgery as "polysurgery addicts." This description fit a 52-year-old homemaker, who'd had 23 different surgical procedures. "I kept trying to make myself look okay," she told me. "I had surgery after surgery, but I was never really happy with the results. My solution was to get more! I was addicted to plastic surgery."

Dieting

While dieting is a common behavior, as well as a feature of eating disorders, it can also be a symptom of BDD. I first became aware of this when reading about BDD before I'd begun my own research. I found the published case of a young man from Germany who thought his cheeks were too "rosy and round"; to make them thinner, he severely starved himself. Since then, I've seen people who've dieted for similar reasons. One young man severely starved himself in the hope that losing large amounts of weight would erase wrinkles from his face. Another lost 30 pounds to make his face less wide.

Other people with BDD diet for more conventional reasons. They try to flatten their stomach or slim their thighs or calves. Some people avoid salty foods or take water pills to decrease eye puffiness, stomach bloating, or facial swelling. Others eat special diets—for example, avoiding chocolate or greasy foods, or taking herbal supplements—trying to make their skin clear. One man I treated went from 160 to 120 pounds because he worried his skin would break out if he ate anything greasy or oily; in fact, he avoided most foods. After treatment with Prozac, his skin worries disappeared and his weight became normal again. Men who think their body is too small may eat high-protein low-fat diets to become larger. One man who did this, however, didn't allow himself to get *too* large and muscular because he feared that compared to the rest of his body, his penis would look too small.

Weight Lifting, Aerobics, and Other Forms of Exercise

Some people with BDD exercise excessively. They may run or do aerobics to decrease cellulite or the perceived flabbiness of their thighs, or to make their arms or legs slimmer or larger. Others do sit-ups to flatten their stomach. These behaviors are carried to an extreme. As a 30-year-old woman said, "My whole day is planned around exercise." A man I treated was so worried about not exercising during his hour-long drive to see me, thinking his muscles would "shrivel up," that he joined 5 gyms between his house and my office, which he worked out at along the way.

Exercise often doesn't have the desired effect, and some people think it makes them look even worse. One woman did what she called "extreme exercises" to decrease supposed facial bloating. "But the exercise didn't have the desired effect," she said. "In fact, it made my legs look bigger and worse. I became obsessed with my legs while I was waiting for them to decrease in size."

Nick, a 32-year-old former car mechanic, carried weight lifting to an extreme, severely damaging his body. He believed his body was too small, which he related to feelings that women didn't find him attractive or "enough of a man." To increase his size, he ate massive quantities of food, weight-gain powders, and special vitamins. He also wore extra shirts and padded his clothes. "But the main thing I did," he said, was lift weights. I lifted for hours a day. In retrospect, I realize I looked fine before I started to lift, and I'm sure everyone else thought I looked fine, too. I looked normal. I was 195 pounds; I wasn't fat, but I wasn't overdeveloped. Now I realize I probably looked even *better* that way. But at the time, I thought I looked too small. I was obsessed with looking bigger. I wanted to be stronger and more masculine. I wanted to be the biggest person on the planet!

"I became *obsessed* with working out. I spent a lot of the day lifting. I *had* to exercise before I left the house. I had to get the feeling and the look of bigness before I went out. I was trying to keep up with my friends who were using steroids. And I did get big—I got a lot of reinforcement for it. People would compliment me. Sometimes I even felt high while I was lifting. But I still felt I wasn't big enough. I had to get even bigger."

Lifting became the focus of Nick's life. "It's embarrassing to talk about this," he said. "I'm ashamed of how it interfered with my life—I stopped working because of it, I dropped out of life. . . . I couldn't concentrate on my work because all I was thinking about was lifting. I actually stopped working because I couldn't get out of the house without exercising. I didn't see my friends—I just stayed in my basement lifting. I lost a lot of them because of it. Once, I got so upset thinking I wasn't big enough that I stayed in my basement for a month, lifting and lifting. I was desperate to be bigger—I couldn't get out of the basement! I was so depressed, thinking I'd never be big enough, that I thought I'd rather be dead. I couldn't let anyone see my body."

Nick injured himself so severely that he had to stop playing sports, and he wasn't able to work. He was often in pain, and even had difficulty walking. When I saw him, he was in physical therapy and had to use crutches to walk. "I totally ruined my body by lifting," he said. "I tore my muscles apart. The irony is that now I can't work out at all—not even a normal amount."

Tanning

Excessive tanning is another risky BDD behavior. People tan for various reasons—usually to darken "pale" skin. Others tan to dry up perceived acne. A young woman repeatedly sunburned and peeled her nose to try to make it smaller. A man in his 50s tanned the top of his head to darken it, so it would blend in better with his hair and he wouldn't look "bald."

Arnie was obsessed with getting a tan—not to darken his skin, but to distract women from what he considered his "jutting" jaw. "I look a little better when I'm tan," he explained. "I get positive feedback from people, so I spend a lot of time in tanning salons. I figure a good tan distracts people from my ugly jaw."

Some people with BDD carry tanning to such an extreme that they severely burn their skin, permanently discoloring and damaging it. Tanning also prematurely ages the skin, and—most worrisome of all—can cause skin cancer.

Ellie always had a very dark tan in the hope that her skin would look better, even though she often burned and knew excessive sun exposure could cause cancer. "My dermatologist told me to stop doing it, but I *have* to get a tan. I don't care if I get cancer. At least I'll look good in my casket. That's how screwed up this whole thing is."

A man in his 40s who couldn't leave his house because he thought he looked so ugly was so desperate for a tan that he developed a severe alcohol problem. He was so self-conscious about his "pale" skin that he'd venture into his backyard to tan every day only after first getting drunk.

Distraction Techniques

Another BDD behavior is accentuating or improving certain aspects of one's appearance as a distraction. The thinking goes like this: by making an acceptable or attractive body part look even better, other people's attention will be directed to the attractive body part, rather than the "defective" one. About 17% of people with people with BDD use distraction techniques. Distracting with makeup is most common (in 10%) followed by clothes (9%), hairstyle (5%), and jewelry (4%).

You may recall that Jennifer used lots of makeup to accentuate what she considered her more attractive features and distract people from her skin. Another woman, who thought her breasts looked fine, was nonetheless considering breast augmentation to distract people from her "ugly" nose.

A man I saw excessively combed his hair, which he considered one of his primary assets, to make it even more attractive and thereby distract people from his "sunken" eyes. "People will be looking at my hair instead of my eyes," he said. "I get a lot of compliments on my hair. It helps me feel less self-conscious about my eyes."

Measuring

Measuring is another form of checking and reassurance seeking. Am I the right size? Do I look okay? People who think they're too short may repeatedly check their height. Maybe I'm not such a midget! Women who think their waist is too large may repeatedly measure it. Muscle girth, breast size, and penis size may be measured over and over again.

One man measured his penis with a tape measure up to 10 times a day, even though a urologist had told him it was normal. When it seemed somewhat larger than usual, he felt better. But, when the measurement confirmed his fear that it was tiny, he felt devastated. When I asked him why he kept measuring it when he was so often disappointed with the results, he responded. "I measure it because I *hope* it will be bigger this time." This response echoes that of people who check mirrors, pick their skin, and seek reassurance: this time it *might* be different.

Reading and Information Seeking

Some people with BDD compulsively seek, buy, and read any information they can find about their perceived defect. Men with genital concerns may frequent bookstores and libraries, perusing every book and magazine they can uncover, searching for information about genital size. Is theirs really small? Or is it okay? Some people with hair concerns read voraciously about hair growth. How quickly does it grow? Once it's lost, can it be regained? They search medical textbooks and the internet, seeking information about agents purported to increase or speed hair growth.

Men and women with body size concerns may spend hours a day reading fashion magazines, weight-lifting magazines, and books on dieting or exercise. They compare themselves with the models, hoping to reassure themselves. Or they search for tips about how to look bigger or smaller, hoping to discover the magical diet or exercise regimen that will finally make them look the way they'd like.

Touching

Rosa frequently touched her hair to make sure it was puffed up. If it didn't feel right, she rushed to the mirror to fix it. Another woman constantly touched her face to "cool it off" so it didn't look so red. Zach frequently touched his lips, which he thought were too small, tense, and "never in the right position," trying to make them look more relaxed and natural. He also compulsively licked them hundreds—perhaps even thousands—of times a day. "I have to lick them to check them, and so they're not so dry and to make them look better. I try to resist, but I get more nervous and upset, and I can't talk to people unless I lick them. But when I do it I usually feel worse, because it looks so strange, and other people must think I'm really weird."

Frequently touching the disliked body part is another form of body checking, which about half of people with BDD do. Touching may also take the form of manipulating the body part to make it look better. A nose may be pushed up to look shorter or sideways to seem less crooked. Judy frequently pressed on her eye to make it more symmetrical with her other eye. She put so much pressure on it that she gave herself a black eye.

Touching, like mirror checking and many other BDD behaviors, can actually fuel the obsession and is best avoided. One woman said, "Touching my face confirms that the defect is there and I feel worse, so I try not to do it." Sometimes it's a trigger for skin picking. Touching often increases emotional distress and may lead to more time-consuming and futile attempts to remove or improve the flaw.

Other Behaviors: Handwashing, Praying, and
Doorknob Touching

There's no end to BDD behaviors. A woman I saw tensed and untensed her facial muscles to make them less "limp." Another person pushed on her eyeballs to improve their shape. One woman made paper cutouts of breasts, which she examined while obsessing about the size of her own.

Symptoms commonly seen in obsessive compulsive disorder can also occur in BDD. People wash their hands to avoid getting dirt on their face, which might cause acne. They may excessively shower as part of their hair ritual, washing their hair over and over to undo previous grooming and set the stage for even more grooming. Excessive and ritualistic praying, and touching doorknobs, may also be done. One woman, for example, repeatedly touched doorknobs to make her eyes brighter.

These cases illustrate the kind of magical thinking that can occur in BDD— that is, the belief that one's actions will cause or prevent a specific outcome in a way that defies commonly understood laws of cause and effect. They also illustrate the interesting overlap between BDD and obsessive compulsive disorder, which I'll discuss further in Chapter 16. And they're examples of some of the less common, varied, and creative BDD behaviors.

These behaviors are unlimited. Claudia swallowed water a certain way so the skin around her mouth wouldn't drop and the lines wouldn't get worse. Nicholas jutted his jaw out to compensate for his cheekbones, so they wouldn't look so prominent. To improve his acne, Tim got up in the middle of the night to put hot towels on his face. To make his face look fuller, Frank slept without a pillow, ate lots of food, and drank more than 3 gallons of water a day. To change the shape of his face, Donald frequently crushed his jaw with his hands. Dennis, who worried about hair loss, searched his pillow each morning for hair, saved his hairs in a plastic bag, and developed complex math formulas to determine the rate of his hair loss. He paradoxically sometimes pulled out his hair, to see how easily it would come out. Somehow the evidence always confirmed that his fear was true.

$\cdot\cdot$ *eight* $\cdot\cdot$

How BDD Affects Lives:
Social Avoidance, Problems at
Work, and Suicide

"I've missed weddings, birthday parties, and funerals because of how I look. I don't go outside, and I'm on medical leave from college because of it. I'm an ugly duckling. I've been teased my whole life. What's the point of living? I thought I was going to die after I overdosed, and I was sorry that I didn't."

Karen

Ian's Experience: "It's Ruined My Life"

I look like a freak of nature," Ian told me. "I look like the Elephant Man. This is the cause of my problems. It's why I went to California. I was trying to look better."

Ian came to see me after his parents discovered that he'd had disappeared to California to get a tan. To scrounge up money for his trip, he had broken into houses across the country, stealing cash and credit cards. "I'm not a criminal," Ian said. "I've never done anything like this before. But I was hoping a good tan would distract people from my ugly face," he told me. "I look a little better with a tan, and I was desperate to get one.

"Maybe I was also sort of trying to get back at society, because people were making fun of how I looked," he added. Ian was also hoping to find a plastic surgeon who would agree to operate. "I was hoping to find a surgeon in California who would redo my whole face. The ones I saw here wouldn't do it because they said I looked fine and didn't need it. But I don't believe them. It's their moral obligation to say I look okay." When I asked how he would have gotten the money to pay for surgery, he replied, "I was thinking of robbing a bank."

Ian had been a good student, athlete, and musician in high school and had never gotten into trouble of any sort. He started having problems when he went to college. That's when his appearance concerns began. He went into the men's room one day after class during his freshman year and felt incredibly ugly. "I feel like my whole face has changed." he said. "I don't really want to say what it is . . . but the skin under my eyes has gotten darker. My face is too wide. My nose looks ridiculous. I have this tape that goes through my head that says 'I hate how I look.' I look in the mirror and it's not me. . . . I feel repulsed by what I see," he said angrily, covering his face with his hands. "It's made my life fall apart. I'm a devastated person because of it. It's ruined my life."

Because he thought he looked so ugly and felt so anxious in class, Ian stopped going to classes and spent most of his time alone in his room. "In high school I was considered good looking and was accepted," he said. "But in college, I started to look bad, and everyone there was Mr. GQ. I don't have to look great—I just want to look normal.

"All I thought about was my face. I didn't go to the dining hall to eat, and I didn't even know if I had classes. I thought about suicide every night," he said. As a result, Ian started failing in school. His professors and a dean met with him and encouraged him to go to class, but he couldn't. "They asked me what was wrong, but I couldn't tell them. I wanted to go to class, but I couldn't. My heart was willing, but my mind wouldn't cooperate.

"All of this happened because of the change in my looks. Why should I go to school or have a job and be productive when people will laugh and make fun of me? I might as well sit in my room." Ian also stopped seeing friends and dating. He'd gone out on a date once in the past year and thought the woman had dated him because she'd felt sorry for him. "I don't go out with girls because I know they'll reject me. So I reject them before they have a chance. I've isolated myself from everyone."

Ian's despair got so severe that he attempted suicide after looking in the mirror and thinking he couldn't go on living any longer. He was hospitalized and then moved back home with his parents.

Carl's Experience: "I Pull Myself Together"

While people with more severe BDD may, like Ian, be unable to function because of their symptoms, others, like Carl, function well despite their emotional pain. Carl was an intelligent man in his late thirties with a good sense of humor. He worked as a partner in a law firm, where he'd been very successful over the years. "I've been a fairly happy person, and I had a good life," he told me. "But a year ago that all changed dramatically.

"I was looking in the mirror one morning, and out of the clear blue sky I noticed unusual thinning of my hair, and I panicked. I feared I was starting to go bald. I looked hideous. I panicked because I thought that within a year or two the whole front would be lost."

Carl started reading about hair loss in dermatology textbooks and seeing dermatologists. "I even talked one of them into giving me minoxidil to make my hair grow, which didn't do me any good. The other dermatologists I saw didn't understand why I was using it. I think about my hair 24 hours a day—it's on my mind all the time. It's like a feeling of hunger that's always there. When I comb my hair or look in the mirror, my focus on it becomes intense, and sometimes I have panic attacks."

In reality, Carl had a full head of thick, curly blond hair. He realized his view was distorted. "I realize I look worse to myself than I do to other people," he acknowledged. "I know I'm distorting how I'll look if I lose more hair. I'll look worse to myself than to others. I'm distorting my perception, but I also believe it. I can't help worrying about it. I'm very tuned in to other people's hair and to changes in my own hair.

"I never really liked how I looked when I was younger. I always thought I was the ugly one in my family," he told me. "Sometimes other kids called me 'curly head.' But I gradually got to like my looks, especially my hair. Now I feel I've lost the best part of my appearance." Because of his concern, Carl felt depressed, and it was hard for him to concentrate at work. "It's affected every aspect of my life," he said. "I don't have enthusiasm for things, and I'm depressed. It's totally due to my hair."

Nonetheless, Carl managed to function well. "I do my best to pull myself together for work," he said. "In the morning I purposely comb my hair without my contacts in so I can't see myself. I try not to look at my hair in my rearview mirror while I'm driving to work." The distraction of work helped him think a little less about his hair. He had to put in some extra hours at the law firm to make up for decreased efficiency, but he performed his job adequately. "But," he said, "I'm afraid that if I continue to lose my hair, I'll be too embarrassed to be around clients.

"Socially, it's caused me some problems," he added. "It affects my relationships because I'm so wrapped up in my hair. It's hard for me to empathize with other people's problems. I feel unappealing because I assume people are looking at me the way I do, which I realize they're not. I feel very self-conscious around women, but I force myself to go out. Even though I look terrible, I'm still asking women out on dates. I worry, though, that this will be an issue if I get into a serious relationship."

Although Ian and Carl had the same disorder, the consequences were somewhat different. Some people, like Ian, can barely function, whereas others, like Carl, function fairly well. The consequences for most people are somewhere between these extremes. Most feel that their social life isn't as good as they'd like, and they may find it harder to do their job, schoolwork, or household duties. But they may compensate reasonably well, doing well enough that others can't tell that anything is wrong. When functioning is severely impaired, others may know that something is wrong but may not realize that BDD is the cause.

Many people with BDD withdraw from the world to at least some extent. Depression and anxiety are common. Accidents and violent behavior can occur.

Occasionally, people do surgery on themselves, with disastrous results. Some people contemplate—and attempt—suicide. Some succeed in killing themselves.

Table 8 provides a summary of problems that the more than 500 people in my studies experienced since their BDD began. Their average age was 31 to 32, and on average, they'd had BDD for 14 years. I'll discuss these problems, plus others, in more detail below.

Figure 1 shows additional specific situations that people in my second BDD series (which has 200 people) currently avoided.

Social Consequences: "I Stay Alone"

"There are traffic lights longer than my social life," Jake said wearily when he met with me. "This problem is ruining my life. It's like fighting demons."

Jake was preoccupied with his arms and legs, which he thought were too skinny, and his "pale" skin. "I have no sex life or love life. I'm almost completely socially avoidant. I hardly ever go out. If I do go to a night club, I feel suicidal. . . . I'm still in shock that I look so horrible after all these years. It amazes me that no one faints when I get on the subway!"

Jake had been married to someone he hated and later divorced. "I married someone I felt no desire for. She was an awful person, but she was the only one who would accept me. She was probably the worst woman in the whole world, but I didn't think anyone else would accept me because of how I look. I felt lucky to have anyone."

Samantha avoided swimming or any activities requiring shorts. She, too, was concerned with pale skin and with freckles on her arms, legs, chest, and back. "The color of my skin is dead looking," she said. "It causes problems in my social life. I miss parties sometimes, and if I go I can't focus on conversations because I'm thinking about my freckles and pale skin. I'm constantly scrutinizing other people's skin. I'm noticing what a nice color it is, or that they don't have any freckles. The only time I really tune into the conversation is when I hear anything about freckles or skin. Then my ears perk up. "This problem also interferes with my sex life. My husband told me to make sure I told you. I feel very self-conscious, and I don't want him to see my body. I can't relax and enjoy anything. My husband can't understand me. He tries but he can't, and he gets angry about it."

The most common problem that BDD causes is interference with relationships and social activities. Ninety-nine percent of the people in my studies reported that at some point their symptoms negatively affected these things. When they considered the period when their BDD was at its worst, 4% said that BDD interfered with their social functioning only mildly, whereas 29% said it interfered moderately, 39% severely, and 28% extremely. Eighty-eight percent have had times in their life when they avoided nearly all social interactions because of BDD.

In my second series of people with BDD, 119 completed the Social Adjustment Scale questionnaire (SAS-SR). On average, their answers indicated that

Table 8. Interference in Functioning

Problem	% of People with BDD Who Experienced the Problem or Average Number
Interference with social functioning (e.g., with friends, family, or intimate relationships) due to BDD	99%
Periods of avoidance of nearly all social interactions because of BDD	95%
Interference with work or academic functioning because of BDD	90%
Periods of complete avoidance of work, school, or one's role (e.g., maintaining a household) because of BDD	80%
Days of work missed because of BDD*	52 days
Days of school missed because of BDD*	49 days
Temporarily dropped out of school because of BDD	14%
Permanently dropped out of school because of BDD	11%
Completely housebound for at least 1 week because of BDD	29%
Ever felt depressed because of BDD	94%
Ever violent because of BDD	28%
Ever psychiatrically hospitalized	38%
Psychiatrically hospitalized at least once because of BDD	26%
Ever thought about suicide**	80%
Ever thought about suicide because of BDD*	63%
Ever attempted suicide	25%
Ever attempted suicide because of BDD	14%

*Since BDD began
**Wouldn't mind being dead, wished you were dead, or considered suicide

Figure I.   Avoidance of Activities*

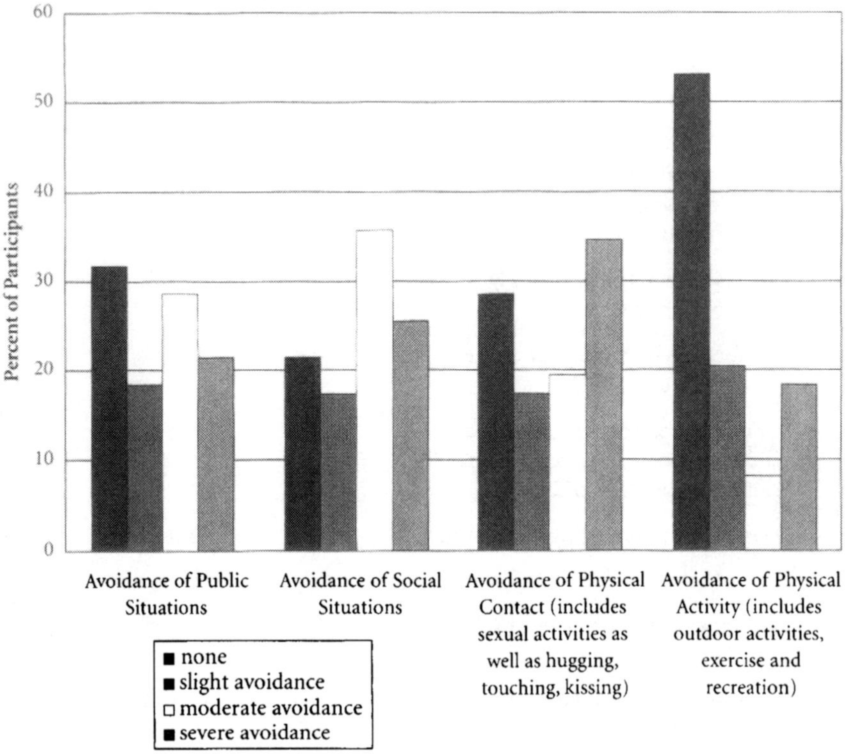

*Assesses avoidance of situations during the past month due to BDD

their social functioning is severely impaired in all areas that the scale assesses (see Figure 2). In fact, on average, the scores of people with BDD were worse than the scores of more than 95% of people in the general population.

People with BDD are often reluctant to go to parties, dances, clubs, weddings, class reunions, or other types of social activities. They feel embarrassed to be seen, so they feel anxious and self-conscious in social situations. They may appear quiet, preoccupied, and withdrawn. They're usually very focused on how they look and how others are appraising their appearance. Are they noticing it? Do they think I look bad? Are they going to reject me because of it? Or they're comparing with others. Such obsessive thoughts and doubts make it hard to focus on a conversation, relax, or enjoy activities. As one man said, "Ninety percent of your mind is on your obsession—you have only 10% left over to focus on what someone is saying."

BDD behaviors can also contribute to problems in social situations. "When I first meet someone, I don't want to be seen," Jake said. "I'm morbidly self-conscious. Then I check out their arms and legs. I think they're lucky, or if

Figure 2. Social Adjustment Scores in BDD and Community Samples

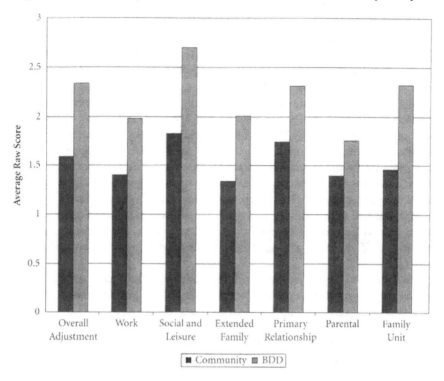

• Lower scores indicate better quality of life.
• On the SAS-SR "Overall Adjustment" scale, BDD subjects' mean score was 2.3 standard deviation units poorer than the community sample score.
• Scores across all SAS-SR domains were 0.9–2.0 standard deviation units poorer than published norms.

someone looks worse than me I feel better for a short while. But not too many people look worse than me. *This* is what I'm thinking about when I'm with other people. I'm not listening to the conversation. I'm totally focused on whether they're noticing my arms and legs and how theirs look compared to mine."

People with BDD feel especially uncomfortable and anxious in situations in which the perceived defects are likely to be exposed. They may avoid swimming, the beach, or events requiring shorts or short sleeves. People with facial concerns feel anxious in most social situations. Many people say that their symptoms typically worsen when they're around other people, which makes them avoid people even more. As one young man told me, "My BDD bothers me less when I'm alone, so I stay alone."

Relationship may be strained or avoided altogether, and intimacy is often forgone. Many people with BDD are very isolated. Spouses, boyfriends, or girlfriends usually have trouble understanding the self-consciousness and avoidance and may become irritated or even angry. "My husband is very frustrated that I don't want to go places with him where I'll have to dress up," Maria told me. She avoided situations, such as parties or dances, in which she couldn't wear bulky sweatpants that covered her thighs. "He doesn't understand why I prefer to stay at home instead of going out or spending time with friends. He's afraid that we're starting to lose our friends because of it."

BDD often stifles intimacy. "I've not only avoided dating because of it," Martha told me, "I finally got a boyfriend, after 20 years of not having one, and my worries about my feet and thighs are interfering with our relationship. It interferes with sex—I'm afraid he'll reject me because of my appearance. It's a burden and a hindrance. I'm afraid I'll never get married because of how I look." Martha never told her boyfriend about her appearance concerns, even after they got engaged. "I'm much too embarrassed," she told me. "I discuss everything else with him, but not this." Because she was so self-conscious she tried to hide her body whenever she was around him. She undressed only in the dark, and she never allowed him to see her feet. "I wear socks at all times," she said.

Sally was able to be intimate with her husband. "But I can't exactly relax," she said. "I worry about my hair the whole time—is it getting messed up? Does it look okay? I jump out of bed right after sex to check my hair. My husband thinks I'm crazy!"

Arnie, who thought his skin was too white, had never felt comfortable with his girlfriends. "It's interfered with my love life and with any intimacy whatsoever. I wouldn't take any clothes off. I wouldn't even roll up the sleeves on a long-sleeved shirt!" Randy attributed his impotence to his BDD. "I'm constantly judging the size of my penis negatively. I'm probably misperceiving, but I think it anyway. The intensity of the feeling is severe. No wonder I'm impotent."

Many people say that BDD caused the breakup of a relationship, even divorce. You may recall Julie, whose first husband left her because of her BDD. "All I talked about was my nose," she explained. "All I talked about was wanting surgery. I was so preoccupied I could hardly take care of my kids or the household. We had no relationship."

Jonathan's wife left him because of his BDD. "She said that was the reason, and I think it was," he said. "And I don't blame her for leaving. I was totally obsessed. I'd spend weekends in bed, and I wouldn't go out with her because of my pimples. I got so wrapped up in the problem that she really didn't have a husband anymore. She called BDD 'the selfish disease.'"

Many people aren't in a relationship at all. About two thirds of the people I've seen (who on average were in their early 30s) have never been married. Twenty two percent were currently married, and 12% were divorced. Many want to be in a relationship but aren't for various reasons—self-consciousness, fear of rejection, shyness, or low self-esteem.

Warren had never pursued a relationship with a woman he liked. "All of my relationships have been with women who pursued me," he said. "I've never been in a relationship with someone I liked because of my appearance. I've felt undesirable. I've stayed single so I don't inflict myself on anyone else." "I'd never ask a girl out," Paul told me. "I'm too shy, and I have the BDD problem. It affects all of my relationships, especially with girls. I totally avoid girls. I don't even think of being intimate with them. It paralyzes me socially."

When people avoid dating and social activities so they aren't rejected, this can create a vicious cycle that makes them more and more isolated. A young man who refused to ask anyone out because of his hair was certain that no woman would ever want to date him, let alone marry him. When I pointed out that in fact he might not ever date if he didn't ask women out and if he continued to avoid social gatherings where he might meet them, he was surprised. He had assumed the reason he wasn't dating was because women found him so unappealing. He didn't realize the extent to which he himself was creating his dateless situation by avoiding women.

Many people have told me that they haven't had children—or never will—because of their BDD. As one patient told me, "I grew up praying that my brothers wouldn't look like me, and I was always reluctant to have children for the same reason." Like this man, many are afraid that their children will be ugly. Others worry that their children will have BDD and don't want them to suffer with such a painful illness.

BDD also often interferes with friendships. Friends may find it hard to understand why social events are missed or attended only after much urging and encouragement. They may be puzzled and frustrated by lateness and last-minute cancellations. Many a person with BDD has ended up spending an evening or day alone instead of with friends as planned.

"I can barely be with friends because I think they're thinking how ugly I am," a 28-year-old woman told me. "I haven't seen my friends in the past 20 years," another said. "The main reason is I'm afraid they'll see how I've aged and that my hair is thinner. I become really upset whenever I see people I haven't seen in a while. I think they'll notice how I've changed. It's gotten to the point where I totally avoid people. I've cut myself off."

Family get-togethers, weddings, and funerals may be anticipated with great trepidation and fear—or missed altogether. "I've missed a ton of social events because of my appearance," Guy told me. "To tell you how bad it is, I missed my two best friends' weddings! I felt too ugly to go. I've missed Christmas get-togethers. If I went, I wouldn't enjoy myself because of how I look. I've hurt other people because of it, by not showing up. My BDD is too overwhelming to go. I've humiliated my parents by not showing up at relatives'. It really bothers me. My family and friends never knew the extent to which I was worried about this."

It's sometimes difficult to determine how much the BDD symptoms themselves are responsible for social problems such as these. It is simply the BDD? BDD is so often accompanied by social anxiety and low self-esteem that it can be hard to tease them apart. But people with BDD generally say that their BDD symptoms are the cause of their social problems or significantly contribute to them. My research findings show that the more severe BDD symptoms are, the poorer social functioning is. This is also true for overall functioning. And when BDD responds to psychiatric treatment, social functioning usually improves, sometimes rapidly and dramatically and sometimes more slowly, especially if symptoms are long-standing and severe.

Researchers have shown that social anxiety and fear of social rejection are more commonly experienced by less attractive people and by those with a negative body image. While people with BDD aren't in reality less attractive on average than other people, they *think* they are.

Teresa summed up what so many people with BDD feel: "I feel so ugly and unpresentable that I avoid parties and dates. I feel too anxious when I'm around other people. I think they're evaluating how ugly I am and that they're thinking I'm ugly and disgusting. I feel like a leper. I've stayed in a lot in the past few years. This problem has utterly and completely limited my social life."

Effects on School and Work: "I Haven't Met My Potential"

"If I'm supposed to be in a meeting at work but I have blemishes, I don't want to go," Dan said. Alicia didn't work at all because of her appearance. "I'm too ugly," she said. "I don't want people to see me and comment negatively."

As I showed in table 8, 90% of the people in my studies experienced interference with work, school, or other important activities. When they considered the period when their BDD was at its worst, 10% of people said that BDD interfered with their work or school functioning only mildly, whereas 30% said it interfered moderately, 23% severely, and 34% extremely. Eighty percent said they had periods when they completely avoided work or school. Like social difficulties, problems in this area range from relatively mild to extremely severe. Most people find that their preoccupations and rituals make it harder to focus and concentrate. They become less efficient. Grades or job performance may drop. Extra time may be needed to make up for time wasted on BDD-related thoughts and behaviors.

People with BDD may be late for school or work or not go at all. They may be reluctant to interview for jobs because they assume they'll be rejected because of how they look. Those with more severe BDD may never even try to get a job or may quit school or work. They may become financially dependent on others. As table 8 shows, a high percentage of people avoid school or work, or drop out of school altogether. And as shown in table 20 in Appendix A, a fairly high percentage are unemployed or not supporting themselves, and 9% are on disability because of BDD.

Elizabeth, a fashion designer in her thirties, had been obsessed with her "rat's nest" hair for ten years, ever since she'd gotten a bad haircut. She thought that the shape wasn't right and that it looked a mess. "It's the first thing I think of in the morning: I think 'My hair looks so awful!' I have nightmares of having it cut. It *really* bothers me. It makes me feel desperate." Although Elizabeth had been widely acclaimed for her innovative work, she hadn't been employed for the past four years. "I've always been told how much promise I have, but I'm so upset by my hair that I can't work," she said. "I've passed up lots of opportunities, all because of my hair. I can't work because I'm so depressed and demoralized. I don't want people to see how I look. I worry I'll *never* be pleased with my appearance."

Erica, fourth-grade teacher, couldn't do her job as well as she'd like. "Sometimes when I'm teaching I feel okay. But then I look in a mirror, and I get down and want to leave school. I start obsessing about my skin—it's what I think about for the rest of the day. It's like a carousel in my mind. The thoughts go round and round and never stop. 'Does my skin look okay? Is it red? Do I look rashy?' It's hard to focus on the students and their needs. By the end of the day, it's affected my teaching. I'm obsessing, and I feel agitated and depressed."

Reggie dropped out of his band because of his appearance worries. "I was too self-conscious to perform," he said, "and I couldn't groom my beard the way I wanted on the road. The other guys in the band thought I was crazy."

People with BDD sometimes avoid taking a job they'd really like. Jobs that involve a lot of interaction with others, especially if the defect will be exposed, are especially avoided. I've seen many people who had a solitary job, such as a night watchman. As one person told me, "I can't do any kind of job where I have to be up close to people. I don't want people to see my facial abnormalities. I think they're noticing how ugly I am, and I worry that they'll think less of me because of it."

Tony took jobs he didn't really like because he didn't want other people to see him. He had always longed to be a high school teacher and football coach, but he hadn't pursued these jobs because of his chin. Instead, he'd worked at office jobs where he sat in a back room doing solitary work. "I've been underemployed because of my appearance problem," he said. "I haven't met my potential or gone after the kind of job I've really wanted. When opportunities for advancement came along I turned them down because they always involved being around people more. I didn't want a job where people would see me. I would have felt too ashamed." Another man said something similar: "I could have a much better job if it wasn't for this problem. I haven't been able to get promotions to positions that involve more social interaction. I've stuck to more technical jobs. I would have liked to advance."

Use of camouflage can also interfere with work. One young man, who wore a hat to cover his hair, told me, "I'm a pretty smart guy, and I should have a much better job than I do. But I can't look for a decent job with this stupid hat. I can't dress up in a jacket and tie and wear this ridiculous thing on my head!" Another man, who thought that his nose was crooked and covered his face with long hair, didn't look for jobs because he couldn't remove the curtain of hair from his face.

People with BDD may drop out of elementary school, high school or college because they can't concentrate, don't want to be seen, or are depressed because of BDD. Sean, a 24-year-old student, was still enrolled in college but hadn't attended classes for the past three years. Instead, he'd been living with his parents. "First I started missing classes and school activities because my hair bothered me so much I couldn't go. I was too embarrassed over it. It always looks strange. It never looks neat or natural. It sticks up and looks bizarre. If I spray it, it looks greased down. Barbers ruin it, so I cut it myself and it looks ridiculous. I spend hours in front of the mirror combing it and trying to fix it. Once I had a perm, and it looked better for a while, but when it grew out I looked like a terrorist.

"First I started missing some classes, and my grades started dropping because I couldn't concentrate. But I was determined to blast through everything, and I pushed myself, but that didn't work. I started missing so many classes that I took a year off. I didn't tell the school officials why because I was too embarrassed. I tried to go back, but I couldn't concentrate so I dropped out again."

Rebecca had also missed many classes. "I wouldn't go to school. I couldn't concentrate because I'd be worrying about my skin or going to the mirror all the time to pick it. And when people saw me, I thought they were judging how it looked. I finally left college because of it. I was very active in high school, and I had lots of friends. But I couldn't leave my room in college. After I left school I stayed in bed for two weeks. . . . I let myself down by leaving. I want to go back in January, but I won't be able to succeed unless I'm feeling better. This problem is an obstacle to getting on with my life."

Students with BDD may find gym class particularly painful because their defects are more exposed or because they have to change their clothes or shower in front of their peers. Rita, who worried about her thighs, told me, "I always flunked gym because I wouldn't wear shorts." Doug skipped gym class because he thought his wrists and body build were too small and didn't want them to be seen. Another man had avoided all sports and skipped gym class because of his shame over his genitals. He eventually dropped out of the ninth grade and never returned because he was so terrified of having a required physical exam and the doctor seeing him naked.

BDD can also interfere with caring for children and managing a household. Ann Marie spent so much time worrying about her facial creases and shriveled eyelids that she was unable to care for her young son. "I've neglected him," she said. "My appearance problems are so time consuming and energy consuming. My ex-husband has to take care of him." A 30-year-old woman told me, "I feel so extremely ugly, I can't get through my day. I'm not mentally or emotionally there for my kids. I'm removing myself from my family. My kids know something's wrong with me, but I haven't told them what it is. I want to lead a normal life so badly."

Other Problems:
Shopping, Bright Lights, and Leisure Activities

"I restrict going places," Jerry said. He was a 45-year-old man who'd had BDD for 20 years. "When I go out, I feel worse and uglier. It's hard to go to the store. I have to boost myself to go. I'm afraid I won't fit in. I constantly worry that people are scrutinizing me and criticizing me. I get incredibly anxious and panicked standing in line because I look so awful, and I think everyone is noticing how ugly I am. Emotionally, I feel like someone's holding a gun to my head. I try to convince myself it's not a big deal, but sometimes I leave the line in a panic, and I go and look at cookware because it calms me down."

People with BDD typically avoid many types of situations and activities because they're so self-conscious, depressed, anxious, or fearful—public transportation, clothes and food shopping, leisure activities, restaurants, going outside on windy days, and other types of everyday activities (see Figure 1, p. 120). Robert avoided all these. "I'm afraid if people see me they might say to themselves 'Oh, gee, look at that guy. Isn't he gross looking?' I think people laugh at me. I avoid public transportation because of it. I can't get on the subway without hyperventilating. I stay in my apartment more. And I postpone grocery shopping. I usually go at night, because people won't see me on the way there, and there won't be as many people in the store."

Like Robert, some people get their mail, shop, and perform other necessary activities under cover of darkness. They avoid clothing stores and shopping malls because of the plethora of mirrors. "There are so many mirrors there— you can't avoid them. Everywhere I look I see myself and how gross I am," one woman told me. "Sometimes I suddenly leave stores when I see my reflection." She eventually bought her clothes only through catalogs. Others keep their distance from mirrors when trying on and buying clothes. One man stood about 20 feet from the mirror when trying on clothes. "Or, if I get up close, I have to look at the clothes with my head down so I can't see my face," he said. "Otherwise I'll freak out." In my second series of 200 people with BDD, about three quarters said they had problems doing household duties, caring for their children, or doing errands because of BDD or another mental disorder (BDD was usually the reason).

Harry rarely went to movies, and when he did he tried to avoid being seen. "I always sit in the back row so people can't sit behind me and laugh at the shape of my head," he told me. Curt walked behind people and sat in the back of the class so no one could see the slight hair thinning on the back of his head. He also always waited for an empty elevator. Jesse avoided dancing, which he loved, because he thought everyone would laugh at his supposedly bowed legs.

Many people, especially those concerned about facial defects, avoid bright lights, which could illuminate the perceived defect. "At parties, I'm very uncomfortable hanging out in the kitchen with bright lights," a 26-year-old computer programmer told me. "I prefer a darker room." Others avoid restaurants with bright lighting, or find a dark booth in the back, so they can't be seen. Some people quit their jobs, or never accept one in the first place, if they have to work under fluorescent lights. In BDD-treatment groups I ran, the group members tried to avoid sitting next to the window, because they feared their defects would be more visible in brighter light. Several men have told me that they know everything about lighting. As one said, "I'm an expert on lights. I'd be a darn good lighting salesman!"

Many people avoid swimming and the beach because the perceived defect will be more exposed—large hips or thighs, small breasts, small body build, thinning hair, skin defects, or cellulite. In addition, wind and water can easily ruin camouflage and painstaking grooming: makeup runs, bronzers streak, and hair styles are destroyed.

Some people avoid the things they love most. Greg avoided sports, even though he'd been an excellent athlete and had played on several varsity teams in high school. Although he was muscular and in excellent physical shape, he feared that people would see his "small and puny" body build, and stopped playing altogether. Loni didn't play on her high school field hockey team because it would mess up her hair. "I missed a very important thing," she told me. "I loved playing team sports—it was what I liked best of all in high school."

Being Housebound

Being housebound is the most extreme kind of avoidance. Twenty-nine percent of the people in my studies have been completely housebound for at least a week because of their BDD symptoms. They didn't leave to go to work or school, or even to do simple errands. Many more stay in for briefer periods, and others remain inside far longer. Some are trapped in their house for years, petrified of going out and being seen.

"I've stayed home for weeks at a time because of my beard," Josh said. "I was in my own world. I worried people were talking about it. It's the root of my paranoia." Kelly stayed in her house for three months. "I stayed in because I didn't want anyone to see me and how bad my skin looked," she told me. "My parents took care of me. This happened after I destroyed my looks by picking at my face at any tiny blemish. I felt unpresentable. My face is ugly. My skin is ugly. I didn't want anyone to see my face."

"I hide from people," Max told me, "especially after I get a bad haircut. I don't want to do anything. I just want to hide. There've been weeks when I didn't leave my house at all. I didn't go into town or shop or go out to eat because I was insecure. I ate my roommates' food and ordered out. I didn't even answer the door when someone came to the house. I was afraid. I was petrified of running into people. I'm afraid they'll think 'Here's this guy who looks awful. I don't want to have anything to do with him.' "

Low Self-Esteem, Depression, Anxiety, and Panic Attacks

Most people with BDD have many negative emotions—low self-esteem, depression, and anxiety. Although it may be difficult to determine whether these feelings *result from* BDD, many BDD sufferers say they do. Others view these feelings as part and parcel of their appearance worries and find it hard to say which causes which. Sometimes they seem to feed each other: low self-esteem, depression, and anxiety worsen BDD, and BDD worsens these feelings.

Other researchers and I have found that people with BDD tend to have low self-esteem. Self-esteem tends to be poorer in people with more severe BDD symptoms, those who are more depressed, and those with poorer insight regarding the perceived defect. The strongest association is with depression. These findings are consistent with what's known about self-esteem more generally. Studies have shown a relationship between perceived appearance and self-esteem across the life span—the worse someone thinks they look, the lower their self-esteem tends to be. Physical appearance is important to the development of healthy self-esteem. Thus, people with BDD—who *think* that their appearance is defective in some way—may have particular difficulty developing healthy self-esteem.

Most people with BDD are depressed, often severely. As Table 8 (p. 119) shows, 94% have felt depressed because of BDD. Many believe that the BDD causes their depression, and indeed, the BDD usually starts first. The depression can be persistent and severe and become an important problem in its own right. On average, people with BDD have more severe depression and anxiety than healthy controls or people with other psychiatric disorders. BDD also typically causes anxiety, which can be severe. "I get so anxious over my physical flaws that it wakes me up at night. I wake up thinking about them and feeling panicked," an interior decorator told me. Chuck, a contractor, told me: "It's like you were just told that you had inoperable, terminal cancer—that fear, that panic. That's what it's like *all* the time."

Anxiety may be psychological, consisting of worry and fear, or it may be physical, with symptoms such as headaches and stomachaches. Panic attacks, which BDD can cause, consist of extreme fear as well as physical symptoms such as heart palpitations, difficulty breathing, and light-headedness. "The stress of BDD has caused me to have a lot of anxiety and even panic attacks," Henry told me. "It's also caused me many stress-related physical symptoms—burning in my stomach, high blood pressure, headaches for which I've had brain scans. I've seen a lot of doctors for these problems, but I couldn't ever tell them what the cause was."

In fact, research has shown that people with BDD have unusually high levels of perceived stress. In a study in which I used the Perceived Stress Scale, a questionnaire that measures the degree to which people appraise life situations as stressful (for example, uncontrollable, overloaded), people with BDD reported very high levels of perceived stress. The more severe their BDD symptoms, the more stressed they felt. Their stress levels were notably higher than for people in the general population or people with a variety of other psychiatric or medical conditions.

These findings fit with Geoffrey's experience. "My worries about my mouth exhaust me," he told me. "Sometimes I'm afraid to get up in the morning because my mouth will consume all my energy and take my time. That's why I'm so tired all the time. It's totally draining. I've had BDD for 16 years, and I honestly don't know how my body has withstood the enormous stress that this obsession causes me."

Poor Quality of Life

As the stories in this book convey, people with BDD have very poor quality of life. Most feel distressed, don't get much enjoyment or satisfaction from life, and have difficulty functioning at work, in school, socially, and in other important areas of their life.

I've studied quality of life in my two series of people with BDD. Both studies used a standard and widely used questionnaire—the SF-36 (also known as the Medical Outcomes Study 36-Item Short-Form Health Survey). The people in these studies reported unusually poor mental health status and mental health-related quality of life (which reflects psychological distress, problems functioning in one's role because of emotional problems, and social functioning). The more severe the person's BDD symptoms, the poorer his or her quality of life. When compared to published norms, mental health-related quality of life for people with BDD is much poorer than for the general U.S. population (see Figure 3). As figure 3 shows, it's also worse than for people with an acute medical condition (a recent heart attack) or a chronic medical condition (type II diabetes). It's even poorer than for people with depression.

My second series of people with BDD also completed the Quality of Life Enjoyment and Satisfaction Questionnaire (Q-LES-Q). On this questionnaire, too, people with BDD reported unusually poor quality of life. As Figure 4 (p. 132) shows, scores were very poor in all areas that the questionnaire assesses: emotional well-being, general functioning, work, school, household functioning, social functioning, leisure, and physical health. The more severe the person's BDD symptoms, the poorer their quality of life tended to be. When compared to a sample of people from the community, 96% of community subjects scored better than the average BDD score. Importantly, scores for people with BDD were also poorer than have been reported for people with major depression, chronic major depression, dysthymia, obsessive compulsive disorder, social phobia, panic disorder, premenstrual dysphoric disorder, or post-traumatic stress disorder. These research results underscore the fact that BDD is a severe illness that needs to be taken seriously.

Unnecessary Medical Evaluation and Treatment

Many people with BDD seek and receive unnecessary medical and surgical evaluation and treatment. Doctors often refuse to provide such treatment because the defect is so minimal they consider treatment unnecessary. Several men I've seen have even been turned down by hair clubs. But some people nonetheless persist in their search for a doctor who will give them what they want. Some receive treatment after treatment—even surgery after surgery—hoping that the next one will finally provide the relief they so desperately seek.

This behavior can take the place of living. Abby, who told me she'd seen just about every dermatologist in Chicago, described this behavior as "just about all I do. The doctors I saw said my skin wasn't so terrible. Some of them thought

Figure 3.   SF-36 Mental Health-Related Quality of Life in BDD, Community, Depressed, Myocardial Infarction, and Diabetes Samples

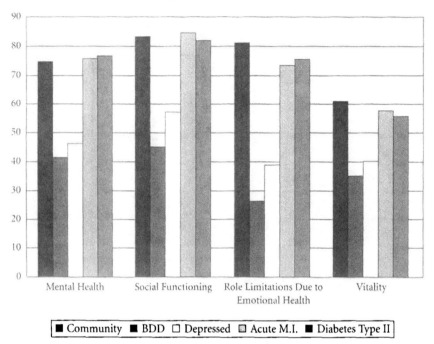

• Higher scores indicate better quality of life.
• Mental health-related quality of life scores were about 1.8 standard deviation units lower (poorer) than U.S. population norms and 0.4 units poorer than norms for depression.

I was crazy. So off I'd go to find another one. It's how I spend my days—going to skin doctors."

While most people who have cosmetic surgery are happy with the result, this doesn't seem to be the case for people with BDD. Most are unhappy with the outcome and blame themselves or the doctor for having made a serious mistake. For some, preoccupation and suffering diminish temporarily, only to return. Or the bodily preoccupation may shift to another area.

Rarely, people with BDD who are dissatisfied with medical or surgical treatment are violent toward the doctor who provided it. There are several reported cases of violence, even murder or attempted murder, toward a physician who the patient thought had ruined his or her appearance. Occasionally, people with BDD sue, even though the treatment outcome appears acceptable to others. Large amounts of money may be spent seeking and receiving such treatments, to no avail. In some cases, life savings are depleted.

Figure 4.   Q-LES-Q Scores in BDD and Community Samples

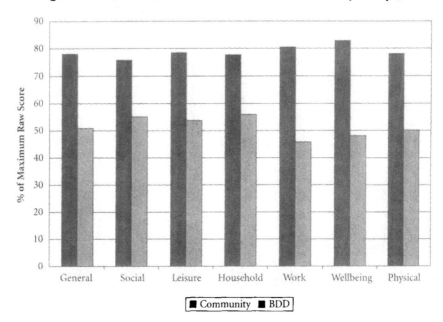

- Higher scores indicate better quality of life.
- On the QLES-Q Short Form ("General" scale), BDD subjects' mean score was 2.0 standard deviation units lower (poorer) than the community sample score; 95% of community subjects scored better than the mean BDD score.
- On the QLES-Q Long Form, scores for all domans were a mean of 2.0 (range 1.2–3.1) standard deviation units poorer than community norms.

Self-Surgery

Some people with BDD are so desperate to fix their perceived defect that they do surgery on themselves. One colleague told me of a patient with BDD who thought the fingers on his left hand were too long, so he cut them off. Some patients scrape their face with coarse sand paper to smooth out their skin. Others try to do a facelift with a staple gun. A nurse tried to change the shape of his forehead by cutting into it with surgical instruments. Another person was so desperate to improve the appearance of his nose that he did his own surgery, cutting his nose open with a knife and attempting to replace his own cartilage with chicken cartilage in the desired shape.

While self-surgery appears infrequent, it's a dramatic manifestation of the severe emotional pain and extreme desperation that some people with BDD feel. More commonly, people with BDD say that they hate their defect so much they'd *like* to do surgery on themselves—for example, cut their nose off—but they don't actually do it.

Bodily Damage

Other types of bodily damage can occur. Some of the damage is inadvertent. Harsh chemicals used on the face or scalp irritate and burn the skin. Excessive face washing leaves skin bleeding and raw. "Stuck-out" ears are superglued. To get rid of acne or white skin, severe sunburns are endured. Excessive weight lifting causes back strain or more serious harm to muscles and joints. Skin picking can cause skin lesions, scarring, and even severe bleeding that requires stitches or emergency surgery.

Other people purposely damage their body in frustration or because they hate it so much. While such behavior occurs only rarely, it does happen. Tara was so frustrated and depressed over how her breasts looked that she cut them with glass from a mirror she'd smashed. "I hated them," she said, "and I wanted to die." A beautiful teenager I saw despised her nipples, thinking they were grotesque and deformed, so she cut them off.

A young man hit his stomach when he got very upset over the "shriveled" skin around his navel. "This problem has made my life really unbearable," he said. "I say to myself 1,000 times a day, 'I hate my guts and want to die.' When it gets really bad, I take my anger and frustration out on myself."

Alcohol and Drug Use

More commonly, people try to cope with BDD by using alcohol or drugs. The intent is to decrease the preoccupation, dull the emotional pain, and lessen anxiety and self-consciousness in social situations. The percentage of people with BDD who've had a problem with alcohol or drugs is high: As shown in Appendix D, 20% of the people in my first BDD series, and 43% of the second series, had an alcohol problem (abuse or dependence) at some time in their life. Seventeen percent of the first series, and 34% of the second series, had a drug problem (abuse or dependence) at some point in their life. You may recall that the Minnesota study I previously mentioned found that 26% of people who were hospitalized on a psychiatric unit with a substance use disorder (drugs or alcohol) had BDD (see Chapter 4).

A very high percentage—70%—of people with BDD who have an alcohol or drug problem (abuse or dependence) say that BDD contributed to their drug or alcohol problem. In 26%, BDD is the main reason or a major reason for their drug or alcohol use. In 27%, it's somewhat of a reason, and in 17% it's a minor reason. Only 30% say that their drug or alcohol problem is unrelated to BDD.

BDD was the main cause of Adam's alcohol and drug problem. He'd had a serious problem with alcohol and drugs for many years, and he'd been in and out of more than 30 detoxification and rehabilitation programs. "You might not believe this," he said to me, "but my alcohol and drug abuse problems were *totally* and *completely* due to my appearance problem. A lot of counselors have told me that's just an excuse, but I think they're wrong. It was a crazy way I tried to block the pain of my obsessions, and it never worked. I tried to numb myself to my perception of my body, but it didn't change. It actually made the pain over my appearance worries worse."

Rick's story was similar. "BDD is the absolute core of what led to my alcohol and drug use. "I slept too much and did alcohol and drugs as an escape, to try to forget my scars," he said. "Sometimes drinking decreased my concern temporarily. But sometimes the alcohol could make my symptoms worse, and it became a problem in its own right. After his BDD improved with the medication fluvoxamine (Luvox), he stopped using alcohol and heroin. In fact, he'd been selling heroin to support his habit, and had been in jail several times. This, too, stopped when he was treated with Luvox.

Emily described her experience as follows. "The only thing that brought relief was drinking. . . . My symptoms were totally debilitating, so intensely painful, and they were making me more and more depressed. Even though I was suffering so much, and drinking too much, no one knew I was suffering from BDD because I managed to look as though I was doing okay. I pulled it together, but the agony inside was totally overwhelming. I couldn't talk about it with other people.

"I finally went to my doctor and told him about the situation because I was worried about my drinking. He told me when I stopped drinking I wouldn't be depressed. But that wasn't true for me. I drank because of body dysmorphic disorder. . . . I drank and slept to deal with it. What causes me the most pain now is the effects of my drinking on my son. I wasn't there for him. That's the part that hurts me the most."

Some men with muscle dysmorphia use anabolic steroids to bulk up. This is a family of drugs that includes the male hormone testosterone as well as numerous synthetic derivatives of testosterone. Unless prescribed for specific medical treatment, anabolic steroids are illegal in the United States and many other countries. They may increase the risk for heart disease, stroke, and possibly prostate cancer. They can also cause irritability, aggression, depression, and physical dependence. And to shed pounds or body fat, some people use ephedra-related products (such as ephedra, ephedrine, or ma huang), dietary supplements which are chemical relatives of speed. In high doses, ephedra may have very serious health risks. It can cause heart attacks, strokes, seizures, and even death.

Accidents

BDD can cause accidents. Janet had several of them. "I'm a mirror-driven person," she said. "I check all the time. The worst part of it is I check in the rearview mirror while I'm driving. A few years ago I had a car accident because I was looking in the mirror instead of the road." Many others describe near misses. "I check the rearview mirror, trying to reassure myself," a salesman told me. "I almost hit a tree once, and I almost ran over someone." Some people, trying to stop this behavior, turn the rearview mirror away from them, or remove it altogether, but then can't see what's behind them—another setup for an accident. Others check a pocket mirror while driving instead of looking at the road.

One woman repeatedly hurt her back while bending into pretzel-like positions to obtain a better look in the mirror. She wasn't satisfied with a standard view—she needed to get an even closer look at a small scar on the side of her neck. Another person fell off a 3-story ladder while examining his reflection in a window.

Violence and Illegal Activities

BDD can also cause anger. Anger has many sources: frustration over looking abnormal, not being able to improve one's appearance or stop it from further deteriorating, lack of control over the perceived defect, or a belief that others are being rejecting or mocking the defect. "I get angry because it isn't fair that I'm the one with the small penis," a college student told me. "And I get very angry at the people who laughed at me in the locker room in high school about my penis size." Some people with BDD smash mirrors when feeling extremely angry about their reflection. Others have violent outbursts.

Research shows that, on average, people with BDD have higher levels of hostility than healthy control subjects or people with another psychiatric disorder. After treatment with an SRI, however, hostility levels drop dramatically. And while most people with BDD aren't violent, 28% say they've been violent at some point in their life because of BDD. (Violence is defined as behavior that damages property or harms a person.)

Some people get so frustrated, despairing, and angry over their symptoms that they throw heavy objects like a brick or put their fist through a wall or door. Others are so certain people are mocking them that they physically harm the person. Violence can also be triggered by the belief that surgery or dermatologic treatment didn't fix the problem, or even made it worse. A young man I saw, who believed face cream created dark spots on his face, went on a rampage around his parents' house, attacking their furniture and splintering it with a hammer.

Sometimes anger and violence are directed toward the surgeon or dermatologist who provided unsatisfying treatment. I'm aware of a man who severely assaulted his plastic surgeon because he was so upset over the outcome of his surgery. Another tried to murder his dermatologist after the treatment didn't work. And there are a number of published reports of people with apparent BDD who threatened, stalked, attempted to kill, or actually killed their dermatologist or plastic surgeon. In a 2001 survey of 265 members of the American Society for Aesthetic Plastic Surgery, 2% said they had been threatened physically, and 10% had been threatened both legally and physically, by a patient with BDD.

BDD can spawn illegal behavior. As I discussed above, BDD can lead to illegal drug use. Ian broke into houses across the country so he could get to

California to get a tan. Todd shoplifted from drug stores. "I don't like to do it," he said, "but I *have* to get stuff for my skin, and I don't have any money." Over several months, he'd stolen nearly $1000 worth of items. "I'm afraid I'll get caught," Todd said, "and I feel guilty doing it. But I can't resist. My acne is destroying my life. I have to make my skin look better!"

Another man had done many illegal things—such as assaulting people and breaking and entering—in the hope that he'd go to jail. He explained, "That way, no one would see me except the other inmates. And it's too hard for me to keep a job because I look so bad, and I wouldn't have to worry about it in jail. Jail would be better than this hell I live in every day."

Hospitalization

BDD commonly leads to hospitalization. Hospitalization occurs for a variety of reasons, including depression due to BDD, accidents, a suicide attempt, or because unsuccessful medical or surgical treatment spurs suicidal thoughts or plans. Nearly 40% of the people in my studies have been psychiatrically hospitalized. Twenty-six percent attributed at least one psychiatric hospitalization primarily to their BDD symptoms.

You may recall that in the only psychiatric impatient study that's been done in BDD, 13% of the patients had BDD. This finding is surprising, because BDD isn't usually looked for or recognized in inpatient settings. In this study, BDD was much more common than many other psychiatric disorders. Thirteen of the 16 patients with BDD considered BDD their biggest problem or a major problem. Those with BDD were more severely ill than those who didn't have it, and their overall functioning was poorer.

I'm aware of several young people who had such severe BDD that they had to go to live in a nursing home. They hadn't responded to numerous treatments and hospitalizations, and they were so incapacitated by their symptoms that neither they nor their family members could care for them.

I met Lawrence in the hospital after he'd tried to kill himself. He was agitated, anxious, and very depressed. This is how he described the reason he was in the hospital. "When I started graduate school in physics, I was troubled by not having many friends and also by a sense of my dramatically receding hairline. My hair had been very slowly receding for some time, but in the past month it became very quick. A few weeks ago I examined my hair and noticed excessive hair loss and decreased density in the front. Even on a daily basis I could see the change. Lots of hair came out in the shower in my hand.

"I worried about how I would have to present myself with my new appearance to my old friends. I also worried about how I could meet new people with my hair the way it was. My self-esteem plummeted, and I felt like a social failure. I couldn't concentrate on my studies. I started to wonder if people were talking about me or laughing at me.

"In the past week I started to panic. I felt very anxious. I was worrying more and more about how I looked and what other people thought of me. I worried that it would get worse and that I'd become bald. I couldn't stop thinking about it, and I felt I was falling apart. I was crying, looking at myself in the mirror. I thought I was collapsing, eroding, and I tried to kill myself."

When his family came to visit him in the hospital, Lawrence hadn't been able to tell them why he was there. "I'm much too embarrassed to tell them about it," he said. "I'm afraid they won't take it seriously. I'm afraid people will think it's trivial, silly, or pitiful. I'm afraid they'll see me as vain. And if I bring it up, I'm afraid they'll notice how bad my hair is."

Even when BDD symptoms are this severe, many people never discuss them. They keep them a secret not only from family but also from hospital staff. BDD symptoms are usually never even mentioned in the medical record, even for patients whose main problem is BDD.

The Cost of BDD

The cost of BDD isn't known, but is certainly high. The economic cost includes medical costs for bodily harm and accidents, the cost of ineffective medical and surgical evaluation and treatment, and the cost of medical and psychiatric hospitalization. It also includes the costs of incomplete education, decreased productivity, lateness, and days lost from work, and the cost of disability payments.

Some people with BDD have significant financial problems because of these costs or because they spend so much money on wigs, clothes, makeup or surgery. One woman was more than $10,000 in debt because she'd spent so much money on clothing and wigs. Several other people were more than $20,000 in debt.

Richard's experience illustrates how costly BDD can be. Richard had dropped out of school because he constantly went to the bathroom to check the mirror and couldn't concentrate on his studies. He tried several jobs, but quit each of them because of his symptoms. He then moved in with his family and went on disability.

Richard had made three suicide attempts, usually after looking in the mirror and feeling devastated by what he saw. After each attempt, he was hospitalized. After he overdosed, he had a long stay in an intensive care unit. In the six months before I saw him, he'd been hospitalized four times. Richard had also had three operations on his lips, which were costly and ineffective. Two had such devastating results, in his view, that he had to be psychiatrically hospitalized. "I had to be hospitalized because after the surgery my lips were black and blue and swollen," he said. "They looked deformed. I went wild, screaming and smashing things. I thought they were worse than ever, and I thought I'd done irreparable damage to myself."

Although Richard had had BDD for only several years, the cost of his illness had been staggering—already well over $100,000. But the greater cost of BDD is the human cost—the severe suffering and pain. Years lost to the illness can't replaced. One man told me, "It's crazy because I've wasted so much of my life. I grieve for all the years this disorder took from me."

Suicide: The Most Devastating Consequence of All

The greatest cost of all is suicide—an irreversible act that reflects intolerable suffering and loss of hope. Luke attempted suicide after an acne medication (Accutane) failed to improve his skin. "It was my last hope," he said. "I got so upset that it didn't work that I had a nervous breakdown. I was constantly grieving over how I looked. I had to be hospitalized because I tried to kill myself."

Suicidal thinking is alarmingly common in BDD (see Table 8, p. 119). Eighty percent—an extremely high percentage—of the people in my studies have had thoughts that life wasn't worth living, that they'd be better off dead, or wishing they were dead. This percentage may be higher than for any other psychiatric disorder. A majority of them attributed such thoughts primarily to their BDD symptoms. As one woman told me, "My appearance is the source of all the pain in my life. I feel hopeless about it. It's a feeling that I'll never belong anywhere or be happy. I feel unacceptable because of it, and sometimes I feel that life isn't worth living."

Juanita felt suicidal because of the hair she perceived on her face, arms, and legs. "It's *severely* upsetting. I fear I won't be able to lead a normal life—date, have sex, and do the other things that people do," she told me. "I feel like a freak, a bad person because I have a defect in my appearance. I fear that no one will ever love me—that I'll be an outcast. So what's the point of going on? I've seriously considered buying a gun to kill myself."

Both Dr. David Veale in England and I have found that about a quarter of people with BDD attempt suicide (see Table 8, p. 119). About half of them attribute at least one attempt primarily or entirely to their BDD. In a recent study I found that the more severe BDD symtoms are, the more likely a person is to think about or actually attempt suicide.

While these numbers might seem high, they make sense. BDD symptoms usually involve a deep sense of shame, low self-esteem, even self-loathing, and feelings of being unworthy, unacceptable, and unlovable. The symptoms often lead to isolation from others and the feeling that others don't understand. Many people have limited social support, poor functioning, and co-occurring disorders such as major depression and substance use disorders—all of which are risk factors for suicide thinking or suicide attempts. Feelings like these can culminate in the belief that life isn't worth living.

These high percentages speak to the unbearable pain and torment that many people with BDD experience. As Luke explained, "I hate myself and how I look. I think to myself that I can't live the rest of my life like this. I think it's possible that I may kill myself someday."

Although auditory hallucinations are rare in BDD, Karen overdosed because she'd heard voices telling her to kill herself because she was so ugly. "These two voices inside me were talking to each other, saying, 'Look at all the pimples she has on her face. Look at her fat thighs. Don't you think she should kill herself? You're fat and ugly, and you should kill yourself.' It's all they talked about. They were laughing at me because of how I looked."

It isn't known how many people with BDD kill themselves, but some do. A study of dermatology patients reported the very sobering finding that of those patients known to have committed suicide over 20 years, most had acne or BDD. The psychiatric literature also contains descriptions of people with BDD who committed suicide because they were so distraught and despairing over their perceived ugliness. And I know of numerous people with BDD who committed suicide. Several were beautiful young women with skin concerns who picked their skin. Another was a young man who had been obsessed with his "misshapen" forehead, and another a young man who hated his hair. Yet another was a man in his 50s who hated his beard and whose life had been devastated by BDD.

Bill told me that there were some people with BDD I'd never be able to interview. When I asked why, he answered, "Because they're dead—they've killed themselves." He should know, because he had attempted suicide 15 times because of the pores on his nose. He could no longer cope with the torment of his perceived ugliness. Another man said something nearly identical: "I think many people have committed suicide because of BDD. I know, because it's so painful. I made two suicide attempts at the time my symptoms were severe. I felt very isolated, and I lost hope."

I have no doubt that in many cases successful psychiatric treatment (SRIs and/or CBT) prevents suicide. In my fluoxetine (Prozac) study (which I'll describe in more detail in Chapter 13), suicidal thinking decreased significantly more with fluoxetine than with placebo (sugar pill) treatment. Juanita had a good response to fluoxetine. She called me years later to say that she'd gotten married and had a great job. She was no longer suicidal over how she looked. Luke also had an excellent response to the same medication plus cognitive-behavioral therapy. After treatment, his appearance no longer tormented him. He went on to a successful career in television, and gave up thoughts of suicide. "It's the furthest thing from my mind now," he told me. "I have a great life. Thank God I got treatment. I owe my life to it."

·· nine ··

Gender and BDD Across the Life Span

"I wish the whole world was bald, including me, so I wouldn't have to worry about my hair!"

Johnnie, age 5

"I still think about how awful my back looks after all these years. I keep to myself because I don't want to draw attention to it. It's one of the things that's made me depressed."

Margaret, age 70

BDD and Gender

Is BDD more common in women or men? Is it different in the two sexes? We don't have definite answers to these questions, but what we do know is intriguing.

It's often assumed that BDD is much more common in women. Aren't women more focused on their looks than men are? And doesn't society place a particularly high premium on attractiveness in women? Indeed, research findings from the general population indicate that more women than men are unhappy with how they look.

Several studies of BDD have contained more women than men. Several others, however, have had as many men as women or even more men than women. Somewhat more women than men (60% vs 40%) have participated in my BDD studies. It's unclear to what extent this ratio reflects the true gender ratio of BDD in the community. It may be harder for men to acknowledge that they have BDD, and men seem less likely than women to participate in BDD studies, especially treatment studies. Thus, the gender ratio may be more equal than these percentages suggest.

In a study done in France of more than 600 patients with obsessive compulsive disorder and similar disorders (e.g., trichotillomania), men and women were nearly equally represented among the 151 patients with BDD. A number of years ago, I reviewed all the published cases of BDD that I could find in the English-language literature as well as a large number published in other languages. In these published cases, the sex ratio was approximately 1.25 female to 1.0 male.

These research findings can't give us as valid an estimate of BDD's sex ratio as we'd like. What's needed to determine it with greater certainty are large-scale surveys, in which the prevalence and sex ratio of BDD are determined in thousands of people in various settings, including the community. The studies I just noted were relatively small and could have various biases. In the meantime, until such surveys are done, we can be certain that BDD affects both women and men.

What about gender differences? In my studies, I've found more similarities than differences between men and women with BDD. Men and women appear similar in terms of most demographic features (e.g., age and employment status) and in terms of most clinical features, such as which body areas they dislike, BDD behaviors, severity of BDD symptoms, degree of impairment in functioning, and number of suicide attempts. Men and women are also largely similar in terms of how many have coexisting psychiatric disorders, including anorexia nervosa, panic disorder, and depression. This latter finding is interesting because, in the general population, these disorders affect more women than men. Why men with BDD appear to have as high a rate of depression as women with BDD is puzzling. Although this finding requires confirmation, there are several possible explanations. One is that depression may often be "secondary" to BDD—that is, resulting from the distress and impairment that BDD causes. My clinical impression and recent research findings suggest that this is often the case. If this theory is correct, then it isn't surprising that men and women are equally likely to be depressed, because they experience similar degrees of distress and impairment as a result of their BDD symptoms. Another possible explanation is that the same underlying biological and psychological mechanisms that cause BDD also contribute to the depression that accompanies BDD; because in our study BDD affected as many men as women, depression would be expected to as well.

But there are some interesting differences between men and women with BDD. I've found that women are more likely to have an eating disorder (see Appendix B for a description), whereas men are more likely to have a problem with alcohol or drugs. Men are more likely to be single. While the sexes are generally similar in the number and areas of bodily concern, men are more likely to think that their body build is too small, skinny, or not muscular enough, whereas women are more likely to dislike their weight and hips, thinking they're too large and fat. While men and women are equally likely to have hair concerns, men are more prone to fear that they're losing their hair. All of the people who worried about excessive body hair were women, whereas all of those with genital concerns were men. Men are more apt to use a hat for camouflage, whereas women are more likely to turn to cosmetics for cover.

These results are interesting because some of them echo normal appearance concerns and behaviors. Research findings indicate that women generally think their bodies are too large, whereas men tend to worry that theirs are too small. A study of college students, for example, found that 85% of the women wanted to lose weight, whereas only 40% of the men wanted to lose weight and 45% actually wanted to gain it. In the general population, concerns about balding are relatively common among men but not women, and women are more likely to use cosmetics than men.

Several treatment findings are also interesting. I've found that men and women are equally likely to seek nonpsychiatric treatment such as surgery or dermatologic treatment for their BDD concerns. They're also equally likely to receive these kinds of treatment. This finding differs from what we know about the general population, in which women are more likely to receive cosmetic treatments than men.

The only other study that to my knowledge has investigated gender differences in BDD was done in Italy in a smaller series (58 people). This study, like mine, found that BDD was generally similar in women and men. And like my findings, women were more likely to have the eating disorder bulimia nervosa, and men were more likely to be concerned with their genitals. Unlike my results, however, the Italian study found that women were more likely to focus on their breasts/chest and legs, check mirrors, and camouflage, whereas men were more likely to focus on their height and excessive body hair. Certainly, we need more research on gender similarities and differences in BDD, not only in clinical settings but also in the general population and in different cultures.

I'm sometimes asked how many people with BDD are homosexual. I systematically assessed this in my series of 200 people with BDD and found that 5% were homosexual and 3% were bisexual. This percentage is somewhat higher than in the general population, but it indicates that the vast majority of people with BDD are heterosexual.

BDD Across the Life Span

BDD usually begins during adolescence, but can start in childhood or adulthood. The people I've studied (more than 500) started disliking their appearance, on average, at age 13. Full-fledged BDD began at an *average* age of 16. The standard deviation was 7.0 years, which means that the majority—two-thirds—were between 9 and 23 years old when their BDD began. The most *common* age of onset of full-fledged BDD was 13. The earliest age of BDD onset in this group was 4, and the oldest was 49.* The graph on the next page illustrates these findings.

*In the studies that have been done, age at onset was usually determined retrospectively rather than prospectively—that is, people who already had the disorder estimated

Figure 5.   BDD Age of Onset

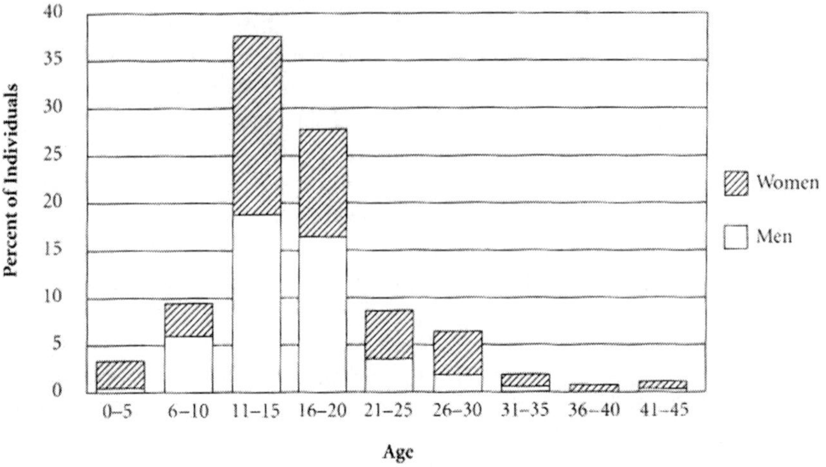

BDD usually begins gradually, but about 20% of people report a sudden onset, going from no concern to a full-fledged concern in less than a week's time. A 21-year-old woman told me, "It started suddenly. I went into the bathroom one day, and I saw a mustache." In some but not all cases, the sudden onset of BDD appears to be precipitated by a negative comment about appearance, a stressful event, or even a benign comment—for example, "Your face looks a little red today." Sometimes it's triggered by disappointing surgery or the acne medicine Accutane. More often, however, BDD begins gradually, with no obvious triggering event.

An important question is: How do people with BDD do over time? Do they get better, stay the same, or get worse? Does BDD tend to be life-long, or do people get over it by early or middle adulthood? Can we predict who will get better and who won't? At this time, we have only very preliminary answers to these important questions. And the answers vary.

When I've systematically asked people I've seen whether their BDD has improved or not over the years, their answers are somewhat discouraging. Looking back over time, 84% report that their BDD symptoms have been continuous

the age at which the disorder began by looking back over time. Because memory can be faulty, this approach is subject to error. Nonetheless, many people with BDD have very vivid memories of their early symptoms, suggesting that retrospective recollections may be reasonably accurate.

Another complicating factor in determining age at onset is that onset of the disorder is usually gradual and sometimes preceded by a dislike of one's body that isn't severe enough to warrant the diagnosis. As one woman said, "I've had hints of concern since I was a child." Determining at what age BDD symptoms become clinically significant— that is, at what age the disorder begins—is sometimes difficult. Nonetheless, the ages at onset found in my own research and that of other researchers are remarkably consistent.

and chronic. That is, they haven't been free, or nearly free, of them for at least a full month since they began. When I ask, "What's the longest time you've gone without worrying about your defect since the problem began?" by far the most common answer is "less than a day." Equally concerning, a majority— 59%—said that their symptoms had gotten worse over time. Only 13% reported that they'd improved. For the rest (28%), BDD symptom severity stayed fairly stable.

While these numbers suggest that BDD tends to be a chronic illness, or even a worsening one, it's important to keep a few things in mind. One is that there may be a bias toward a worse course of illness in people who come to see me, because those who improved wouldn't need to see me. Equally important, relatively few of these people had received adequate treatment for BDD. This is in part because when I started this study, no one knew how to successfully treat BDD. Even now, when we know a lot more about treatment, BDD is still often not correctly diagnosed and treated.

To better understand how people with BDD do over time, we need prospective studies of course of illness, in which symptoms are systematically assessed going forward over time. This is being done in one of my ongoing studies. Preliminary results from this study, too, indicate that BDD tends to be chronic. Over 1 year, the probability of being free of BDD symptoms for at least 8 consecutive weeks was only 9%. The probability of being partially free (not meeting full DSM-IV criteria) was only 15%. Over 2 years, the probability being free of BDD was 14% and of being partially free was 18%. People who had more severe BDD or a personality disorder (see Appendix B for a definition) were less likely to recover. While these numbers may sound dismaying, very few people received adequate treatment for BDD—so for this reason, the results aren't surprising.

People who get effective treatment for BDD (SRIs and/or cognitive-behavioral therapy) tend to do much better than this over time. In a study of people I treated in my clinical practice, all of whom received medication and some of whom also received cognitive-behavioral therapy, 58% had attained partial or full remission from BDD (i.e., they no longer met full DSM-IV criteria for the disorder) at the 6-month point and/or at the 12 month point after beginning treatment. After 4 years of treatment, 84% had attained partial or full remission at at least one of the assessment points (study assessments were done every 6 months during treatment). Those with milder BDD symptoms, and those who didn't have major depression or social phobia at the beginning of treatment, did better over time.

More rigorous treatment studies also yield encouraging findings: in all of the medication studies that have been done so far (which lasted for 8 to 16 weeks), half to three quarters of people improved with an SRI (see Chapter 13). Similarly, studies of cognitive-behavioral therapy show significant improvement in BDD symptoms (see Chapter 14). So taken together, data from patients treated in my clinical practice and from treatment studies are encouraging, indicating that a majority of treated patients do well.

It appears that BDD symptoms often wax and wane over time; that is, when they're present they may be more severe at some times than others. Symptom severity may fluctuate for no apparent reason, or in response to stress or triggering events, such as skin picking or being in a social situation. Women not uncommonly say that BDD worsens premenstrually. Here, too, we need prospective studies to better understand how BDD symptoms fluctuate, and what factors seem to influence this. Ultimately, if we can better understand why BDD improves, we can use this knowledge to alleviate suffering.

BDD in Children and Adolescents

"I Wish the Whole World was Bald!"

"Johnnie, your hair looks so nice today!" the receptionist exclaimed as he walked by. "Oh, Johnnie, your hair looks wonderful!" one of the secretaries echoed. When Johnnie entered the psychiatrist's office, instead of sitting in a chair as asked, he crouched down and intently peered at himself in a thin strip of chrome on the chair. "What are you doing, Johnnie?" the doctor asked him. Johnnie didn't answer. Instead, he tilted his head, examining his hair from different angles, patting it and smoothing it out. He also grinned at himself, examining and touching his teeth.

Johnnie was excessively worried about his hair, which he thought "wasn't right" or flat enough. He was also obsessed with his teeth, which he thought weren't white or straight enough, and his "pot" belly. He frequently checked mirrors and excessively brushed his teeth. He often touched and groomed his hair, using special hair creams. If he couldn't get his hair to look right, Johnnie cried, dunked his head in water, and started his grooming routine all over again. "I wish the whole world was bald," he said, "including me, so I wouldn't have to worry about my hair!"

Over and over again, Johnnie asked his parents, "Is my hair okay?" "Am I fat?" His mother estimated that he spent at least three hours a day focused on his appearance and asking for reassurance. Johnnie was only five years old.

Holly was a shy and attractive 16-year-old high school student, who was reluctant to discuss her appearance concerns because she was so embarrassed. With encouragement, she finally did. "I think my problems first began with shyness," she said. "I felt very self-conscious and uncomfortable being around other people. But then, a few years ago, I started worrying about how I looked. First, it was my body shape. I thought my shoulders and hips were too broad and my waist was too small. Then I got a terrible haircut, and I started worrying about my hair—that it's ugly and never looks right. It's a real rat's nest."

Holly thought about these perceived defects for several hours a day, and frequently checked them in mirrors and windows. "I get down on myself about it, because I shouldn't be so concerned with my appearance," she said. "It's selfish and shallow." Holly spent at least $40 a week on haircuts, permanents, and hair products—money she really couldn't afford to spend. She wore loose-fitting clothes to cover her body. Although she loved to swim, she avoided it because she was so self-conscious about how she looked. "Because I look so bad, I feel I don't fit in anywhere," she said. "I'm avoiding my friends, and I hardly ever go to parties."

As these stories illustrate, BDD occurs in adolescents and even young children. Many adults with BDD have surprisingly vivid memories of their early symptoms. A woman whose symptoms began at age 4, for example, clearly remembered hating her "stubby" fingers and insisting on wearing mittens at her fourth birthday party. Another woman had clear memories of hiding behind her mother's skirt at the playground and refusing to go to nursery school because she looked so ugly. And another told me, "At the age of five I looked in the a mirror and said, 'I'm ugly.' To hide my ugly face, I wore sunglasses to kindergarten."

We don't really know how common BDD is in children and adolescents, because so little research has been done. A study of 208 adolescents in a psychiatric hospital inpatient unit found that 7% had definite or probable BDD. Another study found that 2.3% of 566 high school students had BDD. This latter percentage was obtained with an unvalidated self-report questionnaire rather than an in-person interview, so it's unclear how accurate it is. However, most people with BDD—about 70%—develop it before age 18. So it's important to be aware that BDD can occur in this age group. It's also important to realize that not all appearance concerns in adolescents are normal or simply a passing "phase"—sometimes they're BDD.

Characteristics of BDD in Children and Adolescents

Even though BDD usually develops during adolescence, there's very little published research on BDD in adolescents or children. Nonetheless, what we do know suggests that BDD's characteristics in this age group are very similar to those in adults. Like adults, children and adolescents have prominent, distressing, time-consuming preoccupations that can focus on any body area but often involve the face. Insight is often poor. A majority think that other people take special notice of them in a negative way because of how they look—staring at them, talking about them, or laughing at them. Most perform compulsive behaviors, such as mirror checking. BDD symptoms cause problems with functioning, which can range from mild to extremely severe. This may include poor grades, stopping sports and other activities, and withdrawing from family and friends. In more severe cases, children and adolescents with BDD drop out of school, become housebound, require psychiatric hospitalization, and may even attempt suicide.

The following table summarizes some of BDD's characteristics in 47 systematically assessed children and adolescents. As this table illustrates, BDD in children and adolescents consists of painful and time-consuming preoccupations and compulsive behaviors that cause significant distress and impairment in functioning. Social impairment is nearly universal and often consists of extreme self-consciousness, embarrassment, and avoidance of social interactions.

Table 9. Features of BDD in 49 Children and Adolescents*†

Characteristic	Average, or Percent of Children/Adolescents with This Characteristic
Age	15
Gender	• 90% female • 10% male
Body areas of concern (most common)	• 71% skin • 51% hair • 47% weight
Number of body areas of concern (past or present)	6
Behaviors (most common)	Camouflaging 92% Mirror checking 82% Comparing 80%
BDD severity (as assessed by BDD-YBOCS)	31 (moderately severe)
Ever socially impaired because of BDD	100%
Ever impaired at work or school because of BDD	100%
Currently impaired academically	86%
Dropped out of school due to BDD	18%
Ever psychiatrically hospitalized	39%
Violent behavior due to BDD	38%
Past or current suicidal thinking	73%
Attempted suicide	33%
Ever housebound due to BDD	16%

*These numbers are from 33 children and adolescents from my first research series, as well as 16 children and adolescents from my second research series. All were under 18.
†Published reports in professional journals of individual children and adolescents with BDD describe characteristics similar to those shown in this table.

A majority have problems with school, and some even drop out. Of great concern, a very high percentage think about, or attempt, suicide.

As this table suggests, BDD in children and adolescents appears generally similar to BDD in adults. One apparent difference, however, is that most of the children and adolescents I've seen were female. This may reflect boys' greater reluctance to seek help for appearance concerns, rather than a true difference in how common BDD is in boys versus girls. In the previously mentioned inpatient study in which all hospitalized adolescents were assessed, half were male and half were female. In a recent study, I also found that adolescents had poorer insight than adults and were more likely to have attempted suicide.

Kristin, a 17-year-old adolescent, had many of the classic BDD symptoms shown in Table 9. I met her in the hospital after she'd tried to commit suicide. She said she'd attempted suicide primarily because of her appearance concerns. Since age 13 she'd been excessively preoccupied with her nose, which she thought was too large; her breasts, which were too "small"; and her hair, which "wasn't right." She described her concerns as "very, very distressing—an obsession. They're so horrible I get suicidal; it's why I overdosed. I couldn't stand the pain any more."

Kristin thought about her appearance "every second of every day," and she checked mirrors, store windows, and other reflecting surfaces for hours a day. "I also constantly compare myself to other girls, and I ask my mother a million times a day whether I look okay, but I really don't believe her when she says how pretty I am. . . . Sometimes people compliment me on my hair, but it makes me angry. I think they're saying they like my hair so they don't have to say how ugly the rest of me is." Because she thought she was so ugly, Kristin avoided seeing friends and dating. She also failed some of her courses and eventually dropped out of high school. To feel better about how she looked, she had a nose job, which diminished her concern with her nose, but she then worried more about her breasts.

At the age of 14, Eric became preoccupied with the idea that he had severe acne, wrinkles around his eyes, and "stuck-out" ears—deformities that weren't discernible to others. Eric often checked himself in mirrors and kept lights dimmed so his "defects" wouldn't be visible. He covered his forehead with his bangs and a baseball hat, and he wore makeup to hide his supposed acne. Eric had had many friends and had been a very good student and a star soccer player. But as a result of his appearance concerns, his grades plummeted, and he became increasingly self-conscious, depressed, anxious, and socially isolated. Eventually, after several years of these symptoms, he was unable to attend school and became housebound.

Why It's Important to Recognize BDD in Children and Adolescents

It's important to recognize BDD in children and adolescents. As shown in Table 10, BDD can cause severe problems for children and adolescents. And in the

---

Table 10.   Why It's Important to Recognize BDD in Children and Adolescents

---

- BDD can cause poor grades, dropping out of school, withdrawal from family and friends, suicidal thinking, violent behavior, and other serious problems.
- Normal development can be derailed by BDD symptoms.
- Long-term academic, occupational, and social problems can develop if BDD isn't treated early.

---

inpatient study I've mentioned, adolescents with BDD had significantly greater anxiety, depression, and suicidal thinking than hospitalized adolescents without BDD.

Although the long-term consequences of BDD haven't been well studied, it seems likely that when BDD develops during childhood or adolescence—rather than later in life—it may be particularly problematic. I've found that people who develop BDD before age 18 differ in some ways from those who develop it later. Indeed, we might expect that those with an earlier onset would be more impaired as a result of their symptoms because they've suffered for a longer time and during a developmentally critical period. Indeed, those with onset in childhood or adolescence are more likely to have been psychiatrically hospitalized (for any reason or because of BDD) and more likely to have attempted suicide.

From a development perspective, there are reasons to think that BDD might be especially problematic for children and adolescents. Adolescents must negotiate a number of important developmental tasks: increasing their involvement with peers, becoming more autonomous and independent of their families, developing a stronger and more cohesive sense of identity, and coming to grips with their sexuality, to name just a few. How BDD might affect these processes isn't known with certainty because it hasn't been studied; again, prospective studies that specifically address such issues are needed. Nonetheless, it seems likely that BDD can interfere with these adolescent developmental tasks. Based on my experience treating many parents, this seems to be the case.

Self-consciousness and social withdrawal can interfere with the development of healthy peer relationships—friendships as well as intimate relationships. This can be accompanied by an increased dependence on the family at a time when such dependence is usually decreasing. Indeed, some adolescents with BDD become dependent on their family members to do things for them that they would otherwise do for themselves. They may spend more and more time with their parents—particularly if they're housebound—and rely more on them for their social interaction. They may look to them for financial and emotional support in coping with the disorder. While some dependence on one's family is healthy, BDD can lead to an excessive dependency that interferes with normal development.

It's also my clinical impression that ongoing untreated BDD that begins prior to or during adolescence can interfere significantly with identity formation, one of the central developmental tasks of adolescence. Identity is a broad concept that includes not only a sense of self, character, and personality, but also the establishment of goals, aims, anticipated career and life-style, as well as one's place in the community and the world. If this developmental task isn't successfully negotiated, doubt, insecurity, and aimlessness may result. People with BDD may develop a strong sense of shame and inferiority, about their bodies and themselves, rather than a healthy identity and good self-esteem. They often view themselves in terms of the defect: I am a person with an ugly nose; I am a person who is ridiculed and rejected by others.

BDD may be particularly likely to interfere with the development of healthy self-esteem and identity because physical appearance is important to the development of self-esteem. Of the domains of competence that appear to contribute most to global self-esteem in adolescence—how much one likes oneself as a person overall—physical appearance heads the list. Thus, teenagers with BDD, who believe their appearance is defective in some way, may have particular difficulty developing healthy self-esteem.

In addition, adolescents with BDD may be so excessively and exclusively focused on the supposed defect that they ignore and don't develop their strengths. They may struggle with school and avoid hobbies and other activities. They may neglect other aspects of identity formation, such as career goals.

Other psychiatric disorders that begin during adolescence and have been better studied than BDD have been shown to interfere with identity formation and similar adolescent developmental tasks. Because adolescents' self-concept hasn't yet crystallized, they may be particularly vulnerable to the negative effect psychiatric disorders can have on identity and personality formation. Studies have shown, for example, that school phobia interferes with developmental tasks. One study found that young adults who suffered from school phobia in childhood were more likely than other adults to be dependent, and they had more difficulty completing school and earning a living. They were more socially isolated, were less likely to be in a healthy, intimate relationship, and had more problems in sexual adjustment. BDD may be particularly prone to have these kinds of effects because it's highly interpersonal in nature, perhaps increasing the risk to relationships. In addition, untreated BDD appears to often be chronic, making it difficult to get back on track and resume developmental tasks. Indeed, as Appendix A shows, a significant percentage of adults with BDD (30%) live with their parents; others are unemployed, haven't graduated from school, and aren't dating or socially interacting with others. Some do progress in life but much less than they'd like.

How to Diagnose BDD in Children and Adolescents

I'm sometimes asked whether BDD can even be diagnosed during adolescence, because this is a time when appearance concerns are so common. The answer is yes, it definitely can! While it may sometimes be difficult to differentiate mild BDD from normal adolescent appearance concerns, more moderate and severe BDD can easily be diagnosed in this age group. In fact, as previously noted, adolescence is when BDD is most likely to develop.

It's interesting that BDD usually begins during adolescence—a time when appearance concerns are often prominent and bodily changes dramatic. It has in fact been suggested that BDD may be a pathological response to the various physical and physiological changes of adolescence. Brain development during adolescence may contribute to the disorder's onset. For example, at puberty, across species, the brain seems to increasingly attend to indicators of social status, including appearance, as well as cues of social rejection. Sociocultural factors that emphasize the importance of appearance and acceptance by others are also clearly important at this time. The causes of BDD and the mechanisms by which it's expressed may indeed be linked in some way to the biological, psychological, and social changes that occur during the adolescent years.

As in adults, BDD should be diagnosed when appearance concerns become preoccupying and cause significant emotional distress or interfere with functioning. The adolescent who gets depressed, has problems concentrating in school or whose grades drop, or who misses school, parties, or dates because of appearance worries has concerns in excess of normal, which may be BDD.

The BDDQ, the self-report screening questionnaire for BDD described in Chapter 4, has a version for adolescents, which is in Appendix C. Someone who appears to have BDD based on his or her answers on the BDDQ should then be asked questions from the adolescent version of the BDD Module to determine whether BDD is really present (see Appendix C). Because it's common for adolescents to think a lot about their appearance, it's important to be sure the adolescent is thinking in a negative way about a minimal or nonexistent appearance defect. It may also be helpful to put greater emphasis on impairment in functioning when diagnosing BDD in adolescents, to be sure that the appearance concerns truly are problematic and not just normal concerns.

Kristin's, Eric's, and Holly's concerns were clearly excessive and characteristic of BDD. Kristin avoided social interactions and dating, and she failed some of her courses and dropped out of school. Her suicide attempt and hospitalization were painfully clear signs that what she was experiencing wasn't just "normal adolescence" or something she'd "grow out of." Early on, Eric's grades dropped, and he became anxious and depressed. While these signs weren't dramatic, they signaled that something problematic and serious was occurring—that he wasn't just "going through a phase" or having normal adolescent difficulties. When he dropped out of school and stopped playing soccer, it became crystal clear that his concerns were a serious problem. While Holly's case was milder, the fact that she worried about her appearance for several hours a day and avoided friends signaled the presence of BDD.

All three adolescents also had some typical BDD behaviors—mirror checking, camouflaging, reassurance seeking, and excessive grooming. These behaviors provided additional clues to the disorder's presence.

It's equally important to be aware that BDD can easily be underdiagnosed in adolescents. In fact, in my experience this error is far more common than overdiagnosing BDD. To avoid underdiagnosing BDD in children and adolescents, it's important to be aware that they may minimize BDD symptoms because they're embarrassed by their concerns and reluctant to reveal them. Holly felt that she was selfish and shallow because she was so focused on how she looked, and she was very reluctant to tell anyone about her worries. While adults also have these feelings, secrecy may be particularly common during the teenage years because adolescents may hesitate to confide in and trust adults. Often, adolescents must develop a trusting relationship with an adult before they're willing to divulge their concerns. The best approach to this problem is to simply ask. When adolescents show any signs of BDD, ask them whether they have any appearance concerns. The adolescent versions of the BDDQ and BDD Module can be a useful guide. The most important thing is to not consider such concerns a normal phase of development that will simply pass. It's also important not to tease or criticise the adolescent because of their concerns. BDD is a serious disorder that needs to be treated.

Treating BDD in Children and Adolescents

Effective treatments for children and adolescents have been studied much less than for adults. While more research is greatly needed, at the present time it appears that SRIs and CBT—the treatments that appear effective for adults—are also often effective for children and adolescents with BDD.

Holly, Kristen, and Eric all responded to a serotonin-reuptake inhibitor. After several months of treatment, Eric returned to school and started playing soccer again and seeing his friends. Kristin worried less about how she looked, went back to school, and was no longer suicidal. And Holly stopped covering her body with oversized clothing and started swimming again.

Sally, a 17-year-old girl I treated, dropped out of high school in the ninth grade because she was completely convinced that her face was severely scarred and disfigured—in her words, she looked like a burn victim. In reality, she looked entirely normal, but no one could convince her of this, no matter how hard they tried. She stayed in her bedroom for the next 4 years, refusing to leave because so thought she looked so hideous. She saw no one except her family. She didn't go to school, receive academic tutoring, see friends, or date. She was completely isolated. After taking fluoxetine (Prozac) 20 mg a day for about a month, Sally's BDD symptoms virtually disappeared. For the first time in 4 years she went to the mall, saw friends she hadn't seen in years, attended family get-togethers, and even returned to school. While such a quick and miraculous transformation is somewhat unusual, most children and adolescents do seem to get better with treatment.

While a lot more research is needed on how to effectively treat BDD in children and adolescents, in my experience they respond to SRIs similarly to adults (see details in Chapter 13). It appears that about half to two thirds of adolescents will respond to a particular SRI, and if one SRI doesn't work, another one may. Like adults, adolescents appear to often need fairly high SRI doses (e.g., an average of 50–60 mg/day of fluoxetine or 150–200 mg/day of sertraline), which they usually tolerate well. Like adults, they may need to take an SRI for as long as 3 months before they begin to feel better.

CBT has also been used to treat adolescents with BDD, although no published research has been done in this age group. It's reasonable to expect that CBT approaches that work for adults (see details in Chapter 14) would also work for adolescents. However, the treatment needs to be modified somewhat to make it suitable for adolescents and so parents can participate. Non-CBT psychotherapy, added to an SRI and/or CBT, may also be helpful for some adolescents, to help them with other problems or issues they may have (see Chapter 14). For example, family therapy may help both the adolescent and family members cope better with BDD. Or an adolescent who responds well to an SRI after being out of school and housebound for several years will probably benefit from therapy aimed at helping him or her re-enter school and establish friendships.

It's important to find a psychiatrist, other physician, or qualified therapist who is familiar with BDD and knowledgeable about its treatment (see Chapter 18). This requires first recognizing BDD and taking it seriously. Early and successful treatment has the potential to minimize or even eliminate BDD symptoms and prevent the longer-term disability that the disorder so often causes. It enables an adolescent to get back on track, resume normal functioning, and live an enjoyable and healthy life.

BDD in the Elderly

Mildred was 80 years old and had had BDD for nearly 70 years, since she was a teenager. "I've always felt homely and ugly," she began. "It's shameful to have these concerns, because they're so superficial. It shouldn't matter. . . . Now I realize how excessive and unrealistic they were. When I see pictures of myself, I think I didn't look so bad back then. It doesn't bother me so much now; it was at its worst in my teens and twenties. But I'm still too concerned with how I look."

Mildred grew up in a small town in the Midwest. She described some of her early memories. "There was one main street in town. It was a very small place. I remember sometimes crossing the street to avoid people because I was so ugly. I was always very self-conscious, and I thought people talked about me. I always had the feeling that my mother and her friends talked about how I looked. I remember that when I was very young, one of my cousins commented on how homely I was. Now I think it was just sibling rivalry, but at the time I was devastated. I also remember being told that I looked like my mother. She wasn't a good person, and I thought she was unattractive. I hated it when people told me that I looked like her. I hated to be identified with her.

"I used to wish I were black so I wouldn't have freckles, and I used freckle cream. When people commented on my nice hair I felt bad because it meant I wasn't otherwise attractive. I disliked myself so much I can't imagine people liking me in any way. I didn't feel desirable in any way. My feelings about my appearance were all tied up with feelings of inferiority. I was convinced people thought I was ugly—that I wasn't likable or lovable.

"Seventy-five percent of my life has centered on how I look. I fought back. I tried not to let my appearance concerns interfere much with my life. But high school was an especially hard time. I missed parties, and I was very shy on dates. And I think I might have done different things with my life if I hadn't been so preoccupied. I did raise wonderful daughters, but I would have had more energy for them and for other things, like my music. I think my concerns also affected my personality. People thought I was aloof, but I cared so much about what people thought of me. I was very easily hurt, very sensitive.

"I feel very guilty about my focus on my looks, because it seems so self-centered. There are other things to think about. I've never even told my husband about it, even though we're close, because I think he'd think I'm foolish. I was in therapy for many years, but I never brought it up because it would have been too difficult. I was afraid my therapist would think I was superficial and concerned with unimportant things. I felt so ashamed, especially at my age. I feel I should have enough wisdom not to care about something so silly."

Margaret, who was 70, had also struggled with BDD for many decades. Her concerns, too, had begun when she was a teenager and persisted ever since. She'd been treated in her teens for scoliosis (curvature of the spine), which was severe and required surgery and a brace. But after several surgeries, the scoliosis was much improved and hardly noticeable. Margaret, however, was still pre-occupied with it. "It's been a concern ever since then," she said. "I think my back still looks very ugly. I think about it for hours a day. I can't wear certain clothes because of how it looks. I wear clothes that hide it, and I change them a lot, trying to find an outfit that makes it look better."

Margaret spent approximately 8 hours a day doing BDD-related behaviors: selecting her clothes each morning and changing them during the day, scrutinizing how other people's backs looked, checking mirrors, and asking her husband whether she looked okay. "I still think about how awful my back looks after all these years. I keep to myself because I don't want to draw attention to it. It's one of the things that's made me depressed."

A woman in her sixties, who looked far younger than her age, was obsessed with getting eye surgery to eradicate facial "lines" that resembled those of a 35 year old. She'd seen most of the plastic surgeons in town, and she spent hours a day frantically examining the lines in mirrors and applying creams and makeup. Because of the lines, she restricted her activities and rarely left the house without wearing sunglasses.

Given that untreated BDD may be a fairly chronic disorder, it isn't surprising that it exists in the elderly. However, it isn't known how common BDD is in this age group. The average age of the people I've seen is the thirties; I've seen far fewer elderly people with BDD. Does BDD "burn out" as people age, becoming less severe or remitting altogether? Conversely, can it become more severe over time, and can the elderly be particularly distressed and impaired because of the cumulative effect of suffering over so many years? Might they be particularly embarrassed about seeking help? Further research is needed to answer these important questions.

ten

What Causes BDD?
Clues to an Unsolved Puzzle

"I have no idea why I worry so much about how I look. I wish I knew."
                                                                Anne

Patients' Perspectives

"This problem is chemical," Bridget said. "I can't think of any reason for these gut-wrenching worries about how I look. It must be from a chemical imbalance in my brain." Alison's explanation was quite different. "My mother is very pretty, and so is my sister," she said. "I constantly tried to look like my older sister. She's very feminine, and I idealized her. I wanted her nose, her long hair. I never accepted who I was. I was the ugly duckling, the odd-looking one. I was the runt of the litter."

"I started worrying too much about my skin at a time when I was really stressed," Caroline told me. "It began after I had to take a job working in a place I really didn't want to work. And I started worrying that my rear end was too big after a guy in my class commented on my big ass. My father had also started drinking at the time. But I think these things were mostly triggers. I think my worries have deeper roots, like how I was always put down when I was growing up."

"My father has bad skin," Jamie said. "I look more like my father than like my mother. I worried my skin might end up like his."

"Maybe I learned looks were important," Brad told me. "My family stressed the importance of looks. We always had to look our best and be well-manicured no matter what. . . . Everyone paid lots of attention to my brother—he was the champ of the family and my father's pet. I was always last on my parents' list. . . . I was always very sensitive. I was always sensitive to criticism and rejection. I'm a perfectionist. I've always been hard on myself—since day one. I have high standards. My parents expected a lot from me. I was always the black sheep of the family."

People with BDD have myriad and varied explanations for their symptoms. Some believe the cause is biological—perhaps a chemical imbalance in the brain. Others give a psychological explanation, citing their upbringing, identification with a particular person, or personality traits such as perfectionism or sensitivity to criticism or rejection. Others blame society's emphasis on attractiveness. Some people attribute their symptoms to a comment or to stress in their lives at the time their concern began. Others have no explanation for their symptoms, but they search for one, trying to give their experience meaning. The explanations are varied and bear the stamp of each person's unique autobiography.

This chapter's topic—what causes BDD—is the most complex question in this book. At this time, BDD's cause remains largely unexplored, and there are no definitive answers. This is the outermost edge of the BDD frontier. But even though we're at the beginning of our search, our understanding of what causes BDD is steadily growing.

Theories about BDD's Cause

In past decades, most theories about BDD's cause—a reflection of the times— had a psychological basis. BDD symptoms were assumed to have psychological meaning and a psychological origin. An example of this was the 1920's case of the Wolf Man, whose psychoanalyst suggested that his nose represented his penis and that he unconsciously desired to be castrated and made into a woman. Furthermore, she thought that his nose preoccupation reflected his identification with his mother, in part because it began soon after he saw a wart on his mother's nose. More recent psychological theories don't focus on such concrete symbolism—for example, that the nose really represents the penis. Rather, they focus on the possible role of personality characteristics or life experiences, such as being teased or rejected by other people, perfectionism, or learning to base one's self-esteem largely on appearance.

More recently, biological theories have been proposed. Very preliminary research findings suggest that certain genes and malfunctioning of the brain chemical serotonin might be involved. Do brain chemicals play a role in causing BDD symptoms? Is BDD "hardwired" in the brain? Might research findings about the biological origins of OCD (obsessive compulsive disorder) and social phobia apply to BDD?

Sociocultural explanations have an obvious appeal. You can't watch TV, go to a movie, or read a magazine without being bombarded with images of beauty and perfection. The message we get is that we're supposed to look our best at all times. We're urged to fix any imperfections in our appearance, no matter how small. Might these ubiquitous and powerful messages contribute to BDD's development? Might cultural influences also play a role?

There are other mysteries as well. For example, why do certain people but not others get BDD? Why does one person focus on her nose and another on her legs? Why do some people get BDD during adolescence, whereas others don't develop it until their 30s or 40s?

Most likely, the cause of BDD has multiple sources. That is, factors from all these domains—neurobiological, psychological, and sociocultural—probably contribute to BDD's occurrence. It's likely that both genetic and environmental factors play an important role. This explanation is similar to that demonstrated for other psychiatric disorders as well as nonpsychiatric medical disorders, such as high blood pressure. In the case of blood pressure, genetics plays an important role, creating a biological vulnerability to developing this problem. But psychological factors, such as stress, and sociocultural factors, such as diet, are additional risk factors.

Figure 6 illustrates this theory and shows a possible pathway to the development of BDD. As this figure shows, this theory proposes that genetic and neurobiological factors lay the groundwork, making it possible to develop BDD. In particular, this would include a genetic vulnerability to BDD. Environmental factors probably also contribute—both psychological and sociocultural. In addition, for some people, although not all, an environmental event seems to trigger BDD's onset, presumably in someone who's predisposed biologically and psychologically to developing it. It's likely that numerous genetic/biological factors interact in complex ways with one another and with a number of environmental factors to create BDD. In other words, a complex interaction of factors, rather than a single factor, probably causes BDD. To further complicate matters, the amount of each of these "ingredients" may differ for different people.

To briefly illustrate the model in Figure 6, you probably first need to inherit a genetic predisposition to BDD. This may consist of a vulnerability or susceptibility to developing the disorder BDD specifically or a more general genetic predisposition to worry and obsess—or both. This tendency may involve the brain chemical (neurotransmitter) serotonin and other neurotransmitters, as well as certain areas of the brain. Let's say you're also born with a tendency to have a shy and self-conscious personality (temperament); if this temperament is combined with a tendency to obsess and worry, it may further increase your chance of getting BDD. Environmental factors may further increase this biologically based risk; for example, if you're teased a lot as a child or experience lots of rejection, this may further funnel your genetically based worrying tendency and self-consciousness toward BDD symptoms. And if you're already predisposed in these ways to develop BDD, you may be hyperalert to media images of perfection (such as flawless skin) and buy into them more than the average person does. Then, if your boyfriend breaks up with you, that may trigger feelings of inferiority and full-fledged BDD.

This example is just one of many possible pathways to developing BDD. Nonetheless, as it illustrates, it's extremely unlikely that BDD has a single cause. We can't say, for example, that it's caused simply by the media's obsession with beauty, or by inheriting a certain gene. Instead, it's probably due to multiple contributory factors such as those in Figure 6, each of which may somewhat increase the risk of developing BDD. With enough of these risk factors, the disorder may develop. The factors that contribute to BDD's development may differ somewhat for different people. For example, not everyone with BDD has

Figure 6.   A Possible Pathway to the Development of BDD

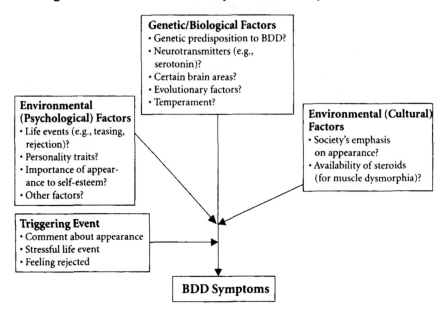

been teased and rejected a lot. And a stressful event, such as a relationship breaking up, isn't usually necessary to bring on BDD symptoms. It may be that if you have a very strong genetic predisposition to developing BDD, environmental factors may play only a relatively small role, whereas if you have a weaker genetic vulnerability, powerful environmental factors may be needed for BDD to develop.

While it's useful to think of risk factors in terms of discrete categories—genetic versus environmental, or biological versus psychological versus sociocultural—these categories are to some extent artificial. Biological and psychological factors overlap and interact with each other in complex ways: biological givens, such as temperament (biologically based personality traits), affect how people interact with the world and influence life events. Conversely, life events, such as repetitive severe trauma and other environmental factors, can actually change the brain. Trying to clearly distinguish biological, psychological, and sociocultural contributions to BDD from one another is complex and to some degree artificial.

At this time, theories about what causes BDD are largely speculative, although recent research findings do give us some important clues. Spinning theories and hypotheses is relatively easy; proving or disproving them is far more difficult. The "why" questions are always the hardest to answer. The cause of BDD is a puzzle that remains to be solved. Nonetheless, we have some intriguing clues to guide us. In the rest of this chapter, I'll discuss Figure 6 and what we know about these clues in more detail.

Genetic/Neurobiological Theories:
Is BDD a Brain Disease?

"A Person with Curious Hair"

How could excessive appearance concerns—which might seem clearly caused by sociocultural factors, such as the media's influence, or by psychological factors, such as low self-esteem—be rooted in a person's genes and brain chemistry? How could BDD be a brain disease?

I start with this perspective because I think it's likely that neurobiology lays the groundwork for BDD—that genetics and biologically based tendencies make BDD possible by creating a vulnerability to developing the disorder.

This hypothesis seems less strange when you consider that some patients themselves believe that BDD has a neurobiological basis. "My obsession may or may not be related to my childhood experiences, but it mostly feels chemical—out of my control," Ron said. "It feels like something biological is driving it." Other people, after searching for a psychological explanation for their symptoms in therapy, are unable to find one. While it could be argued that this therapy outcome reflects unconscious resistance to uncovering a psychological reason for the symptoms, this seems unlikely to be the case for many patients.

A neurobiological basis for body image disturbance actually has a long historical tradition. Early in this century, neurologists explored the neurobiological basis of several types of distorted body image. These included anosognosia (the inability to recognize or acknowledge impaired bodily functioning, such as paralysis) and neglect of one side of the body (e.g., shaving only one side of the face or using only one sleeve of a robe). In 1931, a neurologist reported that some of his patients had interesting reactions toward their left-sided paralyzed limbs, considering them "strange, ugly, disfigured . . . thickened, shortened, or snake like."

Such body-image disturbances are related to brain processes and are often caused by brain damage, such as a stroke, in the brain's parietal region. Injury to the occipital lobes of the brain—the primary visual processing area—can impair visual perception, including perception of facial images. And damage to another area of the brain, the border of the occipital and temporal lobes, can result in an inability to visually identify previously known faces. Some people with damage to this brain area can't identify their own face in the mirror. An example of the bodily misperception that brain injury can cause is a case published in 1947 in which a man described a dog as a person with "curious hair."

An unusual case of BDD-like symptoms also points to the involvement of neurobiological factors in the disorder's development. A 21-year old man who became preoccupied with thoughts that his ears had become smaller, one foot was bigger than the other, and other appearance concerns was eventually discovered to have subacute sclerosing panencephalitis, a rare and diffuse brain disease that was presumably related to the BDD-like concerns. While it's likely that very few cases of BDD are caused by an identifiable neurological disorder, this case illustrates that brain processes gone awry can lead to distorted bodily perception and excessive bodily preoccupation.

The Serotonin Hypothesis

BDD's response to treatment also suggests that neurobiological factors are involved in its development. Although we can't necessarily infer a disorder's cause from its treatment response, this provides valuable clues to the cause or pathophysiological mechanisms involved in a disorder. Evidence that BDD responds to medications known as serotonin-reuptake-inhibitors (SRIs), which affect brain serotonin, suggests that disturbed brain chemistry plays an important role.

Serotonin is one of the brain's natural chemicals, known as a *neurotransmitter*, that carries messages from one nerve cell to another, making the nerve cells communicate with one another and function. Nerve cells release serotonin, which crosses a space between nerve cells known as a synapse and then fits into a receptor on a receiving nerve cell, like a lock in a key. This "unlocking" triggers a variety of chemical reactions in the recipient nerve cell, making it fire an electrical impulse that gets transmitted to neighboring nerve cells by the same mechanism. This process occurs in countless interlocking nerve cell networks and circuits throughout the brain.

The chemical messenger serotonin is important in many critical bodily functions—including mood, cognition, memory, sleep, appetite, eating behavior, sexual behavior, and pain. It inhibits aggressive and destructive behavior. It also plays an important role in a variety of psychiatric disorders, including depression and OCD. BDD, too, may involve dysregulation of serotonin. How does serotonin do so many things? Its multiple roles may be explained by the fact that there are many different types of serotonin receptors located at diverse sites throughout the brain. Serotonin's effects on these receptors are complex and incredibly diverse.

Because the interactions and overlap among brain neurotransmitters (chemical messengers) and their receptors are so complex, and because there are so many neurotransmitters in the brain, it's likely that other neurotransmitters are also involved in BDD. One of these is dopamine, which appears to play an important role in delusional thinking. Dopamine may, in combination with serotonin, be particularly important in the delusional form of BDD. GABA (γ-aminobutyric acid) is another brain neurotransmitter that may be involved in BDD. GABA is a calming neurotransmitter that's ubiquitous in the brain and may be involved in the development of some anxiety disorders.

BDD's many similarities with OCD (see Chapter 16 for details) provides additional support for the theory that BDD involves neurochemical (neurotransmitter) abnormalities. Their similarities suggest that they may have a similar cause. Because much more is known about the neurobiological basis of OCD, it's useful to look at this evidence. Many studies suggest that OCD involves an abnormality in the serotonin neurotransmitter system. This "serotonin hypothesis" is supported by several lines of evidence, including treatment response.

Many treatment studies have demonstrated that OCD responds better to the SRIs than to other medications, implicating the importance of serotonin. Although the SRIs appear to enhance serotonin transmission in the brain, it's unclear exactly how they improve OCD.

Further support for the importance of serotonin in OCD comes from studies showing that when OCD improves with SRI treatment, there are acute changes in serotonin and its metabolites in the body. Pharmacological challenge studies, in which people are given agents that affect serotonin, also tend to support the serotonin hypothesis in OCD. Such agents may, for example, increase OCD symptoms and anxiety in patients with OCD but have no effect in healthy control subjects. Although available data aren't entirely consistent, on balance there's substantial evidence implicating serotonin in OCD. However, this neurotransmitter's exact role, and whether it has a central role in *causing* OCD, remains unclear. Serotonin also appears important in social phobia, another disorder that's similar to BDD (see Chapter 16).

Dopamine, a neurotransmitter important in disorders involving abnormalities in thinking and stereotypic movements, may also play a role in OCD and social phobia. Medications that counteract dopamine can improve OCD symptoms when combined with an SRI. Some forms of OCD may involve an imbalance in the systems controlling serotonin and dopamine. This hypothesis may also apply to BDD, as BDD involves stereotypic behaviors (for example, repetitive grooming) and delusional thinking. Also, dopamine antagonist medications (atypical antipsychotics; see Chapter 13) are sometimes helpful for BDD. Other neurochemical systems, including GABA (γ-aminobutyric acid; see the genetics section below) may also play an important role in BDD.

It's worth keeping in mind, however, that BDD differs from OCD and social phobia in some important ways, as I'll discuss in Chapter 16. So it can't be assumed that everything we know about OCD and social phobia pertains to BDD. Also, research findings that suggest a role for serotonin in BDD are far more preliminary than for OCD. BDD's response to SRIs gives some indirect support to the serotonin hypothesis. A few preliminary reports also implicate serotonin in BDD. One published report published by Drs. Linda Barr, Wayne Goodman, and Lawrence Price described a patient with BDD treated with the SRI clomipramine (Anafranil) and buspirone (Buspar) who ate a low tryptophan diet and drank an amino acid drink without tryptophan. Tryptophan is an essential protein building block (amino acid) that is a precursor of serotonin. This dietary depletion of tyrptophan dramatically exacerbated her BDD symptoms, which was presumably mediated by a drop in brain serotonin levels.

Conversely, there have been several reports of BDD symptoms worsening with the use of agents that antagonize serotonin. One patient's BDD symptoms worsened after he chronically abused cyproheptadine, an allergy medication that counteracts serotonin. And LSD, which affects serotonin, is well known to induce visual illusions, including bodily distortions.

Indeed, serotonin modulates the visual system and visual processing. Animal research shows that serotonin-releasing neurons innervate the primary visual (occipital) area of the brain as well as relay stations along the brain's visual pathways between the eye and the occipital area. Serotonin seems to modulate and regulate the flow of information through the interrelated structures of the visual system. One hypothesis is that serotonin may protect animals from over-reacting to unimportant sensory input. Indeed, destruction of the serotonin system results in over-reactivity to environmental stimuli. Might serotonin also protect humans from overreacting to unimportant stimuli and visual input—that is, to defects in appearance that most people don't see or consider minimal?

A Role for Genes in BDD?

Might a tendency to develop BDD be partially rooted in your genes? Is some-thing "physical" passed on in the genetic material from one generation to the next? Recently, Drs. James Kennedy, Margaret Richter, and I did what is to my knowledge the only genetics study of BDD, in which we looked at serotonin genes and other genes. We used a candidate gene approach, in which we ex-amined certain genes that we hypothesized may be important in BDD. We compared the forms (alleles) of these candidate genes in people with BDD and in people without BDD. A higher percentage of people with BDD had the short allele of the serotonin transporter promoter region gene than the healthy sub-jects without BDD. The serotonin transporter gene codes for a protein (the serotonin transporter) that's like a molecular "vacuum cleaner" which sucks up serotonin from the spaces (synapses) between brain nerve cells. The serotonin transporter is also the main target of the SRI medications. The serotonin trans-porter gene has been implicated as playing a role in other psychiatric disorders. Our result suggests (although does not prove) that the short allele of this gene may increase the risk of developing BDD. Our result is very preliminary, how-ever, and more genetics studies are greatly needed to confirm our finding and to examine other genes. (There are more than 26,000 human genes, so many could be studied!). We also found that one form of a GABA gene was more common in the BDD group than in the control subjects. GABA is a neurotrans-mitter that inhibits the activity of nerves, like a brake. It's ubiquitous in the brain and is implicated in the development of some anxiety disorders. Enhanced GABA release calms the nervous system, reducing anxiety, irritability, and agitation.

It's very unlikely, however, that only one gene (such as the serotonin trans-porter gene or a particular GABA gene) is involved in BDD. Like other psy-chiatric disorders, BDD is likely a "complex" genetic disorder, involving a num-ber of different genes that interact in complex ways with one another and with multiple environmental factors to increase the risk of getting BDD. Also, "BDD genes" may be common in the population and not necessarily defective. Having certain susceptibility genes may simply increase the risk of developing BDD. If a genetic predisposition is involved in BDD, it's unclear whether it consists of a predisposition to develop BDD symptoms specifically, or a more general pre-disposition to obsess and worry, which is then channeled into BDD symptoms by other factors (such as those shown in Figure 6, p. 160). It's also possible that certain genes confer protection against developing BDD.

While it's likely that having certain genes may increase a person's susceptibility to BDD, this doesn't mean that if you have BDD your blood relatives (who share some of your genes) will necessarily develop it too. My research indicates that approximately 20% of people with BDD have at least 1 first-degree relative (parent, sibling, or child) with BDD. About 6% of all first-degree relatives have BDD (although this is probably an underestimate because relatives were not directly interviewed). So the vast majority of blood relatives (more than 90%) don't appear to develop the disorder. This is reassuring. It also suggests that a complex combination of various genetic and environmental factors is necessary for BDD to be expressed.

Twin and adoption studies can help disentangle the extent to which genetic versus shared environmental factors influence the development of a disorder. However, such studies haven't yet been done in BDD. About 6% of first-degree family members appear to have BDD, a rate that's perhaps 3 to 6 times higher than BDD's prevalence in the general population, which suggests that BDD tends to run in families. However, we don't know whether this is because BDD is inherited (i.e., genetic), learned from family members (i.e., environmental), or both.

An excellent family study of OCD, done by Dr. Oscar Bienvenu and colleagues at John's Hopkins University, found that BDD is more common in first-degree relatives of individuals with OCD than in first-degree relatives of healthy control subjects. This finding suggests that BDD may be related to OCD, and that these disorders may share some causal factors (see Chapter 16 for a further discussion).

Yet another reason to think that BDD involves genetic and neurobiological underpinnings is that most, if not all, psychiatric disorders appear at least partly neurobiologically and genetically based. Elegant twin studies of individuals with depression or other psychiatric disorders indicate that genetic factors have a substantial casual role. Even the disorder that might be considered the most environmentally determined of all—post-traumatic stress disorder, which occurs after experiencing an extremely stressful event—is substantially determined by genetic factors.

Are Certain Brain Areas Involved in BDD?

Might BDD also involve certain brain regions—for example, regions that are rich in serotonin? That is, can subtle anomalies in certain brain structures be identified? Recent brain-imaging techniques have greatly advanced the search for abnormalities in brain structure and functioning in a variety of psychiatric disorders. To my knowledge, only one brain imaging study of BDD has been published. Dr. Scott Rauch, his colleagues, and I compared 8 women with BDD to 8 healthy comparison women using a brain imaging technique called morphometric magnetic resonance imaging (MRI), which visualizes the brain's structure. The number of study subjects was small, so the results are preliminary, although the study had many methodologic strengths. We found that the MRI scans of the BDD group differed in some ways from those of the healthy controls. In technical terms, the BDD group had greater total white matter (the part of the brain consisting of myelin, which acts as an insulator and speeds up nerve signal transmission, and connecting fibers). The BDD group also had a "leftward shift" in caudate nucleus asymmetry, meaning that the left caudate was relatively larger than the right. The caudate is a C-shaped structure deep in the brain's core, which is involved in regulating voluntary movements, habits, and cognitions; it may be involved in "pre-packaged" repetitive behaviors such as BDD rituals. The other brain areas we examined were similar in the two groups.

It isn't entirely clear what these results mean. They suggest that, on average, the brains of people with and without BDD differ in some subtle ways, perhaps (but not necessarily) reflecting differences in brain development. (These findings do not, however, indicate that people with BDD have brain "damage.") It's interesting that the brain regions affected in our study are the same regions that tend to be affected in people with OCD. However, the specific findings are actually opposite from OCD: OCD studies have tended to show reduced (rather than increased) white matter volume and a rightward (rather than a leftward) shift in caudate asymmetry. We could conclude from this that BDD and OCD may be related disorders because they seem to involve similar brain regions. However, they don't appear to be identical disorders, because the details of the MRI results differed. Our study also found that the brain regions involved in BDD differ from those involved in depression (e.g., the hippocampus). This finding, while preliminary, suggests that BDD isn't simply a form of depression.

Neuropsychological studies of BDD similarly indicate that the caudate and near-neighbor brain areas (the striatum), as well as the orbitofrontal cortex (an area on the bottom of the front part of the brain just above and behind the eyes), may play an important role in BDD. In these studies, people performed various tasks that require use of these brain areas—for example, remembering a long list of words or drawing a complex figure from memory. When doing these tasks, people with BDD (compared to healthy people without BDD) tended to overfocus on minor details and had trouble "seeing the forest for the trees." This result is interesting because it's consistent with BDD symptoms of overfocusing on minor aspects of appearance and not seeing the "big picture" of how one looks. This "overfocusing" may play a major role in causing and maintaining BDD symptoms, as I'll discuss in more detail in the next chapter. It's interesting that the brain regions suggested to be important in both the MRI and the neuropsychological studies (the striatum [which includes the caudate] and orbitofrontal cortex) are full of serotonin and dopamine receptors.

Functional brain imaging studies, which assess the brain's functioning rather than its structure, haven't been published yet in BDD, but findings in OCD may be relevant. Functional MRI studies in OCD indicate that both the caudate and orbitofrontal cortex are important in OCD. Specifically, these studies have found hyperactivity (increased metabolism) in the orbitofrontal cortex and caudate nucleus in patients with OCD compared with healthy control subjects. These findings have generated models for the basis of obsessions and compulsions, which suggest that there is hyperactivity in a "circuit," or "loop," connecting certain areas of the brain to one another (the orbitofrontal cortex, anterior cingulate cortex, caudate nucleus, thalamus, and other structures). In OCD, certain brain structures in this "worry circuit" (the caudate and other basal ganglia structures) don't "repress" or filter out inputs from the orbital cortex as they should. It's as if a gate that should be closed is left open, allowing the brain impulses that generate certain thoughts and behaviors to repeatedly cycle through the gate and around the loop. This causes intrusive obsessions and compulsive behaviors to occur over and over. Effective treatments for OCD (the SRIs and cognitive-behavioral therapy) appear to reduce this state of overdrive, slowing down this "reverberating circuit" and allowing it to work normally. Serotonin plays an important role in this brain circuit, and the SRI medications modulate nerve transmission in parts of the circuit in a way that could explain both their antiobsessional and antidepressant properties. Whether these findings apply to BDD remains to be studied.

The amygdala—a small almond-shaped structure deep in the brain—also may play an important role in BDD. The amygdala is involved in processing of emotional facial expressions. It's also the command center for our body's fear system, and it's intimately linked with the orbitalfrontal-striatal circuit I've been discussing. One of its main functions is to evaluate the environment for possible threat. When it perceives danger or threat, the amygdala triggers fear and an emergency response (such as escape). You can think of the amygdala as the brain's "panic button." This system allows potential threats to be communicated to other relevant brain areas and responded to quickly. For example, if we step on a snake while walking through the woods, our amygdala evaluates the snake as a threat, makes us afraid, and orchestrates a fleeing response. Interestingly, macaque monkeys without an amygdala show little fear of normally frightening objects, such as rubber snakes. Although the amygdala's role in BDD hasn't been studied, it may be overly activated in BDD. This overactivation may contribute to excessive anxiety and fear (for example, due to feeling negatively judged or mocked by other people). This anxiety may, along with BDD obsessions, drive compulsive BDD behaviors (e.g., excessive checking or grooming).

Other parts of the brain may also be involved in BDD. As noted earlier, certain regions of the parietal lobe have knowledge of body parts. A particular region of the occipitotemporal cortex (the fusiform face area) responds selectively to visual images of human faces, and another (the extrastriate body area) responds to visual images of human bodies and non-face body parts. Studies are needed to determine whether these brain areas, which process the visual appearance of faces and bodies, are involved in BDD.

Evolution, Animals, and BDD

A preference for bodily symmetry, a concern of one-third of people with BDD, may have biologically based, evolutionary underpinnings. Some researchers have found that animals prefer symmetry, as opposed to asymmetry, in their mates. Male Japanese scorpion flies with the most symmetrical wings, for example, obtain the most mates. Female scorpion flies may prefer these suitors because they're more adept at killing their prey. People, like animals, seem to prefer symmetry as well. Studies have found, for example, that college students with more symmetrical features have more sex partners. This preference appears to have an evolutionary neurobiological basis and may signal reproductive fitness or health, or, in animals, provide a way to recognize mates of the same species.

Other animal behaviors give us a fascinating window on possible neurobiological underpinnings of BDD. We don't currently have an animal model of BDD, yet the excessive repetitive behaviors of some animals appear amazingly similar to those of BDD. Some animals, for example, excessively groom themselves or perform other compulsive behaviors. Dogs with acral lick syndrome compulsively lick their fur, particularly their paws, to the point of eroding their fur and skin. This can cause painful sores and infections. Some birds compulsively pluck out their feathers, which may cause infection and even fatal hemorrhage. This behavior has similarities to compulsive skin picking in BDD. Grooming behaviors are evolutionarily adaptive because they keep animals clean, remove parasites that can cause disease, and are important in heat regulation. However, acral lick syndrome, psychogenic alopecia (fur loss) in cats (due to over-grooming), and similar syndromes illustrate how normally adaptive animal behaviors can go awry. A similar process may occur in BDD. It's fascinating that these abnormal grooming behaviors in animals may respond to SRIs but not to non-SRI antidepressants or placebo (a sugar pill). This is similar to BDD.

The brain areas discussed above—the orbitofrontal cortex and striatum—are important in mediating excessive, stereotypic behaviors in animals like excessive grooming. The serotonin and dopamine systems may also be involved. Increasing dopamine levels (one of the neurotransmitters that may be important in BDD) in the caudate can worsen these animal behaviors. Animal and evolutionary models of the need to be accepted by other people and of social dominance and submissiveness may also be relevant to BDD, as people with BDD tend to be unassertive and feel unappealing and inferior to other people. It's interesting that medications that enhance brain serotonin activity (such as fluoxetine [Prozac]) help make certain animals more socially dominant and confident. This is consistent with observations that people with BDD who respond to an SRI typically say they feel more socially confident and comfortable.

Summary

In summary, a genetically based predisposition to worry and obsess—or to BDD specifically—probably provides a necessary cornerstone for BDD's development. This inherited, biologically based tendency may in turn alter the functioning of serotonin and other brain neurotransmitters. It may also cause certain brain areas or circuits to function abnormally. These circuits may involve the orbitofrontal-striatal-thalamic-orbitofrontal "worry loop" and the amygdala, the brain's fear center. Hyperactivity of these brain circuits, combined with neurotransmitter abnormalities, could create obsessions, compulsive behaviors, excessive anxiety, and a tendency to overfocus on minor aspects of appearance. They could also cause normal, adaptive, evolutionarily based preferences and behaviors, such as grooming or a desire for symmetry, to become excessive and go into overdrive. Taken together, these factors may provide the necessary foundation for BDD to develop.

Psychological Theories: Is BDD a Mind Disease?

Kimberly had a psychological explanation for her BDD symptoms. "I never got positive messages from my family, even though I was the good daughter," she told me. "I was never praised, and I felt neglected. I wonder if that's how I developed such low self-esteem and my feelings that I look bad."

Might psychological factors also play a role in causing BDD? Might BDD result from identifying with another person, or from life experiences, such as teasing or rejection? What about the role of personality traits, such as perfectionism or sensitivity to criticism or rejection? Are BDD symptoms the expression or reflection of underlying psychological issues, such as problems in a relationship?

During the past century psychological factors have been considered to play an important role in causing BDD, a reflection of the dominant theoretical framework at the time. This framework—often referred to as a psychodynamic or psychoanalytic perspective—views symptoms as having psychological meaning and causation. Often, the cause is considered to be rooted in childhood experiences.

Some authors, for example, have suggested that BDD arises from the unconscious displacement of sexual or emotional conflict, or feelings of inferiority, guilt, or poor self-image, onto a body part. Conflicts or feelings such as these are considered the underlying problem and cause of BDD symptoms. This displacement process is presumed to occur because the underlying problem is too emotionally threatening or anxiety provoking to be dealt with more directly—thus, it is unconsciously displaced into the more psychologically manageable arena of appearance. It's been further posited that the body part of concern, such as the nose, may represent another, more emotionally threatening, body part, such as the penis. It has similarly been suggested that BDD symptoms may unconsciously be used to "explain" dissatisfying relationships or failures in one's life. According to this theory, blaming your nose for your problems is less threatening to your self-esteem than admitting you're a failure.

Such theories are very difficult to prove or disprove. But in my view they don't provide a satisfactory explanation for BDD symptoms. First, many people respond well to medication or cognitive-behavioral therapy, without any attempt to treat presumed underlying psychological conflict. This suggests that such underlying factors aren't the primary or sole explanation for BDD. In addition, some patients have been in psychoanalysis for many years, searching for or working on psychological problems, without successfully diminishing their BDD symptoms. Such therapy may be very helpful in resolving other problems or life difficulties, but it generally doesn't appear to substantially improve BDD. As I discuss further in Chapters 12–14, SRIs and CBT are currently the recommended treatments for BDD. Simply talking about BDD or trying to understand its psychological origins—even if they exist—doesn't seem to effectively diminish the symptoms. In my view it's a mistake to view BDD as a "displacement" and to focus treatment on something else that is presumed to be causing BDD.

So it seems unlikely that BDD is really a "displacement" for some other problem, or that it's an unconscious way to avoid a more emotionally troubling issue. In fact, it's hard to imagine a more painful problem than BDD. But this doesn't mean that psychological issues aren't important in BDD. In fact, it's likely that they contribute to BDD's development. Figure 1 (p. 120) shows some possible psychological risk factors, which likely combine with genetic/biological factors, and perhaps sociocultural factors, to bring on BDD. It's also possible that psychological factors play a role in determining which specific body areas a person worries about.

Teasing and Other Life Experiences

What psychological factors and life events might contribute to BDD? We don't know with certainty, but one possibility is being teased about appearance. Frequent teasing has been linked to greater body dissatisfaction more generally. Dr. J. Kevin Thompson, for example, found that college women who reported more teasing during adolescence evaluated their body image as an adult more negatively. Individuals with an eating disorder report more past teasing than those without an eating disorder. Using sophisticated statistical methods, Richards found that teasing seemed to cause not only general psychological dysfunction (depression and lowered self-esteem) but also body dissatisfaction.

I've found that about 60% of people with BDD report frequent or chronic teasing about their appearance during childhood or adolescence. This teasing often focused on the body areas they later became obsessed with, but sometimes focused on other body areas. It isn't known whether this percentage is higher than in the general population. If it is, might frequent teasing increase the risk of developing BDD?

It's quite possible that people with BDD have been teased more than people without BDD, and that teasing does increase the chance of developing BDD. This makes sense. After all, if you're teased about how you look—especially if the teasing is frequent or very cruel—this might make you start worrying that you look bad, fueling feelings of self-consciousness, embarrassment, and humiliation. You might start to focus on the belittled body part and zero in on any tiny imperfections. This could further increase your chance of getting BDD.

But it's also possible that people with BDD haven't been teased any more than other people, but that they're more sensitive and take teasing more to heart. It seems that people with BDD tend to be unusually sensitive to criticism and rejection, as I'll discuss below. Perhaps, if by nature you're sensitive, or if you're otherwise predisposed to developing BDD, teasing would affect you and emotionally wound you more than it would affect someone else.

Although teasing may play an important role in BDD, teasing alone isn't the cause. Most of us have been teased about how we look, but most of us don't get BDD. Conversely, many people with BDD say they haven't been teased about how they look, but they get BDD anyway. Nonetheless, teasing—especially frequent and cruel teasing—may make a person more likely to develop BDD at some point in their life. For someone who's already at high risk of developing BDD, teasing sometimes seems to acutely trigger its onset.

Might other life experiences that cause feelings of low self-esteem and rejection contribute to BDD's development? It's been proposed that "unharmonious" family backgrounds or "unfavorable" childhood experiences that lead to enduring feelings of being unloved, insecure, or rejected may contribute to BDD. Some people with BDD confirm this theory, saying they believe that childhood experiences such as these contributed to their symptoms. They say that their parents expected them to be perfect, or that they didn't feel loved or cared for. But plenty of people with BDD don't say these kinds of things.

The only systematic research I know of on early family experiences of people with BDD comes from the Parental Bonding Instrument. This scale is a validated and widely used self-report measure of a person's perceptions of parental care and overprotection before the age of 16. I found that average scores of 40 consecutive people with BDD were notably lower than published norms on parental care and were in the average range on parental overprotection. These findings are consistent with how many patients describe their early life experiences, which often emphasize feelings of rejection and neglect. It's important to note, however, it's unclear whether these individuals actually received less love and care from their parents than the average person, or whether they were unusually sensitive to criticism or rejection at a young age and therefore felt unloved and neglected, even though their parents gave them lots of love and care.

Some people believe their family's or peers' emphasis on appearance contributed to their concern. One woman told me, "In my childhood people doted on my appearance. So I fear if I look bad, people won't like me." Another said, "Appearance was very important in our family, and it became very important to me. The only area of positive feedback from my parents was for my attractiveness. So destroying my appearance was the most destructive thing I could do." Experiences such as these could in theory lead to some of the cognitive distortions (distorted ways of thinking) that I'll discuss in Chapter 14—for example, that one's worth as a person is based only on one's appearance. Occasionally, BDD symptoms seem to begin with a parent's excessive preoccupation with their child's appearance—what might be called "BDD by proxy." Some people with BDD, however, report none of these things. Whether particular family experiences or other early life experiences contribute to BDD isn't clear at this time. This important question needs to be studied.

Another very important question is whether physical or sexual trauma or abuse contributes to BDD's development. In a small preliminary study, Dr. Caron Zlotnick and I found that 20% of 55 women with a history of sexual abuse had BDD—a fairly high rate. Conversely, in my interview study of 200 people with BDD, 9% had post-traumatic stress disorder (PTSD) at some point in their life (see the Glossary for a definition). However, this rate is about the same as the PTSD rate in the general U.S. population, suggesting that people with BDD may not have unusually high trauma rates. To my knowledge, no published studies have assessed what percentage of people with BDD have a childhood history of abuse per se and whether this rate is higher than in people with another psychiatric disorder or in the general population.

Based on my clinical experience, it's clear that some people with BDD have been sexually or physically abused but that some haven't. So it can't be assumed that everyone with BDD has been abused. Nor can it be assumed that if someone is abused, they'll develop BDD. However, sexual abuse may contribute to bodily shame and dislike of one's body. It also makes sense that feeling neglected as a child could contribute to feelings of worthlessness and low self-esteem, including feeling badly about how one looks.

What about the role of other life events? A number of patients I've seen linked their BDD symptoms with moving to a different culture. A man who moved from India told me: "I'm obsessed about my penis and nose and eyes because I feel in general like an unattractive outsider. I'm not as accepted as I'd like to be." Another man from India gave a similar explanation: "I feel like a foreigner in every way—I feel different from others. I'm afraid I'll never have the all-American look."

It's also important to consider whether a previously noticeable physical deformity might contribute to the development of BDD. Some people with BDD—although it's a small minority—report that they had a more severe deformity, such as severe acne, scoliosis, or a facial gash from an accident earlier in their life. With time, their skin healed or their back was straightened, but their view of themselves didn't change. In their mind's eye, they would always be severely deformed. Body-image researchers refer to this as the adaptive failure theory. According to this theory, when a person's actual appearance changes, their self-perception of their body doesn't. Research findings on the validity of this theory are mixed, but some studies have found that obese subjects' perception of their body size—as well as their thoughts, feelings, and concerns about weight—don't necessarily change when they lose weight. After losing weight, they still don't see themselves as thin; a negative "vestigial" body image persists. One woman's comment about her BDD reflected this theory: "I'm like a person who lost 200 pounds and still thinks they're fat. I can't change my view of myself." This theory hasn't been adequately studied and hasn't been studied at all in BDD. But it might apply to some individuals with previous actual deformities.

It's possible that other life events contribute to BDD's development. Perhaps people who later develop BDD experience a lot of rejection or lots of stress. If so, this might increase their risk of developing BDD. Although this hasn't been studied, it's unlikely that life events alone would cause BDD, as some kind of genetic/biological predisposition is probably necessary to develop it. But life events may very well play an important role.

A Role for Personality?

Personality traits are generally both "psychological, or environmental," and "biological, or genetic," in origin. For example, personality traits like submissiveness and extroversion are substantially determined by genetic as well as environmental influences. (For this reason, Figure 6 (p. 160) lists "temperament" (inborn personality traits) in the "genetic/biological factors" box, and also lists "personality traits" in the "environmental (psychological) factors" box.)

Many years ago, some authors viewed BDD as a symptom of an underlying personality disturbance. They proposed that the real problem was the person's personality. However, this is very unlikely to be the case. People with BDD have a variety of personality traits—not everyone with BDD has the same type of personality. In addition, many people with BDD have no personality "disturbance" of any sort. Also, BDD often goes away with an SRI, which wouldn't be expected if it were really a deep-seated personality problem. It therefore is highly unlikely that BDD is *caused* by, or simply a symptom of, certain personality traits or problems.

But might certain personality traits *predispose* people to BDD and act as a risk factor for the disorder? People with BDD are often shy, self-conscious, and hypersensitive to rejection and criticism. Their self-esteem is often low. As I'll discuss in Chapter 16, available research findings suggest that people with BDD tend to be introverted and socially avoidant. They also tend to score very high on "neuroticism," a measure of anxiety, depression, self-consciousness, anger, and feelings of vulnerability. People with BDD also seem sensitive to criticism and rejection. In one study, my colleagues and I found that people with BDD plus depression were more sensitive to rejection than depressed people who didn't have BDD. Specifically, those with BDD said they were more emotionally overreactive to rejection or criticism. They were also more impaired in their functioning at work or school because they tended to overreact to criticism or rejection.

People with BDD also tend to be unassertive. In a study I did using the Rathus Assertiveness Scale, women with BDD scored below the 15th percentile, and men with BDD scored below the 10th percentile compared to normative values. Thus, both genders tended to be unassertive. In another study, I found that 28 people with BDD were even less assertive than those in the first study. They were also much less assertive than depressed people who didn't have BDD.

It makes sense that some of these personality traits—being "neurotic," introverted, sensitive to criticism and rejection, and unassertive—might make a person more vulnerable to BDD. These traits might predispose a person to think negatively about themselves, to worry, to feel unwanted by others, and to think there's something wrong with them.

But the relationship of these and other personality traits to BDD is unclear. It's isn't known whether these traits *predispose to* BDD, contributing to its occurrence or, conversely, whether they *result from* BDD—or both. Certainly, BDD itself makes people anxious, sensitive, and socially uncomfortable and avoidant. Or do certain personality traits and BDD simply *co-occur*, without one predisposing to or causing the other? One reason it's hard to answer this question is that both BDD and personality traits usually develop at a young age and are continuously present, making it difficult to answer this question on the basis of time course (e.g., which started first). However, neuroticism and introversion are partly inherited traits (temperament), suggesting that they may be present before BDD begins and may possibly contribute to its development.

Another personality trait that appears associated with BDD is perfectionism or unusually high standards for oneself. Some people with BDD say that they want to look perfect and that they expect perfectionism in other areas of their life as well. "I have very high standards for myself," a college student said to me. "I expect much more from myself than from anyone else, in terms of my appearance and everything else. It's hard to live up to it." Indeed, one study found that a majority of 50 people with BDD said that they "must have perfection in their appearance." It isn't clear, however, whether this applies just to the perceived defect or to appearance more generally. Using the Frost Multidimensional Perfectionism Scale, Dr. Sabine Wilhelm found that people with BDD had significantly higher levels of perfectionism than healthy controls in areas unrelated to appearance. Might perfectionism contribute to the development and maintenance of BDD? As discussed earlier in this chapter, from an evolutionary perspective trying to look perfect and symmetrical may be adaptive. However, in BDD, demands for perfection might lead to excessive and selective attention to minor asymmetries and appearance flaws, as well as unrealistically high appearance standards.

In another study, Dr. Wilhelm evaluated whether people with BDD tend to feel threatened in various situations—in particular, situations involving appearance or social situations. Study participants completed a questionnaire that presented various ambiguous scenarios and then asked what thoughts occurred to them. For example, an appearance-related scenario was: "While talking with some colleagues, you notice that some people take special notice of you. What thoughts occur to you?" The options are: 1) I am sure they are judging the way I look; 2) They probably agree with my opinion; and 3) They are interested in my conversation. Compared to 22 healthy control participants and 20 participants with OCD, the 19 people with BDD were more likely to select answers like #1. Compared to the other two groups, the BDD group was also more likely to have negative thoughts about general social situations—for example, thinking that they said something foolish in a social situation.

These results suggest that people with BDD tend to have negative and threatening interpretations for appearance-related and social anxiety-related information. This finding is consistent with the theory I mentioned earlier that people with BDD may have an "overactive" amygdala, the part of the brain that responds to perceived environmental threats. It's also consistent with the tendency of people with BDD to be sensitive to criticism and rejection. It's unclear whether this negative interpretive bias predates the onset of BDD, thereby possibly increasing the risk of developing BDD, or whether it results from having BDD. In either case, the tendency to feel threatened in these situations probably helps keep BDD symptoms going, and it may be helpful to try to change this type of negative thinking in cognitive behavioral therapy.

In summary, I would hypothesize that traits such as shyness, social anxiety, low self-esteem, perfectionism, sensitivity to rejection and criticism, and a tendency to feel threatened in certain situations may predispose a person to BDD. In turn, it seems likely that BDD symptoms may strengthen some of these traits. For example, if you avoid social situations because of BDD symptoms, you may become even more socially anxious and shy. For some people, however, these traits might simply be a result of the BDD, in which case they wouldn't have caused the disorder.

Do Psychological Factors Influence the Content of BDD Concerns?

So far, I've been discussing whether certain psychological factors might contribute to BDD's occurrence. But it's also interesting to consider whether psychological factors might influence the *content* of BDD beliefs—the specific aspects of appearance that a person worries about. According to this model, psychological factors or experiences might influence the specific body part of concern, or the theme associated with the concern, such as a fear of aging. For example, are you more likely to worry about your nose, as opposed to your stomach, if that's what you were teased about as a child? Are you more likely to worry about aging, as opposed to femininity, if your parent was very concerned about looking old? Might the content of BDD beliefs be influenced by identification with another person? Some clinical observations have suggested that this may be the case. A young man who was concerned about balding stated, "I'm afraid I'll end up bald like Uncle Joe." Others dislike a particular aspect of their appearance because they associate it with a particular ethnic group. One woman said that she focused on her hair because her grandparents had owned a beauty parlor, and hair was always very important in her family. I think for some people there does seem to be a connection with family values or important life events, but for many other people there doesn't seem to be.

Summary

The role of psychological factors in BDD needs to be studied and better understood. In some cases such factors—such as identification with another person—seem to influence the *content* of BDD concerns. I would also hypothesize that psychological factors, such as certain life events or personality characteristics, may also influence *whether* BDD occurs—that is, they may act as a risk factor for the disorder's development. I think it's likely, however, that psychological factors must act in concert with biological or genetic factors to bring on BDD.

Sociocultural Theories:
Mega-Makeovers and Perfect Thighs

"Mega-Makeovers: Go From So-So to Supersexy!"

"Perfect Thighs in This Lifetime?"

"Fast Fixes for a Bad Hair Day"

"3-D Abs: Work Your Front, Back, and Sides for a Great Middle"

These were messages I read while standing in line one day at the grocery store check-out counter. The most prominent message displayed on the magazine rack was that appearance matters. The covers were adorned with beautiful women and muscle-bound men. You couldn't miss it.

Nor can you miss it on television, in films, or in magazines. We confront airbrushed and retouched images of perfection everywhere. As one person with BDD put it, "You see models everywhere. How can you *not* think about how you look!" Advertisements and magazines reflect our society's incessant focus on appearance. The number of articles on beauty and diets in women's magazines has multiplied in recent decades. We spend huge amounts of money on diets, cosmetics, hair styles, clothing, and makeovers. Increasing numbers of people, including men and teenagers, are having cosmetic surgery. In 1997, plastic surgeons, dermatologists, and ENT doctors in the United States performed about 2 million cosmetic procedures (surgical and nonsurgical); by 2003, that number had risen to nearly, 8.3 million. The marketing of beauty has become a multibillion dollar industry.

Men and boys, too, are increasingly getting this message—from advertising, toys, and other sources. As my coauthors and I describe in *The Adonis Complex*, men are struggling more than ever with the same enormous pressure to achieve physical perfection that women have dealt with for centuries. Dr. Harrison Pope found that the proportion of undressed men (defined as anything too risqué to be seen on a city street) in *Glamour* and *Cosmopolitan* magazines has skyrocketed over the years, from as low as 3% in the 1950s to as high as 35% in the 1990s. Massively muscular men increasingly adorn the covers of men's magazines and also grace women's magazines. G.I. Joe, the action toy that boys have played with for decades, has recently bulked up. Just as Barbie is impossibly thin—if she were the height of an actual woman, she'd have only a 16-inch waist!—GI Joes have become impossibly muscular. If G.I. Joe Extreme were the size of a man, he'd have a 55-inch chest and a 27-inch bicep (arm muscle)—in other words, his arm would be nearly as big as his waist!

But do sociocultural influences fuel not only normal appearance concerns but also BDD? About 60% of the people in my studies said that they believe society's focus on appearance *increases* their BDD concerns. The constant messages about attractiveness, and the incessant portrayal of attractive people on television, in movies, and in magazines, worsens their preoccupation. But only about a quarter believe our society's focus on appearance is a major *cause* of their BDD symptoms. They generally give other explanations or no explanation at all. Or they say that the media and society contribute to their symptoms but aren't the only or the major casual factor. As one woman put it, "Magazines play a role in BDD, but they're not the whole story because everyone sees them but everyone doesn't get BDD." Another agreed: "The media isn't the cause, but it feeds into it."

So it seems that societal messages about attractiveness do trigger increased preoccupation in some people with BDD. Many obsess more about their appearance after seeing attractive people on television or in a magazine. This seems especially likely if they compare themselves with other people or with movie stars or models. Society's emphasis on attractiveness may also contribute to BDD's development. That is, this emphasis may increase the risk of developing the disorder (see Figure 6, p. 160). This theory is similar to that proposed for the eating disorders anorexia nervosa and bulimia nervosa. These disorders are partly biologically based, but their risk appears to be increased by a cultural ideal of thinness.

Muscle dysmorphia is a form of BDD that seems especially likely to result in good part from sociocultural pressures. Men with muscle dysmorphia obsess that their body build is too small and inadequately muscular. They think they look skinny, puny, emaciated, or dwarfed when in fact they look entirely normal or even very muscular (see Chapter 5). Because this form of BDD was rarely seen until recently, it seems likely that society's recent messages that men should be huge and muscular, combined with the availability of anabolic steroids, have channeled a vulnerability to BDD into this particular form of the disorder.

Does the Media Cause BDD?

However, media pressures are unlikely to be the only cause of BDD, including muscle dysmorphia. BDD has been described for more than 100 years, long before the media and advertising attained their current power, suggesting that they alone aren't responsible. BDD also occurs in societies where media messages about appearance are less powerful and pervasive than in ours—or even absent altogether. A colleague told me about a man with BDD from an extremely remote part of Africa. The isolated village he lived in had no TV, no magazines, no billboards, no movies, and no computers. Nonetheless, he had classic and severe BDD that focused on his nose. In addition, BDD responds to psychiatric medications, implicating the fundamental importance of biological factors.

But the media may contribute to, or increase the risk of, BDD. If it does, it would be reasonable to conclude that as we're increasingly exposed to images of physical beauty, BDD is becoming more prevalent. Is BDD more common than it was a century ago, before advertising and other sociocultural messages extolling beauty became such a powerful influence? We don't know the answer to this important question. But just as eating disorders have become more common, BDD may have too.

What About Culture?

Other sociocultural factors probably contribute to BDD's occurrence. If certain cultures or subcultures, for example, value beauty more than others, or are more rejecting of imperfection, perhaps BDD is more likely to develop and is more common in those groups. The only study I know of that's directly compared BDD's prevalence in different countries is one by Dr. Wilhelm and colleagues. This study found that a similar percentage of American and German students— 4.0% vs. 5.3%—had BDD. Other studies indicate that BDD is about equally common in people in Italy, Turkey, and the United States, although these studies didn't directly compare the prevalence of BDD in these countries. Other than these studies, we don't have information on BDD's prevalence in different coun- tries and cultures. Nonetheless, it's clear that it occurs around the world—not only in Western cultures, which heavily emphasize appearance, but also in non- Western cultures. People with BDD have been described not only in the United States, but also in virtually all the European countries, Australia, the former Soviet Union, the Middle East, Canada, many South American countries, China, and Africa. BDD seems particularly well known, and may be especially common, in Japan. So BDD doesn't appear to be a "Western disorder"—rather, it appears universal.

So far we've been considering whether sociocultural factors may be a risk factor for BDD or make BDD more common in some cultures than others. A somewhat different question is whether sociocultural factors may influence the form that BDD takes—for example, its symptoms and effects on people's lives. Culture permeates every facet of human behavior, can influence a disorder's features, and can color the experience of illness. When it comes to BDD, might sociocultural factors influence whether appearance concerns focus on the hair rather than the legs, or whether the nose is considered too large as opposed to too small? Do Western's societies' obsession with youth contribute to BDD con- cerns with aging? Sociocultural forces may also influence how distressed people become when they develop symptoms and how well they're able to cope.

To better answer these important questions, we need to learn much more about BDD in different cultures—for example, by doing in-depth interviews as well as larger cross-cultural comparison studies of BDD. To my knowledge, such studies haven't been done. However, a number of years ago, I compared published case reports and case series of BDD from different countries around the world. This comparison suggested that more similarities than differences exist across cultures—that there is a core, universal disorder (BDD). The sex ratio was generally similar in the different countries, and most people with BDD had never been married. Average age of BDD onset was similar across countries, with a chronic course of illness in the vast majority of cases. People in different countries generally focused on similar body areas and performed similar BDD behaviors, such as mirror checking and camouflaging. Across cultures, there was a high rate of being housebound, high rates of coexisting depression and anxiety, and moderate-severe social and occupational impairment.

Series of patients from the United States, Italy, England, and Turkey also suggest that BDD has many similarities across cultures. From a clinical perspective, I've seen people with BDD from many countries around the world—India, Ecuador, Guatemala, Peru, South Korea, Bahrain, England, Australia, and others. And I've received letters and emails from people from England, Spain, Italy, China, Oman, and countless other countries who appeared to have BDD. Their BDD symptoms were surprisingly similar. In the United States, I've seen many people from minority groups, whose BDD symptoms were also very similar to those of Caucasians.

While these findings and clinical observations require confirmation by more methodologically rigorous cross-cultural comparison studies, they support a "universalist" point of view: culture appears to provide nuances and accents on a basically invariant, or universal, expression of BDD.

These findings are consistent with research on attractiveness. Scientists are finding surprisingly high agreement across cultures on what's considered attractive. When British researchers asked women from China, India, and England to rate pictures of Greek men, their ethnicity scarcely affected their preferences. Certain facial features—such as symmetry and smooth, unblemished skin—are considered beautiful around the world. It's noteworthy that these are common concerns of BDD sufferers. Some researchers theorize that a universal preference for certain facial features may be innate—hard wired into our collective brains over millions of years. Infants only several months old prefer to gaze at certain faces—those that adults consider attractive. Infants prefer attractive faces before they've had any significant exposure to cultural standards of beauty—before they've read Vogue or watched the soaps. Certain types of facial features, such as smooth unblemished skin and symmetrical facial features, may, from an evolutionary perspective, signal health and reproductive fitness, traits selected for by the evolutionary process. This is fascinating terrain, where evolutionary and cultural forces intersect in complex ways.

Nonetheless, it appears that cultural values and preferences may influence and shape BDD symptoms to at least some degree. For example, eyelid concerns appear common in Japan but rare in Western countries. Worry about displeasing other people by being unattractive also seems more common in Japan than in the United States. And while the BDD characteristics of patients in series from the United States, Italy, England, and Turkey are generally very similar, there are also some differences. For example, as discussed in Chapter 9, the United States and Italian studies had some different gender findings. Women with BDD in Turkey appear more likely to focus on their hips and the size or shape of their face or head—and less likely to obsess about their skin—than people in the United States. It's hard to know whether these differences reflect cultural influences, or whether they may be due to other factors (e.g., how the study was done).

Koro, which afflicts primarily men in certain parts of Southeast Asia, may possibly be a culturally related form of BDD. As I'll discuss further in Chapter 16, men with koro believe that their penis is shrinking and acutely retracting into their abdomen, which will kill them. Is this BDD, and is it an example of how culture can shape the form a disorder takes?

It's clear that what's considered beautiful does vary to some degree from culture to culture. Culture affects what's considered the ideal—for example, plumpness or thinness—and this can change over time. Cultural preferences also influence whether a facial scar, for example, is considered ugly and defective or a sign of great beauty. Similarly, culture and societal values may shape the content of BDD concerns. You may recall that in my gender study and the one from Italy (see chapter 8), men and women had generally similar BDD symptoms, but there were also some interesting differences, which might be explained by gender-related sociocultural values and pressures. In my study, men were more worried about their body build being too small and not muscular enough, whereas women worried more about being too big and fat. Men were more likely to camouflage with a hat (e.g., a baseball cap), whereas women more often covered up with makeup.

So the evidence seems to cut both ways. Both attractiveness research and BDD research suggest that there are many similarities across cultures, but that culture may shape appearance preferences and BDD symptoms in some ways. Certainly, we need more research on this very important issue. Yet another important question is whether culture can protect against, or even prevent, BDD's development or expression. Might culture influence BDD severity—and even whether it's expressed at all—in someone with the disorder? A woman in her late seventies described the following experience: "I've felt very ugly my entire life, ever since I was a child," she said. "The only time during the past 70 years that I haven't been preoccupied with how I look was for a couple of years when I lived in Fiji. Maybe it was because the culture was different. In that culture, whites were considered attractive and desirable. I wasn't concerned at all when I was there."

Triggers: Comments, Stress, and Other Possible Precipitants

"I started worrying about my skin when one of my friends in high school called me 'pizza face,' " Patrick told me. "I know he was only kidding, but it stuck in my mind. I started feeling very self-conscious about my skin." Scott started worrying about his appearance when his parents were getting divorced. "My parents split up unexpectedly," he said. "It was especially rough on me, because my father blamed me for the breakup. I remember in the middle of their divorce, when he was really angry about something, he said to me 'You're no longer my son.' I looked in the mirror and I thought I looked different. My whole face seemed to be sagging. I've never looked the same since."

In some cases it seems that a chance remark about appearance may acutely trigger the onset of BDD symptoms. Examples in published case reports include "You certainly resemble your father," "You look very nice but you have got a small mouth," or "Why is your face half red and half white?" G. G. Hay, who wrote about BDD in the 1970s, reported that such a remark was at least partly responsible for the onset of BDD symptoms in 9 of his 17 patients. Several other published case descriptions note the sudden onset of symptoms soon after a distressing event, such as a spouse's affair or abandonment by a boyfriend.

Negative comments about appearance or stressful life events seem to sometimes play a role in BDD's onset. Eight percent of the people in my studies reported that a negative comment about their appearance triggered the onset of symptoms. In most of these cases, symptoms began abruptly and acutely, soon after the comment or stress occurred, as opposed to more gradually. However, as shown in Figure 6 (p. 160), such events probably act as a trigger or contributing factor, but not the only cause of BDD. In other words, they seem to have the potential to precipitate the onset of BDD in someone who is biologically and psychologically vulnerable to developing the disorder. This is sometimes referred to as the vulnerability-stress hypothesis. A high school teacher's comment reflected this view: "My concern about my nose was triggered by a comment about it, in a context of extreme sensitivity and low self-esteem."

One reason to think that comments or stress may act as a precipitant, as opposed to the major or only cause of BDD, is that negative comments about appearance and stress are very common. Virtually everyone has experienced significant stress. Most of us have heard something negative about how we look. But most of us don't develop BDD. In addition, most people with BDD can't identify a trigger of their symptoms, so a trigger doesn't appear necessary for BDD to occur.

Sometimes the comment is clearly negative, such as "Get out of here! You're ugly!" But sometimes it's more benign, such as "Your hair looks different today." When one woman heard the comment, "You're red, white, and blue today," which was referring to the outfit she was wearing on the fourth of July, she thought it meant that she had a red face, which she worried about for the next 20 years. Often the comment—like the "red, white, and blue" one—influences the content of the ensuing preoccupation. One man, whose uncle told him that he had an egg-shaped head, worried about his supposedly egg-shaped head for the next 40 years.

Precipitating stressors are sometimes related to psychological themes that appear particularly relevant to BDD—for example, rejection by other people. Gail's BDD began right after her boyfriend broke up with her. "I was dating a man five years younger than me, and I was worried about being older than him. I was afraid he wouldn't want me because I was older. Shortly after he found out I was five years older, he broke up with me. I wondered if that was why, and I started being preoccupied with my appearance after that—that I looked too old."

In other cases, the stressor seems more general, such as marital or job stress. "My wife and I couldn't agree about whether to have children," Todd told me. "I was feeling guilty and stressed, and I started worrying about my face." The stress of work triggered my concern," Leslie said. "I had the sudden onset of obsessing and picking when things were really bad at work."

Some people report that surgery, dermatologic treatment, electrolysis, or other procedures precipitated their concern. As one woman said, "The electrolysis I had wrecked my face—now it's covered with scars." Another attributed her concern with her supposedly red face to a sunburn she'd gotten when she was 16. A 28-year-old man started obsessing about his face after he'd been hit by a softball, which he thought permanently indented his cheek.

A precipitating comment is often recalled in great detail, with supreme clarity and intense emotional anguish, even though it may have occurred decades earlier. Sometimes, BDD sufferers feel extremely angry and resentful toward the commenting person. They may obsess about the precipitating comment and consider getting revenge. Reactions such as these seem to reflect an unusual sensitivity to negative comments, criticism, and rejection. Instead of brushing off and forgetting wounding comments, as many people do, people with BDD tend to feel them deeply, harbor them, and sometimes suffer enduring emotional pain as a result.

What Doesn't Cause BDD

There are a number of factors that don't cause BDD. Some of them are the following:

- *Moral weakness* People do *not* get BDD because they are morally defective or weak. BDD is a psychiatric disorder with likely biological roots. It isn't caused by weakness of character. For this reason, trying harder, while helpful, isn't by itself an adequate solution to the problem.

- *Vanity* BDD isn't equivalent to or caused by vanity. Simply telling someone to stop being so vain won't end BDD symptoms.

- *Stress* While stress can worsen BDD symptoms, or appears to sometimes trigger its onset in someone vulnerable to the disorder, stress alone doesn't cause BDD. Diminishing stress may be helpful but by itself isn't adequate treatment.

- *Puberty* Some people are told that their BDD symptoms are caused by puberty. It's true that appearance concerns may develop or increase during puberty and that the many physical and emotional changes that accompany puberty may contribute to BDD's development. But to say that BDD symptoms are simply due to puberty implies that they're normal and don't need to be treated. This isn't the case. By definition, BDD symptoms are more problematic than normal appearance concerns and need psychiatric treatment.

What Makes BDD Better or Worse

The question of what makes BDD symptoms better or worse is different from the question of what causes BDD, or what its risk factors are. Rather, once the disorder is present, are there things that seem to affect its intensity, making the symptoms better or worse?

BDD symptoms can wax and wane on their own, for no apparent reason. They seem to have a life of their own. But many people say that certain factors seem to temporarily "turn up or turn down the volume" on their preoccupations and distress.

People with BDD report that the following factors can make their BDD symptoms less intense: exercise, a "positive environment" (e.g., feeling accepted by others), being assertive, and keeping yourself busy with activities. As one woman said, "Work and other activities can decrease my concerns—when I'm impassioned about something, I focus less on my appearance." These factors typically don't cure BDD but can make the symptoms more manageable. People who also have bipolar disorder (manic depressive illness) say that their BDD symptoms temporarily remit when they're manic.

In my experience, the main thing that makes symptoms worse is stopping or lowering the dose of an effective medication (see Chapter 14 for details). Other things that can worsen BDD symptoms include seeing attractive people— in person, on television, in magazines—and comparing yourself with them, having the presence or ugliness of the perceived defect confirmed by other people, a "negative environment" (e.g., one in which the person is put down or undervalued), inactivity or unemployment, social situations, and stress.

People with acne typically say that their preoccupation gets worse when their acne flares. Compulsive hair cutters typically feel worse after a hair-cutting binge, and skin pickers usually feel worse after picking. Many women say their symptoms worsen premenstrually. While social situations can make BDD symptoms more painful for many people, occasionally they're largely limited to social situations. As Zach explained, "When I'm by myself, my symptoms are hardly there. But as soon as I'm around people, I think they're aware of my mouth, and I'm no longer rational. I think that other people are noticing my lips. I become obsessed and anxious, and my rational thinking about them goes out the window." Social situations significantly worsened Zach's symptoms and also decreased his insight into their irrational nature.

It can be helpful to avoid some of these exacerbating factors—for example, comparing with others and looking through magazines at attractive people. But you're better off facing some of them, such as social situations, (see Chapter

14). In the long run, you'll feel better if you expose the defect, if possible, and go to social events.

Concluding Thoughts

A complex chain of steps is likely required for BDD to develop. As appears to be the case for many, if not most, psychiatric disorders—as well as medical diseases—BDD probably results from a combination of factors. There is no one single cause. Genetic and neurobiological factors likely lay the groundwork for BDD, and psychological and sociocultural factors may also contribute. Symptoms most likely result from a complex interaction between genetic and environmental factors that create a circuitous pathway from the underlying genes to BDD symptoms.

Neurobiological factors probably provide a template for BDD, making the process of preoccupation, excessive worry, and ritualistic behaviors possible. This process likely involves serotonin, other brain neurotransmitters, and certain brain structures. Perhaps neurobiological and genetic factors also increase risk for BDD by conferring an unusual sensitivity to the effect of stressful life events or negative comments about appearance.

Sociocultural and psychological factors—including personality traits, certain life experiences, and cultural values—probably combine with this biologically based vulnerability to further increase the risk of developing BDD. Such factors might also influence the *content* of BDD preoccupations—for example, the exact location of the perceived defect. It's possible that evolutionary factors may also influence the content of BDD concerns, as reflected by the high rate of concerns with symmetry and skin blemishes. If BDD and OCD are eventually shown to have similar neurobiological underpinnings, might psychological or environmental factors influence whether BDD, as opposed to OCD, develops? For example, if a family member gets ill, might you be more likely to develop worries about illness and germs (OCD), whereas if you're teased about your hair, might this channel your obsessive tendencies into BDD?

Theories about BDD's cause should account for the age when it usually begins. Does BDD usually begin during adolescence because of the rapid and dramatic appearance changes occurring at this time? Or because adolescents normally become more self-conscious, more interested in their appearance, and may begin to judge their appearance more negatively? Might the brain development and maturation that occurs during adolescence contribute to its onset at this age? All of these factors may play a role.

To answer the critically important question of what causes BDD much more research is needed. We need family studies to elucidate whether BDD is linked to—and therefore might share causal sources with—other psychiatric disorders. Twin and adoption studies are needed to disentangle the role of genetic versus environmental determinants of BDD, both likely contributors. Brain-imaging, genetic, neuropsychological studies, and other studies of BDD's underlying neurobiology, as well as the development of animal models of BDD, are likely to elucidate brain processes in BDD. Studies of psychological factors, including life events, and cross-cultural studies are also needed. The role of earlier risk factors needs to be differentiated from those that occur later in life and appear to acutely trigger BDD's onset in some people. Ultimately, understanding what causes BDD will help us develop more effective treatments and may even enable us to prevent this devastating illness from ever occurring.

·· eleven ··

Aren't We All Concerned with How We Look? BDD, Body Image, and Normal Appearance Concerns

We'd All Like to Look Better

Most of us care about how we look. This is why BDD strikes a chord with so many people. BDD echoes normal appearance concerns.

Most of us want to look acceptable, if not attractive. In a nationwide 1986 survey by Dr. Thomas Cash and his colleagues of 30,000 respondents published in *Psychology Today* magazine, only 18% of men and 7% of women had little concern about their appearance and didn't do much to improve it. The vast majority thought about, paid attention to, valued, and actively worked on their looks. Adolescents, especially females, reported the strongest appearance concerns.

Not only do most of us care about how we look, but most of *dislike* how we look. In a landmark survey of 3,452 women and 548 men published in *Psychology Today* magazine in 1997, more than half of all women—56%—and nearly half of all men—43%—said they were dissatisfied with their overall appearance. Even more were dissatisfied with particular body areas. For example, 71% of women and 63% of men were dissatisfied with how their mid-torso looked. Another, more scientifically sound survey of women done in 1995 by Cash and Henry found that nearly half of women reported overall body image dissatisfaction.

Many other studies support these findings. One survey, for example, found that nearly one-third of teenagers worry that they weigh too much. Yet another showed that 81% of ten year olds had already dieted at least once. In general, studies indicate that women generally want to be thinner, whereas men are just as likely to want added bulk.

There's also a high rate of *distorted* body image in the general population, involving both the body as a whole and specific parts, typically the waist and hips. Researcher J. Kevin Thompson, for example, found that more than 95% of the women he studied overestimated their body size. Their estimates were typically one-fourth larger than their actual body size. Of interest, these same women accurately judged the body size of other people.

Similarly, the previously mentioned 1986 survey by Thomas Cash found that 47% of females and 29% of males who were actually normal weight classified themselves as overweight. Men were equally divided between those who thought they were too heavy and those who believed they were too thin. Adolescents also tend to overestimate body size. Generally, women distort more than men, and distortions are greater when people are asked how they *feel* they look than when asked how they *think* they look.

How to Differentiate BDD from Normal Appearance Concerns

So many of us are concerned about, dislike, and even have a distorted view of how we look. Judith Rodin has referred to these widespread concerns as "normative discontent," a term that reflects how pervasive this unhappiness is. BDD echoes these normal and common appearance concerns. In some ways, the concerns of people with BDD are similar to what most of us experience.

Indeed, the difference between BDD and normal appearance concerns may be largely a matter of degree. Most likely, dissatisfaction with appearance spans a continuum, from mild to moderate to severe and even disabling. BDD may be at the severe end of this continuum of concern and dissatisfaction. BDD-related behaviors may also be conceptualized as more extreme versions of normal behaviors. Grooming, checking our appearance in the mirror, and dieting are things most of us do. When done in moderation, they're common and normal. But people with BDD carry them to an extreme.

In support of this theory that BDD is a more extreme version of normal concern, there's a "gray area" between mild BDD and normal appearance concerns. In some cases it can be hard to determine where normal concern leaves off and BDD begins. Does an adolescent girl who worries that her breasts are too small and feels shy around boys as a result have BDD? Does a man whose slightly thinning hair makes him feel anxious around women and anxious about asking them out on a date have BDD? Severe BDD is easily distinguished from normal appearance concerns. The adolescent boy who won't go to school or go out with friends because of a few pimples on his face, and the man who quits job after job because he thinks his buttocks are asymmetrical, clearly have BDD. But what about milder concerns? How do we differentiate them from BDD? Appearance concerns are very common, and the boundary between mild BDD and normal appearance concerns is fuzzy.

The same dilemma applies to certain other psychiatric disorders that echo normal and common concerns. The boundary between normal grieving and depression, for example, is sometimes unclear. Grief after the death of a loved one is very common and expected. In some cases, it may be difficult to distinguish between a high degree of normal grief and excessive grief that's pathological and requires treatment. It isn't hard to differentiate moderately severe or severe cases from normal. But in milder cases, it's more difficult.

While this "gray area" also applies to certain other psychiatric disorders, the distinction between mild BDD and normal concern may be especially unclear, because appearance concerns are so common. In addition, cultural factors influence how the body is viewed and how much attention its imperfections receive, further blurring the boundary between normal and abnormal concern.

At this time, there aren't any brain imaging tests, blood tests, or other similar tools for diagnosing BDD. Our best guide to differentiating BDD from normal appearance concerns are the DSM-IV criteria for BDD: *preoccupation, distress,* and *impairment in functioning.* To meet criteria for BDD, the person must be preoccupied. Everyone with BDD whom I've seen has at some point worried about their appearance for at least an hour a day. I'm reluctant to make the diagnosis in anyone who worries less than this, because their preoccupation may not be excessive enough to warrant a psychiatric diagnosis. But the hour-a-day guideline isn't fixed in stone and needs further empirical validation.

To be considered BDD, appearance concerns must also cause clinically significant distress or impairment in functioning. Nearly all people with BDD experience both. One potential drawback of this definition is that "clinically significant" is a somewhat imprecise term that involves informed judgment. The opinion of a mental health professional can be helpful in determining whether appearance concerns are clinically significant. In most cases of BDD, however, the degree of preoccupation, distress, and impairment in functioning is clearly greater than what most people experience. Most people may have *BDD-like* concerns, but most people don't have BDD.

It's interesting to hear what people with BDD say about how their BDD concerns differ from normal appearance concerns. In making this differentiation, they often use preoccupation, distress, and impairment as their benchmarks. Kathleen disliked her "wide" nose, "fat" stomach, and "grotesque" veins on her legs. She considered her nose concerns to constitute BDD, but her stomach and vein concerns to be "normal." "With my stomach and veins, it's different," she explained. "I can accept them and put them into perspective. My nose takes up much more of my time. I think about it a lot, and it's getting in the way of my life. My stomach and legs bother me, but they don't cause me such intense anxiety and pain. They don't keep me from socializing. My nose drives me out of my mind."

Melanie similarly described the difference between her appearance concerns and those of other people. "My concern is totally obsessive—it's on my mind for hours a day—and it makes me miserable. Other peoples' appearance concerns don't make them so depressed, stop them from walking out the door, or make them unable to laugh at a joke. My concerns take all of my concentration, and they take over my life."

Kathleen's and Melanie's BDD concerns echoed normal concerns, but they were more intense and severe. They worried too much, and they suffered. Many people with BDD have some additional normal concerns about their appearance, which they can usually easily differentiate from their BDD concerns.

Thus, BDD appears to differ *quantitatively*—by a matter of degree—from normal appearance concerns, lying at the severe end of a continuum or dimension of appearance preoccupation and dissatisfaction. But does BDD also differ from normal concerns in a more substantial and fundamental way? Is it also *qualitatively* different from normal appearance concerns? In other words, is there a point of rarity or discontinuity that suggests a natural cutoff point between BDD and health?

The answer to this question is probably yes. BDD does seem to differ from normal appearance concerns in ways other than its severity. One difference is that BDD appears to affect an approximately equal number of men and women, whereas studies of the general population indicate that more women than men are unhappy with how they look. In addition, surveys of the general population have generally found that people usually dislike their weight or weight–related aspects of appearance, such as the size of their abdomen, hips, or thighs. For example, in a 1972 *Psychology Today* survey, 48% of women were dissatisfied with their weight, 50% with their abdomen, and 49% with their hips and upper thighs. Only 11% were dissatisfied with their face. And in the 1997 *Psychology Today* survey I previously mentioned, 44% of women said that looking at their stomach in the mirror was very upsetting, whereas only 16% said this about their face. Among people with BDD, however, facial concerns are most common.

Another qualitative difference between BDD and normal concerns is that BDD symptoms often diminish with medication. We wouldn't expect normal appearance concerns to improve with medication, because the medication normalizes a "chemical imbalance"; if a chemical imbalance doesn't exist in the first place, medications wouldn't be expected to have this effect.

Perhaps the best evidence for qualitative differences between BDD and normal appearance concerns are the MRI study and the two neuropsychological studies that I discussed in chapter 10. Although the results need to be replicated by other researchers, as a group people with BDD differed from healthy control subjects. In addition, a study I'll discuss below found that people with BDD differed from healthy control subjects in their ability to visually discriminate between similar-appearing objects.

These differences between BDD and normal concern (or between people with BDD and healthy control subjects) suggest that BDD may be qualitatively different from normal concern, with different psychological and biological processes coming into play. This seems especially likely in those with delusional BDD or delusional referential thinking. Additional biological studies (e.g., brain imaging) and other studies are likely to help us solve this puzzle.

The qualitative and quantitative hypotheses are not incompatible. It's possible—even likely—that BDD is *both* qualitatively and quantitatively different from normal appearance concerns. BDD may be on a continuum with normal appearance concerns—differing quantitatively, as a more severe version of normal concern. But it's likely that at some point on this continuum, qualitatively different psychological and/or biological mechanisms (e.g., involving the brain chemicals serotonin and/or dopamine) begin to come into play. This model is similar to that for high blood pressure: higher blood pressure is on a continuum with lower blood pressure, differing quantitatively, or by degree. But at the higher end of this continuum, qualitatively different physiologic mechanisms may come into play that pose dangers to one's health.

What Is Body Image?

Body image—something we all have—is a complex concept. Researchers have offered various definitions over the years. One offered by psychologists Thomas Cash and Thomas Pruzinsky is the following: Body image consists of the internal, subjective representations of physical appearance and bodily experience. Another useful definition from Paul Schilder, is "the picture of our own body which we form in our mind; that is to say, the way in which the body appears to ourselves." Body image is our internal self-portrait. BDD is a problem with body image, not actual appearance.

Body image is an umbrella term for a large number of concepts. It consists of many dimensions and has been said to include such diverse concepts as the body's position in space, perception of bodily sensations, and attractiveness. When even more broadly defined, it's been referred to as body ego, body schema, and self-concept. Body image has been said to embrace our view of ourselves, not only physically but also psychologically, sociologically, and psychologically. Usually, however, narrower definitions (such as those of Drs. Cash and Pruzinsky) are used.

The scientific literature on body image has a long and scholarly history. It's been explored not only by neurologists, psychologists, and psychiatrists, but also by social scientists and philosophers. Luminaries such as Henry Head, Paul Schilder, Sigmund Freud, and Seymour Fisher have investigated such mysteries as how we distinguish self from non-self, and the cause of bizarre body-image experiences such as the phantom limb syndrome (the experience of still feeling the presence of one's limb following amputation) and neglect (denial of the existence of parts of the body after brain damage).

Body Image in BDD

Despite the long and rich history of body-image research, body image in BDD is just beginning to be studied. In recent years, some illuminating work has been done on this interesting and important topic. Figure 7 presents a hypothesized model of body image in BDD, which incorporates research findings and clinical observations. This model also reflects some of what's known about body image in people more generally (i.e., people without BDD). I'll describe this model below.

Figure 7.   A Proposed Model of Body Image in BDD

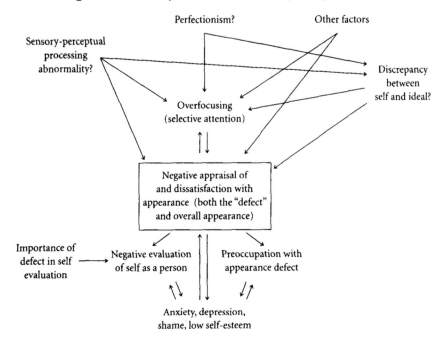

For the sake of simplicity, this model omits certain elements of a model of BDD's development, such as:

1. Genetic and environmental contributions to a possible perceptual abnormality, perfectionism, and other elements in the model (see Figure 6, p. 160);
2. Behavioral elements that may contribute to selective attention, e.g., mirror checking and reinforcement of BDD beliefs, e.g., social avoidance, (see Figure 9, p. 259);
3. Perception of the views of other people

Dissatisfaction with the "Defect" and Overall Body Image

The core of the model (shown in the center box of Figure 7) is negative appraisal of body image and dissatisfaction with body image—both the perceived defect and overall appearance. A small study done in 1982 found that people with BDD were less satisfied with their appearance than healthy control subjects, and they were more likely to feel their body was unacceptable. In a study I did of 97 people with BDD, I assessed body image with the Multidimensional Body-Self Relations Questionnaire (MBSRQ). Compared to scores of 1,070 females and 996 males from a U.S. national survey, people with BDD felt significantly less physically attractive and more dissatisfied with their overall appearance. Compared to the healthy controls, they were also more dissatisfied with discrete body features. However, as a group those with BDD weren't more dissatisfied with their weight. The people who were most dissatisfied with their looks were women, those with more severe BDD, and those with more delusional BDD. Compared to the healthy controls, people with BDD were also more invested (cognitively and behaviorally) in their appearance; men were even more invested than women.

Dr. James Rosen obtained similar results in his CBT treatment study (see Chapter 14) in which he used one of the subscales from the same body image questionnaire (MBSRQ). Before treatment, women with BDD felt physically unattractive and highly dissatisfied with their overall appearance.

Table 11 below shows results from my second BDD series, which illustrate several other parts of the model in Figure 7. Study participants were interviewed with the Body Dysmorphic Disorder Examination (BDDE), developed by Dr. Rosen. The table presents average scores for some of the scale's individual items for 98 people with current BDD. Items are scored from 0 to 6, with 6 indicating

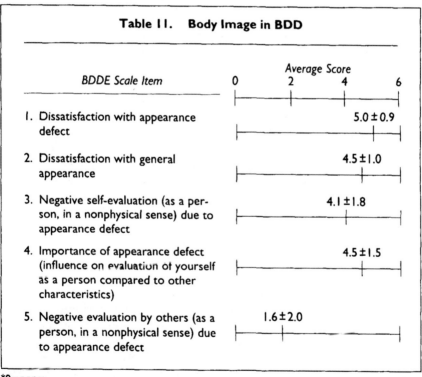

Table 11. Body Image in BDD

BDDE Scale Item	Average Score
1. Dissatisfaction with appearance defect	5.0 ± 0.9
2. Dissatisfaction with general appearance	4.5 ± 1.0
3. Negative self-evaluation (as a person, in a nonphysical sense) due to appearance defect	4.1 ± 1.8
4. Importance of appearance defect (influence on evaluation of yourself as a person compared to other characteristics)	4.5 ± 1.5
5. Negative evaluation by others (as a person, in a nonphysical sense) due to appearance defect	1.6 ± 2.0

*0=none;
2=Slight dissatisfaction, some importance, or slightly negative;
4=Moderate dissatisfaction, moderate importance (definitely one of the main aspetcs of self-evaluation), or moderately negative evaluation;
6=Extreme dissatisfaction, extreme importance (nothing is more important), or extremely negative evaluation
± indicates the standard deviation; two thirds of study participants had a score within 1 standard deviation of the average score

the most severe body image symptoms. As you can see from the first two items in the table, this study, too, shows that people with BDD are dissatisfied with their appearance—both the perceived defect and their overall appearance. However, they're somewhat more dissatisfied with the defect than their overall appearance. In another study, Dr. Martin Antony in England found something similar: compared to healthy control subjects, people with BDD rated both their perceived defect and their overall appearance as very unattractive; however, their ratings of the "defective" feature were even more negative than ratings of overall appearance. These research results and others I'll discuss below suggest that people with BDD tend to: 1) Judge their perceived defect very negatively; 2) Judge other aspects of their appearance more accurately and less negatively; and 3) Give more weight to the "defect" than to the rest of their appearance, which makes their evaluation of their overall appearance negative.

Consistent with these conclusions, when Dr. David Veale asked 50 people with BDD how they'd look if they didn't have their defects, 82% said they would be attractive. Similarly, when I asked people with BDD the question "*Excluding your defect, how would you rate your attractiveness?*" they tended to judge their attractiveness fairly accurately. Most (64%) rated their appearance as average. Thirty percent rated themselves as attractive (above average), and only 5% as unattractive (below average). But when asked to rate their overall attractiveness *including* the defects, self-ratings plummeted. Only 4% said they were attractive, 23% said they were average, and nearly three quarters said they were unattractive. Many people explain the decrease in their overall rating by saying that the defect "takes over"; they weight it more heavily than other aspects of their appearance. As one man said, "Overall, my looks aren't too bad. I'm not ugly. But because of my nose I look ugly. All I can focus on is my nose."So these findings suggest that people with BDD judge their "defective" areas very negatively and inaccurately while evaluating other aspects of their appearance less negatively and more accurately. Ratings of their overall appearance are also negative, suggesting that their negative ratings of the perceived defect seems to unduly impact ratings of their overall appearance.

Overfocusing: Powerful Fuel for BDD

Overfocusing, or selective attention, might cause dissatisfaction with appearance. It may even create a type of visual distortion, in that focusing on one particular aspect of appearance gives that area visual prominence and makes it very noticeable. Other aspects of appearance fade into the background and may even be ignored. The view becomes unbalanced. By emphasizing the defect, it becomes unduly negative. One woman told me, "I can't even see my own face. All I see is my defect." Another said, "I focus on the negative things, and they become too prominent. I lose my balance; I get tunnel vision. I put too much weight on one particular aspect and get bogged down in it." One of my patients said that focusing on a small pimple would cause it to "grow to hideous proportions." He made a mountain out of a molehill. A man I treated said, "It's like when I put my thumb under a microscope—that's how I see my skin. I'm like a walking microscope—my perspective is off. I can't see my whole face the way other people do."

These comments fit with the neuropsychological study results discussed in chapter 10, which showed that people with BDD overfocus on minor, irrelevant details and don't see the big picture. They miss the forest for the trees. Extrapolating to appearance, rather than seeing all of themselves and focusing on liked—as well as disliked—body areas, they seem to overfocus on and selectively attend to disliked areas, which unduly influences their ratings of overall attractiveness and makes them negative (see Figure 7, p. 192). Furthermore, as shown in the figure, individuals come to the conclusion that they look bad based on "selective interpretation"—this conclusion is based on "evidence" that other people don't see as valid (e.g., thinking you're being stared at).

Self-portraits of people with BDD also illustrate this. They tend to emphasize the perceived defect while giving only cursory attention to other body parts. One woman, for example, drew a massive, messy, and detailed head of hair while portraying the rest of her body as a stick figure. A man's self-portrait consisted only of 3 views of his nose, covered with huge and gaping holes.

Does BDD Involve a Sensory-Perceptual Abnormality?

What factors might contribute to this overfocusing and dissatisfaction with appearance? The proposed model in Figure 7 shows several possibilities. One is that at least some people with BDD may have a visual/perceptual processing abnormality (a primary sensory processing deficit). This may cause them to actually see something that other people can't see, or to have a distorted sensory perception of a minor anomaly. This would be expected to lead to overfocusing on and dissatisfaction with the perceived abnormality.

Some people's descriptions of what they perceive seem to support this theory. They say that they actually see a physical anomaly—such as significant balding when they actually have a very full and bushy head of hair. One man said, "There's a clash between what I see and what I think. I think my worries are ridiculous. But I see it!" A woman told me, "I sometimes think I don't see my face correctly, that I'm like my mother after she had her stroke." Some people's self-portraits portray the disliked aspects of appearance in a very distorted fashion, suggesting that perceptual distortion may be present.

Another piece of evidence supporting the theory that some people with BDD experience a perceptual distortion is that when their BDD improves with a serotonin-reuptake inhibitor, they report that the defect has disappeared. They no longer see it! The red spots are gone. The excessive facial hair has disappeared. They now see more hair on their head. One young man told me, after responding very well to fluvoxamine (Luvox), that his hair now looked fuller to him. He actually asked me to tell the pharmaceutical company that Luvox makes hair grow! He thought it was actually growing back. He wasn't sure how to explain this, but it was a definite change that he could see.

A young woman told me that within several days of responding to fluoxetine (Prozac), the "gorilla mask" disappeared from her face. "It's gone?" I asked her, amazed that her supposedly excessive and dark facial hair had disappeared. "Yes, I don't see it anymore. It isn't there," she replied. "Where do you think it went?" I asked, very pleased with the change but also wondering how the hair could have suddenly disappeared. "How could your face have changed so quickly?" "I don't know," she replied. "But it's gone." "Is it still there and looks the same, but you no longer think it's ugly, or does it actually *look* different to you—you actually don't *see* it anymore?" I asked her. "It's *gone*," she replied. "I know what I see. It's not there anymore." When she decreased her dose of Prozac, the hair reappeared.

Some people, like this woman, whose defects disappeared when they took a serotonin-reuptake inhibitor saw the defects again when they lowered their dose or discontinued the medication. One person told me that the holes in his teeth disappeared every time we increased his clomipramine (Anafranil) dose. He didn't *see* them anymore. When we decreased the dose slightly to avoid side effects, the holes came back. This cycle repeated itself many times. He, too, insisted that his teeth changed visually. It wasn't that the holes were still there but he decided they weren't so ugly or that he could tolerate them better. They actually closed up. One possible explanation for these experiences, as discussed in Chapter 10, is that serotonin appears to influence vision. It may protect people from overreacting to unimportant visual input, such as minimal flaws in appearance.

It's also possible, however, that people with BDD don't have a visual/perceptual processing abnormality. They may see themselves accurately but interpret what they see negatively, considering it ugly and unacceptable. Several small preliminary studies suggest that in fact certain aspects of their visual processing may be normal. A study by Dr. Sabine Wilhelm and her colleagues found that people with BDD have a normal ability to recognize other people's faces. And a study by Thomas and Goldberg found that BDD patients' assessments of their own facial proportions were even more accurate than those of normal controls or cosmetic surgery patients (although this study didn't assess perception of the specific body areas the patients disliked).

In a study I did with Elissa Aminoff and Dr. Mike Tarr, BDD participants had poorer visual discrimination ability than healthy controls. This study used a computerized visual discrimination task involving various objects (e.g., snowflakes and faces), but not the study participant's own face. Compared to healthy control subjects, people with BDD had difficulty accurately discriminating different objects from one another. Their visual discrimination problems didn't appear due to a deficit in visual sensory processing, however. Rather, it seemed to be caused by problems paying attention to the task. Perhaps this is because they were distracted by worries about how they looked.

Taken together, the various studies I just described, while preliminary, suggest that people with BDD don't have a primary perceptual/visual processing deficit. Although they're less good than healthy controls at visually discriminating different objects from one another, this appears due to *problems paying attention* to the task, rather than a visual processing problem. And when it comes to their own face, they may have more acute—in fact, hyperacute— visual discrimination. This may be because they *pay more attention* to and *overly focus* on the details of their face. This overfocusing could lead to amplification and distortion of minor irregularities or flaws. Paradoxically, hyperacute visual processing might actually cause a type of visual distortion, in that minor flaws become magnified, and a holistic perspective is lost. The improvement in the defect that some patients see after SRI treatment may result, at least in part, from a decrease in this excessive focus and an improved ability to see the larger picture of how they look.

Are People with BDD Perfectionistic?

To go back to the model in Figure 7, might people with BDD overfocus on and dislike their appearance because they're perfectionistic? Some people with BDD say that they're perfectionistic about their appearance, or about things more generally. This may cause them to overfocus on little flaws they don't like and be unhappy with them. Dr. Veale found that 69% of 50 people with BDD agreed that they had to have perfection in their appearance, although it's unclear whether they're perfectionistic only about the perceived defects or about their appearance more generally. My clinical impression is that for many people with BDD (but not all), it's the former. As I discussed in the last chapter, Dr. Sabine Wilhelm found that compared to healthy controls, people with BDD tend to have high levels of perfectionism in areas unrelated to appearance.

A Discrepancy between Actual Self and Ideal Self

Perfectionism might also fuel BDD symptoms in another way. As shown in Figure 7, research findings suggest that people with BDD tend to have a significant discrepancy between how they see themselves and how they ideally would like to look. A study by Dr. Veale and his colleagues found that people with BDD, compared to healthy control subjects, had significantly larger discrepancies between how they think they *actually look* and both 1) how they *ideally would like* to look and 2) how they think they *should* look.

This finding supports Thompson's "self-ideal discrepancy" hypothesis, in which dissatisfaction is proposed to result from discrepancy between the self and an ideal. As the figure shows, perfectionism may further amplify this discrepancy. "I have a different skin standard for myself," a teacher told me. "It's very high. I have to be perfect in every way." Another person said, "My perfectionism and high standards for my appearance are related to the distortion. It's why I look worse to myself than I do to others." It's unclear, however, to what extent this discrepancy between self and ideal in BDD is due to perfectionism regarding the defect in particular, unrealistically high standards for appearance in general, or underestimation of one's attractiveness—or some combination of these factors. Another possible explanation is that people with BDD may be more aesthetically sensitive than average. Dr. Veale found that compared to people with other disorders, people with BDD were more likely have a job or education in art or design. I have found that 1–2% of people with BDD currently work in art or design, which is about twice as high as in the general U.S. population. As shown in Figure 7, looking much worse than you ideally would like to look would be expected to fuel overfocusing on perceived flaws and dissatisfaction with appearance.

Getting Down on Yourself

People with BDD tend to feel negatively about themselves as a person because of their appearance flaws. As item 3 on Table 11 shows, people with BDD report that the perceived appearance defect has a fairly big influence on how they judge themselves as a person in a nonphysical sense (for example, thinking that the appearance flaws make them uninteresting or undesirable). They also say that the appearance defect is important to how they judge themselves as a person in comparison to other personal characteristics such as their personality, intelligence, life values, and ability at work (see item 4 on Table 11). However, people with BDD tend to believe that other people judge them only slightly negatively as a person because of their defect (see item 5 on Table 11). So people with BDD seem to judge themselves more harshly and negatively as a person than they think other people do.

It's interesting that while the perceived appearance defect has a fairly strong influence on how people with BDD evaluate *themselves* as a person, Dr. Veale found that most people with BDD judge *other people* on the basis of many factors, rather than appearance. In a similar vein, Dr. Wilhelm found that when rating the attractiveness of photos, including their own, people with BDD underestimated their own attractiveness and overestimated the attractiveness of beautiful faces. Taken together, these findings suggest that people with BDD are harder on themselves than they are on others. As shown in Figure 7, this might be expected to fuel anxiety, depression, shame, and low self-esteem, which in turn may further amplify negative evaluation of oneself and appearance preoccupations.

Improving Body Image in BDD

Several studies have investigated whether body image improves when BDD is treated. Dr. Rosen's study of cognitive behavioral therapy (CBT) (see Chapter 14) evaluated body image before and after CBT treatment using a subscale of the MBSRQ. After treatment, the study participants felt more physically attractive and more satisfied with their appearance. In my study of fluoxetine versus placebo (see Chapter 13), which also used the MBSRQ, fluoxetine did not improve appearance satisfaction more than placebo (a sugar pill). However, fluoxetine was more effective than placebo in diminishing the importance of appearance and behavioral investment in appearance (e.g., excessive grooming activities). And in my fluoxetine (Prozac) and fluvoxamine (Luvox) studies, treatment with the SRI generally improved the perceived appearance flaw, in some cases even making it disappear. Of the people who responded to one of these medications, 60% said that the appearance flaw seemed better when they were taking the medication. Of this 60%, two thirds said that it actually looked better visually; the other one third said it looked the same visually, but they liked it better.

It's interesting that in the computerized visual discrimination study I mentioned above, BDD participants who were taking an SRI tended to perform more like healthy control subjects, whereas BDD participants who weren't on an SRI performed more poorly. In other words, those on an SRI had better visual discriminatory abilities. The reason for this isn't clear. However, because SRIs decrease appearance-related preoccupations and anxiety, they may have helped BDD participants better attend to and focus on the computerized task.

Other Insights About Body Image in BDD

The model shown in Figure 7 is very preliminary, and much more research is needed to modify, shape, and expand it. Nonetheless, it's a starting point for trying to understand body image disturbance in BDD and how it may fuel BDD symptoms. The model involves several domains considered important in body image disturbance more generally and in disorders in which body image has been extensively studied, such as eating disorders. These domains are 1) cognitive (e.g., appearance dissatisfaction, negative evaluation of self, preoccupation), 2) emotional (e.g., anxiety and depression), 3) perceptual, and 4) behavioral (behavioral elements of BDD such as avoidance and rituals are shown in the figure in Chapter 14). These domains need to be further researched in BDD and compared to other disorders.

To my knowledge, only one study has compared body image in BDD and another disorder. This study, by Dr. Rosen, compared 51 men and women with BDD to 45 women with an eating disorder (anorexia or bulimia) and to 50 nonclinical healthy control subjects. As might be expected, people with an eating disorder were mainly preoccupied with weight and body shape (e.g., the thighs and stomach), whereas those with BDD were preoccupied with a more diverse array of body areas—most often, the skin. The BDD and eating disorder groups had equally severe body image symptoms overall, which were much more severe than for the healthy control subjects. For example, the BDD and eating disorder groups had similar levels of body dissatisfaction and feelings of unattractiveness. However, people with BDD reported more negative self-evaluation due to appearance and more avoidance of activities due to self-consciousness about how they look.

The "Insider/Outsider" View

Some research on body image more generally appears relevant to BDD. A consistent finding by body-image researchers—and one clearly relevant to BDD—is that there's only a weak association between subjective body image and objective attractiveness. In other words, the view from the "inside" (our perception of our own physical appearance) doesn't match that from the "outside" (other people's view of how we look. As Thomas Cash has stated, beauty is no guarantee of a favorable body image, nor is homeliness a decree for a negative body image.

This common mismatch is a central aspect of BDD. People with BDD view their appearance—in particular, their "defective" body area—very differently than other people do. BDD occurs in people of varying overall attractiveness, some of whom are very attractive. Furthermore, I've found no association between the actual appearance of the perceived defect per se and severity of BDD symptoms—in other words, BDD symptoms are just as severe in those with no defect whatsoever as in those with a present (although slight) defect. Just as in the rest of the population, "insider" and "outsider" views clearly differ in BDD.

Body Image, Depression, and Self-Esteem

In various groups of people—patients with BDD, patients with other illnesses, and nonpatients—body-image distortion and dissatisfaction are associated with depression, low self-esteem, and general psychological distress. The greater the extent of body-image distortion (e.g., size overestimation), the stronger the depression and the lower the self-esteem. Females appear to suffer from these problems more than males. What a person *actually* looks like, however, has little relationship to self-esteem. One of the previously mentioned *Psychology Today* surveys found that more than 90% of people with positive feelings about their appearance, fitness, or health reported favorable psychological adjustment (i.e., a positive self-concept, life satisfaction, and the absence of loneliness and depression). In contrast, negative evaluations of appearanec, fitness, and health were associated with poorer psychosocial adjustment.

Another link between emotional distress and appearance dissatisfaction comes from a dermatology study which found that patients with acne scored far lower than the general population on measures of general emotional well-being. Amazingly, patients with acne reported poorer emotional adjustment than patients with malignant melanoma, a type of skin cancer. The authors hypothesized that the low scores of acne patients were due to the lowered self-esteem that acne can cause.

In these studies, the direction of causality is generally unclear. Do body-image distortion and dissatisfaction *cause* depression, low self-esteem, and poorer psychological adjustment? Or do these latter factors cause poor body image? Or both? Or are poor body image and other psychological factors simply associated, without a causal connection? Despite this lack of clarity, the association between poorer psychological adjustment and a dislike of, or a distorted view of, one's appearance is clear.

The Burden, Pain, and Isolation of Actual Disfigurement

Erving Goffman, other researchers, and authors such as Lucy Grealy have vividly and movingly described the burden, emotional pain, and social isolation of people with visible physical deformities. Such disfigurements may result from birth defects, illnesses, accidents, or other causes. I've been struck by how similar the experiences of many of these people are to those of people with BDD. This makes sense. Because people with BDD think—and may be completely convinced—that their defect looks unattractive, even grotesque, it's not surprising that their experience might be similar to that of people with actual disfigurement. Indeed, some people with BDD describe themselves this way: "I'm the third ugliest person in the world," "I look like a burn victim," "I look like the Elephant Man."

Research suggests that people with facial disfigurements are very aware of their deformities and other people's reaction to them. They feel stigmatized. They may assume that all of the behavior of others who interact with them is a reaction to their appearance. This awareness of being obviously deviant in a negative way profoundly shapes their self-concept and self-esteem, which may be quite low. The visibly damaged often feel a profound sense of shame and vulnerability to exposure, devaluation, and rejection. They may feel deeply defective and not quite human. These experiences are similar to those of many people with BDD.

Disfigured people generally need more energy to prepare for going out in public and must cope with emotional hurdles in social situations in which the defect will be visible. When they do go out into the world, they may hide the defect by disguising it. They often try to fade into the background rather than stand out "deviantly" in the crowd. They struggle to maintain self-esteem and be accepted by others. McGregor describes one reaction to facial disfigurement as "social death"—that is, badly disfigured individuals may cut off their relationships with the world and go into a closet existence. People with BDD—especially more severe BDD—experience strikingly similar feelings, fears, behaviors, and isolation.

You might think that people with actual deformities bear an extra burden because the world may actually respond to them less positively, or even with revulsion. But many people with BDD firmly *believe* that this is how others react to them. A majority believe—and many are completely convinced—that people take special notice of their defects. They may be so absorbed in their perceived defect that they interpret virtually any kind of response by another person as a reaction to the defect.

The body-image literature also notes that different people with actual physical deformities adapt quite differently to them. Some cope fairly well, whereas others don't. Various factors influence how a person reacts to a disability. This is also true in BDD, as some people are able to function relatively well while others are disabled by their body-image concerns. It's been said that to psychologically overcome a disability, one must stop thinking about it all the time and get on with living. Paradoxically, to stop thinking about the defect is exactly what's so difficult in BDD.

Shedding Light on Our Internal Self-Portrait

Body image in BDD is clearly important. Indeed, the fundamental problem in BDD is with body image, not actual appearance. However, our knowledge of this topic is still rudimentary. What I discussed in this chapter is preliminary and needs to be confirmed. Some of the excellent research that's been done in other groups (e.g., women with eating disorders) needs to be done in BDD. How do body image dissatisfaction and distortion develop in BDD, and how are they maintained? Do they involve a sensory perceptual distortion? Or do people see themselves accurately but simply dislike what they see? What other factors might contribute to body dissatisfaction? How is body image in BDD similar to and different from that of other disorders, such as eating disorders?

We clearly need to learn more about body image in BDD—to shed more light on that elusive, internal self-portrait. And most important, we need more research on how to improve body image in people with BDD. The preliminary findings above suggest that SRIs and CBT may accomplish this for some people. However, we still need to search for ways to help people with BDD feel more satisfied with their appearance and view themselves more accurately.

·· *twelve* ··

Getting Better:
A Treatment Guide

In the next four chapters, I'll discuss the important topic of how to overcome BDD. In this chapter, I'll give an overview of treatments and a brief general treatment guide. First, I'll describe a few patients and what treatments worked for them (and for many patients like them). Then, I'll discuss some common barriers to treatment and how you can overcome them. You'll need to do this before you can be successfully treated. Then I'll make some key points about effective treatments—specifically, medications known as serotonin-reuptake inhibitors (also called SRIs, or SSRIs) and a type of therapy known as cognitive behavioral therapy (CBT). I have so much to say about these two core treatments for BDD that I'll devote entire subsequent chapters to them (Chapters 13 and 14). In those chapters I'll describe these and other potentially helpful treatments in much more detail and will make additional practical treatment recommendations. Then, in Chapter 15 I'll discuss treatments that many people with BDD get (such as cosmetic surgery) but which don't seem to work, and which you're probably better off avoiding.

I'll make lots of specific treatment recommendations in the next four chapters. However, it's important to keep in mind that these are general guidelines and that there isn't a one-size-fits-all treatment approach for people with BDD. In general, the treatments I'll describe work well for most people, but they need to be tailored to some degree to each person. For example, most people can potentially benefit from an SRI, but the exact dose you need might differ from what someone else needs. And while you might respond best to the SRI Escitalopram (Lexapro), your friend might respond best to the SRI sertraline (Zoloft) or to another SRI. If you have another psychiatric disorder that an SRI doesn't work for, you may need additional medication or therapy for that problem. For example, some people with problematic anxiety do fine with an SRI alone, whereas some benefit from adding a medication like buspirone or a benzodiazepine (I'll describe all of these medications in the next chapter).

While CBT is often effective, the exact CBT approach that's used needs to be tailored to each person. Some people do better with a greater emphasis on cognitive therapy (which focuses on evaluating and changing beliefs), whereas others do fine with less emphasis on this and more on behavioral techniques (which focus on changing behaviors). Some people benefit from non-CBT therapy (for example, insight-oriented or supportive therapy, which I'll also discuss in chapter 14) in addition to CBT or an SRI. Other people don't need this. Some people do well with CBT alone, others with an SRI alone. Still others benefit most by combining these treatments.

I'd suggest that you become familiar with the basic treatment strategies in this book and then get the input of a doctor or therapist who's knowledgeable about BDD and has met with you for an evaluation. It's ideal to work as a team with a knowledgeable professional to tailor these treatments to you.

Patients' Responses to Treatment

Christina: A Good Response to Medication

When I first met Christina, she was worried that her skin wasn't clear enough. "It has red blotches on it and too many pimples," she said. "I've gotten depressed because of it. Every time I talk to someone they look at my skin, and they're thinking how bad it looks. It's really hard for me to be around other people at work and school."

Christina was indeed depressed. She felt sad and anxious, was tired all the time, and couldn't concentrate. She thought about her skin for more than eight hours a day and believed that other people took special notice of how bad it looked. Although she was very conscientious, she had missed several days of school in recent weeks. "I couldn't get myself out of the mirror, and I didn't want other people to see me," she explained. She was also having trouble doing her part-time job. She was avoiding people at work and was very quiet when she was around them because she felt so self-conscious.

Christina was reluctant to take medication but decided to give it a try. "If there's a chance it'll help, I'll try it," she said. "I don't like to take pills, but this is getting to be too much." She started fluvoxamine (Luvox), one of the serotonin-reuptake inhibitors. For the first few weeks nothing much happened. But during the third week, Christina thought she noticed that she was starting to obsess a little less and that she wasn't quite as depressed or anxious. During the fourth week, she called me. "I just want you to know how much better I'm feeling," she told me. "I really noticed a change yesterday. I went out with friends instead of staying home, and I had a great time!"

Over the next few weeks Christina continued to further improve. After 8 weeks of fluvoxamine treatment, her symptoms were essentially gone. "I can't believe this has happened," she said. "I had this problem for so long, and now it's gone!" Christina had had BDD for ten years; this was the first time since her symptoms began that she'd felt well. She was now thinking about her skin for only five minutes a day. Her emotional pain and depression were gone. She was going out with friends and dating for the first time in years. She was also doing very well in school and in her job.

Christina also realized that she had been distorting how bad she looked. Her skin looked fine to her now. "I just wasn't seeing myself clearly before," she said. "I feel like I've been blind, and now I have my sight back! I feel calmer, happier, and more confident. It's hard to believe the medication has made this much of a change, but it has. I feel the way I used to feel, before the BDD ever started. I feel great!"

Jason: A Good Response to Cognitive-Behavioral Therapy

Jason had tried several serotonin-reuptake inhibitors for his BDD but hadn't given them an adequate try because he was reluctant to take them religiously. He had also tried cognitive-behavioral therapy but hadn't really given this a good try either. He'd had BDD for 20 years and had been disabled by his symptoms.

Jason's concern focused on his lips. He thought that they were large and ugly and that they offended other people. He frequently licked them to improve their appearance, covered them, checked them in mirrors, and tried to keep them in a more attractive position. He also avoided other people as much as possible. He came for treatment because he wanted to improve his social life and return to work. He wanted to give cognitive-behavioral therapy another try. He was a good candidate for this treatment, because he was highly motivated to do CBT.

Jason's therapy consisted of several key CBT techniques. First, with his therapist's help, he cut way down on his mirror checking. It wasn't easy, but it helped a lot to resist the urge to check his lips in excruciating detail for hours a day. Instead, he looked in the mirror, at his entire face, for only a few minutes a day while grooming and brushing his teeth. He told me, "It's *much* better to stay about a foot away and not zero in on my lips an inch from the mirror for hours a day—now I realize when I get that close and stare at them that long they look really weird and distorted, and then I really freak out!" He also stopped licking his lips and covering them with his hand. Jason also did behavioral experiments to test his belief that his lips offended other people. This helped him learn that other people weren't bothered by his lips—in fact, they didn't seem to even notice them. He also learned how to identify and fix errors in his thinking that made him think he was very ugly and that other people thought so too. With his therapist's help, he gradually started going places that he feared and avoided. He began talking more with other people, speaking up in groups, and even went to some parties.

After five months of treatment, Jason felt much better. He was much less self-conscious and more relaxed around other people. He had better control over his thoughts. If he did start thinking his lips were ugly and that everyone was staring at them, he could recognize that these thoughts weren't realistic, and he could come up with more accurate and helpful beliefs. Jason was very pleased with his progress and felt he'd learned skills he could use in the future if his BDD ever flared up. "I really feel better after the CBT," he told me. "The BDD isn't controlling me anymore!"

David: A Good Response to Medication
plus Cognitive-Behavioral Therapy

David was feeling desperate. A 32-year-old disc jockey, he was at the point of quitting his job. He couldn't focus on his work because of his hair obsessions, and was often late because he couldn't tear himself away from the mirror in the morning. Even the expensive new hairpiece he'd bought to hide his slightly receding hairline didn't help him feel any better. "I don't like going out in public, and I've given up on dating," he said. "I don't want to date because someone will run their fingers through my hair and know it's a hairpiece. I can't focus on conversations because I think people are looking at my hair. At times I stay in completely; I don't even food shop."

In the week before he first saw me, David missed work three times and had considered going to an emergency room because he was so panicked about his hair. "I hate myself and how I look. I'm really down on myself. I've even had thoughts of ending my life. I can't live the rest of my life like this. How can you live in your own body if you can't stand it?"

David started taking fluoxetine (Prozac) right away. He continued supportive psychotherapy (see description below) which had helped him cope a little better but didn't diminish his BDD symptoms. As expected, the medication didn't work immediately, and the first month of treatment was rocky. David and I considered hospitalization several times. But with the support of friends, family, and his therapist, he maintained his will to live. About a month after beginning treatment, David started to feel somewhat better. His hair preoccupation began to wane, and the thoughts were less painful. He was more willing to see his friends. He didn't check mirrors all the time, and he sought reassurance less often. He was no longer considering suicide.

He then started CBT while continuing the medication. His CBT therapist helped him stop mirror checking and reassurance seeking. He started going out more and seeing friends. Finally, he even gave up his hairpiece. He received many compliments on his new hair style, and his self-confidence greatly improved.

Overcoming Barriers to Treatment:
The Critical First Steps to Success

Before they overcame BDD, David, Christina, and Jason all took some important initial steps, which made successful treatment possible. First, they acknowledged that they had a problem—that they worried too much about their appearance and that their worrying was a problem for them: it caused them too much emotional pain, made them depressed and anxious, and interfered with their functioning or caused difficulties for their family or friends.

They also recognized that they needed professional psychiatric help. Jason and David had attempted other approaches—trying harder, trying to reassure themselves that they looked okay, surgery, and hair clubs. They finally acknowledged to themselves that these approaches hadn't worked and weren't likely to ever work. Although Christina and David didn't like the idea of seeing a psychiatrist or taking medication, they did. They realized they had nothing to lose and potentially much to gain.

There are, unfortunately, many barriers to getting effective treatment for BDD, which need to be overcome. Some of them are the following.

- **Overcoming lack of knowledge about BDD**   Many people are unfortunately uninformed or misinformed about BDD, or are even unaware that it exists and often responds to psychiatric treatment.

What To Do: It's important to learn about BDD and its treatment. This is an essential first step to a successful outcome. In addition to reading this book, you may want to look at some of the suggested reading in Chapter 18. Also, researchers are learning more about BDD all the time. These research results get published in professional journals as they become available. While these articles are written for professionals and can be somewhat technical, many people with BDD, as well as friends and family, benefit from reading them. You can access these articles through Medline and PsychLit (see Chapter 18). This is a good way to learn about the latest research findings on BDD, including up-to-date information about treatment advances. Up-to-date articles are also sometimes written for nonprofessionals in various publications.

- **Overcoming embarrassment and shame**   Embarrassment and shame can be significant barriers to obtaining effective treatment. Many people never mention their BDD symptoms, even to a mental health professional, even though they consider them a major problem or their biggest problem. They may instead talk only about depression, anxiety, or relationship problems.

What To Do: Get up your courage and let someone know you have BDD. It may help to first confide in a family member or friend. Then see a mental health professional who's knowledgeable about the disorder (many, but not all, are) and tell them about your concerns. Approach this as you would if you were having stomach pains or chest pains. Tell the professional that you worry a lot about how you look and think you have BDD. Some people say it's helpful to bring an article about BDD or this book to their appointment to break the ice when raising the topic. Don't just say you're anxious or depressed, because you may get the wrong treatment.

- **Overcoming guilt and blame**   Some people with BDD are bogged down in guilt and blame. They may feel guilty because they think they caused their defect (for example, by picking their skin) or because they feel they've wasted their life by being so focused on how they look. Or they blame other people, such as a surgeon who operated on them or people they think made fun of how they looked. For some people, the guilt and blame are so paralyzing that they don't even try to get better.

What To Do: Focus on the present rather than the past. You can't undo the past, so it doesn't help to ruminate about it. Try to let go of your guilt; you aren't responsible for having BDD. Feeling guilty just unnecessarily adds to your pain. And feeling angry and blaming others isn't helpful either. It doesn't help you fix the problem, feel any better, or get on with your life. It's far better to acknowledge these feelings and then try to let them go. Focus instead on the present and future: try to make today and your future days as good as possible by getting treatment that works.

- **Diagnosing BDD**   Accurately diagnosing BDD is a necessary step toward effective treatment. If BDD isn't diagnosed, it probably won't be successfully treated. Unfortunately, BDD is still unfamiliar to some mental health professionals, and many people with BDD seek nonpsychiatric treatment, such as surgery, which doesn't seem to work. Perhaps most important, secrecy about BDD prevents the diagnosis from being made. In fact, studies have shown that although BDD is relatively common, it nearly always goes unrecognized and undiagnosed in clinical settings.

What To Do: Fill out the BDDQ, which is in Chapter 4, to see whether you may have BDD. The information in Chapters 3–8 should also help you figure out whether the diagnosis applies to you. Then I'd suggest following the advice above—getting an evaluation from a mental health professional familiar with BDD and telling them you think you have this disorder and want treatment for it.

- **Overcoming trivialization of BDD**   It's easy to trivialize BDD. Why should she care so much about how she looks? The fact that the person looks okay only compounds the problem. It may lead to reassurance—don't worry, you look fine—rather than effective treatment. Sometimes BDD is mistaken for vanity. For BDD to be diagnosed and adequately treated, family members and clinicians need to take the symptoms seriously; BDD must be recognized as a serious psychiatric disorder that can cause severe suffering.

What To Do: I hope that after reading this book, you're convinced that BDD is a serious disorder. If you want someone else in your life to take it seriously, you can talk with him or her about it. Or, you may want them to read this book; many people tell me this has helped other people understand BDD and realize that it's bona fide disorder and a serious problem.

- **"Your appearance concerns aren't your real problem"** This kind of statement is a common example of trivialization. When a person with BDD hears something like this, and are told that they need to figure out what their "real problem" is, they generally feel misunderstood. They may also feel angry, as did one person who told me "I've been told that BDD isn't my real problem. It's very frustrating, and I get angry over it—they don't get it! There's no mystery about what my problem is—*my nose* is what bugs me. It's painful!" Or, to be compliant, they may no longer discuss their BDD and even leave treatment. As one patient said, "If you treat BDD as something other than the real problem, the patient will never bring it up again."

What To Do: Although people with BDD may have other problems as well, it's important to recognize BDD as a real problem that in and of itself requires diagnosis and adequate treatment. It's best not to tell someone else that BDD isn't their "real problem." If you have BDD and someone tells you this, you don't have to accept it. Most important, if a doctor or therapist tells you this, and won't focus on BDD in treatment, he or she may not be the right therapist for you. Keep in mind, though, that if you do have other problems, it may help to get treatment for those problems as well as BDD.

- **"But I don't have BDD: I'm really ugly!"** In some cases, other people (such as friends, family members, or a health-care professional) realize the person has BDD, but the BDD sufferer doesn't. Insight before treatment is usually poor or absent, so the person with BDD thinks they're truly ugly and don't have BDD.

What To Do: Realize you can have BDD even if you think you don't—that it's typical for people with BDD to think they're truly ugly and don't have the disorder. If other people tell you that you look fine and that you have BDD, give them the benefit of the doubt—they could be right. If you're worrying a lot about how you look, and this concern is upsetting you and causing you emotional pain or problems in your life, you'll probably benefit from BDD treatments regardless of how you look. Effective treatment is likely to help you worry less and give you more control over your thoughts. It will also probably help you function better and feel less distressed and depressed. As one patient said to me, "It's hard to accept it's an actual illness. Once you can accept it and get the right treatment, you'll get your life back." So give the right treatment a try! There's nothing to lose.

- **Overcoming stigma** To some extent, psychiatric disorders are still unfortunately associated with stigma, which may make people reluctant to seek psychiatric treatment. However, this view is changing. Increasingly, psychiatric problems are being recognized as medical problems that deserve treatment, thanks in good part to the advocacy of consumer groups.

What To Do: Accept that BDD is a medical condition like diabetes or heart disease. It just happens to involve the brain, as many other medical conditions do too. You'd probably go to the doctor if you had bad chest pain, so why not go and get treatment if you're obsessed and have time-consuming behaviors you feel compelled to do? Remember that stigma is decreasing, and isn't something you need to buy into anyway. Would you feel stigmatized if you got treatment for a heart attack? Would you stigmatize someone else if they did? I hope not! BDD really isn't any different. It just happens to involve the brain rather than the heart.

- ***Overcoming reluctance to try psychiatric treatment***   Some people are reluctant to try psychiatric treatment. The reasons vary. Sometimes, it's a concern about stigma. For others, it's fear of the treatments themselves, which is often based on a misunderstanding of them and possible side effects. Others insist that surgery is the solution. Sometimes this reluctance stems from a desire to "do it on my own," and the person feels like a failure if they accept psychiatric care. While reluctance may be understandable, it shouldn't keep you from getting treatment and getting better. Although SRIs can have side effects and CBT can be challenging, most people fare well with these treatments and easily tolerate them. You shouldn't feel or look "drugged" while taking an SRI, and these medications aren't addictive. If medication side effects occur, or CBT is too difficult, a good doctor or therapist will work with you and probably succeed in making them tolerable. I'll say more about surgery in chapter 15, but as best we know it usually doesn't work for BDD and may even make you worse. It isn't a good substitute for psychiatric treatment. And trying to get better on your own is unlikely to work. Perhaps, if your BDD is mild, you may benefit from trying accepted CBT techniques on your own. But most people—and certainly those with moderate or severe BDD—will need professional help. As best we know, herbs, diet, "natural" remedies, and other strategies (other than SRIs or CBT) are unlikely to work.

When you overcome these barriers, the stage is set for a successful—in some cases a lifesaving—outcome. Anne, who had an excellent response to Celexa (citalopram) told me, "I'm feeling terrific, for the first time in 30 years." Like some people I've treated who responded to medication, Ann "tested" the medication by trying to bring her obsession back. But she couldn't. Sandy told me something similar: "The medication definitely curbs the obsession. It released a logjam. My life felt like a stream that had thousands of huge boulders and logs in it—the water couldn't flow through smoothly. Now it flows with ease. I feel full of energy and creativity." And after CBT, Jason felt that he—not the BDD—was in change of his life.

Key Points About Recommended Treatments

As I've already mentioned, several psychiatric treatments (serotonin-reuptake inhibitors [SRIs, or SSRIs], and CBT) appear to often be effective for BDD. Research has shown that they significantly diminish symptoms in a majority of people with BDD.

Many treatment research studies have been done since I wrote the first edition of this book. All of these studies support earlier and more preliminary indications that SRIs and CBT help a majority of people with BDD. These studies have also provided more detailed and very useful information about how to use these treatments successfully.

Despite these important advances, there's still much less research on treatments for BDD than for many other disorders, and more treatment research is greatly needed. For example, we need more research on the effectiveness of SRIs and CBT for BDD, and whether CBT or medication is more effective. We also need more research to determine whether other medications may boost the effectiveness of SRIs when SRIs aren't completely effective. We need to ascertain which elements of CBT work best. The only way we can answer these and many other important questions is to do research studies. These studies can be done only with funding and if people with BDD participate in them. I'm optimistic that much more treatment research will be done in the coming years, which will greatly benefit people suffering from BDD.

In the meantime, we already know a lot about treatments that work for BDD. Here is a brief summary of what we know at this time. These are the key points I'll be making about treatment. I'll say much more about each of them in the next three chapters:

Key Points about Treatment

- *Serotonin-reuptake inhibitors (SRIs, or SSRIs)—antidepressant medications with antiobsessional properties—appear effective for a majority of people with BDD.* With these medications, appearance-related preoccupations, as well as associated behaviors such as mirror checking usually diminish. Functioning often improves. People feel better—less depressed and anxious. Symptoms often diminish partially but may resolve completely. They are currently the medications of choice for BDD.

- *The following medications are SRIs:* Celexa (citalopram), escitalopram (Lexapro), fluoxetine (Prozac), sertraline (Zoloft), paroxetine (Paxil), fluvoxamine (Luvox), and clomipramine (Anafranil).

- *If an SRI doesn't work for you, be sure you've tried a high enough dose for a long enough time.* Often, too low a dose is used, which may not work. Don't give up before trying a high enough dose. Also, you should try the medicine for at least 12–14 weeks (and be on a high enough dose for at least 3 of these 12–14 weeks) before concluding that an SRI won't work for you. A briefer try may be inadequate to see if an SRI will work for BDD.

- *If an SRI alone doesn't work well enough, even after you've tried a high enough dose for a long enough time, you may improve by adding another medication to the SRI or by switching to another SRI.* Other medications, such as buspirone, may be helpful when added to an SRI. Also, one SRI may work better than another for you, so trying another SRI may work. There's no way to predict which one will be best for you—you just have to try them.

- *Between half and three quarters of people with BDD improve significantly with a particular SRI; about 80%–90% of people eventually respond to one of the SRIs.* Studies so far have found that 53% to 73% of people who take a given SRI will experience significant improvement in BDD. If you don't respond to the first SRI you try, you may respond to another one, either alone or when combined with other medications. In my clinical practice, about 90% of people who stuck with treatment and tried different medications if the first one didn't work eventually got better. It's important to note that these encouraging percentages were achieved by following the medication dosing and duration guidelines discussed in this book.

- *Cognitive-behavioral therapy (CBT) that focuses on BDD symptoms also appears effective for many people.* This treatment, too, can help people with BDD feel and function better. Since many therapists aren't trained to do CBT, it's important to find a therapist who does this treatment and is familiar with BDD.

- *CBT for BDD generally consists of several approaches:* CBT is a practical, "here-and-now" treatment that teaches you skills and focuses specifically on improving BDD symptoms. CBT approaches usually include cognitive restructuring, behavioral experiments, exposure, and response prevention. Additional approaches, such as mirror retraining, may also be helpful.

- *A majority of people with BDD respond to CBT.* CBT is often effective. It's important to note that these encouraging percentages were achieved by CBT-trained therapists familiar with BDD who used the specific CBT techniques that I'll describe further in Chapter 14.

- *If CBT doesn't work well enough for you, you may need to have more sessions or talk with your therapist about modifying the CBT approach:* Like medication treatment, CBT has to be tailored to the individual person and sometimes needs to be modified during treatment to make it more effective.

- *SRIs and cognitive-behavioral treatment—what I consider the "core treatments" for BDD—may be successfully combined.* You may want to try an SRI and CBT together, right from the start. Or, you may want to try an SRI first; if that doesn't work well enough, you can add CBT. Or, you could try CBT first; if that doesn't work adequately, you can add an SRI.

- *It isn't known whether SRIs or CBT are more effective or whether they're equally effective:* We don't know whether an SRI is more effective for certain types of people with BDD, and CBT for others, or vice versa. So, based on current knowledge, either, or both, are worth trying.

- *If you have more moderate or mild BDD, you can try an SRI, CBT, or both.* An SRI can be used regardless of how severe BDD is. CBT can also potentially be helpful regardless of the severity of BDD.

- *However, if you have severe BDD, are very depressed, or are considering suicide, I strongly recommend an SRI, whether or not you also try CBT:* BDD can be a life-threatening illness, and an SRI can be life saving. An SRI is definitely needed if you are very suicidal or very depressed. I also recommend CBT in such cases, but some people are too depressed to even participate in CBT. In such cases, an SRI can help you feel better enough that it's possible to do CBT.

- *Regardless of whether you try an SRI or CBT or both, it's important to find a doctor and/or therapist who's knowledge about BDD, takes your appearance concerns seriously, and is willing to focus on BDD in treatment.* Simply focusing treatment on depression, anxiety, or other symptoms may not work for BDD. My website (which can be reached at www. BodyImageProgram.com or through the Butler Hospital or Care New England web sites) lists doctors and therapists who treat BDD. There are many other professionals not listed on this website who can also treat BDD.

- *Other types of psychotherapy may be useful when combined with an SRI or cognitive-behavioral treatment.* Although they haven't been well studied, such psychotherapeutic approaches do *not*, however, at this time appear to be effective for BDD when used alone. These treatments include insight-oriented psychotherapy, supportive psychotherapy, and family therapy.

- *Surgery and other medical treatments (e.g., dermatologic treatment) generally don't appear helpful for BDD and may even make it worse.* As best we know, it's best to avoid such treatments and to try CBT and/or an SRI instead. There's an exception to this, however: people who compulsively pick their skin and damage it as a result may need dermatologic treatment in addition to an SRI or CBT.

Key Points about Treatment (*continued*)

- *A number of other approaches appear ineffective for BDD.* These include natural remedies, efforts to uncover a presumed trauma, and reassurance that the person looks fine. There is no evidence whatsoever that herbs or other "natural" remedies improve BDD.

- *Give an SRI or CBT a try!* You have nothing to lose by trying these treatments. Most people tolerate them very well, and a majority get much better. You deserve to feel better and have a better life. These treatments can make this possible.

- *Don't give up!* It may take a while to find the exact approach that works for you, but most people with BDD eventually get better with an SRI or CBT. Some people respond to the first SRI they try, whereas others have to try another one, or even many of them, to find one that works for them. Some people respond to CBT fairly quickly, whereas others need more intensive and longer treatment. But if you persist, and keep trying the recommended treatments, you'll probably get better: you'll be less obsessed, less distressed, will function better, and will enjoy your life a lot more.

·· *thirteen* ··

How to Successfully Treat BDD
with Medication

You might wonder why we would even consider treating a body image problem with medication. Well, there are a number of reasons to think it might help. Some of BDD's core features—obsessional preoccupation and compulsive, repetitive behaviors (such as mirror checking)—are similar to those of OCD, a disorder for which SRIs often work. In addition, many people with BDD are depressed because of their BDD symptoms, which suggests that antidepressants might help. Certain medications can improve insight in other disorders and therefore might help people with BDD, whose insight is often poor. In addition, BDD's development probably involves neurobiological factors, including abnormalities in serotonin functioning (see Chapter 10). This in turn suggests that SRIs, which correct serotonin functioning, might help.

Serotonin-Reuptake Inhibitors (SRIs):
First–Line Medications for BDD

Many people I've described in this book improved with serotonin-reuptake inhibitors (SRIs, or SSRIs). The SRIs are a type of antidepressant medication that also diminish obsessional thinking and compulsive behaviors. They effectively treat depression; in addition, they effectively treat obsessive compulsive disorder (OCD). While *all* antidepressants effectively treat depression, it appears that only the SRI antidepressants effectively treat BDD.

In addition to effectively treating depression and OCD, the SRIs are effective for a number of other psychiatric disorders. These include panic disorder, bulimia, binge eating disorder, and social phobia. They may help people with anorexia who've regained some weight keep this weight on. The SRIs are also helpful for aggression, impulsivity, and anxiety, and they are used for nonpsychiatric problems, such as headache and pain syndromes. Like other psychiatric medications, the SRIs are prescribed by psychiatrists, other physicians, and, in some states, nurses.

As shown in Table 12 on the next page, the SRIs currently available in the

Table 12. Serotonin-Reuptake Inhibitors		
Medication		*Typical Dose Range (milligrams per day)**
Generic name	*Brand name*	
Citalopram	Celexa	20–60
Escitalopram	Lexapro	10–20
Fluvoxamine	Luvox	100–300
Fluoxetine	Prozac	20–80
Paroxetine	Paxil	20–60
Sertraline	Zoloft	50–200
Clomipramine	Anafranil	100–250

*This is the usual dose range for a variety of disorders: later in this chapter I discuss the average doses used for BDD

United States are citalopram (Celexa), escitalopram (Lexapro), fluvoxamine (Luvox), fluoxetine (Prozac), paroxetine (Paxil), sertraline (Zoloft), and clomipramine (Anafranil). The first six medications are sometimes referred to as SSRIs (*selective* serotonin reuptake inhibitors) because they affect the brain chemical serotonin far more than other brain chemicals. Serotonin is one of the brain's natural chemicals that transmits signals between nerve cells. These chemicals (neurotransmitters) are the chemical messengers that make the brain's nerve cells fire and function. Healthy functioning of serotonin is important in many bodily functions, including mood, sleep, and appetite.

The SRIs increase the amount of serotonin at the junction between nerve cells by preventing its reuptake, or reabsorption, into the releasing nerve cell (neuron). As a result, less serotonin is broken down, and more is then available to act on neurons that are "downstream." This increased amount of serotonin between nerve cells in turn influences the activity of brain neurons. It appears that the SRIs increase overall serotonin transmission in the brain. They probably work by increasing serotonin availability at key brain areas. However, the serotonin system in the brain is extremely complex, and the SRIs' overall effect on this system needs to be better understood. In addition, because different neurotransmitter systems are highly interconnected, the SRIs also influence other neurotransmitters, such as dopamine. Furthermore, it's possible that the SRIs' effect on serotonin isn't what actually leads to decreased symptoms. This effect may simply be one step in a complicated chain of events.

The work of Dr. Lewis Baxter and his colleagues, as well as other researchers, on the effect of SRIs in obsessive compulsive disorder is extremely interesting and sheds some light on how these medications might work in OCD. Because BDD has many similarities to OCD, the SRIs may have similar effects in BDD. (Such studies haven't been done yet in BDD.) These researchers studied patients with OCD before and after treatment with an SRI or CBT (specifically, exposure and response prevention). They found that each of these treatments *normalized* abnormal brain functioning. Before treatment, brain scans showed abnormalities in certain areas of the brain; after either of these treatments, brain functioning became normal. The normalization occurred only in patients who responded to treatment, not in nonresponders or untreated healthy control subjects. SRIs may also make the amygdala (the brain's "panic button") function more normally and stop overreacting.

What's fascinating is that these studies showed that an SRI actually makes the brain *normal*. Some people worry that medications will somehow disrupt their brains or create artificial changes or an artificial state. But research findings suggest the opposite is true. They indicate that SRIs correct a "chemical imbalance" in the brain—that they alleviate symptoms by normalizing an abnormal state. Patients who respond to an SRI feel more "normal." They say that they feel like themselves again, or that they have more control over their mind— the way they used to, or the way other people do. Similarly, SRIs aren't "happy pills"—that is, they don't create an artificial state of happiness; rather, they correct abnormal brain functioning. Researchers have also found that antidepressants such as SRIs may make the brain healthier by protecting brain cells from damage and stimulating the healthy growth of new brain cells. They also appear to protect depressed people with heart disease from a poor cardiac outcome, and stroke patients treated with an antidepressant are more likely to survive than untreated patients.

What's the Evidence That SRIs Work?

A number of research studies demonstrate that SRIs substantially improve BDD symptoms in a majority of people. These studies also suggest that SRIs are more effective than other medications for BDD. It's important, however, to use a high enough SRI dose for a long enough time to give the medicine a chance to work.

Prior to the late 1980s, no one really knew whether BDD got better with medication and, if so, which medications might work. At that time, Dr. Eric Hollander and I started treating our patients with SRIs and found that many got better. This was the case for both adults and adolescents. SRIs even helped some severely ill and chronically hospitalized patients after many other medications had failed. In my clinical practice (in 90 patients), I found that 63% of SRI treatments (given at a high enough dose for a long enough time) led to substantial improvement in BDD symptoms. In contrast, other types of psychiatric medication that patients had received were usually ineffective.

These are the kinds of things my patients told me. "With Anafranil I can talk to people without feeling they're staring at me," Nathaniel said. "It's easier to stay out of the mirror. I spend less time worrying. It comes into my mind less and it's easier to get rid of the thoughts. I can argue with myself that my obsession is irrational—I tell myself, 'just shrug it off!' I'm not so self-conscious around people anymore. It's not a life or death problem for me now."

"I'd say I got 95% better on Prozac," Ned said. He'd had severe BDD for 30 years and had been hospitalized more than 10 times for his symptoms. He had also tried 13 non-SRI medications, without results. "My obsessions mostly went away, and I could stay out of the mirror. I stopped being hospitalized. I was so impressed that I bought stock in the drug company!"

Patient comments like these spurred me and other researchers to do more scientifically rigorous and systematic studies of SRIs. In these studies, patients were seen at specified time points during treatment, and standard rating scales were used to carefully assess their symptoms. These studies provided more scientifically credible information about these medications' effects. These studies are summarized in Table 13.

The first two studies, which were "randomized," "double-blind," and "controlled," are the most scientifically rigorous and convincing, because neither the doctors nor the patients knew whether patients were getting the SRI (which was hypothesized to be effective) or the comparison treatment. (The comparison treatment in the fluoxetine study was placebo—also known as a sugar pill; the comparison treatment in the clomipramine study was desipramine, a non-SRI antidepressant.) A double-blind design allows treatment response to be evaluated more objectively. In addition, "random assignment" minimizes differences in patients in the two groups which might affect treatment outcome. In the "open-label" trials, which used escitalopram, citalopram, or fluvoxamine, there was no comparison treatment, so both patients and doctor knew the patient was getting the SRI. All of the SRI studies included patients with varying degrees of BDD severity—ranging from mild to extremely severe. On average, study patients had moderately severe BDD.

As you can see from the "Study Results" column in the table, all of the studies found that the SRI that was tested was often effective for BDD symptoms. In the fluoxetine (Prozac) study, fluoxetine was more effective than placebo for BDD symptoms and daily functioning. In the clomipramine (Anafranil) study, the SRI clomipramine was superior to the non-SRI antidepressant desipramine in improving BDD symptoms and functioning. In the "open-label" studies, escitalopram (Lexapro), citalopram (Celexa), and fluvoxamine (Luvox) were effective for most patients.

One of the most intriguing results from these studies is that SRIs often work for delusional BDD (see chapter 3 for a description of this form of BDD). In fact, people with delusional BDD appear as likely as those with nondelusional BDD to respond to an SRI. That is, people who are *completely* convinced that their view of the defect is accurate, and who can't be talked out of this belief, have a high rate of response to an SRI. I've found this in all of my SRI studies, as did Dr. Hollander in his clomipramine study. As I'll discuss in Chapter 16, people with delusional BDD would actually qualify for a diagnosis of delusional

Table 13. SRI Studies in BDD[a]

Medication Tested	Study Design	Number of Patents Who Received Treatment	Length of Study and Average Medication Dose (mg/day)[b]	Study Results[c]	References[d]
Fluoxetine (Prozac) vs placebo (sugar pill)	Randomized, double blind, placebo-controlled, parallel group trial[e]	67	• 12 weeks • 77.7 ± 8.0 (range: 40–80)	Fluoxetine was significantly more effective than placebo for BDD symptoms (response rate of 53% vs 18%) and daily functioning	Phillips, 2002
Clomipramine (Anafranil) vs desipramine	Randomized, double blind controlled cross-over trial[f]	29	• 16 weeks (8 weeks on each medication) • Clomipramine: 138 ± 87 • Desipramine: 147 ± 80	Clomipramine was significantly more effective than desipramine for BDD symptoms (response rate of 65% vs 35%) and daily functioning	Hollander, 1999
Citalopram (Celexa)	Open-label trial[g]	15	• 12 weeks • 51.3 ± 16.9 (range, 10–60)	73% of subjects responded to citalopram; quality of life and functioning also significantly improved	Phillips, 2003
Escitalopram (Lexapro)	Open-label trial[g]	15	• 12 weeks • 28.0 ± 6.4 (range= 10–30)	73% of subjects responded to escitalopram	Phillips, un-published data

Fluvoxamine (Luvox)	Open-label trial[g]	30	• 16 weeks • 238.3 ± 85.8 (range, 50–300)	63% of subjects responded to fluvoxamine	Phillips, 1998
Fluvoxamine (Luvox)	Open-label trial[g]	15	• 10 weeks • 208.3 ± 63.5 (range, 100–300)	10 of 15 subjects responded to fluvoxamine	Perugi, 1997

[a]These are all of the controlled and open-label BDD medication studies that had been published in scientific journals at the time this book was revised (excluding case reports, case series, and chart review studies).

[b]The "±" sign indicates the standard deviation. In 68% of cases, the dose was within 1 standard deviation of the average dose. (See the text for an explanation.)

[c]In all of my studies, "response" was defined as 30% or greater improvement on the BDD-YBOCS; while a 30% decrease in BDD symptoms may seem relatively small, this degree of improvement corresponds well to a rating of "much improved" by both patients and clinicians. Dr. Hollander defined "response" as 25% or greater improvement on the BDD-YBOCS; Dr. Perugi defined "response" as "much" or "very much" improved on the Clinical Global Impressions Scale.

[d]Reference for these studies are listed in Chapter 18.

[e]Half of the patients were randomly assigned to fluoxetine and half to placebo; neither the doctor nor the patient knew which treatment the patient was receiving.

[f]Half of the patients were first treated with clomipramine and then desipramine; the other half received desipramine first and than clomipramine. Neither the doctor or patient knew which treatment the patient was receiving.

[g]Only one treatment (the SRI) was given; both the doctor and patient knew they were receiving it.

disorder in addition to BDD. While the treatment of delusional disorder is an understudied area, medications known as neuroleptics (antipsychotics) are commonly used to treat such patients. Available research findings, however, suggest that the BDD type of delusional disorder may actually respond to SRIs. At this time, I first treat patients with delusional BDD with an SRI. If they don't respond adequately, I may then add a neuroleptic (antipsychotic) medication to the SRI. But if a patient with delusional BDD is severely ill (e.g., hospitalized), I sometimes begin treatment with an SRI and a neuroleptic simultaneously. Finding that SRIs work for people with delusional BDD has been an unexpected and welcome discovery.

What Gets Better with an SRI?

People who respond to an SRI generally improve in a variety of ways. They spend less time obsessing and, if they start thinking about the perceived defect, it's easier to push the thoughts aside and think about other things. The thoughts are less tormenting. Some people think they actually look better than they used to, so the thoughts are less painful for this reason, whereas others think they look the same but they're better able to cope with their appearance problem emotionally. BDD-related behaviors generally improve as well. It's easier to resist the mirror checking, comparing, skin picking, reassurance seeking, and other behaviors. Many people have a better social life. It's much less painful to be around other people, and many find it easier to work or do schoolwork.

There are usually other benefits as well. Anxiety, depression, and suicidal thinking often diminish. Self-consciousness often decreases, and self-esteem and self-confidence get a boost. One of my patients said that she felt "wonderful—like a new person." She had stopped worrying about her nose and hair for the first time in 30 years.

Let's take a closer look at what symptoms improve with an SRI. The extent of improvement varies for different people, with many responding to the medication only partially and others responding completely. Generally, responders experience improvement in a variety of ways:

Preoccupation People who respond to an SRI say they're *less preoccupied with their appearance.* Those who respond completely may spend only minutes—or no time at all— instead of hours a day obsessing. A partial responder may still be preoccupied, but the time decreases—for example, from six hours a day to three. The decrease in preoccupation is usually due to the thoughts' entering the person's mind less frequently and to a better ability to resist and push them away. This change alone can be liberating. Time is freed up to think about more important and enjoyable things. Concentration improves because the distracting thoughts aren't present as often. Feelings of control increase.

Ability to resist and control the obsessional thinking A particularly distressing aspect of BDD is the feeling of not being in control of your own mind. SRIs often change this. People who respond find it *easier to resist and control the distressing thoughts.* This results in less time obsessing about the appearance problem. They regain control over their thinking and their mind. They—not the obsessions—are in charge.

Emotional pain   *The emotional pain and suffering that BDD causes usually diminish as well.* The pain may become more tolerable or even vanish. The thoughts are no longer as depressing, anxiety-provoking, or tormenting. In part, this is because they occur less often; in addition, when they do occur, they're less emotionally painful. Their power is diminished. As one person said to me, "They've lost their punch. It used to be a huge battle to get out that door. Now it's just a twinge."

BDD-related behaviors   *BDD behaviors usually improve.* Less time is spent checking mirrors, skin picking, hair cutting, reassurance seeking, and perform- ing other BDD behaviors. They're easier to resist and control, and the anxiety caused by doing them, or not doing them, diminishes. "The main thing Prozac did for me was help me stay out of the mirror," one person told me. "I go into the bathroom, and my heart races, but I have the fortitude not to look. It's a very important change. The mirror no longer controls me."

Daily functioning   *Functioning also often improves.* It becomes easier to go to work or school and to concentrate. It's not as hard to be around other people or leave the house. BDD sufferers may repair wounded relationships, start so- cializing more, or begin dating. "Our social life improved dramatically every time my wife took Prozac," an engineer told me. "Every time she stopped it, our social life stopped too."

Several of the SRI studies I've described specifically evaluated whether people were able to function better in their daily life when treated with an SRI. All of them found that with SRI treatment, functioning improved in numerous areas: work and school functioning, household functioning, interpersonal relation- ships, and recreational activities. These changes can occur rapidly and may be dramatic. A woman I treated started school again within several weeks of re- sponding to fluvoxamine, a change she'd wanted to make for 10 years but which her symptoms had made impossible. But other people change more slowly and make smaller gains. Habits can become very ingrained; it isn't always easy to effect major changes. But most people who respond to an SRI do make some progress toward functioning the way they would like.*

---

*It's fascinating to consider that animal research shows that enhancement of serotonin with medications like Prozac leads to more "social" behavior—decreased avoidance, vig- ilance, and social solitude. Animals with extreme depletion of serotonin show signifi- cantly less "social" interaction than other animals.

Avoidance *Avoidance usually lessens.* It's easier to do things, go places, and be around others. People become more active—their life becomes more colorful and interesting. Spending less time obsessing or checking the mirror frees you to do other things. It's also easier to do things and be around others when the thoughts and compulsions are less painful and powerful. In addition, self-consciousness and fear around other people may diminish, making it easier to socialize.

Quality of Life Of great importance, *SRIs also often improve overall quality of life.* In other words, people function better, enjoy their lives more, and get more satisfaction from life. In my citalopram (Celexa) study, quality of life improved significantly. In my fluoxetine (Prozac) study, quality of life tended to improve more with fluoxetine than with placebo. In both studies, the more BDD symptoms improved, the more quality of life improved. Table 14 illustrates changes in some of the preceding areas among medication responders in my fluoxetine, escitalopram, citalopram, and fluvoxamine studies. Keep in mind that these are *average* scores—some SRI responders had less of a response and others had more. Each item is rated on a five-point scale (0–4), with higher scores reflecting more severe symptoms. So, for example, before SRI treatment, patients on average experienced moderate to severe interference in functioning, whereas after treatment they experienced no interference to mild interference in functioning.

While the items listed in Table 14 and discussed above are standard symptoms assessed by many BDD researchers, other symptoms may also improve with an SRI.

Depression and anxiety *Depression and anxiety often improve with SRI treatment of BDD.* Depressive symptoms that improve include depressed or irritable mood, lack of interest and motivation, poor energy, impaired concentration, low self-esteem, and problems with sleep and appetite. Suicidal thinking also usually diminishes. Anxiety symptoms, such as worrying, being on edge, and tension, usually improve as well. In all of my SRI studies, standard measures of depression revealed significant improvement in depression and suicidal thinking in a majority of patients.

Hostility and anger In my fluvoxamine study, *hostility and anger significantly diminished* with treatment. This result is consistent with studies of SRIs in other disorders, which show that anger, hostility, and aggression often decrease with SRI treatment.

Body image This aspect of treatment response has been less well studied than the others I've discussed so far. My clinical experience suggests that *some, although not all, SRI responders experience improvement in body image.* In my

Table 14. BDD-YBOCS Scores Among SRI Responders Before and After Treatment with an SRI*

BDD-YBOCS Item	Average Score Before Treatment with an SRI	Average Score After Response to an SRI*
BDD PREOCCUPATIONS		
Preoccupation due to thoughts	3.1 hours a day	1.7 hours a day
Interference due to thoughts (social, occupational/academic, other)	2.3 (between moderate and severe)	0.5 (between none and mild)
Distress due to thoughts	2.7 (between moderate and severe)	1.2 (between mild and moderate)
Resistance of thoughts	2.1 (between some effort and little effort)	0.9 (between always makes an effort and makes an effort most of the time)
Ability to control thoughts	3.1 (between little control and no control)	1.3 (between much control and moderate control)
BDD BEHAVIORS		
Time spent on behaviors	2.7 hours a day	1.5 hours a day
Interference due to behaviors (social, occupational/academic, other)	2.1 (between moderate and severe)	0.6 (between none and mild)
Distress if behavior prevented	2.6 (between moderate and severe)	1.2 (between mild and moderate)
Resistance of behaviors	2.8 (between some effort and little effort)	1.1 (between makes an effort most of the time and some effort)
Ability to control behaviors	3.1 (between little control and no control)	1.2 (between much control and moderate control)

Table 14. *(continued)*

BDD-YBOCS Item	Average Score Before Treatment with an SRI	Average Score After Response to an SRI*
INSIGHT	2.9 (between fair and poor)	1.5 (between good and fair)
AVOIDANCE		
(due to thoughts or behaviors—e.g., other people, work/school, going places, doing things)	2.0 (moderate)	0.4 (between none and mild)
TOTAL SCORE	31.5 (moderate to severe BDD)	13.1 (subclinical BDD—i.e., not meeting criteria for the disorder)

*For actual scale items, see Appendix C; scores after treatment would be higher if non-responders were included

fluoxetine versus placebo study, those treated with fluoxetine reported greater improvement in "appearance orientation" on the MBSRQ. In other words, their appearance was less important to them, and they weren't as "behaviorally invested" in it (e.g., they cut down on excessive grooming activities). However, fluoxetine didn't improve appearance satisfaction significantly more than placebo.

I've also looked at this question in a different way, and got somewhat different results. In my fluoxetine (Prozac) and fluvoxamine (Luvox) studies, I systematically asked study participants whether their defect had changed while taking the SRI. Sixty percent of the responders said it had improved.* The changes fell into two categories: (1) One third of the 60% said the defect visually looked the same, but *it wasn't as distressing or anxiety provoking* as it used to be. People said things like, "It still looks the same, but I can live with it. It doesn't upset me as much. It's more of a normal dislike." Or "I'm not overreacting the way I used to. I can live with it now. It's no longer consuming me and ruining my life." (2) Two thirds of the 60% said the defect actually *looked different (and better) visually.* As discussed in chapter 11, parents said such things as "The marks on my face are gone. I don't *see* them anymore." Or "My face

*In contrast, only 20% of medication nonresponders said the defect had improved while taking the SRI.

used to look blotchy and red. Now it looks fine. I must have been misperceiving." One woman told me, "My features seem to have fallen into place. I look more attractive." She said that her appearance had physically and visually changed—it wasn't just that she could cope better with it. Occasionally, SRI responders not only don't despise the defect any more—now they really *like* their body! After treatment, a woman who responded to escitalopram (Lexapro) told me, "I used to think I looked hideous! But now when I look in the mirror I say to myself: 'you look pretty darn cute!'" About half reported that both kinds of changes occurred—both a cognitive/emotional change and what seems to be a perceptual change.

This raises the fascinating question of whether SRIs can actually improve visual perception. Serotonin appears to play an important role in vision in animals and may do the same in humans. The SRIs may correct a chemical imbalance involving serotonin that leads to faulty perception, overfocusing, or faulty interpretation of visual images.

Insight *Some SRI responders experience improved insight*, becoming more aware that their view of the defect was distorted. Many also experience less referential thinking. In the fluvoxamine (Luvox), citalopram (Celexa), and escitalopram (Lexapro) studies, responders experienced significantly improved insight.* As one woman said, "I used to be 97% convinced that I looked horrible. Now I'm 97% convinced that I don't. I realize I was distorting." In his clomipramine versus desipramine study, Dr. Hollander found that insight improved more with the SRI clomipramine than with the non-SRI desipramine. In my fluoxetine versus placebo study, however, the results were more mixed. Insight improved more in study participants treated with fluoxetine than in those treated with placebo, but not to a "statistically significant" degree. However, insight did improve significantly more in treatment responders than in treatment nonresponders.

Concern with more noticeable appearance problems *Sometimes the SRIs decrease an obsessional preoccupation with a noticeable aspect of appearance*, such as obesity. Some people whose appearance problem wouldn't qualify for BDD (because the defect is obvious) may become less preoccupied with and less upset by these problems when treated with an SRI. For example, some people who are quite overweight become less consumed by their weight obsessions—they're still not happy with their weight, but they're no longer obsessed with it. Both their BDD-related concern and their concern with a more noticeable appearance problem diminish.

*Insight was assessed with the Brown Assessment of Beliefs Scale (BABS), a scale developed by Dr. Jane Eisen of Brown Medical School, myself, and Drs. Doug Beer, Katherine Atala, Steven Rasmussen, and Lee Baer. This scale has been shown to be a reliable and valid measure of insight (degree of delusionality).

In a way, this observation makes sense. The medication can't distinguish between a slight appearance problem (i.e., BDD) and one that's more noticeable. The medication doesn't have eyes! The SRIs probably work by decreasing excessive, obsessional thinking, regardless of what someone actually looks like. This issue requires more research and goes beyond BDD. It raises the question of whether accident victims or people with congenital deformities who are overly preoccupied with and distressed by very noticeable defects might benefit from SRI treatment. Might they become less consumed by their concern—less preoccupied, less distressed, and better able to function? It's possible.

How To Treat BDD with an SRI

The recommendations below are based on all of the research studies that have been published to date, as well as extensive experience treating patients with BDD. Keep in mind, though, that your treatment will need to be individually tailored to you, in consultation with your doctor.

1. Use an SRI as a first-line medication for BDD, including delusional BDD: The studies I've reviewed, as well as my and other clinicians' clinical experience, indicate that *SRIs are effective for a majority of people with BDD. Importantly, the SRIs appear more effective than other types of medications, such as other antidepressants or neuroleptics (antipsychotics).* They appear equally effective for "delusional" and "nondelusional" BDD (see Chapter 16 for a description of these forms of BDD).

2. You can try any SRI: *All of the SRIs appear effective for BDD, so you can use any of them.* As you can see from Table 13, fluoxetine (Prozac), clomipramine (Anafranil), escitalopram (Lexapro), citalopram (Celexa), and fluvoxamine (Luvox) have been best studied, but clinical experience suggests that sertraline (Zoloft) and paroxetine (Paxil) are also effective. No scientifically rigorous studies have directly compared the effectiveness of any SRI to that of any other, so we don't know with certainty whether one is more effective than another. Clomipramine would generally not be used first, however, because it's a little more likely to cause side effects and can be toxic if a patient overdoses.

In my escitalopram (Lexapro) and citalopram (Celexa) studies, a somewhat higher percentage of patients improved than in my other SRI studies. In addition, a higher percentage were "very much improved" (as opposed to only "much improved"). In addition, many patients responded earlier (within 2–6 weeks) than people usually respond to an SRI. While we can't conclude from these preliminary observations that escitalopram (Lexapro) or citalopram (Celexa) are more effective for BDD than other SRIs, these observations are very encouraging.

At this time, there's no way to predict which SRI (or SRIs) will work (or work best) for you. The only way you'll know is to try them. It's best to discuss the options with your doctor.

3. Reach the maximum SRI dose that's recommended by the pharmaceutical company or that you can tolerate, unless a lower dose works for you: *It's very important to use a high enough SRI dose.* The most common error I see is use of too low an SRI dose for BDD, so the person doesn't get better. If your dose is too low, you may not improve, or you may improve only a little. Taking a low dose of an SRI for BDD (for example, 10 mg or 20 mg per day of citalopram) can be like taking only one aspirin for a severe migraine headache. You wouldn't really expect that to work. Although no research studies have rigorously compared different SRI doses in BDD (such studies are greatly needed), it appears that *people with BDD usually require higher doses than those typically used for depression and many other disorders.* Table 15 shows the average SRI doses I've used in my clinical practice for patients with BDD.

As you can see by looking back at Table 12, which shows the usual dosing ranges for these medications in a variety of disorders, the doses I typically use are at the higher end of, or even higher than, the usual dosing range. For many patients, I've tried to find the lowest effective dose, but often ended up with a fairly high dose because symptom relief was better. *It really doesn't matter what SRI dose you end up on, as long as it works for you. Since you're taking the medicine anyway, you might as well take the dose that helps you feel best. The most important thing is not to give up on a medicine—and assume it won't work for you—until you've reached 1) the highest dose recommended by the pharmaceutical company (see Table 12 for these doses) or 2) the highest dose you can*

Table 15.   Average Doses Used in My Clinical Practice to Treat BDD

Generic Name	Brand Name	Average Dose	Standard Deviation*
Citalopram	Celexa	66 mg per day	36 mg per day
Escitalopram	Lexapro	29 mg per day	12 mg per day
Fluoxetine	Prozac	67 mg per day	24 mg per day
Fluvoxamine	Luvox	308 mg per day	49 mg per day
Paroxetine	Paxil	55 mg per day	13 mg per day
Sertraline	Zoloft	202 mg per day	46 mg per day
Clomipramine	Anafranil	203 mg per day	53 mg per day

*The standard deviation indicates the typical range of doses used. In about two thirds of cases, the SRI dose used was within one standard deviation of the average. For example, for fluoxetine, about two thirds of people received between 43 mg/day (67 minus 24) and 91 mg/day (67 plus 24), with an average dose of 67 mg per day. (However, for clomipramine, the dose never exceeded 250 mg per day.)

tolerate if the highest recommended dose causes side effects you can't handle. You're more likely to get good results this way. It's a mistake to keep the dose too low and then conclude that the medicine isn't working.

Some people feel even better with a dose that's higher than the typical maximum dose (see Table 12). I've treated many patients with 30 to 50 mg per day of escitalopram, 80 to 100 mg per day of citalopram or paroxetine, 100 mg per day of fluoxetine, or 400 mg per day of sertraline or fluvoxamine. In fact, as Table 15 shows, the average doses of citalopram (Celexa), escitalopram (Lexapro), fluvoxamine (Luvox), and sertraline (Zoloft) I've used in my clinical practice exceed the typical maximum doses. The higher the dose, the more likely you are to have side effects, but many people tolerate these higher doses well and have minimal or no side effects. The main reason to try doses like these is if you've had only a partial response to the highest dose recommended by the pharmaceutical company and you're tolerating the medicine well. There's nothing to lose by trying a higher dose; it may work even better. Sometimes I use one of these higher doses if a patient hasn't responded to many adequate SRI trials, and we're getting low on treatment options. One important caveat is that clomipramine doses shouldn't exceed 250 mg per day. And you won't need to try a high dose if a lower dose is working well enough for you. If a dose higher than the maximum recommended dose doesn't work better than a lower dose after you've tried it for 3 weeks or so, it makes sense to lower the dose back down to the lowest dose that worked well.

I often see people who've already tried an SRI at a low dose, without results. It can be worthwhile to try the same SRI again at a higher dose—sometimes this works. You may be better off, however, first trying an SRI you haven't tried before.

4. How quickly to raise the SRI dose: There's no one-size-fits-all formula for how quickly to do this. It will depend on a number of factors. Generally, I recommend raising the dose more quickly for people who are more severely ill (especially those who are suicidal) and those who are tolerating the medicine well. Your preference also matters. *A reasonable goal, however, is to reach the maximum dose that the pharmaceutical company recommends (if a lower dose doesn't work) by 4 to 9 weeks from the start of treatment, assuming side effects aren't a problem.* In my fluoxetine study, participants received 20 mg per day for the first two 2 weeks; the dose was then raised by 20 mg per day every 10 days (every 2 weeks would also have been fine) to a maximum dose of 80 mg per day if tolerated. Patients tolerated this dose increase very well, and no one dropped out of this study because of side effects. In my citalopram study, participants started out with 20 mg per day; the dose was raised to 40 mg per day after 2 weeks and to 60 mg per day after 4 weeks, if tolerated.

This dosing strategy has several potential advantages: 1) you're less likely to undertreat BDD, because you're likely to reach a high enough dose, and 2) you'll probably respond more quickly than if you raise the dose more slowly. A potential disadvantage, however, is that the faster you raise the dose, the more likely you may be to get side effects. Also, you may end up on a higher dose than you really need, because you didn't stay on a lower dose for long enough to see if that dose would work. On balance, though, I usually have more success raising the dose fast enough so I reach the highest dose by the 5th to the 9th week of treatment. Side effects can usually be successfully managed, if they occur. And the problem with raising the dose more slowly than this is that it can end up taking a long time to reach an effective dose, especially if you end up needing a relatively high dose. If you do raise the dose more quickly (as I prefer to do), once you've felt better for a while you can always slowly lower the dose bit by bit to see if a lower dose works equally well.

As you're raising the dose, if a low dose seems to be working, you can always stay at that dose for a few more weeks and see what happens. For example, if you're feeling better with 10 mg per day of escitalopram, you may want to stay at that dose for another 2 to 3 weeks to see if you improve even more. If you do, you may want to stay there even longer, to give the dose even more of a chance to work. On the other hand, you may decide that you want to raise the dose anyway, even if you start getting better on 10 mg per day, because a higher dose may work even better for you. This is a personal decision that's best made with your doctor after thinking through the pros and cons of each choice. There's no way to predict ahead of time which medication, or what dose, will be best for you. You'll just need to give different doses a try.

5. Don't give up on an SRI until you've tried it for 12 to 16 weeks, while reaching a high enough dose: *It's also important to try the SRI for a long enough time.* Taking the SRI for 12 to 16 weeks, and reaching a high dose (unless a lower dose works for you) for at least 3 of those weeks is called an *"adequate"* *trial.* If you don't take a high enough dose, or if you don't try it for long enough, the SRI trial is considered "inadequate." In other words, it may not be sufficient to successfully treat BDD.

In most published BDD studies and in my clinical practice, people needed to take an SRI, on average, for 6 to 9 weeks before BDD symptoms substantially improved. In my fluoxetine (Prozac) study, two thirds of people substantially improved (i.e., "responded") between the 4th and 11th week of treatment. In my fluvoxamine (Luvox) study, two thirds improved between the 3rd and 10th week of treatment. However, in my citalopram (Celexa) and escitalopram (Lexapro) studies, people responded to the medicine, on average, after only 4 to 5 weeks (two thirds responded between weeks 1–2 and 7–8). So some people respond to an SRI within several weeks, whereas others have to try it for as long as 12 weeks—or occasionally even 16 weeks—before they respond. This means you'll need to be patient and wait for the medicine to work. But don't get discouraged: it often does work!

It's worth emphasizing that these numbers and recommendations are based on studies that increased the SRI dose, and reached the high end of the dosing range, fairly quickly (see the examples above). If you raise your SRI dose more slowly (i.e., if you take more than 9 weeks or so to reach the maximum rec-

ommended dose), you may need more than 12 to 16 weeks to get better. If you haven't gotten to a high enough dose by week 12 to 16, it's usually advisable to try to raise your dose at that point to see if a higher dose works better than a lower dose. But if you've already reached the highest dose recommended by the pharmaceutical company, or the highest dose you can tolerate, by 12 to 16 weeks—and if you've been on that highest dose for at least 3 weeks—then it's probably best to make a change by switching to another SRI or adding another medicine to the SRI. (I'll say more about these options later in this chapter.)*
In my experience, it doesn't make sense to just continue taking a low SRI dose (or even a high dose), if it isn't working for you, for many months or years.

I often see patients who've tried lots of SRIs without getting better. A common problem is that they tried the SRI for too brief a time (e.g., only 4 to 8 weeks). In my fluoxetine study, nearly half of the people who eventually responded to the medication still hadn't responded by the 8th week of treatment. This was the case for one third of the people in my fluvoxamine study. These people generally responded between weeks 8 and 12 of treatment. In addition, many people I've seen who didn't respond to a past SRI never reached a high enough dose. Often such patients have been diagnosed with depression while their BDD was missed. Because their BDD wasn't recognized or diagnosed, it wasn't effectively treated. For many, depression didn't improve either.

6. SRIs usually begin to work gradually: Occasionally, the medication begins to work in a dramatic fashion. Sometimes people can pinpoint the day, or even the hour, that it starts working. But typically it starts working gradually. People say things like "I felt a little better three days ago and today, but not for very long, so I don't know if it's really working." Don't get discouraged if this happens, because it's expected. These ups and downs—what I call a "sawtooth pattern" of improvement—gradually give way to more sustained periods of feeling better. Good hours gradually turn into good days, and good days transform into good weeks. With time, you'll notice more and more improvement in many, if not all, of your symptoms.

7. You need to take the medicine every day as prescribed: It's very important to take the medication every day, exactly as prescribed. It usually takes a while to work, so you need to take it every day even if it doesn't seem to be helping. *If you take less than prescribed, or you take it sporadically, it may not work as well or at all.* If you have trouble remembering to take it, try a pill box, which you can buy at a pharmacy. This can help you stay on track. If you don't want to take the medicine as prescribed because of side effects or because you have concerns about it, it's better to discuss your concerns with your doctor than to stop the medicine or not take it as prescribed. The whole point of taking

---

*While it's possible that some people might begin to respond to an SRI after 12 to 16 weeks, this important question hasn't been well studied. Based on my clinical experience, however, it's unlikely that an SRI will start working after 16 weeks (assuming a reasonably high dose has been attained by then).

it is to feel better, and you're more likely to feel better if you actually take it and don't miss any doses.

8. If you respond to an SRI, you're likely to continue to feel well for as long as you take it: In my clinical experience, the vast majority of people who respond to an SRI continue to feel well over months and even years while taking the medication. Some patients I've treated who responded to medication ten years ago are still taking it and doing well. In fact, many people say that the longer they take the SRI, the better they feel. I've found that about 40% of people who improve with an SRI in the first three months of treatment continue to improve even more over the next 6 months. I've also found that fewer than 10% of people who respond to an SRI experience a full return of their BDD symptoms while continuing to take the SRI. However, there is a great need for formal research studies to investigate these important issues.

9. Continue an effective SRI for a year or two, or longer: If you do improve with an SRI, for how long should you take it? Unfortunately, no scientifically rigorous studies have addressed this very important question. However, based on my clinical experience treating BDD patients for nearly 15 years, *I'd generally recommend staying on an effective SRI for at least a year or two, even if you're feeling better. You may want to stay on it longer than that, especially if you've tried stopping an SRI and your symptoms returned, or if your BDD has been severe.* After all, you need a break. A year or more of decreased symptoms can allow you to get back to work or do your job more effectively, socialize more, and start enjoying your life.

After a year or two, my patients and I discuss their options. Some people decide they'd like to try to stop the medication to see what happens. In my clinical experience, about 85% of people who stop an effective SRI experience some return of their symptoms although sometimes they're less severe than they were originally. If your symptoms recur, you can always start the SRI again, and in my experience the symptoms usually improve again when this is done. (Occasional people however, don't respond quite as robustly as they did the first time.) But since it appears that many people—if not the majority—experience symptom return after discontinuing an effective SRI, some people opt to stay on it over the longer term. They don't want to risk a recurrence of their symptoms. For people with very severe BDD, especially those who've attempted suicide because of their symptoms, this is probably the wisest choice.

The SRIs have been extensively studied over decades in many other disorders, and they appear safe when taken for many years. Nonetheless, you should discuss how long to stay on an SRI with your doctor. If you plan to get pregnant, it's especially important to discuss ahead of time whether or not to continue the SRI while you're pregnant or breastfeeding.

10. If you decide to stop an effective SRI, plan this carefully with your doctor: Based on my clinical experience, BDD symptoms often return after an effective SRI is stopped (although this important question hasn't been well studied). After stopping an effective SRI, some people find that their BDD symptoms are as severe as before they took it, whereas others find they're milder and more tolerable. And some people remain relatively symptom free. We don't know whether BDD symptoms are less likely to return after stopping an effective SRI if you've also had CBT. This is an important question that needs to be studied.

Because your BDD symptoms may return if you stop an effective SRI, I'd suggest that taking the following steps if you decide to discontinue one:

1) *Lower the SRI dose slowly and gradually over several months rather than discontinuing it abruptly.* (However, as I'll discuss below, if you switch immediately to another SRI, you can stop the first SRI more quickly than this). The more severe your BDD symptoms were in the past, the more slowly I'd suggest lowering the dose. This way, if the symptoms recur and you decide to increase the dose again, some medication is already "on board," which might decrease the time needed to regain response. In addition, a slow tapering can allow the lowest effective dose to be found; that is, the lowest dose that keeps the symptoms at a tolerable level can possibly be identified, which is useful information. My clinical experience also suggests that reemerging symptoms may be less severe if the medication is gradually tapered rather than abruptly discontinued. It's also possible (although it really isn't known) that BDD symptoms may be less likely to recur at all if the SRI is slowly tapered over a number of months rather than abruptly discontinued.

2) *Try discontinuing the effective SRI when you aren't very stressed and your life is relatively stable.* This way, if BDD symptoms return, you may be able to handle them better. It makes sense, for example, that you could deal with returning symptoms better if your job and relationships are stable and going well than if you're looking for a new job and ending an important relationship. It's also possible (although we don't really know) that BDD symptoms may be less likely to reemerge if you're less stressed rather than more stressed.

11. What to do about side effects if they occur: In general, the SRIs are well tolerated. Reviewing lists of all these medications' possible side effects can lead to unrealistic worry; some lists contain side effects that occur only rarely or no more often than with a placebo (sugar pill). Like all medications, the SRIs have the potential to cause side effects, but they're often quite minimal and may improve or disappear with time. Most people have no side effects or fairly minimal and tolerable ones. Like other antidepressants, the SRIs aren't habit forming or addicting. Antidepressants have been safely used for nearly half a century, and SRIs have been prescribed for decades. SRIs are one of the most commonly prescribed classes of medication. They've been taken by many millions of people, often for many years.

Nonetheless, side effects can occur. Some of the more common ones are nausea, insomnia, feeling jittery, fatigue, decreased sex drive and sexual functioning, sweating, and decreased appetite. Anafranil can cause side effects such as dry mouth and constipation. These side effects are problematic in a minority of people, and they go away after stopping the medication. None of the SRIs have been documented to have life-threatening side effects. In my experience, people with BDD who experience side effects are often willing to tolerate them because they so appreciate the symptom relief they obtain.

When side effects do occur, they can often be diminished. Approaches include increasing the dose more slowly (if the dose is being raised), slowly decreasing the dose (while watching carefully for the reemergence of BDD symptoms), or adding other medications to counteract side effects. Often, such strategies are helpful. If they aren't, you can try another SRI. You may tolerate one better than another.

It helps to be patient! I say this because side effects, if they occur, often appear before the medication has had time to work. This can be frustrating. Keep in mind that some side effects get better, or even disappear, as treatment is continued. And the longer you stay on the medication is (up to a point), the more likely it is to start working.

12. An important reminder: Be sure your doctor knows from the beginning that you have BDD—don't tell him or her that you just have depression or anxiety: The most common clinical error I see is treatment focused on depression but not BDD. This often leads to use of an antidepressant other than an SRI, too brief an SRI trial, or use of SRI doses that are often too low for BDD. In such cases, the BDD (and the depression) may not improve. *An effective medication regimen for depression will not necessarily effectively treat BDD. However, an effective medication regimen for BDD will usually effectively treat depression, whether or not the depression is due to BDD.*

What If an SRI Doesn't Work Well Enough?

What if an SRI doesn't work or works only partially? This is an important question that you may face. Some people are pleased enough with a partial response that they don't want to pursue additional treatment. Others, however want to further improve. While there are very little research data on this question, my clinical experience suggests that a number of approaches may be effective.

1. Optimize the SRI you're already on: *This means following the above guidelines to the extent that you can, taking a high enough dose for a long enough time.* It doesn't make sense to give up on an SRI if you haven't given it a good enough try. As I've mentioned, some people benefit from exceeding the maximum dose recommended by the pharmaceutical company (excluding clomipramine [Anafranil]) and tolerate it fine. If optimizing the SRI doesn't work well enough for you, there are two major approaches you can take:

1) "Augment" the SRI: One approach is called *augmentation*. With this approach, you continue the ineffective or partially effective SRI and add another medicine to the SRI to augment, or boost, the SRI's effect.

2) Switch to another SRI: The second approach is called *switching*. With this approach, you discontinue the SRI and try another SRI. I'll discuss each option below.

2. You can "augment" an SRI or "switch" to another SRI; it isn't clear which strategy is better: Unfortunately, we don't know whether it's better to augment an inadequately effective SRI, or discontinue the SRI and switch to another SRI, because this question hasn't been well studied. However, in my clinical practice, I found that among patients who hadn't responded well to an adequate SRI trial, augmenting the first SRI was successful in 33% of cases, whereas switching to another SRI was successful in 44% of cases. This difference wasn't significantly different statistically.

However, I found something interesting when I considered whether the patient had had no response, versus a partial response, to the first SRI. Of those people who hadn't responded to the first SRI (i.e., were not "much improved" or "very much improved"), only 18% responded when I added an augmenting medicine to the SRI. But among people who'd had a partial response to the SRI (i.e., were "much improved" or "very much improved"), 41% responded when I added an augmenting medicine. This difference was statistically significant. This finding suggests that you may be better off augmenting an SRI if you've partially responded to it, but it may be better to switch to another SRI if you haven't responded to the first SRI. However, because this study was relatively small and not very scientifically rigorous (because it was based on my clinical practice), it's best not to draw firm conclusions about which approach is more effective.

There are other things you might want to consider when deciding whether to augment or switch. If you haven't responded to numerous SRIs (for example, 3 of them) without any attempt at augmentation, it would make sense to try augmentation. Conversely, if you haven't responded to several augmentation strategies with one SRI, it's probably best to switch to another SRI.

Another consideration is that the better you've responded to an SRI, the less appealing it is to discontinue it and try another one. For example, if you no longer feel suicidal, and your BDD and depression are a lot better (even if not completely better) on an SRI, it may be too risky to discontinue that SRI and try a new one. It's possible that the second one won't work or won't work as well as the first one, and your symptoms could get worse again (although it's possible that another SRI could work better). Continuing the SRI and adding another medicine allows you to maintain your partial response to the SRI, whereas if you stop the SRI you risk losing whatever response you had.

So when deciding whether to augment or switch, there are several things to consider, including your individual situation and your and your doctor's preference. The approach you take needs to be tailored to you. If the approach you choose doesn't work, you can always try the other one.

3. Augmenting a partially effective SRI: As I just discussed, SRI augmentation has some potential advantages. Although augmentation is commonly used and has been well studied in many other disorders, such as depression and OCD, it's hardly been studied in BDD. To the best of my knowledge, the only data on the effectiveness of SRI augmentation in BDD comes from my clinical practice and my study of pimozide (Orap) augmentation of fluoxetine (Prozac), which I'll discuss below. Because many people don't experience complete symptom relief with an SRI, more BDD augmentation studies are greatly needed.

Table 16 shows the augmenting medications I've most often used for BDD, typical dosing ranges, and average doses. Augmentation approaches for BDD have been studied so little that it's premature to say which is most effective. However, as I describe each augmentation strategy below, I'll convey my impression of their effectiveness.

Often, I add the augmenting medicine to the SRI only after I've tried the SRI for at least 12 weeks and at a high enough dose. I do this because the SRI may work well enough by itself, so the augmenting medicine isn't even needed. This approach can keep the medication regimen simple. Sometimes, however, it makes sense to add the augmenting medication to the SRI sooner, before the SRI alone has been adequately tried. This may be reasonable, for example, for someone with very severe BDD. Or the augmenting medicine may be more helpful than an SRI alone for certain symptoms (e.g., agitation) or a co-occurring disorder other than BDD.

Because there's so little research on SRI augmentation for BDD, it's unclear how long you should try an augmenting medicine before giving up. Based on my clinical experience and augmentation studies of other disorders, I'd suggest trying an augmenting agent for about 6 to 8 weeks, and reaching the higher end of the dosing range in table 16 during that time if possible, before making a final decision about whether it's working or not.

Buspirone (Buspar):   I've had some success by adding buspirone (Buspar) to an SRI. Buspirone is an antianxiety medication with effects on serotonin. It's sometimes used as an augmenting agent to treat depression and OCD. Unlike other antianxiety medications, buspirone is generally not sedating and has no potential for causing physical dependence or addiction.

In my clinical practice, adding buspirone to an SRI has been effective in about one third of patients. The magnitude of the improvement is fairly large. People with delusional BDD appear as likely to respond to buspirone as those with nondelusional BDD. Buspirone augmentation is appealing because this medicine has so few side effects and is usually so well tolerated. It may also improve coexisting anxiety and possibly depressive symptoms.

I've also treated a small number of patients with buspirone alone who preferred not to take an SRI. Several experienced some improvement in BDD symptoms, although none had the robust response that can occur with an SRI.

Clomipramine: I sometimes combine the SRI clomipramine (Anafranil) with one of the selective SRIs (fluvoxamine [Luvox], fluoxetine [Prozac], paroxetine [Paxil], citalopram (Celexa), escitalopram (Lexapro), or sertraline

Table 16. Potential SRI Augmentation Medications in BDD[a,b]

Medication		Type of Medication	Common Dosing Range in BDD (mg per day)	Average Dose Used in My Clinical Practice (mg per day)[c]
Generic name	Brand name			
Buspirone	Buspar	Antianxiety	30–80	57 ± 15
Clomipramine	Anafranil	SRI[d]	Therapeutic blood level	128 ± 76
Venlafaxine	Effexor	Antidepressant[e]	150–450	365 ± 89
Bupropion	Wellbutrin	Antidepressant[e]	150–400	400 ± 0
Olanzapine	Zyprexa	Psychotropic agent (Neuroleptic)[f]	5–20	8.3 ± 2.9
Ziprasadone	Geodon	Neuroleptic[f]	10–180	60 ± 67
Risperidone	Risperdal	Psychotropic agent (Neuroleptic)[f]	1–6	3.8 ± 1.7
Methylphenidate	Ritalin	Stimulant	10–60	32 ± 7
Lithium	Lithobid, Eskalith	Mood stabilizer	Therapeutic blood level	825 ± 568

[a]"Augmentation" refers to adding another medication to the SRI to try to boost the SRI's effect. Often, augmenting agents are added to the SRI after the SRI by itself has been given an adequate try, but they can also be added to the SRI before this is accomplished. Technically, using two antidepressants at the same time is sometimes referred to as a "combination" strategy.

[b]It's important to be aware that augmentation strategies in BDD have been only minimally researched and need to be better studied.

[c]The "±" sign indicates the standard deviation. In 68% of cases, the dose was within 1 standard deviation of the average dose. (See the text for an explanation.)

[d]Clomipramine can be added to one of the SSRIs, or vice versa, although clomipramine blood level must be carefully monitored because SSRIs can dramatically raise the clomipramine blood level, which can be toxic.

[e]Other antidepressants may also potentially be combined with an SRI (e.g. mirtazapine [Remeron]). The one important exception is that an MAO inhibitor (e.g., tranylcypromine [Parnate]; phenelzine [Nardil], selegeline [Deprenyl]) must NEVER be combined with an SRI under any circumstances.

[f]Other neuroleptics may also potentially be useful, although I've used them less in my practice. These include quetiapine (Seroquel) and arapiprazole (Abilify). Other atypical neuroleptics are likely to be developed and marketed in the future.

[Zoloft]) if response to an adequate trial of one of them isn't sufficient. Some patients do better on the combination than on either medication alone. In my clinical practice, 44% of patients responded when I added clomipramine to a selective SRI or vice versa. This response rate was somewhat higher than for other augmentation strategies, although the magnitude of the response wasn't quite as large as for some of them. Nonetheless, because clomipramine is an excellent antidepressant, it may be a particularly appealing augmentation choice for people who are severely depressed. Although I generally recommend trying an augmenting agent for 8 weeks, I'd recommend trying clomipramine for 12 weeks before deciding whether it's working well enough. I generally wouldn't recommend combining clomipramine with a selective SRI without first attempting to optimize a trial with just one of them.

Because the selective SRIs have the potential to greatly increase clomipramine blood levels, which can be highly toxic at very high levels, a lower dose of clomipramine should generally be used than when clomipramine is used without another SRI. If a patient is already on an SSRI, I generally begin by adding only 25 mg a day of clomipramine and then gradually raise the dose, depending on the person's clomipramine blood level. You should always check a clomipramine level when this medication is combined with a selective SRI to ascertain that it isn't too high.

Other Antidepressants: Antidepressants other than clomipramine can be added to an SSRI. These medications include venlafaxine (Effexor) and bupropion (Wellbutrin).* Some patients do quite well with this approach. Some of my patients with severe depression who hadn't responded to lots of medications did particularly well on 400 mg per day of bupropion (Wellbutrin) plus 80–100 mg per day of citalopram (Celexa). It's possible that adding bupropion (Wellbutrin, which doesn't directly affect serotonin) is more effective for people whose depression doesn't seem largely due to BDD (in other words, who seem to have a "separate" depression), but this is speculative at this point. We need to learn a lot more about the effectiveness of this approach, as it appears promising for at least some people with BDD.

Neuroleptics: The neuroleptics (antipsychotics) are a class of medicines often used to treat psychotic symptoms but which are also effective for a broad range of other symptoms (e.g., agitation and anxiety). (Because some of the newer ones are effective for so many different kinds of symptoms, they are now officially classified under the very broad term "psychotropic agent"—meaning they have effects on psychiatric symptoms—rather than neuroleptics or antipsychotics.) For several reasons, these medications are potentially promising SRI

---

*A class of antidepressants known as MAO inhibitors should *never* be added to an SRI *under any circumstances* because of the risk of severe toxicity related to the MAO inhibitor. Also, care should be taken when combining an SRI with venlafaxine (Effexor) or clomipramine (Anafranil) because of the risk (although it's very low) of a rare syndrome called serotonin syndrome, which is caused by excessive amounts of serotonin.

augmenters for BDD. First, they are effective SRI augmenters in OCD and depression. Second, many people with BDD have prominent delusions of reference and delusional conviction about the perceived appearance defect; neuroleptics are the best treatment for delusional thinking in other disorders.

There are two types of neuroleptics: "typical" (or "first generation") and "atypical" (or "second generation"). The typicals are older medications; the atypicals are newer. Although neither type has been well studied in BDD, the atypicals appear more promising. Some of my patients have responded well when we added atypical neuroleptics such as olanzapine (Zyprexa), ziprasidone (Geodon), or risperidone (Risperdal) to an SRI. Ziprasidone (Geodon) seems especially promising.

These medications can also diminish severe distress and agitation resulting from BDD. In patients with these symptoms I often combine an atypical neuroleptic with an SRI from the beginning of treatment. Using an atypical neuroleptic early in treatment can provide quicker relief than the SRI alone—producing a calming effect, helping the person function better, and in some cases preventing hospitalization.

Only one study has, from a scientific perspective, adequately studied a neuroleptic as an SRI augmenter. This study tested pimozide (brand name Orap), a typical neuroleptic that's effective for Tourette's disorder (characterized by repetitive, uncontrollable verbal utterances or physical movements known as tics, which are similar to the compulsive behaviors of OCD). I decided to use pimozide rather than another neuroleptic because when I started the study the atypical neuroleptics weren't available yet. Also, pimozide is an effective SRI augmenter in OCD. Most important, pimozide has long had the reputation (which wasn't based on much scientific evidence) of being uniquely effective for delusional BDD and certain other types of delusional disorder. In fact, it was often used to treat BDD, so it seemed important to determine whether or not it worked.

The pimozide study was a randomized, double-blind study in which patients who hadn't had a good response to an adequate trial of fluoxetine (Prozac) were randomly assigned to receive treatment with either pimozide or placebo, while remaining on fluoxetine. The study found that pimozide wasn't more effective than placebo, even for people with delusional BDD. Nor did pimozide improve insight more than placebo. While one study alone can't definitely determine whether a treatment works, these results are not promising. Nonetheless, I don't think we can assume that because pimozide wasn't effective that the atypicals won't prove effective. At the time of this writing, I would tend not to augment an SRI with a typical neuroleptic such as pimozide, but I'd consider augmenting with an atypical neuroleptic. Because neuroleptics are effective for Tourette's syndrome, it's possible that neuroleptic augmentation is more effective for BDD symptoms that are tic-like—for example, skin picking or hair plucking—although this question hasn't been studied.

Methylphenidate (Ritalin): Occasional patients (10%–20% in my experience) improve significantly when methylphenidate or another stimulant is added to an SRI. I'm more likely to use this approach with patients who are severely depressed and fatigued, because the stimulant can improve depressed mood and energy as well as BDD. One concern, however, is that stimulants are potentially habit forming and are best not used in people at risk for substance abuse or dependence. Because stimulants can potentially worsen tics, there's a theoretical concern that they might worsen skin picking (which has some features in common with tics), but I haven't seen this happen.

Lithium: Lithium is a natural substance that's best known as a treatment for bipolar disorder (manic depressive illness). However, it's also effective for a broad range of other disorders and symptoms (e.g., mood swings, depression, aggressive behavior, suicidal thinking). In my clinical experience, about 20% of BDD patients substantially improve when lithium is added to an SRI.

Benzodiazepines: Benzodiazepines (e.g., clonazepam [Klonopin], lorazepam [Ativan]) are used primarily to treat anxiety and insomnia. Strictly speaking, I don't consider them augmenting agents, because I add them to an SRI at any point during treatment—whenever they're needed. Benzodiazepines can be very helpful for severe distress, anxiety, or agitation that an SRI doesn't adequately diminish. They can also greatly improve poor sleep. They can be used temporarily or over the longer term. Temporary use of benzodiazepines during the first few weeks of treatment (while waiting for an SRI to work) can be especially valuable for people who are severely anxious, agitated, unable to sleep, or suicidal. Benzodiazepines are potentially habit forming, but in my experience, few people with BDD abuse them. I tend not to prescribe them, however, for people who've abused alcohol or drugs. For these individuals, an atypical neuroleptic may be a helpful alternative.

Anticonvulsants: Medications such as valproic acid, gabapentin, leviteracetam, and lamotrigine are sometimes helpful for anxiety or depressive symptoms. Valproic acid and lamotrigine can be very helpful for mood swings in people who have bipolar disorder in addition to BDD. Results from my genetics study (see Chapter 10) raise the question of whether these medications (which boost calming GABA the brain) have promise in treating BDD; they need to be studied.

Cognitive-Behavioral Therapy (CBT): It's worth briefly mentioning here that if medication doesn't work well enough for you, you should strongly consider adding CBT. CBT can also be used along with an SRI from the start of treatment. Most of the next chapter is devoted to CBT.

4. Switching to another SRI: If you don't respond to an adequate trial of one SRI, you may respond to another. My approach is, if necessary, to try one SRI after another, in the hope that one will work better than others. You may have to try several SRIs before you find one that works.

It appears that all of the SRIs are about equally effective for BDD. This means that *on average* they all appear about equally likely to work. However, this doesn't mean that they will all work equally well *for you*. One (or several) may be more effective than another for a given person. There's no way to predict which SRI (or SRIs) will work best for you. If you don't respond to one, it's worth trying another (although you might want to first try SRI augmentation). I've treated many patients who responded to an SRI after failing many others. In some cases, the sixth one worked after 5 had failed! In my clinical practice, 43% of patients who didn't improve with an initial adequate SRI trial responded to at least one subsequent SRI, and 44% of subsequent adequate SRI trials received by these patients were effective.

What if you've responded to an SRI (i.e., had at least a 30% decrease in BDD YBOCS score) but want to try another one because of side effects, or to see if another SRI works even better for you? The good news is that if one SRI has worked for you, other SRIs appear highly likely to also work. In my clinical practice, among people who responded to an SRI and then switched to a different one, 92% of subsequent SRI trials also led to improvement. The subsequent SRI may work better than the earlier one, about the same, or not as well. There's no way to predict which outcome will occur.

5. Other potentially effective approaches: So far, I've focused on trying SRI augmentation or switching to another SRI if an SRI doesn't work well enough. But there are a few other approaches that may also work:

1) Venlafaxine (Effexor) is an effective antidepressant that may work for BDD when used by itself (I mentioned above that it can also be effective when combined with an SRI). Even though, technically speaking, venlafaxine isn't classified as an SRI, it has potent effects on serotonin. In an open-label study of 11 patients done by Dr. Hollander and his colleagues, venlafaxine significantly improved BDD symptoms in those patients who completed the study. In my experience, too, it's often effective for BDD. Because the SRIs have been much better studied, I'd suggest using them first. But if an SRI doesn't work, venlafaxine (Effexor) is worth trying.

2) MAO Inhibitors (MAOIs): (phenelzine [Nardil], tranylcypromine [Parnate], selegeline [Deprenyl]) are older but very effective antidepressants that are sometimes effective for BDD. Although most of my data comes from patient reports of past treatment, they appear effective in about 30% of cases. I haven't used them much in BDD because so many SRIs, and venlafaxine, are now available, which are generally better tolerated. However, an MAOI may be worth trying if lots of other medications haven't worked for you. If not taken exactly as prescribed, they can have toxic effects, so it's critically important to carefully follow prescribing directions if you try one and to *never* combine an MAOI with an SRI.

3) Opioids (opiates): I know a few people who took a prescription opioid medication (e.g., Percocet) for a medical problem and unexpectedly experienced relief from severe BDD symptoms. I also know several who unfortunately became addicted to an illegal opioid (e.g., heroin) because it alleviated intolerable BDD. The potential benefits of opioids (e.g., morphine) are being studied in OCD. I don't routinely recommend opioids or prescribe them, because they're potentially highly addicting. Also, I know of only a few cases in which they've been tried. Nonetheless, they remain an option for a severely ill person who has failed all standard treatments. Treatment with an opioid is preferable to life-long hospitalization, living in a nursing home for the rest of your life, or suicide.

6. A Reminder: Each person with BDD requires individualized assessment of BDD and other symptoms. If other disorders are present along with the BDD, this may influence the medication selected. I recommend a comprehensive evaluation by a psychiatrist and development of an individualized treatment plan. Creativity and expertise in psychopharmacology are needed in more treatment-resistant cases. So is persistence. With enough tries, in my experience most people eventually improve with medication. Don't give up!

Medications That Don't Appear to Work for BDD

Medications other than SRIs have barely been studied in BDD. So what I say about them may be modified as more treatment studies are done. In the meantime, the limited research data we have suggest that non-SRI antidepressants (with the possible exception of venlafaxine and MAO inhibitors) don't often work when used alone to treat BDD. You many recall that Dr. Hollander found, in a very good study, that the non-SRI antidepressant desipramine was usually ineffective for BDD, and it was significantly less effective than the SRI antidepressant clomipramine (Anafranil). However, as I've already discussed, some non-SRI antidepressants (e.g., bupropion [Wellbutrin] and venlafaxine [Effexor]) may be helpful when combined with an SRI.

Although neuroleptics (especially atypical neuroleptics) are promising when added to an SRI, they don't appear to work for BDD—even delusional BDD—when used alone. However, the only research that's been done on this very important question is a retrospective look at what medicines have worked or not worked in the past for people I've seen with BDD. So to know with greater certainty whether neuroleptics alone (i.e., without an SRI) work for BDD, we need good prospective treatment studies of these medications. There are a few published case reports in which an atypical neuroleptic (olanzapine [Zyprexa]) was effective for a patient with BDD. The effectiveness of atypical neuroleptics, in particular, needs to be studied. Other types of medications—such as mood stabilizers, stimulants, and benzodiazepines—also don't seem effective for BDD when used without an SRI (although as I've discussed above, some may help in combination with an SRI). However, there's very little research on these medications, and they, too, need to be more rigorously studied to better evaluate their effect on BDD symptoms.

In a study I did in the early 1990s, before we knew how to treat BDD, I asked my patients what medications they'd taken in the past, and which ones had worked. My aim was to get some clues about which medicines might be effective for BDD and were worth studying. What I found is that only 8% of treatment trials with medications other than SRIs resulted in clinically significant improvement of BDD symptoms. With a class of antidepressants known as tricyclics (excluding the SRI clomipramine [Anafranil], which is a tricyclic), only 15% of 48 treatments resulted in improvement. In a similar type of study, Dr. Hollander found that among 50 BDD patients, tricyclic antidepressants (excluding clomipramine) led to no overall improvement in BDD symptoms, whereas SRIs did improve BDD symptoms. These medications sometimes improved depression but usually not accompanying BDD symptoms.

I found that MAO inhibitors worked for approximately 30% of people. An encouraging finding, however, is that some patients responded well to an MAO inhibitor after not responding to one or more SRIs. Only 2% of neuroleptic (antipsychotic) trials, and 6% of trials with a variety of other psychiatric medications, such as benzodiazepines, resulted in improvement in BDD when used alone (i.e., without an SRI). Neuroleptics also appeared ineffective even for people with delusional BDD, a group they might be expected to help. Keep in mind, though, that these medications may be helpful when combined with an SRI.

So, in summary, SRIs are currently the medication treatment of choice. Some non-SRI medications appear potentially helpful when combined with an SRI, but at the present time most don't appear effective for BDD when used without an SRI.

ECT, Neurosurgery, and Other Treatments

In published case reports, ECT, or shock therapy, was reported to be effective for BDD in two of eight patients. My data suggest a similarly low response rate, with 0 of 8 people responding. I'm aware of approximately 10 additional cases, in none of which ECT was effective for BDD, although several patients had transient improvement, primarily in depressive symptoms. These findings, while limited by the very small number of patients, suggest that this treatment isn't promising for BDD. Nonetheless, because ECT is the most effective treatment available for depression, it may may be worth considering for someone with BDD who is also severely depressed, especially if the depression doesn't appear largely due to BDD. Because ECT is a very effective treatment for depression and has the potential to be lifesaving, it should remain an option for someone with BDD who is very depressed and suicidal.

While brain surgery might seem like a drastic measure, some people are so severely tormented and incapacitated by their BDD symptoms that they seriously consider it or have it done. I'm aware of several people with BDD who tried this. A published case reported improvement in BDD symptoms with a procedure known as a modified leucotomy. A colleague told me about a young woman with debilitating and intractable BDD who had an excellent response to a similar procedure (bilateral anterior cingulotomy and subcaudate tractotomy). Procedures like these interrupt brain circuits implicated in OCD (see Chapter 10).

I know of four people with unusually severe BDD who, after failing countless other treatments, had a neurosurgical procedure known as an anterior internal capsulotomy. This treatment is being studied in severe treatment-refractory OCD. Two people didn't respond, but two did. One woman who improved had been completely devastated by BDD concerns that focused on her hair. She lost her job and friends, was housebound, had many lengthy hospitalizations, and tried to electrocute herself and kill herself in many other ways. Her husband told me, "Before the surgery, her life was desperation and despair; the procedure was miraculous and lifesaving." However, in a study of this procedure in people with intractable OCD, those who also had BDD-like symptoms (BDD per se wasn't assessed) tended not to respond as well as people without BDD-like symptoms.

It's hard to know what to make of these conflicting reports. The main thing to consider is that the data we have on neurosurgery is still extremely limited. There are reports on only a few cases; no scientifically rigorous and systematic studies have been done in BDD. Therefore, I don't at this time recommend brain surgery for BDD, especially if many other treatment options haven't been tried or haven't been adequate. But it will be important to see whether future studies demonstrate that certain types of neurosurgery offer hope for severely ill people with BDD who don't respond to other treatments. In the meantime, it's worth considering neurosurgery for extremely severe, life-threatening BDD for which many other available treatments have been tried but haven't worked. It's a better alternative than life-long hospitalization, living in a nursing home for the rest of your life, or suicide.

Other new treatments are being pioneered and tested in a variety of psychiatric disorders, especially depression and OCD. These cutting-edge treatments include vagal nerve stimulation (in which an electrode that's surgically implanted in the neck stimulates the vagus nerve, which travels to the brain), transcranial magnetic stimulation (in which a coil held near the head induces changes in the brain's magnetic field), and deep brain stimulation (in which electrodes implanted in the brain create reversible changes in nerve cell functioning). None of these treatments have been studied in BDD (or at the time of this writing, even used for BDD to my knowledge), so we don't know whether or not they're effective for this disorder.

A Suggested Approach To Treating BDD with Medications: A Proposed Algorithm

In this section, I'll discuss a proposed "algorithm" for treating BDD with medications, which pulls together and visually presents the information in this chapter. The algorithm is shown in Figure 8. It's a visual flow diagram that you can follow when treating BDD.

1) Diagnose BDD Starting at the top of the algorithm, you can see that the first step is to diagnose BDD.

Figure 8.   A Proposed Medication Treatment Algorithm for BDD[a,b,c]

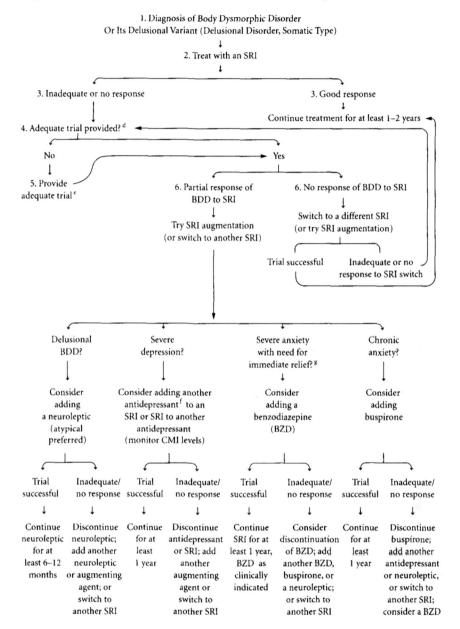

[a] This is an abbreviated version of a proposed medication treatment approach to BDD; see the text for more detail.

[b] This algorithm incorporates and is consistent with scientific evidence, but because such evidence is currently limited, the algorithm is also based on clinical experience.

[c] The algorithm is for medication treatment only and does not include CBT, which appears effective for BDD (see the next chapter).

(continued)

*2) **Treat with an SRI*** If you follow the arrow down, you can see that if BDD is present, the next step is to treat with an SRI, regardless of whether you have delusional or nondelusional BDD.

*3) **Response to an SRI*** If you have a good response to the SRI, you then follow the line that goes down to the right. In this case, the algorithm suggests continuing the effective SRI for at least 1 to 2 years. If you haven't had a good response to the SRI, you follow the line to the left, which asks if you had an adequate trial.

*4) **Have you had an adequate SRI trial?*** I've discussed in the text what an adequate SRI trial is; footnote d briefly reminds you of this.

*5) **Be sure you have an adequate SRI trial*** If you *haven't* had an adequate SRI trial, you follow the line that goes over to the left and down, which indicates that the next step is to have an adequate SRI trial (see footnote e and the text for a description). If you *have* had an adequate SRI trial, you follow the line to the right and down. At the fork, you then go to the right or the left, depending on whether your BDD has partially responded (follow the line to the left) or not responded (follow the line to the right) to the SRI.

*6) **Augment or switch*** If your BDD has *partially responded* to an adequate SRI trial (at least "much improved" or a 30% or greater decrease in your score on the BDD-YBOCS (which is in Appendix C), the algorithm suggests that you try SRI augmentation. However, the information in parentheses indicates that switching to another SRI is also an option. If your BDD *hasn't responded* to an adequate SRI trial, you follow the line to the right. The algorithm suggests that you can switch to another SRI. Trying SRI augmentation is also an option.

*7) **Augmentation options*** You then continue to follow the lines of the algorithm, depending on your response. Augmentation options are shown at the bottom of the algorithm. I've discussed several additional treatment options above in the text that aren't included in the algorithm.

I won't describe the algorithm's contents in any more detail here, because I've previously discussed them. However, there are a few important caveats about the algorithm. First, this algorithm (and algorithms in general) shouldn't be used in a cookbook fashion or in place of your doctor's clinical judgment. The algorithm contains general treatment suggestions and may need to be mod-

Figure 8 *(continued)*

d Has the highest SRI dose recommended by the pharmaceutical company or that you can tolerate been reached and used for a minimum of 3 weeks, and has the total SRI trial duration been 12–16 weeks?

e Try to reach the highest dose recommended by the pharmaceutical company or the highest dose you can tolerate for at least 3 weeks; be sure that you take the SRI for a total duration of 12–16 weeks.

f Options include clomipramine (brand name Anafranil), venlafaxine (brand name Effexor), bupropion (brand name Wellbutrin) and others.

g In some cases (e.g., for severe anxiety and suicidal thinking), consider combining a benzodiazepine or neuroleptic with an SRI as initial treatment.

  CMI=clomipramine; BZD=benzodiazepine

ified to reflect your unique clinical situation. For example, you may also have non-BDD disorders or symptoms that will influence the medications you take. For example, if you have another disorder, such as bipolar disorder, you would need additional medications that aren't shown on the algorithm. For people with an alcohol or drug problem, it may be unwise to use a benzodiazepine or a stimulant. Other factors may influence the treatment decisions that you and your doctor make. They include potential medication side effects, your treatment preference, or a need for immediate symptom relief. So the algorithm is a general proposed treatment guide that will need to be tailored to you in consultation with your doctor.

Another important caveat is that although the algorithm incorporates and is consistent with available empirical data from scientific studies, there are still relatively few treatment studies of BDD. In particular, there's very little scientific data on SRI augmentation strategies for BDD. Therefore, this algorithm—especially the augmentation section—is also based on clinical experience. Furthermore, clinical experience with certain treatment approaches is still limited. Finally, the algorithm itself hasn't been systematically tested. For all of these reasons, this algorithm is "proposed"; it isn't written in stone. More treatment research on BDD is greatly needed and will likely modify and improve the algorithm as we learn more about effective treatments.

Needed Treatment Research

More BDD treatment research studies are greatly needed! We need more and better studies of the treatment options discussed in this chapter and the development of new and more effective treatments for BDD. We need more placebo-controlled SRI studies, including studies that compare SRIs to one another and to other types of medications, to further establish that SRIs really are the most effective medication for BDD. Because many people respond only partially to SRIs, we also need studies of SRI augmentation options to help people become symptom free. Studies of longer-term treatment are also critically important; such studies will help us learn more about how people do on medication over time and what happens when they stop effective medication. We also need to determine how many people get even better if CBT is added to medication.

Research studies like these are very expensive; they require funding and take time to complete. They can be done only if people with BDD participate in them. Nonetheless, I'm optimistic that more treatment research will be done in the coming years and that this research will continue to alleviate the terrible suffering that BDD so often causes.

·· *fourteen* ··

Cognitive-Behavioral Therapy
for BDD

An Overview of Cognitive-Behavioral Therapy (CBT)

Cognitive-behavioral therapy is the best-studied and most promising type of psychotherapy for BDD. Cognitive-behavioral therapy, or CBT, is a broad term encompassing a number of specific therapeutic approaches. It is a practical "here and now" treatment approach that focuses on changing problematic thoughts and behaviors. When used by trained therapists, CBT is effective for such disorders as depression, phobias, panic disorder, obsessive compulsive disorder, and eating disorders. Available data indicate that it is also effective for BDD.

The *cognitive* aspect of cognitive-behavioral therapy focuses on cognitions—that is, thoughts and beliefs. The goal of cognitive therapy is to identify, evaluate and change unrealistic ways of thinking. The *behavioral* aspect of cognitive-behavioral therapy focuses on problematic behaviors, such as checking and avoidance of social situations. The aim is to stop such behaviors and substitute healthier behaviors. Usually, cognitive and behavioral approaches are combined—hence, the commonly used term "cognitive-behavioral therapy," or CBT.

CBT for BDD usually consists of the following core techniques:

- *Response (ritual) prevention*
- *Cognitive restructuring*
- *Behavioral experiments*
- *Exposure*

I'll briefly describe each of these techniques here and will discuss them in more detail later in this chapter.

1) Response (ritual) prevention:

- *What it is:* You resist performing excessive, repetitive BDD behaviors, such as mirror checking, excessive grooming, and reassurance seeking.

- *Goal of response prevention:*   The goal is to stop doing certain BDD behaviors (such as reassurance seeking) altogether and to do others (such as grooming) only a normal amount.

- *How to do it:*   First, start with the easier behaviors, trying to cut them down and eventually stopping them. Then move on behaviors that are harder to resist. Try to cut those down and eventually stop them, too.

- *Why it's important to do response prevention:*   It's understandable that you do BDD behaviors over and over again, but they really don't help. Even if you feel a little better right after you do them, the relief doesn't last very long. Plus, these behaviors just feed BDD and keep it going (I'll say more about this later in this chapter). Even worse, for some people the behaviors greatly increase obsessions, anxiety, and depression.

2) Cognitive restructuring:

- *What is it:*   You learn to identify and evaluate negative thoughts and beliefs you have about your appearance as well as "errors" in your thinking. You learn to objectively evaluate whether your appearance-related beliefs are accurate and helpful, and to generate more accurate and helpful beliefs.

- *Goal of cognitive restructuring:*   The goal is to develop more accurate and helpful beliefs about your appearance, rather than automatically assuming that your BDD-related beliefs are true.

- *How to do it:*   You first notice and identify "negative automatic thoughts" about your appearance and the importance of appearance. These are negative thoughts that you have so quickly and automatically you may not even be aware that you're thinking them. You objectively evaluate the evidence that supports and doesn't support your beliefs. You also determine whether the negative automatic thoughts involve distorted thinking (also known as "cognitive errors"). You then use this information to generate more accurate and helpful appearance-related beliefs.

- *Why it's important to do cognitive restructuring:*   People with BDD have very negative beliefs about their appearance and the importance of appearance. Most just assume their beliefs are true. It's important to objectively evaluate the accuracy of these beliefs, rather than just assuming they're true, and to develop beliefs that are more accurate and helpful.

3) Behavioral experiments:

- *What they are:*   You design and carry out experiments to test BDD beliefs to find out if they're accurate or not. This approach is similar to cognitive restructuring in the sense that you're evaluating whether your beliefs are accurate. However, cognitive restructuring is done by writing and filling out a form on paper, whereas a behavioral experiment involves actually going into a situation (e.g., the grocery store) to do the experiment and to collect actual evidence for and against your belief.

- *Goal of behavioral experiments:*   The goal is to objectively evaluate whether your beliefs are true rather than just assuming they're true.

- *How to do them:*   First you make a very specific hypothesis about what you think will happen in a certain situation. Then you go into the situation and test out your hypothesis, collecting evidence for and against it. Let's say you believe that 75% of people will look at you in horror and move away from you within 5 seconds in the grocery store because you look so bad. You would write this down and then go into the grocery store (alone, with a friend, or your therapist). You would observe what people actually do in the store and write down your observations.

- *Why it's important to do behavioral experiments:*   Many people with BDD have appearance-related beliefs that they never really check out. They just assume their beliefs are true. It's important to test whether they really are.

4) Exposure:

- *What it is:*   You gradually face situations that you avoid (for example, social situations) because of your BDD.

- *Goal of exposure:*   The goal is to not avoid any situations because of BDD and to feel more comfortable in those situations.

- *How to do it:*   First, you make a list of the situations you avoid and number them from 0 to 100 according to how anxious they make you feel and how much you avoid them. You start by going into one of the easier situations (one that's rated about a 30) and staying there until you feel less anxious. The more you do this, the easier it will get, and you can then face harder situations. Exposure may work better if it includes a behavioral experiment and cognitive restructuring.

- *Why it's important to do exposure:*   Avoidance of anxiety-provoking situations (like social situations or school) just feeds BDD symptoms and keeps them going. Avoidance also prevents you from having a fulfilling and enjoyable life.

Although I've listed these core techniques separately, in reality they overlap to some degree and are often combined in treatment. Several other cognitive and behavioral techniques are sometimes also used for BDD, usually in combination with the core elements described above. These techniques include mirror retraining, habit reversal, mindfulness, refocusing, activity scheduling, and scheduling pleasant activities. I'll describe these techniques later in this chapter.

More CBT Basics

Here is some more basic information about CBT for BDD:

- *CBT teaches you helpful skills:*   The purpose of CBT is to learn practical skills that can help you cope with and overcome BDD. These are skills you can use now and in the future to keep your BDD under control. Like any kind of learning, it's important to be motivated and to take an active role in your treatment. CBT isn't something that's done to you; rather, it's something you learn how to do, and it requires work on your part. In many ways, your therapist is like a coach or guide who teaches you skills and helps you master them.

- *Homework is important:*   You do homework between treatment sessions and then review it with your therapist at your next session. It consists of doing various assignments and practicing CBT skills. At various stages in your treatment, you'll probably do response prevention, cognitive restructuring, behavioral experiments, and exposure as homework (although the order in which you learn these skills can vary). You'll also do some of these things during your therapy sessions. Although homework may be a somewhat unpleasant word, it's a very important and helpful part of treatment. It gives you a chance to practice CBT skills and try out things that it may not be possible to do during treatment sessions. Research of other disorders has shown that doing CBT homework increases the likelihood that CBT will work (this hasn't been researched in BDD but is probably true for BDD too).

- *Number of sessions:*   The number of sessions can vary a lot, depending on how severe your symptoms are, how motivated you are to do CBT, and other factors. It isn't known what the optimal number of sessions is for BDD. Published studies have used from 8 to 60 sessions. It's hard to predict at the beginning of treatment exactly how many sessions you'll need; this is something that you and your therapist can discuss and decide as your treatment goes along. Some additional "booster sessions" after the treatment is finished can be very helpful.

- *Frequency of sessions:*   Often, CBT is done once a week, although it's possible that it will work faster and better if it's done more frequently (e.g., several times a week or even every day). If weekly sessions don't work, you may want to try more frequent ones. Patients with more severe BDD and difficulty functioning may benefit from more than one session a week.

- *Length of sessions:*   Often CBT sessions last for an hour, but sometimes they're longer than this. Most published studies have used 90-minute sessions. 90-minute, or even longer, sessions may be more effective than shorter session, because they allow you to do more things (e.g., exposure or behavioral experiments) during the session with your therapist (rather than just doing them on your own at home as homework).

- *Group or individual treatment:*   CBT can be done individually (with just you and your therapist) or in a group (with one or two therapists and 4 to 10 other people with BDD). Some people participate in both individual and group CBT.

- *Stages of treatment:*   Treatment typically begins with an evaluation by a physician or therapist to confirm that you have BDD, to assess other problems or disorders you may have, and to discuss treatment options. If you decide to do CBT, you'll then have another session or two to lay some important groundwork for treatment (e.g., learning more about BDD and CBT, which is called psychoeducation). Then you'll move on to learning and practicing the core aspects of treatment and perhaps some of the other techniques listed above; this is what most of the treatment will consist of. Toward the end of treatment, you'll learn "relapse prevention," which will help you maintain your gains after you end treatment. "Booster sessions," in which you check in with your therapist from time to time after you end treatment, can also help you maintain your gains and keep your CBT skills sharp.

- *You need a therapist trained in CBT:*   For CBT to work, you need to find a therapist with training in this treatment who is also familiar with BDD (I'll say more about this below).

What's the Evidence That CBT Works?

In the 1980s a few clinician-researchers (e.g., Isaac Marks in England) published papers in scientific journals that illustrated the effectiveness of CBT for several patients with BDD. These clinical reports spurred other researchers to conduct more scientifically rigorous studies of CBT. In these studies, larger numbers of patients were evaluated, and they were assessed with standard rating scales.

CBT is the only type of therapy that has been systematically studied in BDD. Available research studies indicate that CBT substantially improves BDD symptoms in a majority of people. Most of these studies, which are summarized in Table 17 below, used a combination of cognitive and behavioral techniques. Research hasn't been published which teases apart which components of CBT are most effective. Nor have studies compared CBT to other forms of therapy, so it hasn't been proven that CBT is more effective than other types of therapy. Nonetheless, clinical impressions suggest that this is probably the case. Studies

Table 17. Published Studies of Cognitive-Behavioral Therapy (CBT) for BDD[a,b]

Study Design	Individual or Group Treatment[c]	Number of Patients	Number and Length of Treatment Sessions	Study Results	Reference[d]
Patients were randomly assigned to CBT or a no-treatment control condition[e,f]	Individual	19	• 12 weekly sessions • Each session was 60 minutes	BDD symptoms improved significantly more with CBT than no treatment	Veale, 1996
Patients were randomly assigned to CBT or a no-treatment control condition[e]	Group (4 to 5 members per group)	54	• 8 weekly sessions • Each session was 2 hours	CBT was significantly more effective than no treatment; significant improvement occurred in 82% of the CBT group at the end of treatment, and in 77% at follow-up 4.5 months later	Rosen, 1995
Case series[g]	Individual	5 in the first series; 17 in the second	• First series: 4 weeks of daily CBT (20 total sessions), 12 weeks of daily CBT (60 sessions), or 8 or 12 weeks of weekly sessions • Second series: 4 weeks of daily sessions • All sessions were 90 minutes	4 of 5 patients in the first series improved; in the second series BDD severity decreased by 50% or more for 12 of 17 patients	Neziroglu, 1993

Case series[g]; at the end of 6 weeks of treatment, patients were randomly assigned to a 6-month relapse prevention program versus a no-treatment control condition	Group (4–5 members per group)	13	• 12 weekly sessions • Each session was 90 minutes	BDD symptoms significantly improved	Wilhelm, 1999
Case series[g]	Individual	10	• 6 initial weeks of daily sessions (30 total sessions) • Each session was 90 minutes • The 6 months of relapse prevention sessions occurred every other week	BDD symptoms significantly improved by 6 weeks and remained stable at follow-up after another 6 months. Relapse prevention treatment resulted in stable gains for anxiety and depression, which worsened in the control group during the 6-month follow-up, although the groups did not differ in BDD symptom severity at the end of the 6-month follow-up.	McKay, 1997, 1999

[a]These are the controlled studies and larger case series published in scientific journals at the time of this writing. Single case reports, small case series, and chart review studies are excluded. However, it's worth noting that in a retrospective chart-review study of 30 patients with BDD, Drs. Juan Gomez-Perez, Isaac Marks, and Juan Gutierrez-Fisac reported improvement in about half of the 21 patients who completed CBT treatment. Also excluded are studies of body image dissatisfaction that did not determine whether participants had the disorder BDD per se.

[b]All of the studies except for McKay's used a combination of cognitive and behavioral techniques; McKay and colleagues used only behavioral techniques.

[c]Patients who received individual treatment met alone with their therapist; those treated in a group received treatment with other patients with BDD.

[d]References for these studies are listed in Chapter 18.

[e]Patients were randomly assigned to CBT or to a waiting list; those on the waiting list didn't receive treatment. This study design has some advantages over a case series, because the no-treatment condition controls for changes in BDD that might occur simply with the passage of time or for other reasons. The randomization process minimizes differences in the patients in the two groups which might affect treatment outcome.

[f]In this study, no patients were delusional.

[g]In the case series design, all patients received CBT.

have demonstrated that CBT is more effective than certain other therapies in disorders with similarities to BDD, such as OCD and social phobia.

The first two studies shown in Table 17, which were "controlled" studies, are the most scientifically rigorous studies done so far. In these studies, patients who received CBT were compared to patients on a waiting list who received no treatment. The no-treatment condition controls for changes in BDD that might occur simply with the passage of time or for other reasons. Another advantage of these two studies is that patients were randomly assigned to these two treatment conditions, which minimizes differences in the patients in each group that might affect treatment outcome. The other studies shown in the table were "case series," in which a series of patients was treated with CBT (without comparison to another condition, such as a waiting list).

Some of the studies provided individual treatment, in which patients met alone with their therapist, whereas others used group treatment, in which patients received treatment in a group along with other people with BDD. Most published studies contained only or primarily women. The study by Dr. Rosen included only women, most of whom had weight and body shape concerns, whereas the other studies included people with more typical BDD concerns. Dr. Rosen's study also appeared to contain many people with milder BDD, whereas the other studies appeared to contain many people with more severe BDD.

As you can see from the "Study Results" column in the table, all of the studies found that CBT was often effective for BDD symptoms. In the two studies that used a waiting list control condition, patients who received CBT improved significantly more than those on the waiting list who didn't get CBT. Two of the studies had the advantage of assessing how patients were doing many months after CBT had ended; both studies found that patients maintained their improvement. Thus, the results of CBT appear to last, at least for the 4-to-6-month time periods assessed in these studies.

The results in Table 17 aren't definitive, because none of the studies compared CBT to another type of therapy. It's possible that simply meeting with a therapist every week is what makes people better, not CBT specifically. However, this seems unlikely. Data I've obtained by asking patients what types of treatment they've received in the past, and which treatments helped them, suggest that other types of therapy (for example, standard "talking therapy" or general "counseling") are generally ineffective for BDD. Nonetheless, we need studies that rigorously compare the effectiveness of CBT to other therapies. In the meantime, the studies that have been done so far all indicate that CBT is often effective and a very promising treatment for BDD.

Only one study to my knowledge has looked at the important question of who gets better with CBT—in other words, for whom is CBT most likely to work? This study, by Dr. Neziroglu and colleagues, found that the better the person's insight (i.e., the less delusional their BDD beliefs were), the better they responded to CBT. We need research to determine whether certain cognitive techniques are particularly effective for delusional thinking.

My clinical impression is that people with milder BDD are more likely to do well with CBT, but this doesn't mean that more severely affected patients shouldn't try it; in fact, they're the ones who need it most. It also appears that people who are more motivated and willing to do homework are more likely to improve. This may be the best predictor of who gets better with CBT. Finally, if you're very depressed, it will be much harder to do CBT. Depression can sap your motivation and concentration, and can make it hard to do even the simplest task, let alone CBT homework. If you're very depressed, I'd recommend trying an SRI along with CBT, or trying an SRI first and then doing CBT after the SRI improves your mood, energy, concentration, and motivation.

What Gets Better with CBT?

Many aspects of BDD, as well as related symptoms, improve with CBT. These improvements are generally similar to those found in medication studies. The studies in Table 17 found improvement in the following areas with CBT treatment:

- **BDD symptoms**   All of the studies found that core BDD symptoms significantly improved by the end of treatment. Treated patients spent less time obsessing and performing BDD rituals, and they could better resist and control their obsessions and rituals. In addition, after treatment BDD obsessions and behaviors caused less distress and interfered less with day-to-day functioning. Treated patients also avoided situations less because of BDD.

- **Depressive symptoms**   A number of the studies examined change in depressive and anxiety symptoms, and found that they also improved significantly. In the study by Dr. McKay and colleagues (see Table 17), patients who participated in a 6-month relapse-prevention program after 6 weeks of intensive treatment maintained their improvement in anxiety and depression. In contrast, patients who received only the initial 6 weeks of treatment without the subsequent relapse prevention program experienced worsening of depression and anxiety after the initial 6-week treatment program. While they're preliminary, these results suggest that longer-term treatment may be needed to maintain improvement in depression and anxiety.

- **Insight**   Dr. Neziroglu has looked at the important question of whether insight improves with CBT treatment. In her case series, she found that insight tended to improve. In other words, people who had CBT developed more realistic and accurate beliefs about their body defects.

- **Body image**   In Dr. Rosen's study, women who received CBT felt less unattractive and became less dissatisfied with their appearance than those who didn't receive CBT. Feelings of low self-worth in connection with weight and shape also improved more in the women who had CBT.

- **Self-esteem** Dr. Rosen also found that self-esteem improved more in women who received CBT than in women who were on the waiting list and didn't receive CBT.

- **Social anxiety** In his study, Dr. Veale examined social anxiety and found that it diminished significantly more in people treated with CBT than in those on a waiting list who didn't receive CBT.

CBT studies done so far haven't examined whether quality of life improves with CBT or whether functioning improves in a variety of domains (e.g., work, household functioning, social functioning). However, studies have shown that CBT reduces global (overall) impairment in functioning due to BDD obsessions and rituals. In addition, clinical observations suggest that multiple domains of functioning and quality of life appear to often improve with CBT.

Taken together, these results are very promising and encouraging. They indicate that CBT often improves not only the core BDD features of preoccupation, distress, and impairment in functioning but also many other important aspects of the disorder.

Rationale for Using CBT for BDD

The strongest rationale for treating BDD with CBT is that research studies (summarized in Table 17) indicate that CBT is often effective (although more and better studies are needed to confirm these promising results). Another rationale is that research has convincingly shown that CBT is often effective for disorders with similarities to BDD, such as OCD and social phobia. In addition, theoretical models of how BDD develops suggest that CBT should work for BDD. I'll now discuss this last point.

In Chapter 10, I provided a more general theoretical model of how BDD develops (see Figure 6). In Chapter 11, I proposed a model of body image in BDD (see Figure 7). I'll now expand upon these two models in a way that's relevant to CBT and how CBT works. The CBT model, shown in Figure 9, provides a more detailed theory about how BDD develops and is maintained. This model is adapted from one developed by Dr. Sabine Wilhelm. Several other BDD researchers have also contributed to a CBT model of BDD—in particular, Drs. David Veale, Fugen Neziroglu, and James Rosen. At this point, this model is largely theoretical and hypothetical, and more research is needed to verify it.

I'll now go through each step of the model shown in Figure 9. Boxes that contain italicized and capitalized typeface show CBT interventions and how they weaken BDD. The top of Figure 9 shows the factors (discussed in Chapter 10) that are proposed to contribute to BDD's development: it's likely that genetic/biological factors, psychological factors, and sociocultural factors combine to create selective and excessive attention to certain aspects of appearance (some of the factors shown in Figure 7 in Chapter 11 may also contribute to this). In other words, people with BDD overfocus on normal appearance features or minor flaws, thereby interpreting visual input in a biased way. (As I discussed

Figure 9.   A CBT Model of BDD

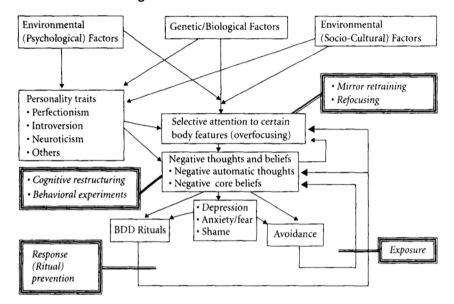

in Chapter 11, some people may also experience a visual "illusion.") They tend to ignore global aspects of appearance, which further distorts self-perception. This selective attention and overfocusing triggers negative thoughts and beliefs about appearance, such as thoughts that you look abnormal and that other people share this view, the belief that other people don't accept you because you look abnormal, and a sense of shame and general defectiveness as a person. There's a feedback arrow going from negative thoughts and beliefs back to selective attention, because having negative thoughts about how you look can cause you to focus even more on the disliked body areas. This creates a vicious cycle in which selective and intensive attention to disliked body areas fuels more negative thoughts and beliefs about those areas, which in turn fuels more selective attention to them, and so on.

As I discussed in Chapters 10 and 11, personality traits such as perfectionism may also play a role in BDD. Although trying to look perfect may be adaptive from an evolutionary perspective, the problem in BDD is that these beliefs become too important and are held rigidly. They probably fuel selective attention to minor asymmetries and appearance flaws as well as negative appearance-related thoughts, perhaps by increasing the discrepancy between how you view yourself and your ideal (see Chapter 11). Other personality traits, such as neuroticism (a tendency to worry, and to be depressed, anxious, and self-conscious) might also contribute to selective attention to appearance "flaws" and to negative thoughts about appearance.

As Figure 8 shows, the CBT techniques of *mirror retraining* and *refocusing* target this selective attention to disliked body areas. With mirror retraining, you learn to notice your entire body, rather than zooming in and overfocusing on the disliked areas. Mirror retraining also helps diminish the negative thoughts by helping you describe and think about your body in less negative ways. With refocusing, you learn to gently refocus your attention on what's going on around you, rather than focusing in on your perceived defects. The CBT techniques of *cognitive restructuring* and *behavioral experiments* help you to objectively evaluate your negative appearance-related thoughts and beliefs, and to develop more accurate and helpful ones.

The next step of the CBT model in Figure 8 proposes that negative thoughts and beliefs about appearance trigger negative feelings, like depression, anxiety, fear, and shame. These painful feelings (and the negative thoughts) fuel BDD rituals—attempts to neutralize and diminish the feelings and thoughts (e.g., reassurance seeking). They also fuel avoidance of situations (e.g., social situations) that trigger the feelings and thoughts. Although it's understandable that people with BDD do rituals and avoid anxiety-provoking situations, these behaviors actually maintain BDD—they reinforce it and keep it going (this is indicated by the heavy arrows going back to the selective attention and BDD thoughts).

Rituals reinforce and feed BDD thoughts and feelings in several ways. First, they keep you focused on your appearance. Also, because they sometimes temporarily diminish painful emotions, you want to do them more and more. The problem is that they don't usually help you feel better, and they keep you focused on your perceived flaws, which feeds and maintains the BDD. Rituals can also maintain BDD by preventing disconfirmation of your appearance-related beliefs. For example, if you go out of the house only after you spend two hours styling your hair, you never have the chance to learn that nothing bad will happen if you spend only 10 minutes. Avoiding situations and people reinforces BDD because it robs you of the opportunity to test your beliefs and learn that terrible things won't happen if you don't avoid these things. It also prevents you from enjoying life and being productive. Like BDD rituals, avoidance may temporarily diminish painful feelings, but in the long run it makes them worse. The CBT technique of *response (ritual) prevention* helps you stop excessive BDD rituals. (In Figure 8, response prevention is shown blocking the rituals.) *Exposure* helps you stop avoiding things so your life becomes more enjoyable, fulfilling, and less focused on BDD. (In Figure 8, exposure is shown blocking avoidance as well as the rituals, because rituals shouldn't be performed during exposure.)

Doing CBT for BDD

I'll now say more about how CBT for BDD is done. Because of space limitations, it isn't possible to do this in a detailed way. Several books in Chapter 10— especially Dr. Wilhelm's book—offer much more detailed information about doing CBT for BDD, and I highly recommend them. The section below will describe the CBT treatment approach, but it isn't intended to substitute for treatment with a trained CBT therapist. At present, no CBT treatment manuals for therapists have been developed. (A treatment manual provides a more detailed, step-by-step program for therapists to follow when treating a patient.) However, Dr. Wilhelm, Dr. Gail Steketee, and I are currently developing one, which we hope will enhance treatment for people with BDD.

The CBT approach that's discussed below has some things in common with approaches that have been proven effective for disorders that have similarities to BDD, such as social phobia, OCD, and depression. However, the approach has been modified specifically for BDD because BDD differs in important ways from these other disorders (see Chapter 16). Clinician/researchers who have taken the lead in developing CBT for BDD include Drs. David Veale, Sabine Wilhelm, Fugen Neziroglu, James Rosen, Thomas Cash, and Rocco Crino. These individuals have made great strides with this; nonetheless, we are still figuring out the best ways to do CBT for BDD, and it's likely that some of the currently recommended techniques will be more fully developed and further modified over time as we gain more clinical experience with different approaches and do more research studies.

The First Steps

Before you start CBT, it's important to take a few essential steps. First, you need to overcome the treatment barriers I discussed in Chapter 13. In addition, you need to take a few critical steps that are more specific to CBT:

1) First, you need to find a therapist who's specifically trained in CBT and is familiar with treating BDD: Most therapists and counselors aren't trained in CBT. You can ask over the phone, before you even make an appointment, whether the therapist does CBT and has treated patients with BDD. If you have trouble finding a CBT-trained therapist, some of the resources listed in Chapter 18 may be helpful. You'll need to meet with the therapist for an evaluation to confirm that you have BDD and to discuss treatment options.

2) You need to be motivated and willing to do the treatment during sessions and to do homework between sessions: CBT isn't just done to you. You aren't a passive recipient of the treatment, which magically makes you better. Rather, you learn specific skills with your therapist's guidance so you can eventually learn to be your own therapist. CBT is often hard work. So you need to be motivated, involved in the treatment, and willing to do the required work during and between treatment sessions. If you aren't sure whether you're motivated, you can meet with the therapist to learn more about the treatment approach and decide whether you want to try it.

3) If you have severe BDD or are very depressed or suicidal, consider taking an SRI before or during CBT: If your BDD is very severe or you're very depressed, it may be too hard to do CBT without an SRI. Depression can sap your energy and diminish your motivation, making CBT difficult. An SRI can diminish your BDD and depressive symptoms to the point where you're motivated to do CBT and able to fully participate in it. *If you're considering suicide because of BDD symptoms, in my view it's essential to take an SRI, whether or not you do CBT.*

Starting CBT for BDD

Once you decide to start CBT, there are a few things you and your therapist will do to lay the groundwork for learning the core CBT skills. These building blocks include (but aren't limited to) the following:

1) Learning more about BDD and CBT: Your therapist will discuss BDD and CBT with you (i.e., provide psychoeducation) and answer your questions.

2) Developing a model of your BDD: It's helpful to discuss your BDD symptoms in detail with your therapist so you can develop a model of how your symptoms seem to have developed and are maintained. You can use Figure 8 as a guide, filling in whether you experienced any life events that seem to have contributed to BDD, what rituals you do, what situations you avoid, etc. You and your therapist can use this model to help tailor the treatment specifically to you.

3) Setting goals: It's important to set goals for your treatment—what you'd like to accomplish. This will help you and your therapist stay on track during treatment. For example, one goal might be to return to school. Another might be to go shopping during the day rather than only at night when fewer people are in the store. The more specific you make your goals, the better.

You'll then begin to learn the core CBT skills defined above and discussed in more detail below. It isn't known what's the best order to learn them in, although some experts begin with response prevention or cognitive restructuring. Response prevention will probably give you some immediate relief. And learning cognitive techniques early in treatment may make exposure easier. It isn't known whether all core aspects of CBT are necessary, or whether some are more effective than others. Usually, they're all combined. Until research is done which answers these questions, it's probably best to learn all the core skills, as well as some additional skills such as habit reversal (for skin picking), refocusing, and mirror retraining.

Response (Ritual) Prevention

Response (ritual) prevention is stopping compulsive behaviors (rituals). The goal is to stop checking mirrors, asking for reassurance, comparing with others, measuring your body, excessively changing your clothes, or engaging in any other repetitive BDD-related behaviors. The ritual should be minimized—and ideally stopped altogether.

As I mentioned earlier, the rationale for this approach is that these behaviors sometimes decrease anxiety and thus are done again and again, in the hope that this will be one of those times. But relief of anxiety is usually only temporary, if it occurs at all. Rituals also keep you focused on your appearance, and rituals may actually worsen anxiety. In addition, the behaviors can maintain your fear and prevent disconfirmation of your beliefs about the perceived defect. For example, if you always cover a scar with makeup, you never have the opportunity to see that people won't shun you if it's uncovered.

Many experts start response prevention early in treatment, because bringing excessive behaviors/rituals under control will diminish your preoccupation and distress. You start by making a list of your behaviors/rituals. You can use the Ritual Form (see below) to do this. You rate each behavior from 0 to 100 according to how hard it would be to stop the behavior—for example, how much anxiety you would feel. You can ask yourself questions such as "How much anxiety would I feel if I stopped asking my mother if I look okay?" or "How anxious would I get if I didn't wear a hat when I leave the house?" Susan's Ritual Form is shown below.

Once you make these ratings, you start cutting back on the behaviors, beginning with the one with the lowest rating (the least anxiety-provoking one). If possible, you should try and stop that particular behavior altogether, especially if you find that when you do it once you end up doing it over and over. For example, if asking another person for reassurance triggers asking many times, it may be better to try and not ask for reassurance at all, as it may be especially hard to resist the urges to ask again and again. However, some behaviors may be far too difficult to initially stop cold turkey. In this case, cutting back gradually until you stop the behavior altogether may be the best approach. For example, putting a total stop to mirror checking right away is usually very difficult, so it may work better to cut out particular checking times, such as your morning checks or your afternoon checks. Once you master this, you could then move on to stopping the mirror checks that are harder to resist—for example, before going out for the day—until you eventually stop all mirror checking.

Initially, doing response prevention can increase your anxiety. And some response prevention (e.g., going out of the house without makeup) involves exposure, which is anxiety provoking. However, the more you do it, the easier it gets, and ultimately your anxiety will diminish. You gradually move up your behavior/ritual rating scale, stopping or cutting back and then stopping behaviors that are harder to resist. You can stop or cut down on one behavior at a time or on several simultaneously. Eventually, you stop all of them.

Susan rated reassurance seeking the lowest but still found it hard to completely stop it all at once. So she started with this behavior and cut it down gradually. For the first week she asked her mother for reassurance only 10 times a day instead of 20 times a day, for the second week only 5 times a day, and for the third week only 2 times a day. Then she stopped altogether. Both she and her mother were very pleased! You could cut down on your behaviors faster or slower than this, depending on what you think you can challenge yourself to do and successfully accomplish. Susan then moved up her hierarchy on the behavior/ritual form, cutting down and then stopping each excessive behavior. For example, when she got to grooming, she cut her grooming time down from 5 hours a day to 4 hours a day, then to 3 hours a day, 2 hours a day, and 1 hour a day. Eventually, she did it for only 30 minutes a day.

Of all of the CBT techniques, response prevention is probably the easiest to do without the assistance of a professional therapist. Even if you don't do formal CBT with a therapist, I'd encourage you to try response prevention on your

Ritual Form

Behavior/Ritual	How Hard It Would Be To Stop the Behavior
#1 (most difficult):	
#2:	
#3:	
#4:	
#5:	
#6:	
#7:	
#8:	
#9:	
#10:	

Susan's Ritual Form

Behavior/Ritual	How Hard It Would Be To Stop The Behavior
#1 (most difficult): Using lots of makeup (camouflaging)	100
#2: Grooming (spending too much time in the morning)	80
#3: Buying lots of beauty products	65
#4: Checking mirrors	60
#5: Changing my clothes lots of times in the morning	50
#6: Comparing myself with other people and models in magazines	40
#7: Asking my mother for reassurance	30

own. The key to success is to always be consistent in cutting down the behaviors. Once you cut down, don't let yourself start doing them more again. The more consistent you are in cutting down and stopping the behaviors, the more relief you'll experience because you won't be feeding the BDD anymore.

Stop excessive mirror checking   Checking mirrors and other reflecting surfaces (e.g., windows, backs of spoons) is one of the most important behaviors to control. Many people say they quickly feel better when they cut back or stop this behavior. Mirror checking is time consuming and often makes people much more anxious and depressed. In addition, most BDD sufferers check reflecting surfaces so excessively, closely, and in such minute detail that they get a very distorted view of themselves and then feel even worse about how they look. Have you ever intensely stared in the mirror at something on your face (a mark, pimple, or pore) from only an inch away? Or closely examined your face with a magnifying mirror? Minor flaws become gigantic! This is what many people with BDD do, many for hours a day. Other reflecting surfaces (e.g., car bumpers, shiny plastic or chrome surfaces) will also give you a very distorted picture of yourself.

The goal is to have a normal relationship with mirrors (mirror retraining, which I'll describe below, can help you achieve this). This means not going out of your way to check them, not checking them many times a day or for long periods of time, not staring in them from only an inch or two away, and being able to look in them briefly when necessary (for example, when grooming each morning). For example, it would be reasonable to stand several feet from the mirror for 5 to 10 minutes each morning while washing your face, combing your hair, and brushing your teeth—without zeroing in on your flaws. It's also reasonable to intermittently look in a mirror for a few minutes when washing your face and brushing your teeth at night. What you don't want to do is gaze at yourself for longer periods of time, make extra trips to the bathroom or other places during the day to check, or sneak peeks in a pocket mirror or reflecting surfaces you encounter during the day. It's probably also a good idea to take down extra mirrors if you have lots of them. For example, no one needs five mirrors in their living room.

Stop asking for reassurance   Getting reassurance that you look okay may decrease your anxiety temporarily, but soon the anxiety returns, as does the urge to ask again. Quite often, a reassuring reply isn't believed, so anxiety doesn't diminish even temporarily. The best thing to do is to stop asking people how you look or if you look okay. If a BDD sufferer asks you to reassure them, it's best not to respond. Instead, you could give a response like "I know you're upset about how you look, but it doesn't help for me to respond to you," or "We've agreed that it isn't useful for me to reassure you; this is a BDD ritual that I don't want to reinforce." It can help to then encourage the BDD sufferer engage in some activity other than a discussion of appearance. With time, if reassurance isn't provided, the behavior and the need for reassurance may eventually become less frequent or even stop.

Limit grooming time Try to limit grooming activities, such as applying makeup, shaving, or styling your hair. Keep it to a reasonable amount of time, for example, 15 minutes a day. Time, rather than how you feel, should be used to determine when to stop the behavior, because people with BDD typically never feel really satisfied with how they look. If you spend a lot of money on beauty products, it's a good idea to limit this as well, keeping the amount well within your budget.

Stop other compulsive BDD-related behaviors Avoid comparing yourself with models in fashion magazines if they trigger increased obsessions and anxiety. Stop comparing yourself with other people; try, for example, to focus on the conversation you're having with them instead. Stop measuring yourself, frequently weighing yourself, and frequently changing your clothes. Tell yourself that these are BDD rituals—not things you *have* to do.

Recording the time spent doing these behaviors facilitates success. You may also want to keep a diary of situations that seem to trigger or worsen the checking behavior. This can help you anticipate difficult situations, devise techniques for dealing with them, and monitor progress.

Keeping busy is also useful. It can help to develop a list of enjoyable activities, which you can refer to and do instead of ritualizing when the urge to ritualize occurs. Some people find it helpful to put this list on the refrigerator, where they can easily find it. Reminding yourself to go for a walk, pick up a crossword puzzle, listen to your favorite music, or go jogging instead of checking the mirror are just some examples of activities to substitute for BDD thoughts and behaviors. Keeping busy can decrease the obsessions and behaviors to some extent by shifting attention away from them, although it isn't, by itself, adequate treatment for BDD.

Be creative, and try to come up with other ways to resist your BDD behaviors. One woman I treated posted reminder signs outside her bathroom door which said "Are you SURE you really want to go in there???" This reminded her that if she did go in, she'd probably pick her skin and end up feeling much worse. She told me, "Reading the sign reminded me that I'd regret it; it got me to stop, turn around, and do something else instead." Try making the signs creative and colorful so you notice them. You can also record these kinds of messages (for example, "Don't pick") on a tape recorder and play them.

You can also make a list of the advantages and disadvantages of skin picking, mirror checking, and other BDD behaviors, listing the advantages of each behavior in one column and the disadvantages of it in another. You can then rate each advantage and disadvantage from 1 (not very important to me) to 10 (very important to me). This can potentially help you and your therapist find ways to help you deal with the problem. For example, if one of the advantages of skin picking is stress relief, it may be helpful to learn ways to deal with anxiety and stress.

Cognitive Restructuring (Cognitive Therapy)

Whereas response prevention focuses on changing problematic *behaviors*, cognitive therapy focuses on identifying and changing cognitions—that is, the negative *thoughts and beliefs* that underlie and fuel problematic behaviors. Cognitive therapy aims to help people overcome negative attitudes about themselves, and may also make it easier to do exposure.

Cognitive therapy was initially developed by a psychiatrist, Aaron Beck, and has been further developed by many others over the past several decades for the treatment of depression, anxiety disorders, and other disorders. Several experts have further modified cognitive restructuring for BDD, including Drs. David Veale, Sabine Wilhelm, Fugen Neziroglu, and James Rosen. This type of therapy is based on the premise that our internal world can be divided into thoughts, feelings, and behaviors, which interact in a complex way with the environment, as illustrated in the figure below. This figure is similar to the bottom portion of the CBT model shown in Figure 9.

Cognitive therapy (cognitive restructuring) focuses on evaluating and changing negative thoughts and feelings such as these, which should in turn change painful emotions and problematic behaviors. As the term "cognitive" implies, the focus in cognitive therapy is on evaluating and changing *thoughts and beliefs.* A reason for this focus is that cognitions (thoughts) drive emotions. For example, if you hear a loud noise in the middle of the night while you're in bed, after your initial startle you'll feel frightened if you think a burglar is in the house but simply annoyed if you think your cat knocked a book off a shelf. How you *feel* will depend on what you *think* is going on. Another reason cognitive therapy focuses on changing thoughts and beliefs is that it's hard to change your feelings directly; it's easier to change the thoughts and beliefs that create the feelings.

Cognitive restructuring involves following a number of steps, which you write down on a form called a *"thought record."* A blank thought record you can use is provided below, as is Kelly's thought record, which has been filled out for the example in Figure 10. I'll first give an overview of the steps involved in filling out a thought record and will then explain it in more detail.

1. Identify the *negative automatic thoughts* that trigger upsetting feelings and behaviors (for example, "My lips are too small in proportion to the rest of my face"). Write down how strongly you believe the thoughts (0% to 100%). Also write down the triggering situation for the thoughts (e.g., seeing a model on TV).
2. Identify the *maladaptive interpretations (core beliefs, attitudes, and rules)* that *underlie* the negative thoughts and drive the BDD symptoms (e.g., "If I don't look right, I'll always be alone").
3. Identify and write down the unpleasant *feelings/emotions* that the negative automatic thoughts and beliefs cause. Often, these feelings are

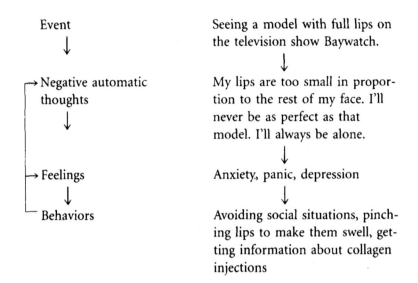

Event	Seeing a model with full lips on the television show Baywatch.
Negative automatic thoughts	My lips are too small in proportion to the rest of my face. I'll never be as perfect as that model. I'll always be alone.
Feelings	Anxiety, panic, depression
Behaviors	Avoiding social situations, pinching lips to make them swell, getting information about collagen injections

Figure 10.   An Example of BDD-Related Thoughts, Feelings, and Behaviors and How They Interact with the Environment

sadness, anxiety, panic, or shame. Rate how strongly you feel them (0%-100%)

4. Identify any *"cognitive errors"* (also known as "thinking errors") that your negative automatic thought involves. I'll explain cognitive errors further below, but for the time being I'll note that the thoughts and beliefs on Kelly's thought record involve cognitive errors called "catastrophizing," "fortune telling," and "discounting the positive."

5. As shown in Kelly's thought record, you then generate a *rational alternative thought*. What's the evidence that your negative automatic thoughts and beliefs are true? What's the evidence that they aren't true? Is the thought/belief helpful? (If your thought makes you anxious, depressed, ashamed, or angry, it isn't helpful.) Is there an alternative thought/belief that's more helpful or that might be true, even if you don't believe it 100%? Write down your more realistic or helpful alternative in the "Alternative Thought/Belief" column. Also write down how strongly you belief the alternative thought (0% to 100%).

6. Complete the thought record by writing down your *feelings/emotions after focusing on the alternative thought*. Also write down how strongly you feel it.

The purpose of using a thought record to do cognitive restructuring is to stop simply assuming that your negative thoughts and beliefs are true. Many BDD-related thoughts are unrealistic and unhelpful. Filling out a thought record gives you an opportunity to identify and then *objectively evaluate* your negative

Thought Record for Cognitive Restructuring

Triggering Situation	Negative Automatic Thoughts* (Also rate how strongly you believe them)	Feelings/Emotions (Also rate how strongly you feel them)	Cognitive Errors (Thinking Errors)	Rational Alternative Thoughts/Beliefs** (Also rate how strongly you believe them)	Feelings/Emotions (Also rate how strongly you feel them)

*You can also write down core beliefs in this column

**Some sample questions to ask yourself to challenge your negative automatic thoughts and to generate alternative thoughts:

• What's the evidence that my belief is true? What's the evidence for it and against it?
• Is there an alternative explanation?
• Is my belief helpful? Are there other, more helpful beliefs?
• Identify the cognitive errors and respond to the errors with more realistic statements

Kelly's Thought Record for Cognitive Restructuring

Triggering Situation	Negative Automatic Thoughts* (Also rate how strongly you believe them)	Feelings/Emotions (Also rate how strongly you feel them)	Cognitive Errors (Thinking Errors)	Rational Alternative Thoughts/Beliefs** (Also rate how strongly you believe them)	Feelings/Emotions (Also rate how strongly you feel them)
Seeing a model with full lips on Baywatch	Thought: "My lips are too small in proportion to my face. (80%) Core Belief: If I don't look right, I'll always be alone (80%)	Anxiety, panic, depression (70%)	• Catastrophizing • Fortune-telling • Discounting the positive	I may not look perfect. But that doesn't mean I'll be alone forever. I don't have any evidence that I'll always be alone. Plus, I can't predict the future. And I have many positive traits that people like (60%)	A little sad and anxious (40%)

*You can also write down core beliefs in this column

**Some sample questions to ask yourself to challenge your negative automatic thoughts and to generate alternative thoughts:

• What's the evidence that my belief is true? What's the evidence for it and against it?

• Is there an alternative explanation?

• Is my belief helpful? Are there other, more helpful beliefs?

• Identify the cognitive errors and respond to the errors with more realistic statements automatic thoughts and to generate more accurate and helpful thoughts. As you can see from Kelly's thought record, the strength of her unpleasant emotions (sadness and anxiety) dropped from 70% to 40% after she completed the thought record.

You can fill out a thought record after a situation has occurred, to evaluate it and think it through in a different way. Or, you can fill one out before you go into a situation that you anticipate will be difficult (i.e., during exposure), to prepare yourself and cope with the situation better. The more you fill out thought records as homework, and the more you practice the alternative beliefs (shown in the 5th column of the thought record), the more helpful this exercise will be. It's important to actually fill out the thought record on paper; this process clarifies your thinking and improves the quality of your cognitive re-structuring. However, once you get the hang of it, you'll want to do cognitive restructuring in your head, while you're in a triggering situation, so you can cope with the situation better while you're in it.

I'll now say more about the steps (1 to 6) that I just described and which are shown on the blank thought record and on Kelly's thought record.

1) Triggering situation: The "triggering situation" is any situation in which your negative automatic thoughts occur. For people with BDD, it's often a situation where other people are around. *To identify a triggering situation, ask yourself: "What situation was I in when I felt upset or had an upsetting BDD thought?"*

2) Negative automatic thoughts: It can take a lot of practice to learn how to identify these. Negative thoughts about appearance can be so "automatic" that we hardly realize we're thinking them. They're like a thinking "habit." Often, it's easier to identify the painful feelings (such as anxiety) that you're experiencing. *To identify the negative automatic thought that caused a painful feeling, ask yourself "What was just going through my mind? What thought made me feel upset?"* Here are some more examples of negative automatic thoughts— the frequent yet often-fleeting thoughts that trigger painful emotions in people with BDD:

Some Examples of Negative Automatic Thoughts in BDD

- She must be thinking I look hideous.
- I'll never have a good time at the party because everyone will be staring at me.
- No one will want to talk with me because of my ugly hair.
- This haircut is a total disaster! I definitely can't go out tonight.
- Those boys must be laughing at me because my skin is so bad.

3) Core Beliefs: It can also be very helpful to identify the core beliefs that underlie the negative automatic thoughts, as these beliefs can also be unrealistic and can trigger distressing feelings. These are generally "deeper" beliefs about yourself as well as assumptions or rules that you have about your appearance. *To identify core beliefs, ask yourself: "What does this negative thought mean about me? What would it mean for me if it were true?"* Here are some examples of core beliefs:

Some Examples of Core Beliefs in BDD

- I have to look perfect.

- My worth as a person depends on whether I look good.

- If I don't look right, I'll always be rejected and alone.

- I must always be approved of by everyone.

- Life would be fine if it weren't for this ugly feature.

- I'm unlovable and worthless as a person.

---

4) Cognitive Errors: The next step in cognitive restructuring and filling out a thought record is to determine whether there are any "cognitive errors" (also known as "thinking errors" or "cognitive distortions") in your thoughts and beliefs. Cognitive errors are faulty ways of thinking that fuel our negative automatic thoughts. Cognitive errors don't occur only in BDD, and they aren't made only by people with psychiatric disorders. In fact, we all make cognitive errors every day in our normal thinking. The problem with cognitive errors is that they cause distortions in our thinking, which in turn make us feel bad— for example, sad, angry, anxious, or worried. *To identify cognitive errors you need to become familiar with the common ones and ask yourself: "What cognitive error did I make when I had this thought"?* It's helpful to study the list below and learn to identify the cognitive errors in your thoughts. People with BDD often experience more than one of them. This can in turn help you develop more realistic and accurate ways of thinking. Shown below is a list of some of the cognitive errors that are particularly common in BDD, along with some BDD examples.

Common Cognitive (Thinking) Errors

All-or-nothing (black or white) thinking	You see yourself or the world in extremes—all good or all bad, or black versus white. You view things in all-or-nothing terms. The subtle shades of gray get lost. A BDD-related example: "With hair like this, I'll always look *totally* ugly," or "I'm the only one in the mall who looks like a freak."
Mind reading	You believe you know what other people are thinking—and you assume they're having negative thoughts about you—without having sufficient evidence or considering other, more likely, possibilities. A BDD example: "I *know* that person is thinking my nose looks funny."
Fortune telling	You predict that things will turn out badly, as if you were looking into a crystal ball. A BDD example: "I know everyone will laugh at me if I leave the house," or "I'll *never* get over this hair problem."
Thinking with your feelings	You think something *must* be true because you feel it so strongly, and you ignore evidence to the contrary. You take your emotions as evidence for the truth. A BDD example: "I feel unattractive, so I must look that way."
Labeling	You put a fixed, global, and negative label on yourself without considering evidence to the contrary. A BDD example: "I'm just an ugly loser!"
Discounting the positive	You claim that positive things you do, or positive aspects of yourself, don't count. You transform neutral or even positive experiences into negative ones. A BDD example: "I know that I'm nice and a smart person, but that doesn't matter! All that matters is my stomach." Or when someone tells you that you look good, you think they're just being nice. This cognitive error is responsible for why people with BDD have trouble accepting compliments.
Negative filtering	This is similar to "discounting the positive." You focus on the negatives and ignore the positives and the bigger picture: "All my positive traits don't really count. All that really matters is how my chin looks."
Personalization	You believe that other people are reacting to you, without considering other, more likely, explanations for their behavior. A BDD example: You assume that a look of disgust on someone's face is directed toward you and a reaction to your appearance.

Overgeneralization	You make far-reaching, global conclusions on the basis of a single interaction or event. BDD-related examples: "I didn't get asked out this weekend. I'm never going to go out on a date. No one in the whole world likes me!"
Catastrophizing	You exaggerate the negative aspects of an event and view negative events as catastrophic, without considering other possibilities. BDD-related example: "This haircut is such a disaster that life's not worth living anymore."
Unfair comparisons	You have unrealistically high standards and focus primarily on the few people who meet those standards, finding yourself inferior in comparison. A BDD example: You compare yourself with airbrushed models in magazines and feel upset that you don't look as good as they do.

For each negative automatic thought and underlying core belief you may be able to identify one cognitive error or many. In Kelly's example, there were at least three: catastrophizing, fortunetelling, and discounting the positive. Tom's first example, shown in the thought record below, has the same ones as Kelly. His second example has mindreading, black and white thinking, labeling, discounting the positive, and fortune telling

It's helpful to identify cognitive errors for several reasons. First, it should help you recognize that your thoughts and beliefs may not be completely accurate. Second, it will help you come up with rational alternative thoughts and beliefs for your thought record.

5) Alternative Thoughts/Beliefs: This is the crux of cognitive restructuring and the most difficult step. If it were easy to think in a different (more accurate and helpful) way, you'd probably already be doing it. To generate alternative beliefs, you take the approach of a scientist and objectively ask yourself the following kinds of questions:

- Is there any evidence to support my negative automatic thought/core belief?
- What is the evidence for and against my thought/belief?
- Is there an alternative view or explanation?
- Is the thought/belief helpful? If not, is there a more helpful thought/belief?
- Use the cognitive errors you've identified as a springboard to developing an alternative belief. For example, if you identified "fortune telling" in your negative automatic thought (as both Kelly and Tom did),

Thought Record for Cognitive Restructuring

Triggering Situation	Negative Automatic Thoughts* (Also rate how strongly you believe them)	Feelings/Emotions (Also rate how strongly you feel them)	Cognitive Errors (Thinking Errors)	Rational Alternative Thoughts/Beliefs** (Also rate how strongly you believe them)	Feelings/Emotions (Also rate how strongly you feel them)
Getting a haircut	Thoughts: This haircut is a total disaster. I won't be able to go out tonight (80%). Core Belief: People won't want to be with me if I don't look right.	Panic and shame (70%)	• Catastrophizing • Fortune telling • Discounting the positive	This haircut isn't perfect, but it isn't the end of the world. I may not like it, but I can live with it and go out tonight. I can't predict how my friends will react, anyway. Besides, they like me for who I am (sense of humor, friendliness), not because of my hair (70%)	Anxious but not panicked; some shame (45%)
Buying groceries	Thought: That woman must be looking at me and thinking I'm totally ugly because my jaw's so wimpy. Core Belief: Appearance is the only thing that matters. I'll always be inferior to everyone else.	Humiliation, anxiety, anger (80%)	• Mindreading • Black and white thinking • Labeling • Discounting the positive • Fortune telling	She might be thinking I'm ugly, but there's no evidence she is; she probably has lots of other things to think about, like whether she's buying the right groceries. I really can't read people's minds. Even if she is looking at me, she could be thinking that I seem like a nice person or whether she should buy the brand I'm buying. There's no evidence that I'm totally ugly and will always be inferior. I don't have a crystal ball. Also, people tell me how smart I am and what a good personality I have. Other people don't think appearance is the only important thing, and I have to admit they have a point. I like my friends because they're nice and fun to be with—not because of how their jaw looks!	

*You can also write down core beliefs in this column

**Some sample questions to ask yourself to challenge your negative automatic thoughts and to generate alternative thoughts:
- What's the evidence that my belief is true? What's your evidence for it and against it?
- Is there an alternative explanation?
- Is my belief helpful? Are there other, more helpful beliefs?
- Identify the cognitive errors and respond to the errors with more realistic statements

an alternative thought/belief might be "I really can't predict the future; this (fill in feared event) could happen, but it probably won't." Or, if you identified "mind reading," you could respond by saying that you don't have special powers and you really can't read people's minds.

• After doing all of the above, ask yourself: "After considering all the evidence, is there an alternative thought/belief?"

Try to identify as many alternative beliefs that you can. Some people find it helpful to identify at least one alternative belief in response to each cognitive error.

A therapist can teach you to use some additional and helpful techniques to examine the evidence and generate alternative beliefs. I won't describe them in detail here but will note that they involve approaches such as the pie chart technique, role playing, and the downward arrow technique.

6) Re-rate your feelings and emotions: Now that you've identified and written down some alternative beliefs, how do you feel? Focus on the alternative belief and then write down your emotions and feelings in the last column of the thought record. Are they less painful than they were originally (in column 3)? They should be, if you've identified some useful alternative beliefs. If you don't feel much better, you'll need to try to generate more useful alternative beliefs. Keep in mind that it's unrealistic to think that all painful emotions will completely disappear with one round of cognitive restructuring (that's all-or-none thinking!). It's more realistic to expect that they'll diminish to some degree. The more they diminish, the more successful your cognitive restructuring has been, and the more you'll want to use similar alternative beliefs in the future in similar triggering situations.

7) Rating the strength of your thoughts/beliefs and emotions: You probably noticed that the thought record asks you to rate the strength of your belief in the negative automatic thought and in the rational alternative thought (as well as the strength of your emotions before and after you've generated the rational belief). It's important to do this so you can determine what kinds of alternative thoughts are particularly helpful to you. If you don't believe your alternative belief very much, you'll want to go back to try to generate a better one by more thoroughly examining the evidence (as I discussed above, you'll also need to do this if your emotional distress doesn't diminish). Sometimes people don't believe their alternative belief very strongly because they aren't objectively evaluating the evidence for and against their belief.

Cognitive restructuring isn't the same as positive thinking. Positive thinking involves simply trying to convince yourself of something positive. The problem is that your positive thought may not be true, and so you might not believe it. As a result, you might not feel much better. In contrast to this, with cognitive restructuring you *objectively evaluate* the evidence for and against your belief and *generate a more realistic belief.* It should be more helpful than positive thinking because it's based on *facts,* not on what you wish or hope is true. If you think something terrible is likely to happen, an example of positive thinking is: "Nothing bad could ever happen!" This isn't realistic, because something bad possibly *could* happen. In contrast, an example of cognitive restructuring is identifying the cognitive errors of fortune telling and catastrophizing and then generating an alternative belief such as: "It's possible that something bad could happen but it's unlikely because it hasn't ever happened in this situation before. Besides, I can't predict the future, so how do I know it will happen?" The latter is likely to be more helpful because it's more accurate and believable.

Behavioral Experiments

Many people with BDD have appearance-related beliefs that they believe are true but never really check out. For example, if you assume that people are staring at you intently but you avoid looking at them (because you're sure you're being stared at and are too anxious), you don't have much of a chance to see if your assumption that they're staring at you is true or not. Or if you always wear a hat or heavy makeup when you go out, you don't have a chance to see if people react to you in an unusual way if you go out without them.

Behavioral experiments allow you to test whether your beliefs are actually true. They combine cognitive techniques, exposure, and response prevention. They're similar to cognitive restructuring in the sense that the goal is to learn how to objectively evaluate the accuracy of your BDD-related beliefs and to develop more accurate and realistic beliefs. And, as with cognitive restructuring, you act like a scientist, collecting objective evidence for and against your beliefs. However, cognitive restructuring is done with pen and paper, by filling out thought records, whereas behavioral experiments are done in *real-life situations*. Another difference is that behavioral experiments involve *actual testing* of your beliefs, rather than *thinking* them through as you do with cognitive restructuring. Behavioral experiments also involve exposure and response prevention, in that you go out into situations that you might usually avoid, and you do the experiment without doing your rituals (a blank form is shown below).

In a nutshell, a *behavioral experiment* involves the following steps:

Steps of a Behavioral Experiment

---

1. You come up with a very specific *hypothesis* about what you think will happen in a certain situation;

2. You *design a specific experiment* that will test your hypothesis, and you write it down on a behavioral experiment form (see below);

3. You then *go into the situation and carry out the experiment,* collecting evidence about what actually happens and determining whether your hypothesis is confirmed or not;

4. You then complete the behavioral experiment form, writing down *what actually happened, whether your prediction came true, and what you learned* from the experiment.

Here's an example of a behavioral experiment, which is shown on Lorenzo's behavioral experiment form below. Lorenzo believed that his skin was "beet red" and that his hair looked "really weird" and "stuck out all over the place." He believed that his face was so red and his hair looked so strange that he stood out in a crowd and that people took special notice of him. Lorenzo decided to do a behavioral experiment of going to the grocery store and seeing how people reacted to him. His hypothesis was that because his hair and skin looked so bad, if he went into the grocery store 80% of people would look at him with disgust and move away from him within 5 seconds. Initially, he wasn't sure that people would react with a look of disgust, but after he gave it more thought he agreed that if he really looked that strange, people would react this way and wouldn't be able to totally suppress their feeling of disgust. When people see an amputee or burn victim, for example, they take special notice (even if they try to pretend they don't) and have a look of revulsion, disgust, or even horror on their face, even if it's fleeting. Lorenzo wrote this hypothesis down on his behavioral experiment form. He also rated how certain he was that this would happen, using a percentage (80%) as well as the level of anxiety he predicted he'd feel when doing the experiment (80). Before he carried out the experiment, Lorenzo and his therapist discussed the fact that it was likely that a somewhat higher percentage of people would move away from him than toward him, because people wouldn't want to bump into him. Also, in our society people have a fairly large personal space around strangers and wouldn't want to get too close to him for this reason.

Lorenzo decided to do the experiment with his girlfriend, Juanita, so they could both collect evidence. They went to the grocery store at a busy time, because if very few people were in the store it would be hard to collect much evidence. They bought some groceries and also watched to see how people reacted to Lorenzo. They were careful, however, not to act in an unusual way or to stare at people while collecting the evidence, since this behavior could make people uncomfortable and make them move away from Lorenzo.

What Lorenzo and Juanita observed was that about 30% of people didn't move at all when they were around Lorenzo. They seemed to be busy deciding what food they wanted to buy. About 40% of people moved away from Lorenzo, and about 30% moved toward him. Neither Lorenzo nor his girlfriend observed any looks of disgust, even fleeting ones.

When Lorenzo got home he completed his behavioral experiment form. He met with his therapist a few days later to review it. After the experiment he believed his initial hypothesis only 50% instead of 80%. He decided he'd learned that maybe people weren't disgusted by his looks, and maybe they didn't particularly notice him at all. In fact, they seemed much more interested in check-

---

Behavioral Experiment Form

Before the Behavioral Experiment:

1. Behavioral experiment to be completed (describe in specific terms):

2. Your hypothesis and feared consequences (what you predict will happen; be specific):

3. Rate strength of your belief that the feared consequences will occur (from 0%–100%):

4. Rate level of anxiety (from 0–100):

The Experiment:

5. Date: Time to complete:

6. Actual consequences:

7. Did your predictions (feared consequences) come true?

After the Experiment:

8. Rate strength of your belief in the feared consequences:

9. What did you learn from the experiment?

This form is adapted from a form developed by Dr. Sabine Wilhelm

ing the food prices or ingredients, looking at their shopping list, or keeping their children well-behaved. Lorenzo also realized that perhaps he had initially believed his hypothesis because he went to the grocery store only when it was nearly empty, and he barely looked at people when he was there because he was so worried that they were staring at him. Thus, he'd never had much of an opportunity to test out his belief or disconfirm it.

Lorenzo's Behavioral Experiment Form

Before the Behavioral Experiment:

1. Behavioral experiment to be completed (describe in specific terms):

I'll go to the grocery store on a Saturday afternoon when it's busy to buy groceries with Juanita.

2. Your hypothesis and feared consequences (what you predict will happen; be specific):

Because I look so bad, 80% of people will look at me with disgust (at least briefly) and will move away from me within 5 seconds.

3. Rate strength of your belief that the feared consequences will occur (from 0%–100%):

80%

4. Rate level of anxiety (from 0–100):

80

The Experiment:

5. Date: *Saturday, April 7*   Time to complete: *30 minutes*

6. Actual consequences:

About 30% of people didn't move at all; they seemed busy picking out food or watching their kids. About 40% moved away from me. But no one looked disgusted. They were mostly looking at other things and hardly seemed to notice me. About 30% moved toward me. Juanita and I both agree on this.

7. Did your predictions (feared consequences) come true?:

No. Some people moved away from me, but no one looked disgusted, and no one really even seemed to notice me much. Only about 3 people moved away from me in 5 seconds but they didn't even look at me. And a lot of them stayed where they were or even moved toward me.

After the Experiment:

8. Rate strength of your belief in the feared consequences:

50%

9. What did you learn from the experiment?:

Maybe people aren't taking special notice of me after all, and maybe I don't look really weird or disgusting.

This form is adapted from a form developed by Dr. Sabine Wilhelm

The next week Lorenzo did the same experiment in the grocery store. He then tried a harder experiment. He did the same experiment but went to a hardware store with especially bright lights. Because the lights were so bright, and because the hardware store was very crowded on a Saturday morning, this was an even better experiment. This is because Lorenzo's negative beliefs were even stronger in this situation and was one he usually avoided.

There are several things to keep in mind when designing a good behavioral experiment:

1) Developing the Hypothesis and Planning the Experiment:

The hypothesis has to be testable: It makes sense that you have to have a hypothesis you can actually test in a direct way. If, for example, Lorenzo had gone to the grocery store at midnight, when it was empty, he wouldn't have been able to test his hypothesis very well. As another example, if you have a hypothesis about what people are thinking, to test it you'd have to actually ask them (rather than trying to figure it out by looking at their facial expression, for example), so you'd want to reserve this type of experiment for situations in which it would be socially appropriate to ask people what they're thinking.

The hypothesis has to be specific: If you have a very specific hypothesis, it will be much easier to confirm or disconfirm. Notice that Lorenzo specified the percentage of people he thought would look at him with disgust, and he identified a specific amount of time within which they would move away from him. He and his therapist also specified what a disgusted facial expression would look like. If you have a vague hypothesis (for example, "people will look at me in the store"), it will be hard to collect good evidence. Some people may look at you but many won't. If 10 people look at you but 25 don't, would your hypothesis be confirmed or disconfirmed? If they just look at you, without staring intently or looking at you with horror or disgust, are they really having negative thoughts about you? It would be hard to know.

Come up with a hypothesis that won't be "confirmed" for reasons unrelated to your appearance: In other words, you don't want to predict something that could happen for reasons unrelated to your appearance or by chance. For example, if you predict that 25% of people will leave the checkout line in the grocery store because you look so bad, the problem is that this could happen for many reasons that have nothing to do with you. People not uncommonly leave the line to get some food they forgot, because they noticed that another line was shorter, because they realized they're in the "cash only" line and don't have any cash, etc. Lorenzo's hypothesis—that 80% of people would look at him with disgust and move away from him within 5 seconds—would be unlikely to occur for other reasons.

Make a hypothesis that you'll learn something from: To get the maximum benefit from a behavioral experiment, do an experiment that's likely to influence your thinking to at least some degree. If your hypothesis is refuted but your reaction is "so what," then it probably wasn't worth doing the experiment in the first place.

Specify your hypothesis before the experiment, not after it: Remember that to collect believable evidence, you need to plan beforehand exactly what you're testing. Developing your hypothesis afterward isn't as convincing as developing it beforehand.

2) Doing the Experiment:

Start with easier experiments and then move on to more challenging ones: It's important to design an experiment that you're pretty sure you can successfully complete. If you pick one that's too hard, you may not do it at all, or you may abandon it before you collect your evidence because you're too nervous. On the other hand, you don't want to pick one that's too easy, because you may not learn much from it. Once you successfully complete an experiment, do it again. Then try a more challenging one—for example, in a situation with more people or one that involves getting closer to people, being under brighter lights, or using less camouflage or none at all. If you generally use camouflage, such as makeup or clothing that covers you excessively, you should eventually do behavioral experiments without it.

Behave as normally as possible while collecting your evidence: If you behave in an unusual way—for example, stare at people or follow them around—in order to collect your evidence, they may notice this and become nervous themselves. Because they're nervous, they may take special notice of you or react toward you in an unusual way. This behavior would be a reaction to your behavior, not your appearance. Guido, who was 6 feet 4 inches tall and 220 pounds of solid muscle, intensely stared at people while doing his behavioral experiments. This made people feel very uncomfortable and anxious, so they reacted to him with fear and anxiety. Unfortunately, Guido interpreted this to mean that he really was ugly.

You can do a behavioral experiment alone or with your therapist or a friend: It can be an advantage to take someone with you, because you can get someone else's input as to whether the hypothesis was confirmed or not. It's best, at least initially, to do experiments with your therapist, but whether this is feasible will depend on factors such as where your therapist's office is located and whether there's enough time during your session.

Do lots of experiments: It takes lots of experiments and lots of practice to get the full benefit of behavioral experiments. It isn't realistic to think that just a few experiments will get rid of your BDD.

You can combine your behavioral experiments with cognitive restructuring: It can help to try to anticipate the negative thoughts you'll have about your appearance during the experiment and to do some cognitive restructuring on a thought record form to help you prepare for the behavioral experiment. For example, Lorenzo could have filled out a thought record form for the thought "People will look at me with disgust because I look so bad" before he did his experiment.

3) After the Experiment:

Complete the behavioral experiment form right after you do the experiment: It's important to put your observations in writing and to write down what, if anything, you learned from the experiment. Actually filling out the form will clarify your observations and thinking. After you complete the experiment, also write down the percentage to which you now believe your initial hypothesis. It's unrealistic to expect that the strength of your belief will drop to 0%, but the percentage should drop at least somewhat. If it doesn't, you'll need to rethink the hypothesis or the experiment; often, this indicates that there was some problem with the experiment itself.

Review the experiment and your Behavioral Experiment form with your therapist: You'll want to discuss whether the expected outcome occurred and what you learned from the experiment. You'll also want get your therapist's feedback. For example, he or she may have some useful suggestions for how to design better experiments in the future. Designing good experiments takes practice and skill.

Here are a few suggestions for behavioral experiments you may want to try, if you believe the hypothesis to at least a fair degree and think you'd learn something from them. But you'll also want to design your own experiments; it's best to tailor them specifically to you.

- If I walk down a crowded sidewalk, at least 75% of the people walking toward me will cross to the other side of the street before they pass by me because I'm so ugly.
- If I walk down a crowded sidewalk, at least 80% of the people will look at me with a look of disgust (at least fleetingly) because I look so hideous.
- When I pay the cashier for an item, she'll look at me with disgust and recoil from me because my hands look so deformed and withered.
- If I get on the bus without any makeup, 70% of people will be distracted from what they're doing and intently stare at me because I'll look so bad.

Exposure

Exposure involves gradually facing situations that you fear and avoid because of BDD. Often, these are social situations. The goal of exposure is to not avoid any situations because of BDD and to feel more comfortable in those situations. As I discussed above and showed in Figure 9, avoidance feeds BDD and maintains it.

For exposure to work, you need to enter avoided situations repeatedly, exposing the perceived defect until your anxiety diminishes. While doing exposure, it's important to not perform your rituals. The theory behind exposure is that with enough exposure of the defect, anxiety and fear gradually decrease.

Exposure can be done in several ways. It can be done by imagining yourself in the anxiety-provoking situation with the defect exposed (imaginal exposure). Or you can actually put yourself in the feared situation (in vivo exposure). In vivo exposure is probably more effective, but if it's too anxiety provoking, doing imaginal exposure first may make in vivo exposure possible. The two approaches can be effectively combined.

Here are the basic steps you take to do exposure:

The Basic Steps of Exposure

1. **Make an exposure hierarchy:**   You first list situations you avoid, rating them from the least to the most anxiety provoking and how much you avoid them (see form below);

2. **Start by facing a situation with a lower rating:**   Do exposure in a step-wise fashion, going from easier to harder situations;

3. **Stay in the situation long enough for your anxiety to diminish:**   It's important not to leave the situation before your anxiety has dropped; if you do, the exposure probably won't help, and it may be even harder to face the situation again;

4. **Then enter a situation with a higher rating:**   Increasingly put yourself in situations that are more and more difficult, so you eventually enter the hardest situation;

5. **Do exposure repeatedly and frequently:**   The more often you do it, the easier it gets;

6. **Don't do rituals during exposure:**   Doing rituals (such as leaving a situation to check a mirror) dilutes the effectiveness of the exposure;

7. **Don't use camouflage during exposure:**   This will also dilute its effectiveness;

8. **Don't distract yourself from feeling anxious during the exposure:**   This, too, will make exposure less effective;

9. **It's probably best to do exposure as part of a behavioral experiment:**   In other words, it's probably best if you test a specific hypothesis during the exposure;

10. **It can also help to do cognitive restructuring before, during, and after the exposure:**   This can help keep you thinking straight and make the exposure more tolerable.

I'll now discuss these steps in more detail and give an example.

1) Make an exposure hierarchy: With your therapist's assistance, you first develop a list of situations that make you anxious. (See Hierarchy for Exposure Therapy form below.) For many people with BDD, these are social situations. Using the Subjective Units of Distress Scale (SUDS), you rate the amount of anxiety you experience in each situation. The numbers 0 to 100 are used, with 0 representing no anxiety and 100 representing a state of panic. The number assigned often reflects such factors as the number of people in the situation in which the defect is exposed, the familiarity of these people, and the distance of

Hierarchy For Exposure Therapy

Feared/Avoided Situation	Anxiety Rating (0–100)	Avoidance Rating (0–100)
#1 (most difficult situation):		
#2:		
#3:		
#4:		
#5:		
#6:		
#7:		
#8:		
#9:		
#10 (least difficult situation)		

Remember that you can do a behavioral experiment while you're doing exposure. You can also do cognitive restructuring before, during, and after the exposure.

the exposed body part from others. You also rate how much you avoid each situation.

Sandra's exposure hierarchy is shown below. She rated going out to the mailbox 10 for anxiety and 5 for avoidance on a scale of 0 to 100. She gave shopping a higher rating, because this involved being around more people, who might notice the slight scar on her face. She rated talking to a classmate or a stranger face-to-face from several feet away 60, whereas talking with them from a foot away was a 70 and 80 because the scar would be more visible. The list of feared situations and the numbers assigned will differ for each person and should be individualized.

2) Start by facing a situation with a lower rating: After developing a hierarchy, the next step is to expose yourself, and the perceived defect, to a feared situation with a relatively low number. The key is to identify a situation that produces some anxiety but not too much. You can use the Exposure Form below for these exercises. Starting with an activity rated a 5 or 10 would have been too easy, so Sandra started with jogging around the neighborhood with the scar exposed. Initially, she was very anxious, but the more she did this, the less anxious she became.

Sandra's Hierarchy for Exposure Therapy

Feared/Avoided Situation	Anxiety Rating (0–100)	Avoidance Rating (0–100)
#1 (most difficult situation): Going out ona date	100	100
#2: Talking with a man at a party	90	90
#3: Speaking up in class	80	85
#4: Talking to a classmate or stranger face-to-face from a foot away for at least 5 minutes	70	80
#5: Talking to a classmate or stranger face-to-face from several feet away for at least 5 minutes	60	60
#6: Going to class and sitting near classmates	50	50
#7: Asking a store clerk about an item	40	45
#8: Going shopping—for example, grocery shopping	30	30
#9: Jogging around the neighborhood	20	20
#10: Getting the mail	10	5

Exposure Form

Exposure #1:

Date: Time:

Exposure task:

Hierarchy number (from Hierarchy Form):

Time spent doing exposure:

Anxiety rating before exposure (0–100):

Anxiety rating after exposure (0–100):

How did it go?

What did I learn?

Exposure #2:
Date: Time:

Exposure task:

Hierarchy number (from Hierarchy Form):

Time spent doing exposure:

Anxiety rating before exposure (0–100):

Anxiety rating after exposure (0–100):

How did it go?

What did I learn?

---

3) Stay in the situation long enough for your anxiety to diminish: Initially, your anxiety will probably get worse. For exposure to work, you need to stay in the anxiety-provoking situation until it diminishes. This will make it easier to face the situation again. If you leave before your anxiety has dropped at least somewhat, the exposure probably won't work. In fact, you may be even more anxious the next time you enter the situation.

When first entering the situation, anxiety usually increases (and it should for exposure to work), but after a long enough time it should actually fall again, to a level that is lower than your original anxiety level. It's important not to discontinue the exposure until your anxiety falls again. Therapists use the term *habituation* to refer to this phenomenon. If you leave a situation prematurely, when anxiety is still very high, it will be that much harder to go back to the situation the next time.

4) Then enter a situation with a higher rating: Once you feel more comfortable in the exposure situation, you'll need to challenge yourself more by facing a situation with a higher rating. The goal is to move up your hierarchy as quickly as possible, but not so quickly that you can't put yourself in the harder situation or leave it prematurely. After she felt more comfortable jogging around the neighborhood, Sandra moved up her hierarchy, frequently going to the grocery store and doing other kinds of shopping. At first, she felt very anxious because she worried that others would notice her scar, but the more she went, the better she felt. She then continued moving up the hierarchy. She eventually pushed herself to go to night school again, first three times a week and then five times. (See Sandra's Exposure Form below). Gradually, over several months, she did activities with higher anxiety ratings. Eventually, she even talked with a man at a party. Gradually, her fear and avoidance diminished.

Sandra's Exposure Form

Exposure #1:

Date: *May 17*   Time: *3:00 pm*

Exposure Task: *Going to class and sitting near classmates*

Hierarchy number: *6*

Time spent doing exposure: *90 minutes*

Anxiety rating before exposure (0–100): *50*

Anxiety rating after exposure (0–100): *35*

How did it go?: *Not too bad. After I sat there for about a half an hour I started feeling less nervous and started listening to the teacher more. The longer I stayed, the less nervous I was.*

What did I learn?: *I felt nervous, but I felt a little better by the end of the class. I can probably handle going to class. It's worth it because I want to get my degree.*

Exposure #2:

Date: *May 20*   Time: *4:30 pm*

Exposure task: *Talking to a classmate from several feet away for at least 5 minutes*

Hierarchy number: *5*

Time spent doing exposure: *10 minutes*

Anxiety rating before exposure (0–100): *60*

Anxiety rating after exposure (0–100): *45*

How did it go? *OK. I talked with a girl I met a few weeks ago who seems nice. We talked about how to do one of the homework problems.*

What did I learn? *I did OK having the conversation, and it helped me with my homework. I'll try talking with her again. It would be good to get to know some of my classmates.*

---

5) *Do exposure repeatedly and frequently:* It's important to face the situation repeatedly—usually many times a week—so habituation will occur and it will become easier and easier to do. In other words, you'll need to do exposure for homework. If you face the situation only occasionally, you may find that your anxiety doesn't diminish that much. The more often you do exposure, the quicker you'll make progress.

6) *Don't do rituals during exposure:* This can make exposure less effective. If you temporarily leave the situation to fix your hair, for example, you won't learn that you can tolerate the situation regardless of whether your hair is perfectly in place. You may think something like: "I stayed at the party, but it doesn't really count, because my hair didn't look as bad as it usually does." Then it may not be much easier to go into the situation the next time, without checking and fixing your hair.

7) Don't use camouflage during exposure: The rationale for this is the same as for not doing rituals. If, for example, you cover your mouth, turn away from people, or use heavy makeup, you won't learn to tolerate situations without doing these things. So it's important to stop using camouflage in the exposure situations, unless it allows you to enter the avoided situation early in treatment. Stop wearing covering makeup, a hat or wig, bulky clothing, and sunglasses. Shave off your mustache or beard if it's hiding a defect, and avoid covering the defect with your hands or hair. If it's too hard to stop using camouflage right away, you can stop using it more gradually. For example, you could inch your hat back a little more each time you go out, gradually exposing more of your hairline. Or you could use a little less makeup each time you go to class.

It's also important to refrain from doing other things that might minimize the anxiety you experience during the exposure. Don't engage in avoidance behaviors. For example, when you're with other people, it's better not to hide in the dark part of the room. It's important to experience some anxiety during the exposure, which should gradually diminish with time.

8) Don't distract yourself from feeling anxious during the exposure: To minimize their anxiety, some people try to think about something neutral, sing a song in their head, or think that they'll do their rituals later. Unfortunately, these kinds of behaviors will also make exposure less effective. In fact, for exposure to work, you need to experience some anxiety. This is how you'll make progress.

9) It's probably best to do exposure as part of a behavioral experiment: Exposure often seems to work better if you do a good behavioral experiment at the same time. In other words, fill out a behavioral experiment form and test out a specific hypothesis during the exposure. Many people with BDD have poor insight, so habituation may not occur with exposure alone, as it does in many other disorders such as OCD. This is because people with poor or absent insight can easily misinterpret what's happening around them, so their anxiety may not diminish with exposure alone. Combining exposure with a good behavioral experiment should help you to recognize that your beliefs may not be accurate, which should help diminish your anxiety.

10) It can also help to do cognitive restructuring before, during, and after the exposure: This can help you get your thinking straight before you go into the anxiety-provoking situation. You can also do cognitive restructuring during the exposure, while you're actually in the situation, by identifying your cognitive errors and thinking alternative, more realistic thoughts. Filling out a thought record after the exposure may also be helpful, especially if the situation made you very nervous. This can help you reappraise what happened in a more accurate way.

If exposure therapy is too anxiety provoking, move back down to a lower-rated activity on your hierarchy. If this, too, is too anxiety provoking, you may need to modify the hierarchy, so less anxiety-provoking situations are included. Sometimes the SUDS levels need to be reevaluated and modified because you may underestimate the actual anxiety level you'll experience in the situation. The important thing is not to give up! If you do it right, exposure will make you somewhat anxious, but the more you do it, the easier it will get. And the rewards can be enormous: you'll be able to live a much freer and more enjoyable life.

Other Potentially Helpful CBT Techniques

The techniques below may be combined with the core techniques above. They shouldn't be used alone to treat BDD, because it's unlikely that they're adequate treatment by themselves.

1) **Mirror Retraining:** As the CBT model (Figure 9) shows, this technique interrupts the selective attention to appearance that feeds BDD obsessions. Mirror retraining consists of:

1) Learning to look at your *entire* face or body (not just the disliked areas) while looking in the mirror, and

2) Learning to *objectively* (rather than negatively) describe your body while looking in the mirror.

The rationale for mirror retraining is that when people with BDD look in the mirror, they usually zoom in on the negative body areas and examine them in excruciating detail while ignoring the rest of their body. They also tend to say very negative things to themselves about the disliked body areas. These behaviors cause lots of anxiety and feed the BDD. Mirror retraining teaches you to see *all* of yourself, which gives you a much more accurate view of your body and is how other people see you. It also teaches you to *objectively* evaluate your appearance rather than doing it in a negative way. So when you have to look in the mirror during the day (for example, when washing your face in the morning) or when you happen to catch a glimpse of yourself in a reflecting surface, you can call upon your mirror retraining skills to get a more accurate view of yourself. Initially, mirror retraining will probably make you anxious, but with practice, your anxiety will diminish. You'll also feel less anxious when you have to look in a mirror (for example, when grooming) or if you encounter a reflecting surfaces unexpectedly, because you'll be able to see yourself more objectively and accurately.

To do mirror retraining you stand several feet in front of a full-length mirror and objectively describe your body parts, going from head to toe (e.g., the color of your eyes, the length and width of your nose, the length and width of your feet). You do this without saying negative things to yourself about how you look (this will take practice!). It's best to do mirror retraining only at specified times of the day (e.g., 5 minutes in the morning and 5 minutes at night). It's very important that you don't do any mirror checking rituals while doing the retraining; in other words, don't zero in on the disliked body areas and excessively check them, as this will defeat the purpose of the mirror retraining.

2) Habit Reversal: This is an established treatment for trichotillomania (hair pulling) that is increasingly being used for other problematic habits, such as skin picking. In BDD, it can help skin picking, hair plucking, and body touching. You first write down detailed information about your picking behavior (or hair plucking or touching) in a diary so you become more aware of your picking (this is called "awareness training," or "self-monitoring"). This could be the situation in which you picked and the length of the picking episode. Then you learn to substitute other behaviors (a "competing response") for the picking. This could be things such as clenching your fist, squeezing a soft ball, or knitting. You also learn relaxation techniques, how to reward yourself for not picking, and how to use habit reversal in a wide range of situations.

3) Mindfulness: Mindfulness skills are psychological and behavioral versions of meditation practices from Eastern spiritual training. They have been developed by Dr. Marsha Linehan for borderline personality disorder and Dr. Jeffrey Schwartz for OCD. They are increasingly being used as part of the treatment of a number of disorders. Mindfulness skills balance your emotions and rational thinking to achieve a "wise mind." They involve a particular way of observing and being aware of your thoughts and emotions by focusing on them "in the moment." Rather than actively resisting your thoughts, you just watch them float by, like clouds across the sky, and gently let them go without engaging them. You observe your thoughts in a nonjudgmental way, without criticizing them or yourself. You also become fully involved in what is happening in the moment (e.g., what your friend is saying to you, or the feel, smell, and taste of the plum you're eating). This approach can potentially help you disengage from the powerful BDD obsessions that grip your mind.

4) Refocusing: Refocusing could be considered an element of mindfulness in the sense that it focuses your mind and awareness on the current moment's activity rather than your obsessive thoughts. As Figure 9 shows, refocusing can interrupt the selective focus on appearance and negative BDD thoughts. This technique involves gently focusing your attention and thoughts on what's going on around you (for example, a conversation you're having with a friend) rather than on BDD thoughts. When you notice your thoughts straying to BDD (e.g., "She looks so good and I look really ugly"), you gently bring your attention back to what you're supposed to be mindful about—for example, what your friend is saying to you. You don't try to actively fight the thoughts or push them out of your mind, because this actually increases your focus on the thoughts and may paradoxically worsen them. For example, try to *not* think about a pink elephant. Paradoxically, you think about one! Instead of focusing on a pink elephant at all (your BDD thoughts), nonjudgmentally observe that you are having the thoughts and then gently focus your mind back on what is happening around you in the moment. This technique sounds deceptively simple, but it takes practice to learn.

5) Activity Scheduling: This approach is often used in the treatment of depression. It consists of scheduling activities throughout the day by writing them down in an appointment book and then doing them. This approach doesn't directly target BDD symptoms, but it minimizes idle time, leaving less time for BDD obsessions and rituals. It can also improve your mood. Activity scheduling may be especially useful for people with severe BDD and depression who find it hard, for example, to even get out of bed.

6) Scheduling Pleasant Activities: This approach is similar to activity scheduling. It consists of scheduling and then doing pleasant and enjoyable activities—ideally every day. This technique, too, can minimize idle time, so there's less time available for BDD obsessions and rituals. It can also improve your mood.

Some people find that additional techniques may also be helpful for them, such as relaxation techniques (like deep breathing, progressive muscle relaxation, or meditation). Other people find it helpful to learn assertiveness training or how to accept compliments.

Relapse Prevention

The last few sessions of CBT usually consist of relapse prevention. The goal is to help you maintain the gains you made in treatment. In these sessions, you plan ahead for challenging situations you anticipate you'll face after you finish CBT. Some ups and downs in BDD symptoms are to be expected; recognizing your vulnerable times (for example, when you're stressed) and being sure to use your CBT skills at those times will help keep your symptoms under control. If your symptoms persist despite using your relapse prevention strategies, you'll want to see your therapist for one or more booster sessions (see below).

Booster Sessions

It can help to have occasional "booster sessions" with your therapist after your therapy has ended. If your relapse prevention strategies aren't effective enough, you may benefit from checking in with your therapist to brush up on your CBT skills and to trouble shoot rough spots you're encountering. Not much is known about how BDD sufferers treated with CBT do after treatment has ended, although the few studies that have looked at this question (see Table 17) found that they tend do fairly well. Nonetheless, it isn't uncommon for people to need an occasional booster session and to benefit from this. Even if you don't have booster sessions with your therapist, you're more likely to do well if you keep practicing your CBT skills after your therapy has ended.

What You Can Try if CBT Doesn't Work

If CBT doesn't work for you—or doesn't work as well as you'd like—the following approaches may be helpful:

1. Talk with your therapist about this: If you're discouraged with lack of sufficient progress, it's important for your therapist to be aware of this. He/she may be able to modify the approach to make it more successful.

2. Try to figure out if you're doing the CBT skills right: Most people learn to master CBT skills, but they can take a while to learn. They can also be challenging to learn and keep using correctly. Some people learn them well but then backslide a little (usually because they aren't practicing them enough). For example, some people do mirror checking (a ritual) during mirror retraining, which makes the mirror retraining less successful. Faulty ways of thinking can creep into "alternative thoughts" when doing cognitive restructuring. And it can be challenging to design a good behavioral experiment or to stay in a situation long enough for your anxiety to diminish when doing exposure. To get your skills back on track, it may help to review the skills with your therapist, look back at notes you wrote down during your sessions, review this chapter and books on CBT for BDD (see Chapter 18), and practice even more.

3. Ask yourself if you're practicing your CBT skills enough: CBT requires practice and effort on your part. Are you doing homework every day? Are you frequently practicing and using all of the skills—doing response (ritual) prevention, filling out thought records, and doing behavioral experiments, exposure, mirror retraining, and other skills you may have learned? If not, this is probably why the treatment isn't working. If the treatment is too hard, tell your therapist so he or she can make it more doable for you. Remind yourself that it's worth it to work hard at CBT so you really learn the skills. Remember that most people get better with CBT!

4. Consider more frequent or longer treatment sessions: More intensive treatment may be more effective for you. Longer sessions, in particular, may allow you to learn things in your session by actually doing them with your therapist (e.g., going out of the office and doing a behavioral experiment). This may be more effective than just discussing them in your therapist's office and then doing them by yourself at home.

5. Consider involving a family member or friend in your treatment: Sometimes it helps to have a family member or good friend learn something about CBT and help out by being an "ancillary coach" at home. They won't be able to take your therapist's place, but they may be able to help by encouraging you to do your homework and practice your skills. They may also be able to participate in some of your homework (for example, by doing a behavioral experiment with you). Having them read this book and come to one or a few of your sessions with your therapist may be all that's needed for them to help.

Also, some therapists provide treatment in the patient's home, which may be helpful for very ill people who have a hard time leaving their house.

6. Consider taking an SRI: If CBT has helped you somewhat, an SRI may help you improve even more. Or if you're too depressed to do CBT, an SRI can make it possible to do CBT by improving your mood, energy, concentration, and motivation. If your BDD is very severe, an SRI can also make you less anxious and make it easier for you to leave the house and try exposure and behavioral experiments. SRIs and CBT work very well together.

Needed Therapy Research

CBT is clearly a very promising treatment for BDD. Nonetheless, we need much more research on this treatment! Most important, a CBT treatment manual needs to be developed to guide therapists as they provide CBT. Once a manual is developed and tested, we need more rigorous studies of CBT's effectiveness using the manual. Studies need to compare CBT to other treatments, such as other types of therapy and SRIs.

Research is also needed to determine the optimal session length and number of therapy sessions (although these may vary somewhat for different people). Future studies need to include broader samples of patients (e.g., men as well as women, members of minority groups, people with delusional BDD, and a range of BDD severity). A broader range of outcomes needs to be assessed—not only improvement in BDD but also in body image, functioning, and quality of life.

There are many other unanswered questions about CBT that research is needed to answer. Is individual therapy better than group therapy—or vice versa? Each may have its advantages. For example, group therapy enables people to meet others with BDD and involves a lot of exposure (sitting in a room with other people), whereas individual treatment can be better tailored to the individual person. Does CBT help protect against relapse in people who discontinue an effective SRI? Until studies of this important question are done, it shouldn't be assumed that if you have CBT you'll do fine if you stop an SRI, although it's possible that CBT will diminish the risk of relapse. It also needs to be determined whether adding an SRI to partially effective or ineffective CBT makes people even better; clinical experience suggest that it often does. We also need to study for whom CBT works best. In addition CBT needs to be adapted for use in adolescents, since this is the age when BDD usually develops.

Even though we need a lot more research, at this point CBT is the psychotherapy of choice for BDD. What we know so far indicates that it is often very effective for people with BDD, and it has the advantage of teaching helpful skills that can be used whenever they're needed.

Therapies That May Be Useful When Combined with an SRI or CBT

The following treatments appear useful for some people when combined with the "core" treatments I've described (an SRI and/or CBT); they do not, however, appear to be effective for BDD when used alone. This impression is based on information I've systematically obtained from study participants about their past treatment response as well as my clinical experience. At this time, however the effectiveness of these treatments haven't been adequately studied in BDD, so definitive judgments about their effectiveness can't be made. Five, ten, and twenty years from now, it will be possible to make more definitive statements about whether they work for BDD, either alone or in combination with an SRI or CBT.

Insight-Oriented Psychotherapy

Insight-oriented psychotherapy, also known as psychodynamic or exploratory psychotherapy, is a type of "talking therapy." This approach focuses on increasing self-awareness and bringing about behavioral change (e.g., improving relationships with others) through exploration of one's perceptions and interactions with others. Better understanding of yourself, awareness of your inner life and motivations, and improvement in your problems may result.

Available evidence, although it's very limited, suggests that this type of treatment alone—as well as psychoanalysis alone—is generally ineffective for BDD. I've seen countless patients who have been in insight-oriented psychotherapy for months or years, as the only treatment for their BDD, only to end up unimproved and frustrated over their lack of improvement. They never figured out the "reason" for their BDD. Even if they thought they did, their symptoms generally didn't improve as a result. They may have understood themselves—and perhaps even their BDD symptoms—better, but most say they didn't obsess any less, stay out of the mirror less, or otherwise have improvement in BDD. Most of the psychoanalysts I've asked have said that in their experience psychoanalysis alone usually doesn't work for BDD.

Having said this, insight-oriented psychotherapy or psychoanalysis may be useful for some patients as an adjunct—that is, in addition—to the core BDD treatments. Psychologically minded people may benefit from an insight-oriented therapy that explores BDD-related themes—for example, low self-esteem, sensitivity to rejection, or relationship problems. This type of therapy may also be very helpful—if not essential—for certain problems unrelated to BDD.

Supportive Psychotherapy

Supportive psychotherapy is another type of talking therapy that emphasizes the creation of emotional support and a stable, caring relationship with patients. The therapist focuses more on providing support than on increasing patients' understanding of themselves. Components of this approach often include advice, learning new social skills, and assistance in problem solving. The goal is to help patients attain the highest possible level of functioning. In reality, many therapists combine elements of supportive psychotherapy with those of insight-oriented psychotherapy. Supportive psychotherapy is also often usefully combined with other therapeutic approaches, such as medication treatment or cognitive-behavioral therapy.

For people with BDD, this kind of therapy offers understanding and support for their struggles with the disorder. It can help BDD sufferers cope better with life—for example, the effects of BDD on friendships, intimate relationships, school, or work. It can also be very helpful when dealing with stressful life events or relationship problems. For some patients, the support offered by a doctor who is prescribing medications, or by a therapist doing cognitive-behavioral therapy, may suffice. Some patients do, however, benefit from additional supportive psychotherapy, and for some it's essential.

While supportive psychotherapy can be a very helpful addition to the core BDD treatments (SRIs and CBT), I don't recommend it as the only treatment for BDD. By itself, it appears unlikely to effectively diminish BDD preoccupations or behaviors. Like insight-oriented psychotherapy, the role of supportive psychotherapy in the treatment of BDD needs further study.

Couples and Family Therapy

Family meetings and couples or family therapy may be another helpful approach in combination with CBT and/or medications. Such meetings may include spouses, parents, or other family members. I often meet with family members, at least once, to get to know them and hear their view of the problem. They often find it helpful to learn about BDD—what it is and what the treatment options are. If family members participate in BDD-related rituals, we discuss ways in which they can avoid being part of these behaviors.

More extended family meetings or formal couples or family therapy may be helpful for selected individuals, particularly families of children and adolescents. This approach may increase understanding of BDD's effect on the patient and the family, provide a forum for devising coping strategies, and teach family members how to assist in CBT. Other family problems, if present, can also be addressed. Also, parents or guardians will need to be involved to at least some extent in the treatment of their children or adolescents, regardless of what type of treatment they receive.

Group Therapy

Any of the therapies described above—CBT, psychodynamic psychotherapy, supportive psychotherapy, or family therapy—can be provided in a group rather than individually. Based on current knowledge, it seems likely that only group CBT will be effective specifically for BDD symptoms, although the other forms of group therapy haven't been studied in BDD. The other forms of group therapy, however, may be helpful for other problems you may have.

My clinical impression is that groups that aren't focused on BDD aren't likely to be effective for BDD. Many people with BDD have great difficulty participating in non-BDD-focused groups and may drop out because they're so embarrassed by their appearance and their symptoms. They're usually reluctant to divulge their appearance concerns, and they may simply spend the group time comparing themselves with others and thinking that everyone else is noticing how ugly they are.

Vocational Rehabilitation

While medication and CBT may improve work or school functioning, some people—particularly those who've been underemployed or unemployed for a long time—also benefit from a formal vocational program. Response to medication or CBT may get these individuals to the point where they can usefully participate in such a program. For someone who hasn't been working, the first step may be a volunteer job, with gradually increasing hours, then a paying job, perhaps first on a part-time basis. Other people with BDD won't need to take this stepwise approach and can start working immediately.

It's generally best for individuals with BDD who abuse drugs or alcohol to also be in a treatment program that focuses on their drug or alcohol problem, even if they think their substance abuse is caused by BDD. It's important, however, that the treatment program's philosophy supports your getting an SRI and/ or CBT for your BDD symptoms.

Self-Help Groups

I'm sometimes asked whether self-help groups are helpful. My answer is that it depends on the group, and that self-help groups alone are unlikely to effectively treat BDD. I do recommend certain self-help groups, but in addition to the core treatments I've described.

To the best of my knowledge, there are currently no national, or even regional groups, that focus on BDD. Some people however, benefit from participation in groups sponsored by the Obsessive Compulsive Foundation (OCF), because of the many similarities between BDD and OCD. Others benefit from participating in such organizations as the National Alliance for the Mentally Ill (NAMI), Freedom From Fear, or, especially if they have accompanying depression or manic-depressive illness, the Manic Depressive and Depressive Association (MDDA). These are national organizations with local chapters that offer education and support groups for people with psychiatric problems. I recommend groups like Alcoholics Anonymous and Narcotics Anonymous for people with a coexisting alcohol or drug problem.

Self-help groups that don't educate members about psychiatric illness or don't support psychiatric treatment are unlikely to be helpful and may be harmful. I hope that in the near future groups will form that are specifically geared to people with BDD.

Combining Treatments

All the psychotherapy treatments I've described in this chapter can be combined, sometimes with a better outcome than with any one treatment alone. As I've previously emphasized, I advise everyone with BDD to take medication or be in cognitive-behavioral treatment.

How do you know which combination of therapies, if any, should be used? It depends on the individual. Your treatment plan should be tailored to your individual needs and life situation. If you have severe BDD and are very depressed or suicidal, supportive therapy may be a helpful addition to an SRI and CBT. In such cases, family meetings or family therapy can help family members better cope with BDD or other problems the family may have.

If you have significant problems in addition to BDD, you may benefit from one of the non-CBT therapies in addition to medication and CBT. You may, for example, benefit from an insight-oriented therapy or couples' therapy aimed at resolving relationship difficulties, self-esteem problems, or sensitivity to rejection, problems that don't always adequately resolve with medication or CBT. You may also benefit from vocational rehabilitation or a partial hospital program in addition to medication and CBT. Coexisting disorders may require additional medications or therapy. You should get the advice of a psychiatrist or other licensed mental health professional to make this determination.

Being busy, staying active, and having meaningful activities and people in your life can also help you overcome BDD. By themselves, they won't cure BDD, but many BDD sufferers say they help. As one of my patients told me: "My job has been one of the saving graces." Another patient with unusually severe BDD always felt and functioned better when she scheduled lots of things to do. Doing this, combined with taking escitalopram (Lexapro) and doing CBT, was very helpful for her. When you're idle, BDD obsessions and rituals can expand to fill your empty hours. Being busy can be a welcome distraction and take your focus off of BDD. And the more pleasurable and meaningful these activities are, the happier and more productive you'll be.

·· *fifteen* ··

Treatments That Don't Work

Even though there are effective treatments for BDD, most people with this disorder seek and receive treatments that don't seem to work. These ineffective treatments include surgery, dermatologic treatment, and other nonpsychiatric treatment (for example, dental treatment). Still other people get electrolysis to remove unwanted facial or body hair, join hair clubs, and try other useless remedies. People with BDD can waste lots of time and money pursuing these treatments, and can end up bitterly disappointed when they don't obtain the relief they're so desperately seeking.

Although more research is needed to confirm that these treatments don't work for BDD, in the meantime, based on current knowledge, I'd recommend that you avoid them: they don't seem to help, and they can even make BDD worse. Instead, I'd recommend that you try an SRI or CBT, which appear far more effective for BDD.

Sophie's, Jack's and Kate's Experiences

Sophie was initially happy with her nose surgery, but after several months she became increasingly dissatisfied and had another operation. This time, she thought the surgeon ruined her nose. She even considered suing him, even though other people told her how nice her nose looked (although it had also looked fine before surgery).

"I don't care what other people say," she said. "He made me look like an idiot!" A third nose operation was also unsuccessful. "People still look at my nose and think it's ugly," she said. "They're thinking I look like a dog." Sophie believed this even though she'd often been asked to work as a model. Her explanation for these requests was, "They've asked me to model because they feel sorry for me because of my atrocious appearance."

Jack estimated that he'd seen 10 to 15 dermatologists and plastic surgeons for the scars on his face. The problem began during childhood, when he had chicken pox. "My father forced me to go to school, even when I still had some scars, and I freaked out because people could see the scars. I picked to get rid of them, which made them even worse." For many years, Jack wore his hair long so it covered much of his face. Most of the surgeons and dermatologists told Jack he looked fine—that his scarring was minimal—and didn't provide treatment. "They thought it wasn't really a problem," Jack explained. But recently he'd found a dermatologist who'd agreed to do dermabrasion. "I was so happy with having it done that I cut my hair short," he said. "Then I took the bandages off, and I realized the scars were still there." Jack was so upset over this that he quit his job as a cashier.

Kate saved up her money and spent thousands of dollars on skin remedies. She'd seen many dermatologists and plastic surgeons as well as countless cosmetologists and aesthetisists. She'd also tried numerous acne medications, cosmetics, and facials. She'd even managed to buy liquid nitrogen through a mail-order catalog to remove a few freckles from her face. "I felt desperate for treatment—I'd try anything. I knew I'd have no peace until I could solve the freckle problem. I constantly called the doctor when the treatment didn't seem to be working. I was an obnoxious patient."

How Many People Get Surgery, Dermatologic Treatment, and Other Nonpsychiatric Medical Treatment for BDD?

Studies have found that 6%–20% of people seeking cosmetic surgery have BDD. One of these studies found that only 7% of women seeking cosmetic surgery had BDD, whereas 33% of the men did. While more studies are needed to confirm these findings, they suggest that a substantial proportion of people— especially men—who have cosmetic surgery may have BDD. In a study that I and my dermatologist colleagues did, 12% of 268 patients seen by the dermatologists had probable BDD. In a study in Turkey, 9% of 159 patients seen by a dermatologist had BDD. These percentages, too, are fairly high.

What about the flip side of this question: the percentage of people with BDD who seek and receive these types of treatments? In a study I did of 250 adults with BDD who saw me for an evaluation or treatment, a majority of them (76%) had sought surgery or medical treatment for their perceived appearance flaws. These 250 individuals requested a total of 785 treatments, so most of them had requested multiple treatments. One person had sought 35 different treatments! Two thirds of the 250 people had actually received surgery or another medical treatment. The group as a whole had actually received a total of 484 such treatments. The results from my series of 200 people with BDD were very similar. In other words, people with BDD seek and receive a lot of nonpsychiatric treatment.

The graph below shows the results from the first study. As you can see, dermatologic treatment was the type most often asked for and received. It was sought by 55% and received by 45% of the 250 people with BDD. This makes sense when you consider that skin and hair preoccupations are the most common BDD concerns. People most often were treated with antibiotics, but they also received other treatments such as minoxidil for perceived hair thinning. Some even got very powerful treatments—isotretinoin (Accutane) or dermabrasion—for perceived or minimal acne.

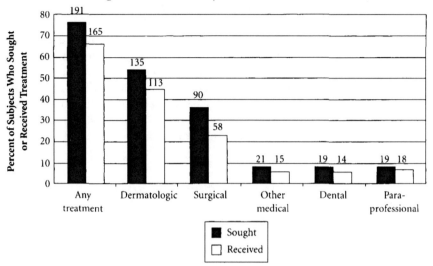

**Figure 11   Dermatologic, Surgical, Dental, and Other Medical Treatment
Sought and Received by 250 Adults with BDD**

Figure 11 also shows that 36% of people requested surgery, and nearly a quarter actually had surgery for their perceived appearance flaws. Drs. Veale and Hollander found that 26% of 50 people and 40% of 50 people with BDD had had surgery. In my study, people who received surgery had an average of 2 to 3 surgical procedures, so multiple surgeries were the rule. One woman had 9. Rhinoplasty (a nose job) was the most common procedure (42% of all surgeries). This was followed by chin surgery and breast surgery. People in this study also received dental treatment (e.g., tooth filing or orthodontia), other medical treatments, and paraprofessional treatment (for example, electrolysis).

Occasional patients have surgery on a body part that looks acceptable to them to make it even more attractive and thereby "distract" attention from the "defective" body part. One handsome man was planning a total facial reconstruction, even though his face looked fine to him because, if it looked even better, people might not notice his supposedly thinning hair. A beautiful young woman had a cheekbone implant so people would look at her cheekbones instead of her "ugly" lips.

People with BDD didn't receive more than one third of all the treatments they requested. And they didn't receive more than half of all the surgeries they requested. The most common reason is that the physician considered the treatment unnecessary (because the person looked fine) and didn't provide it. So many people had to see a lot of doctors before they could find one who would finally agree to provide the requested treatment.

It can be very difficult, though, to turn down requests for surgery or other medical treatment. Some people with BDD suffer so greatly that it can be very hard to deny them the treatment they so desperately seek. "The doctors and my friends and family tried to talk me out of surgery," Andrew told me. "But they couldn't turn me down because I was so miserable." Another man said, "I can't believe the doctor did liposuction because now I know I look fine. But I was so unhappy back then that he gave in and did it."

One man thought he looked like an "alien" and believed he was the third ugliest person in the world (after Gomer Pyle and Tiny Tim). He'd gone to 3 dermatologists and 3 dentists, none of whom agreed to treat him. He'd also seen 16 plastic surgeons, all of whom turned him down. One surgeon told him that if he got all the surgery he wanted, he'd look "mutilated." Finally, the 17th surgeon agreed to do a nose job, but the patient hated the result so much that he sued the surgeon. When I saw him he was so desperate for more surgery that he was planning to get into a massive car accident that would destroy his entire face.

Do These Treatments Work?

The answer to this question seems to be no—they usually don't. In the study I've been describing of 250 people with BDD who received these treatments, 72% of the treatments resulted in no change in overall BDD severity. Table 18 below shows this.

This table shows that, considering all types of nonpsychiatric treatment combined ("any treatment"), only 11.7% of all treatments improved overall BDD symptoms, and 16.3% were followed by worsening of overall BDD symptoms. Most often, BDD didn't change. In my series of 200 additional people, even fewer treatments improved BDD: only 3.6% (91.0% led to no change, and 5.4% led to worsening). What about surgery, which is generally the most definitive and expensive treatment that's received? In the study shown in Table 18, 58.3%

Table 18.   Outcome of Nonpsychiatric Treatment for 250 Adults with Body Dysmorphic Disorder

	Improved	Same	Worse
Any treatment	11.7% (53)	72.0% (326)	16.3% (74)
Surgery	17.4% (20)	58.3% (67)	24.3% (28)
Dermatologic	9.8% (26)	81.9% (217)	8.3% (22)
Dental	14.7% (5)	29.4% (10)	55.9% (19)
Other medical	0.0% (0)	88.2% (15)	11.8% (2)
Paraprofessional	9.1% (2)	77.3% (17)	13.6% (3)

Number of treatments received in each category: Any treatment: 453, surgery: 115, dermatologic treatment: 265, dental: 34, other medical: 17, paraprofessional: 22

of surgeries resulted in no change in BDD symptoms, and 24.3% were reported to make BDD symptoms worse. In other words, after surgery nearly one quarter of patients were even more preoccupied with the perceived appearance flaw, more distressed, and more impaired by their appearance concerns. Eighty five percent of treatments received from a dentist, 100% of other treatments received from other types of doctors (e.g., endocrinologist), and 91% of treatments received from a paraprofessional led to no change or worsening of BDD symptoms. It's worth noting that surgery and dental treatments were particularly likely to worsen BDD symptoms.

Dr. Veale's study, done in England, had similar results. He found that 81% of the 50 BDD patients he saw in a psychiatric setting were dissatisfied or very dissatisfied with the outcome of nonpsychiatric medical consultation or surgery. Repeated surgery tended to fuel increasing dissatisfaction. Although I didn't ask patients about their satisfaction per se, it's my impression that experiencing no change in the appearance concern—and certainly experiencing a worsening of this concern—causes people with BDD to feel quite dissatisfied. Sometimes the dissatisfaction is intense, leading to panic, despair, and sometimes even suicidal or violent behavior.

Although only some patients find that BDD gets worse after surgery or medical treatment, in some cases the outcome is extremely poor—even life-threatening. One man I saw who had multiple ear surgeries became suicidal and violent each time the bandages were removed after surgery, necessitating repeated emergency hospitalization. A young man whose surgeon turned him down for forehead surgery but who gave him some facial cream thought the cream created huge, dark spots on his face. He became so enraged over this that he went on a rampage around his parents' house, threatening them with a hammer and splintering their furniture. A number of patients threatened to sue, or expressed fantasies of harming, their surgeon.

"I hated the results of my surgery," Nicole told me. "Too much bone was taken off one side of my nose. Now you can see a shadow on the smooth side and a bump on the other side. It was the biggest mistake of my life. It took all of my looks away." Jeff, who had multiple surgeries, told me, "Overall, surgery made my appearance worse. I wouldn't do it if I could do it over." Some people feel temporarily better, but the improvement doesn't last. "My nose looked better for a while after I had surgery," a 35-year-old salesclerk told me. "But then it seemed to grow back after six months, and I wasn't happy with it anymore." One man thought that orthodontia had pulled his ears down. Another man became more preoccupied after trying minoxidil for his supposedly thinning hair. "I was much more obsessed," he said. "I kept wondering, 'Was it growing?' I spent even more time in the mirror."

What's especially concerning is that about 40% of children and adolescents with BDD seek surgery or medical treatment for their perceived defects. About one third actually receive it. Unfortunately, these treatments don't seem to work.

So far, I've been discussing what happens to overall BDD symptoms after these treatments. But what about the specific body part that's treated? Does concern with that body area in particular get better or worse? My study found that in most cases (about three quarters), worry and distress over the treated body area didn't diminish after surgery or other medical treatment. About one quarter of all treatments did result in less preoccupation and distress with that particular area. But in most of these cases, overall BDD symptoms didn't improve. What often happened is the person subsequently obsessed more about some other body area. Some worried more about a previous appearance concern; others started obsessing about a new body part. Dr. Veale found that this happened after half of all surgeries. As a 50-year-old business executive said, "My obsession stayed regardless of my appearance. After surgery, it just moved on to something else."

After dermatologic treatment, Ellen became more sensitive to smaller imperfections in her skin. And another woman told me, "I've seen six dermatologists, and I think they made my skin look better, but I don't worry any less because I worry just as much about small pimples as big ones. And now I'm hypervigilant. I worry my skin will get bad again."

This type of outcome isn't surprising, considering that the problem in BDD isn't physical—it's obsessional and involves distorted body image. Changing a surface characteristic generally doesn't cure the tendency to worry, obsess, and see yourself in a distorted way. As G. A. Ladee wrote in the 1960s, BDD is "the self-detested body image . . . which no mirror and no surgeon can correct." What's needed is psychiatric treatment that gets at the root of the body-image problem by treating the tendency to worry, obsess, and overfocus on minor or nonexistent flaws.

So what percentage of people reported *both* decreased concern with the treated body area per se *plus* improvement in overall BDD? In other words, what percentage of treatments results in less preoccupation and distress with the treated body area without being followed by increased concern with another body area or development of a new appearance concern? I found that *this happened with only 7% of all treatments—a very small percentage.*

Some people with BDD seem to have very high and unrealistic expectations for surgery, expecting the surgical outcome to be perfect. Darrel was an example of this: "The surgeries I had helped a little, but they weren't good enough. I'm a perfectionist." Surgery after surgery may be obtained in pursuit of this elusive perfection. Others with BDD have a very particular idea of how they should look after surgery, which may not conform to conventional views of beauty, including the surgeon's view. They may expect an outcome that to others would be undesirable. As the husband of a woman with BDD said, "The surgeons always focus on something different than my wife wants them to." One man was so desperate over his nose that he asked to have it completely removed!

In other cases, people with BDD may not have conveyed their desire to the surgeon or may feel that their directives weren't followed; some requests are vague. Or they may not have anticipated how they'd actually look after the desired change was accomplished. A 30-year-old man told me, "I wanted my nose shorter, but the surgeon changed the whole shape because he thought it would look better that way. He took my whole nose off. I didn't want him to do those things. I feel I lost my identity, and I'm sorry I ever had it done." Another person, whose nose had been changed exactly as he'd wanted, was nonetheless disappointed because he hadn't anticipated how his new nose would look in relation to the rest of his face, and he was angry at the surgeon for not telling him how he'd look.

Even when the treatment outcome is good by objective standards, which it usually is, some people blame the surgeon for ruining their looks. This can fuel a desire for even more surgery, leading to procedure after procedure. "I first saw a plastic surgeon who refused to operate because he said nothing was wrong," Claire said. But she subsequently did have surgery, first liposuction of her neck as well as chin and cheekbone implants. "Overall I felt somewhat better, but my chin was still off center. I needed another operation to center the chin and build up the right jaw." After another surgery, Claire still thought that her chin wasn't centered. "After my third surgery, I was happy with the chin centering but not my jaw." She was planning a fourth surgery to fill out her jaw and make it look symmetrical, even though her savings were nearly depleted.

"My life has never been the same since my surgery," Walter said. "I went to have my nose done, and the surgeon volunteered that I could use an implant in my chin, even though my chin had never bothered me. It ruined my life. I was horrified by the surgery. My nose was ruined—I have awful scar tissue there. I was very angry and upset. I got suicidal because of it. I also got swallowing and saliva problems because of the chin implant. I had to go to the emergency room because I was so upset."

Some people repeatedly visit the surgeon after surgery, asking for reassurance about the "faulty" operation. Others sue. Very rarely, they become violent toward the doctor. Still others get extremely depressed and even suicidal after having surgical or medical treatment that they believe has ruined their looks. A woman lawyer, who had many unsuccessful surgical procedures, told me that she thought she might ultimately kill herself over the results of future surgery.

I've treated many patients who were suicidal over their belief that Accutane (a powerful acne medication) caused irreversible damage, such as dry and flaky skin, or a change in their skin color. "In using the Accutane, I threw gasoline onto the fire," one patient told me. "I've caused irreparable damage to myself. The tragic mistake I made is always on my mind. . . . Because of this, I prefer not to live." Accutane treatment more generally has been associated with depression and even suicide; I wonder how many of these people had BDD and to what extent BDD—rather than the Accutane—may have been responsible for their depression and suicidality.

You may recall from Chapter 8 that some people with BDD are so desperate for surgery that they harm themselves intentionally, so surgery will have to be done. One man smashed his nose with a hammer so the surgeon would have to operate. Still others do their own surgery. They do a facelift with a staple gun, sandpaper their face to smooth it, or cut off their nipples. Others file their teeth down to make them even, or cut into their forehead, nose, or other body parts with a knife or surgical instruments.

So although most people are satisfied with cosmetic surgery, this doesn't appear to be the case for people with BDD. While no one can predict with certainty how a particular person with BDD will respond to surgery or other medical treatment, it appears that virtually none have improvement in their BDD overall, and some are devastated by the results. Psychiatric treatment is more likely to be helpful and is a much more conservative approach. The results aren't irreversible, as they may be with surgery. There's nothing to lose by trying it.

Having said this, there is a group of people with BDD who may benefit from a combination of psychiatric and dermatologic treatment. These are people who pick their skin, some of whom seriously damage it. They can create infections and scarring. Some even need emergency surgery to stop the bleeding and repair the damage caused by the picking. But while some people require and may benefit from dermatologic treatment to repair this damage, this treatment generally doesn't decrease the BDD symptoms—the preoccupation and picking behavior—that caused the skin damage in the first place. Psychiatric treatment is needed to break the picking cycle and prevent further skin problems. I found that 85% of 20 people with BDD who picked experienced no decrease in their skin obsessions or skin picking with dermatologic treatment but that 75% subsequently improved with a serotonin-reuptake inhibitor.

Most of the research findings I've discussed in this chapter are from people who saw a psychiatrist. What about people with BDD who don't go to a psychiatrist but only see a surgeon, a dermatologist, or a dentist? You may recall that 6%–20% of people who receive cosmetic surgery, and 9%–12% of people who receive dermatologic treatment, appear to have BDD. Are they any happier with the outcome of these treatments than people who eventually see a psychiatrist? Or are they even less happy? Although little systematic research has been done on BDD in dermatologic, surgical, and other medical settings, these patients have been well described in the professional medical literature. In the dermatology literature, BDD has been referred to as "dermatologic hypochondriasis," "hypochondriacal preoccupation with trivial lesions," and "dermatological non-disease." Skin picking associated with BDD is subsumed by the term "neurotic excoriations." In some reports the term "monosymptomatic hypochondriacal psychosis" is used, which refers to delusional BDD.

BDD is even less precisely identified in the surgery scientific literature. Scientific papers discuss patients with characteristics that overlap with BDD, such as "insatiable" surgery patients, "polysurgical addicts," and patients with "psychological problems" or "minimal deformity." The problem is that these terms aren't clearly defined, and can't be assumed to pertain to BDD because it isn't clear which patients in these studies, if any, had BDD.

One study from Japan was an exception in that the patients were identified as having BDD. This was a study of 274 patients with BDD who went to a surgery clinic requesting cosmetic surgery. A review of the patients' medical records indicated that many were dissatisfied with the results of surgery. The researchers concluded that surgery in people with BDD is risky because they often have unrealistic expectations, are often unhappy with the outcome, and may be angry with the surgeon about the outcome, even though it looks fine to other people. These surgeons therefore tended to avoid operating on people with BDD. Other articles in surgery journals have also cautioned surgeons against performing surgery on people with BDD because of poor outcomes that include patient dissatisfaction with the procedure or even violence toward the surgeon. There are several well-known cases of surgeons who were murdered by people who appeared to have BDD. A review of BDD in a German surgery journal concluded that such patients should not be treated with surgery.

In an important 2001 survey of 265 members of the American Society for Aesthetic Plastic Surgery (ASAPS), 84% of the surgeons who responded said they had operated on a patient who they thought was appropriate for surgery, only to realize after the operation that the patient had BDD. Eighty-two percent of these surgeons thought the patient had a poor outcome with surgery: 43% said the patient was more preoccupied with the perceived defect than before surgery, and 39% said the patient was now preoccupied with a different perceived defect. Eighty-four percent had refused to operate on people with BDD.

It's interesting that only 30% of the surgeons who responded to the survey thought that people with BDD should never have cosmetic surgery. This may reflect the fact that some people don't tell the surgeon about their unhappiness with the surgical outcome. Others do worry less about the perceived defect after surgery, but the problem is that most don't experience improvement of BDD overall (for example, their concern may shift to another body area); often, the surgeon isn't aware of this.

In my experience, most people with BDD are not litigious, physically aggressive, or violent, but 40% of the ASAPS survey respondents said that a patient with BDD had threatened them. Twenty-nine percent of the surgeons said they were threatened legally, 2% physically, and 10% both legally and physically. Certainly, this is a terribly unfortunate outcome for the surgeon and BDD sufferer alike, and it's yet another reason to avoid surgery.

Recent surgery studies from Sweden and Finland may be relevant to BDD. These studies found that women who have cosmetic breast augmentation surgery are more likely to commit suicide (about three times more likely) than women from the general population. An American study also showed an increased risk of suicide in women opting for breast augmentation. One wonders how many of these women had BDD, and whether BDD might have contributed to at least some of the suicides.

Many articles in dermatology journals state that patients with BDD frequently have a poor response to dermatologic treatment. Of great concern is a study done in two dermatology practices in England, which found that the most frequent causes of patient suicide were acne and BDD. I've talked with dermatologists who told me about BDD patients of theirs who committed suicide. One dermatologist said that six of his patients with probable BDD had committed suicide in the past year alone. Reports like these underscore how serious BDD is and how important it is for people with this disorder to get effective psychiatric treatment.

There's a great need for more studies of this important issue. What's especially needed are prospective studies, in which patients are followed over time and carefully assessed before and after surgery or dermatologic treatment to see whether their BDD improves, is unchanged, or worsens. Patients should be clearly identified as having BDD, and their outcome after these treatments should be assessed over a long period of time.

Even though BDD appears unlikely to get better with these treatments, some people who initially consult surgeons, dermatologists, or dentists may be reluctant to see a psychiatrist. If this is true for you, keep in mind that as best we know, these treatments usually don't work. Seeing a psychiatrist or therapist doesn't mean you're "crazy." It simply means that you have a potentially treatable illness that in many ways is no different from heart disease or any other medical illness. Psychiatric treatment is very likely to help you feel a lot better. There's a good chance it will give you more control over your obsessions, help you get your life back on track, and relieve your mind of worry, anxiety, and depression.

It may be hard for you to accept this advice if you think your defect is real and truly looks bad, as almost all people with BDD do. Most people with BDD have the hope that a physical change in their appearance will solve their problem. But look back at what my patients have told me about how they wish they'd never had surgery. Remember that as best we know, these treatments almost never help. And keep in mind that regardless of what you actually look like, if you're obsessing about an appearance flaw, and if you're distressed over it or it's causing problems in your life, psychiatric treatment is likely to quell your obsessions, alleviate your suffering and distress, and help you function better and start enjoying your life again.

Other Ineffective Treatments for BDD

There are a number of other treatment approaches and coping strategies that are sometimes used for BDD but appear ineffective.

- *Diet* I once saw a magazine article on my research that blazoned the headline: "Feeling ugly? Eat a banana." After noting that SRIs may lessen appearance preoccupations, the author went on to recommend that BDD sufferers eat chicken, avocado, corn, and bananas to cope with their symptoms. While certain foods do contain precursors of serotonin, there is no evidence whatsoever that foods affect serotonin levels enough to diminish BDD symptoms. I don't recommend diet alone to treat BDD.

- *Natural remedies* Some people try "natural remedies," such as homeopathic approaches, megavitamins, St. John's wort, and other substances found in health food stores or on the internet. *These treat-*

ments don't seem to work. None of them have been studied in BDD, and there's no evidence they're effective. Just because substances like tryptophan and 5-HTP (5-hydroxytryptophan) are natural and have links to serotonin doesn't mean they effectively treat BDD. While some of these substances are potentially harmless, others may actually be harmful. In fact, a number of years ago the U.S. Food and Drug Administration withdrew tryptophan from the U.S. market because a toxic variant of this compound was inadvertently produced, which caused at least 37 deaths and 1,500 cases of a severe syndrome called eosinophilia myalgia syndrome. 5-HTP, too, may be dangerous. The weight loss herbal supplement ephedra (ma huang) was linked to many heart attacks, strokes, and even deaths. So not everything that's "natural" is healthy; arsenic, too, is natural but can kill you.

The problem is that the Food and Drug Administration generally doesn't regulate herbs and dietary supplements, and they can be marketed without any proof of safety or effectiveness. Some are contaminated with toxins like mercury lead, or dangerous pesticides. Prescription medicines, such as SRIs, in contrast, must undergo extensive and rigorous scientific testing to demonstrate that they're both safe and effective before they can be marketed. You're much better off trying an SRI, since they've been extensively tested for safety, safely taken by many millions of people, and shown by research studies to often effectively treat BDD.

- *Uncovering a presumed trauma*   There is no evidence that BDD is caused by childhood trauma. While some people with BDD have experienced trauma, it's a mistake to assume that everyone with BDD has undergone serious trauma, that the presumed trauma is necessarily related to the development of BDD, or that uncovering a presumed trauma will cure the disorder. Some patients who clearly have experienced trauma may find it helpful to deal with this issue in psychotherapy, but this doesn't constitute treatment for BDD.

- *Reassurance*   BDD does not respond to reassurance alone. Trying to talk a person with BDD out of their worries doesn't cure the disorder and generally makes everyone feel more frustrated.

- *Hypnosis*   Some of my patients have tried hypnosis for their BDD, but many were too anxious, tense, and preoccupied to be successfully hypnotized. One person improved with hypnosis but only temporarily. Similarly, while relaxation techniques may be a useful part of cognitive-behavioral therapy, they don't appear to be effective when used alone.

- *Trying harder*   Many people try this approach alone, thinking it will be enough. But trying harder, by itself, won't treat BDD. Nor does it help for others to tell the BDD sufferer to "pull themselves up by their bootstraps." The problem with this approach is that, in addition to not diminishing BDD symptoms, the BDD sufferer may feel even worse about themselves—not only because they think they look bad, but also because they can't talk themselves out of being so concerned about it.

But making an effort and having a healthy attitude are important components of getting better. The right attitude needs to be combined with treatments that appear effective for BDD. It's important, for example, to try harder by doing the following:

Helpful Ways to Try Harder

- Make a commitment to psychiatric treatment
- Make a commitment to CBT:
  - Work with your therapist to resist your rituals, do exposure and behavioral experiments, and evaluate your BDD-related beliefs
  - Do assigned homework
  - Be patient if the therapy takes time to work, and maintain your effort even if it's challenging at times
- Try an SRI:
  - Stay with it even if you have side effects; they may improve or disappear with time
  - Be patient if the medicine takes time to work
  - Try another SRI if previous ones haven't worked for you
  - Remember that a healthy attitude and medication work hand in hand—they're powerful allies
- Don't give up!
  - Remember that most people with BDD get better with the right treatment
  - Keep in mind that in upcoming years, more treatment studies will be done and better treatments will be developed. Our knowledge about BDD, and hope for BDD sufferers, will steadily grow

---

·· *sixteen* ··

Anorexia Nervosa, Obsessive Compulsive Disorder, Koro, and Other Disorders—Are They Relatives of BDD?

"For the past three months I've been giving off a body odor. It smells like a swamp, dug up mud, a rotten smell; it comes from my guts. I can't go anywhere. I don't want to go with my friends, and I think I've lost them on account of that."

This person sounds a lot like people with BDD. What they have in common is an embarrassing preoccupation with a bodily concern, the fear that others perceive the problem when in fact they don't, and the resulting loss of friends. The quotation above refers to olfactory reference syndrome (ORS), an underrecognized syndrome characterized by a concern with emitting a foul body odor—often flatulence, sweat, bad breath, or an anal or genital odor. Is ORS related to BDD? Might they even be the same disorder? And what is BDD's relationship to other disorders, such as anorexia nervosa, a disorder involving distorted body image in which people think they're too fat when in reality they're too thin?

And what about the relationship between BDD and obsessive compulsive disorder or koro? Like BDD, OCD consists of obsessional thoughts that are difficult to resist or control. Instead of focusing on appearance, they focus on contamination, a fear of harm occurring, or other themes. And most people with OCD, like those with BDD, compulsively do things over and over that are hard not to do—such as washing their hands again and again or checking the stove or a lock 30, 50, or 100 times a day.

Koro is a fascinating syndrome that usually afflicts men and occurs primarily in epidemics in China. Men with koro fear that their penis is retracting into their abdomen, which they think will kill them. Understandably panicked, they implore others—family members or emergency-room doctors—to pull on their penis with various types of clamps and retractors.

Whether BDD is related to these other disorders is an interesting, controversial, and important question. If it is, the same treatment approaches might be effective for BDD. Or, because they would probably run together in families—as related disorders tend to do—we could predict that relatives of people with BDD would be at increased risk for a related disorder, and vice versa.

Although scientific evidence isn't available to definitively answer all the questions I'll pose in this chapter, it does allow us to come to some reasonable conclusions—for example, that BDD is not a form of schizophrenia. While BDD may be related to depression, BDD isn't simply a symptom of depression. BDD and OCD are probably closely linked and yet have some important differences. And BDD's relationship with koro? This is yet another mystery to be solved.

BDD: Symptom or Illness?

Before I discuss BDDs relationship to other psychiatric disorders, I'll first briefly address a larger issue that's been debated over the years. Is BDD a separate psychiatric disorder, as DSM-IV indicates, or is it instead a nonspecific symptom that can occur in a variety of disorders, such as schizophrenia, depression, or personality disorders? Table 19 presents three hypotheses on this issue:

Table 19. Is BDD a Symptom or an Illness?	
Hypothesis	*Medical Analogy*
1. BDD is a *nonspecific symptom* that can occur in a *wide variety* of psychiatric disorders (such as schizophrenia, depression, or personality disorders)	BDD is like a fever
2. BDD is a symptom or form of another specific psychiatric disorder (not of a wide variety of psychiatric disorders, as proposed by hypothesis 1)	BDD is like the butterfly rash in lupus
3. BDD is a distinct diagnostic entity—that is, a *separate disorder*	BDD is like diabetes

Hypotheses 1 and 2 propose that BDD is a symptom, of either a variety of illnesses (hypothesis 1) or of a specific illness (hypothesis 2). Hypothesis 1 proposes that BDD is like a fever, which is a nonspecific symptom that can occur in a wide variety of illnesses, from chicken pox to strep throat to cancer. Hypothesis 2 proposes that BDD is similar to the butterfly rash in lupus, an autoimmune disease. The rash occurs on the face and is a fairly characteristic symptom of lupus. In keeping with hypothesis 2, some authors have considered BDD a form of schizophrenia. In Japan, BDD has been viewed as a type of social phobia. And in ICD-10, DSM-IV's international counterpart, BDD is classified as a type of hypochondriasis. In contrast, hypothesis 3 proposes that BDD is a separate disorder—like diabetes—rather than a symptom of another underlying disorder.

Which hypothesis is correct is important for several reasons. If hypothesis 1 is correct, then treatment would presumably be directed at whatever the underlying disorder was thought to be in a particular person. If in one person it were schizophrenia, the schizophrenia would be treated. If in another person it were OCD, the OCD would be treated. The BDD symptoms would be expected to resolve as the underlying illness did.

If BDD is a symptom of a particular other disorder (hypothesis 2), then treatment would in all cases be directed at that one underlying disorder. But if BDD is a separate illness (hypothesis 3), then treatment would be directed at the BDD itself. Treatment directed at another coexisting illness—if one were present—wouldn't necessarily successfully treat the BDD.

What I've written about BDD to this point has implied that it's a separate disorder, and indeed DSM-IV classifies it that way. But some authors have proposed that hypotheses 1 or 2 are more accurate. G. G. Hay, a British psychiatrist, proposed hypothesis 1 when he wrote in 1983 that "dysmorphophobia is a symptom, not a diagnosis or an illness"; he believed that it could occur as a symptom of a "variety of psychiatric syndromes." Hay thought that the underlying illness could vary from a personality problem (such as a "sensitive" personality type) to schizophrenia to mood disorder.

It seems unlikely that this hypothesis is valid. While it's true that various types of body image symptoms can occur in other disorders, the syndrome BDD—as described in the published scientific literature and in this book—is a well-defined syndrome. It has characteristic symptoms that have been consistently described around the world for more than 100 years. Research that's been done, especially in the past 10 years, has increasingly clarified its clinical features, which aren't identical to those of any other disorder, let alone a variety of disorders. Also compelling is what patients say: 62 percent of those I've seen have reported that BDD is their most severe and primary problem or their only problem, suggesting that BDD isn't simply a nonspecific symptom of other psychiatric problems or disorders. In addition, BDD can occur in the absence of other psychiatric disorders. If BDD were simply a nonspecific symptom of other disorders, it would be expected that symptoms of some other disorder, such as schizophrenia or depression, would always be present. This isn't always the case.

Furthermore, when BDD does coexist with another disorder, it shouldn't be assumed that the BDD is "secondary," or due to, the other disorder. It used to be thought that if a person had both OCD and major depression, then the OCD was a symptom of the depression, or, similarly, that if panic disorder and major depression coexisted, the panic disorder was a symptom of the depression. This view is no longer considered correct. If a person has two disorders, one isn't necessarily a symptom of the other; both disorders should be diagnosed and targeted in treatment. BDD is no different.

Finally, data indicating that BDD responds to a specific medication treatment—SRIs—but not to other medications casts serious doubt on hypothesis 1. With the exception of OCD, no other psychiatric disorder has been well demonstrated to respond *preferentially* to SRIs.

What about hypothesis 2 versus 3? Is BDD a symptom of a *particular* other psychiatric disorder, such as OCD, or is it a *distinct disorder?* The best way to answer this question is to determine what causes these disorders. If their causes are the same, we would consider them the same disorder. But we still don't know exactly what causes them and how they develop. So in the meantime, we need to approach this question by assessing similarities and differences between BDD and other disorders in a variety of domains, such as symptoms, age of onset, course over time, treatment response, and results from studies such as brain imaging, genetic, and neuropsychological studies. The more similar two disorders are in these various ways, the more likely they are to be related. Unfortunately, there are no direct comparison studies of other disorders with BDD, except for BDD and OCD and BDD and eating disorders. This limits the conclusions we can draw. However there are other clues we can use. If particular disorders commonly coexist with each other, or if they occur at a relatively high rate in family members, this is further evidence that they may be related.

In this chapter, using clues such as these, I'll discuss a number of disorders and how closely related to BDD they seem to be. I'll conclude that BDD has some things in common with these other disorders, but also has some important differences. Whether there are more similarities than differences varies for each disorder. Schizophrenia, for example, is quite different from BDD, whereas OCD has many similarities with BDD. However, BDD appears to differ in some important ways from all of the disorders I'll discuss. These differences suggest that BDD isn't identical to any of them—that it's a distinct disorder. This conclusion supports hypothesis 3 rather than hypothesis 1 or 2. The differences between BDD and other disorders have important practical implications. It's important to keep these differences in mind so BDD is correctly diagnosed and treated.

Obsessive Compulsive Disorder: Obsessional Worries and Compulsive Behaviors

Nina constantly worried that she'd throw her children out the window or cut them with a knife. She frequently checked to make sure she hadn't harmed them and that they were okay. "The thoughts don't make any sense to me," she said, "I would never hurt anyone, especially my children, but I can't stop thinking them." Mark worried that he'd get sick from dirt or germs. He feared that his house would become dirty, which could make him and his family ill. To prevent contamination and illness, Mark washed his hands for several hours a day. He refused to allow visitors in his home, and whenever he, his wife, or his children entered the house he made them change their clothes and take a shower.

Similarities Between BDD and OCD: As these stories illustrate, obsessive compulsive disorder (OCD) is characterized by obsessions, which are intrusive, recurrent, unwanted ideas, thoughts, or impulses that are difficult to dismiss despite their disturbing nature. OCD is also characterized by compulsions, which are repetitive behaviors, either observable or mental, that are intended to reduce the anxiety caused by obsessions. Obsessions and compulsions are also hallmarks of BDD. The most common OCD obsession is fear of contamination, followed by pathological doubt (e.g., a fear that the house will burn down because the stove wasn't turned off), need for symmetry, and aggressive obsessions. The most common compulsion is checking, followed by washing, symmetry (a need to order or arrange things "perfectly" or perform certain behaviors symmetrically or in a balanced way), a need to ask or confess, and counting.

Similarities between BDD and OCD have been noted for more than a century. In the late 1800s, Enrico Morselli stressed the obsessional and compulsive nature of BDD symptoms. He noted that people with BDD are frequently "caught by the doubt of deformity" and that they compulsively check their appearance. In 1903, Pierre Janet classified BDD symptoms within a class of syndromes similar to OCD, referring to BDD as *obsession de la honte du corps*, or obsession with shame of the body.

In addition to shared obsessions and compulsions, the *content* of thoughts in the two disorders can overlap. Both BDD and OCD can consist of a desire for symmetry (of a body part in BDD and of other things in OCD), a concern that something "isn't right" (a body part in BDD and other things in OCD), and a need for perfection. Both disorders are also characterized by checking (e.g., mirrors in BDD and locks in OCD), skin picking (to improve appearance in BDD and to remove contaminants in OCD), and repeated requests for reassurance (about appearance in BDD and other things in OCD—e.g., that someone wasn't harmed).

Because I was intrigued by BDD's and OCD's apparent similarities, I and my colleagues did a study in which we compared 53 people with BDD to 53 people with OCD. BDD and OCD were similar in terms of most of the variables we examined: sex ratio and other demographic variables, age at onset of the disorder, past course of illness (often chronic), impairment in functioning, and lifetime rates of most of the coexisting disorders that we assessed. BDD and OCD also commonly co-occurred: 15% of OCD patients also had BDD, and about a third of those with BDD also had OCD. Illness severity scores were nearly identical. The two groups were also largely similar in terms of family history of psychiatric disorders.

In addition, available treatment studies indicating that BDD responds preferentially to SRIs offer strong support for important similarities between BDD
and OCD (OCD has been convincingly shown to respond preferentially to
SRIs). And in the neuropsychological studies I described in Chapter 10, people
with BDD had memory difficulties because they overfocused on small and irrelevant details. Although they weren't directly compared to people with OCD,
this is similar to what's found in OCD. And a number of studies have found
that BDD occurs more often in people with OCD than in people without OCD,
suggesting that BDD and OCD may be related disorders.

Differences Between BDD and OCD: However, in the BDD/OCD comparison study I noted above, we also found some significant differences between
the two disorders. People with BDD were less likely to have ever been married
(13% versus 39%) and more likely to have had suicidal ideation (70% versus
47%) or made a suicide attempt (22% versus 8%) because of their disorder.
Those with BDD had an earlier onset of major depression (19 versus 25 years)
and a higher lifetime rate of major depression (85% versus 55%) and social
phobia (49% versus 19%). They also had a higher rate of alcohol or drug abuse
or dependence in their first-degree relatives. Taken together, these results suggest
that BDD and OCD have many similarities and are probably closely related, but
that they also have some notable differences and are probably not identical.
People with BDD appear to be more socially anxious, depressed, and suicidal.

Another obvious difference between BDD and OCD is the content of the
preoccupations. Although the content is sometimes similar, it's usually quite
different. Whereas people with BDD focus on defective appearance, those with
OCD often fixate on such fears as becoming ill, causing harm, and the possible
occurrence of dire events. In OCD, the fear underlying such negative thoughts
often is *"What if something terrible happens and I'm responsible?"* In contrast, in
BDD, the underlying fear often involves feelings of shame and low self-esteem,
and is often interpersonal in nature: *"What if I'm rejected or go unloved?"* or
"I'm not acceptable; I'm inadequate and defective as a person." In addition, it's
my impression that BDD rituals (such as mirror checking) are less likely than
OCD rituals (such as handwashing) to temporarily relieve anxiety—in fact BDD
rituals often increase anxiety. BDD appears to cause more social difficulties,
including problems in intimate relationships.

People with BDD also tend to have poorer insight than those with OCD. In
a study Dr. Jane Eisen and I did, we compared insight into the underlying belief
in 85 people with BDD and 64 with OCD. A typical belief in BDD is looking
ugly or deformed; OCD beliefs vary but often consist of a belief that something
bad will happen if a ritual isn't performed (e.g., the house will burn down if
the stove isn't checked 30 times). On average, insight in BDD was poor, whereas
in OCD it was good to fair. Specifically, we found that people with BDD are
more convinced that their belief is true and are more likely to think that other
people agree with them. They're also less willing to be convinced by someone
else that their belief isn't true, and they try less often to convince themselves
that it isn't true. They're also less likely to think that their belief has a psychiatric

cause (for example, due to a disorder such as BDD or OCD) and more likely to think it's actually true.

The poor insight of people with BDD is one of the reasons that cognitive approaches (cognitive restructuring and behavioral experiments; see Chapter 14) are usually emphasized when treating BDD with cognitive behavioral therapy. Cognitive approaches target the unrealistic thinking and poor insight that's usually present in BDD. Many expert therapists think that behavioral approaches (exposure and response prevention) when used alone (that is, without cognitive approaches) tend to be less effective for BDD than for OCD. Cognitive approaches are therefore usually combined with behavioral approaches when treating BDD (see Chapter 14).

While BDD and OCD both appear to respond preferentially to SRIs, they may respond somewhat differently to other medications. In Chapter 13 I described a study in which I added a typical neuroleptic (pimozide) or placebo to an SRI (fluoxetine). This study found that pimozide wasn't more effective than placebo. This differs from findings in OCD, for which pimozide and other typical neuroleptics are often effective when added to an SRI. While the BDD study findings need to be confirmed, this is another way in which BDD's treatment response may differ from OCD's.

A published case report suggests that there may be physiological differences between BDD and OCD. A patient with BDD who underwent acute experimental dietary depletion of the amino acid tryptophan, which likely led to decreased serotonin levels, experienced dramatic worsening of her BDD symptoms as well as her depression. But her OCD symptoms didn't get worse. This finding suggests that BDD and OCD may have a somewhat different underlying pathophysiology and are not identical disorders. Also suggesting differences between BDD and OCD was Dr. Wilhelm's finding (discussed in Chapter 10) that people with BDD tend to have negative and threatening interpretations for appearance-related and social anxiety-related information, whereas people with OCD don't. This points to a fundamental difference in the way people with BDD and OCD process information from the environment. In addition, the results of the BDD brain imaging study described in Chapter 10 differed from those typical of OCD (although this study did not directly compare BDD and OCD, which would ideally be done). Finally, in the preliminary genetics study I did with Drs. James Kennedy and Margaret Richter (see Chapter 10), our results for the serotonin transporter promoter region gene were actually opposite what's been found in OCD. Furthermore, we did not find a difference between BDD patients and healthy controls for the 5HT1B gene, whereas a difference has consistently been found in OCD. Finally, we directly compared patients with BDD to patients with OCD and found that they differed. Those with BDD tended to have a particular form of the serotonin transporter promotor region gene, whereas this was not the case for people with OCD. While preliminary, these results point to a fundamental difference in the cause of these disorders.

Conclusions: Taken together, all of this evidence suggests that BDD is closely related to OCD but that they have some important differences and aren't identical. A reflection of this hypothesis, BDD is often referred to as an "OCD-spectrum disorder"—a disorder that isn't the same disorder as OCD but that's one of a number of disorders (including Tourette's disorder, hypochondriasis, eating disorders, and trichotillomania [hair pulling]) that share clinical features with OCD and are postulated to be related to it.

A recent, well-done study by Dr. Oscar Bievenue and colleagues strongly supports the hypothesis that BDD is related to OCD (i.e. that it's an OCD-spectrum disorder). This large and methodologically strong family study assessed the rate of BDD in first-degree relatives of people with OCD versus the rate of BDD in first-degree relatives of people in the community without OCD. They found that BDD was significantly more common in first-degree relatives of the people with OCD than in relatives of the community group (4% versus 1%). Showing that BDD runs in family members of people with OCD supports the theory that BDD and OCD are related.

It's interesting to hear what patients with both BDD and OCD say about similarities and differences between their BDD and OCD symptoms. One patient often tells me that the symptoms seem so similar that he's certain that BDD and OCD are the same disorder. But, like many people with both disorders, Renee saw some differences as well as similarities. "My BDD concerns seemed more reasonable to me, whereas my OCD concerns had *no* basis in reality. They seemed crazy and senseless. . . . My BDD seems pettier than my OCD, and yet it affected my self-esteem more because appearance is so important, especially during adolescence. Even though my OCD was more severe than my BDD, the BDD hurt me more socially because people could see the problem; I couldn't keep it a secret. It's harder to discuss the BDD because it's harder to describe the sadness and loneliness that goes with it. . . . I felt worse and more self-conscious around people with the BDD than with the OCD." Bill's comparison was similar: "They're alike in a lot of ways, but the OCD is irrational and senseless. The BDD is true; it makes sense. The BDD has a much worse effect on your social life. Everyone can see it. You can't hide it like you can hide OCD. . . . My OCD rituals gave me some relief—each check temporarily relieved my anxiety. The BDD rituals didn't relieve my anxiety even temporarily. The BDD made me suicidal."

Practical Implications: The research findings above and clinical experience suggest that people with BDD tend to be more socially anxious and depressed than people with OCD, and that they're more likely to have suicidal thinking and attempt suicide. So it's important to closely monitor these things in people with BDD, especially those with severe BDD. Clinical experience also suggests that because of their poor insight, it may be more difficult to convince people with BDD to try psychiatric treatment (in Chapter 17 I suggest ways to accomplish this).

Because treatments for BDD and OCD have much in common, if you can't find a clinician experienced in treating BDD, try finding one experienced in OCD (see Chapter 18). However, as discussed above, somewhat different medications and psychotherapy approaches may be needed for these disorders, so be sure to tell the clinician you have BDD. Also, when a person has both BDD and OCD, the two disorders sometimes respond differently to the same treatment. For example, although a particular SRI will usually work for both BDD and OCD, it sometimes works for OCD but not BDD, or vice versa. This is yet another important reason to diagnose BDD and OCD separately and to target them individually in treatment.

Social Phobia:
Social Anxiety, Embarrassment, and Avoidance

BDD also has many similarities to social phobia (also know as social anxiety disorder). This anxiety disorder is characterized by an excessive fear of social or performance situations in which the person is exposed to unfamiliar people or to scrutiny by others and fears they'll do something embarrassing or humiliating. The excessive fear may occur in most social situations (generalized type) or in specific situations, such as speaking in public or eating or writing in front of others.

Natasha had felt extremely anxious and fearful in social situations since she was a child. "I've always been really nervous around other people," she said. "Even in grade school. I'd miss school on days I had to give a book report in front of the class. I've never gone to parties because I'm afraid I'll do something embarrassing, like blushing or saying or doing the wrong thing." As a result, Natasha didn't date and had no friends. She spent most of her time alone at home.

Similarities Between BDD and Social Phobia: Studies have shown that untreated people with BDD tend to be introverted and have high levels of social anxiety and distress. Like people with social phobia, many people with BDD try to avoid social situations because they cause anxiety and distress.

In Japan, BDD is considered a member of a larger group of disorders (Taijin Kyofushu) that is similar to social phobia. People with Taijin Kyofushu fear offending or hurting others through their supposedly awkward social behavior or supposed physical defect. In support of the view that BDD is related to social phobia, people with BDD often report that their BDD symptoms intensify in social situations. Occasional people with BDD say they worry about their appearance only in social situations.

The underlying beliefs in BDD and social phobia are similar. Typically, they focus on ways in which the person feels defective. They often involve feelings of shame, preoccupation with others' views of the person, fear of being scrutinized and negatively evaluated, and fear of being embarrassed, humiliated, and rejected.

Some symptoms have features of both BDD and social phobia, underscoring their similarities. For example, a fear of blushing (erythrophobia) in social situations has features of both social phobia (fear of looking embarrassed) and BDD (fear of facial redness). The disorders' sex ratio, age at onset, and course over time also appear generally similar. In addition, BDD and social phobia often co-occur, suggesting they may be related.

It's interesting that Dr. Wilhelm's study (discussed in Chapter 10) found that people with BDD tend to interpret social situations in a threatening way, like people with social phobia. (None of the participants in her study had a diagnosis of social phobia, so co-existing social phobia wouldn't account for this result.) These findings point to an important similarity between BDD and social phobia (and an important difference between BDD and OCD; see above).

Differences Between BDD and Social Phobia: A key difference is that repetitive behaviors (compulsions) are a prominent feature of BDD but not social phobia. In fact, some people with BDD consider these behaviors (e.g., skin picking) to be their most distressing and problematic symptom.

BDD and social phobia may also respond somewhat differently to medication. Social phobia responds to SRIs, but it also responds to certain other medications. The generalized type of social phobia also responds to MAO inhibitors, and the specific type of social phobia responds to beta-blockers. Although adequate studies of these medications are lacking in BDD, available data and clinical experience suggest that BDD sometimes responds to MAOIs but not in most cases and that it doesn't respond to beta blockers. In addition, the results from my preliminary BDD genetics study differ from results in social phobia.

Conclusions: BDD and social phobia have many similarities, and in fact social phobia is probably one of the disorders (along with OCD) that's most closely related to BDD. In fact, I'd hypothesize that BDD is closely related to *both* OCD and social phobia. However, BDD and social phobia also have some important differences and are not identical disorders.

Practical Implications: It's important to differentiate BDD from social phobia, especially because their medication response can differ. Also, response (ritual) prevention is a very important component of cognitive-behavioral therapy for BDD (see Chapter 14), but not social phobia. So when a person has prominent social anxiety, it's important to determine what makes them anxious and whether their anxiety is triggered largely by appearance concerns. If it is, BDD is the more accurate diagnosis.

It's also important to be aware that BDD and social phobia commonly co-exist (i.e., are present in the same person). In fact, about 12% of people with social phobia also have BDD, and close to 40% of people with BDD also have social phobia (unrelated to appearance concerns). So it's important to look for social phobia in a person with BDD and vice versa so both disorders, if present, are diagnosed and treated. I've found that people with both BDD and social phobia are more likely than those with BDD alone to have past or present alcohol abuse or dependence (51% vs 20%). They're also more likely to have past or present drug abuse or dependence (36% vs 20%), which will also need treatment. Finally, while both BDD and social phobia often respond to SRIs, in some cases a person's BDD responds but their social phobia doesn't, or vice versa. For this reason it's important to identify both disorders and monitor the response of both of them to treatment.

Eating Disorders: Distorted Body Image and Problematic Eating Behavior

Might BDD and anorexia nervosa be related disorders, or even the same disorder? Their similarities make this a reasonable and intriguing question. I've in fact received letters from young women who assume they have BDD—yet, they appear to actually have anorexia or another eating disorder. In some cases, BDD and eating disorder symptoms closely overlap, making it difficult to differentiate them.

Similarities Between BDD and Eating Disorders: The eating disorders (anorexia and bulimia) and BDD share a preoccupation with appearance and a distorted body image. People with anorexia think they're too fat, which leads to excessive weight loss, usually to the point where they appear emaciated and very malnourished. Yet the person with anorexia thinks she looks fine, or even—at a weight of 60, 70, or 80 pounds—too fat. Dr. Rosen's study (described in Chapter 11) found that people with BDD and people with an eating disorder have equally severe body image symptoms, such as similar levels of body dissatisfaction and feelings of unattractiveness. For both groups, appearance unduly influences self-esteem and how one evaluates oneself as a person.

BDD can fixate on body areas that are typically focused on in anorexia and bulimia, such as the size of the stomach, hips, or thighs. BDD and eating disorders also both involve compulsive behaviors such as mirror checking and body measuring. Like the eating disorders, BDD sometimes involves unusual eating or excessive exercise or dieting—for example, when trying to make one's face less wide.

BDD and eating disorders also often co-occur, which provides some indication that they may be related. I've found that about 12% of people with BDD have anorexia nervosa or bulimia (which is higher than in the general population). Conversely, Dr. Jon Grant found that 39%—a very high percentage—of 41 women with anorexia nervosa had BDD unrelated to weight concerns. Yet another similarity is that both BDD and eating disorders typically begin during adolescence and, when untreated, often persist over time.

Differences Between BDD and Eating Disorders: However, there are some differences. One difference is that people with BDD actually look normal. People with anorexia don't. They look emaciated—in some cases skeletal—but the more abnormal their appearance becomes, the better they think they look. As they lose weight, they often feel more satisfied and more in control of their body and their life. They typically defend their strikingly abnormal, skeleton-like appearance as looking right, or even too fat. If they camouflage their body with bulky clothing, the purpose is generally to prevent others from seeing how thin they are and telling them to gain weight. In contrast, people with BDD nearly always feel very distressed and out of control. They camouflage out of a deep sense of shame and a desire to prevent further embarrassment by exposing the defect to others.

Another difference is that people with eating disorders typically focus primarily on overall body weight, whereas people with BDD more often focus on specific body parts, often facial features. However, this distinction can break down to some degree, in that individuals with anorexia often also have more focused complaints—for example, the size of their stomach or thighs. And some people with BDD are concerned with their weight, hips, thigh or overall body build. Muscle dysmorphia, which is considered a type of BDD, consists of a preoccupation that one's overall body size is too small. This form of BDD may be more similar to eating disorders than other forms of BDD are, in that it often involves an obsession with eating a special diet, excessive exercise, and striving to eliminate body fat.

BDD and eating disorders differ strikingly in their male-to-female ratio (more than 90% of people with eating disorders are women). Furthermore, effective treatments for BDD and eating disorders differ in some important ways. Although recent preliminary data suggest that anorexia may respond to SRIs, the SRIs seem to mostly help people maintain their weight after they've regained it. People with anorexia don't respond as often or as robustly to SRIs as people with BDD do. And while bulimia responds well to the SRIs, it also responds to a wide range of antidepressant medications, unlike BDD. Another difference, found in Dr. Rosen's comparison study of eating disorders and BDD (see Chapter 11), is that people with BDD evaluate themselves more negatively because of how they look, and they avoid activities more because of self-consciousness about their appearance.

Conclusions: BDD and eating disorders have some important similarities—most notably, a preoccupation and dissatisfaction with appearance and unrealistic body image. The muscle dysmorphia type of BDD, in particular, has similarities to anorexia nervosa, although "in reverse." However, BDD and eating disorders have some important differences, including their sex ratio and treatment response, which indicate that they aren't identical.

Practical Implications: Because of their differences, it's important to differentiate BDD from eating disorders and diagnose them separately. This will allow the correct treatment to be provided for each disorder. It's easy to differentiate classic BDD from an eating disorder. For example, a man who's obsessed with his nose is clearly different in many ways from an emaciated woman who thinks she's too fat. However, in some cases, it isn't so easy to distinguish BDD from an eating disorder and to figure out which diagnosis is correct. Jean, for example, obsessed about her supposedly large hips. She occasionally dieted but didn't otherwise have symptoms of an eating disorder. Did she have BDD or an "eating disorder not otherwise specified" (an eating disorder that doesn't fulfill all of the diagnostic criteria for anorexia or bulimia)? If a person's concerns focus on the hips, stomach, or thighs but not on overall body weight, and the person doesn't have notably abnormal eating behavior or otherwise meet criteria for an eating disorder, I diagnose BDD. Most of the people I've seen who focused on these areas also had other classic BDD concerns, such as an excessive preoccupation with facial features, supporting the BDD diagnosis. It's unclear whether BDD should be diagnosed if the only preoccupation is body weight; the concern is that an eating disorder may be the more appropriate diagnosis.* But some researchers do consider a concern with weight alone to constitute BDD. This issue remains controversial, and we need more research to determine the correct approach to diagnosis in cases such as these.

As I discussed in Chapter 3, it's unclear whether DSM-IV's diagnostic hierarchy is correct. This hierarchy states that BDD shouldn't be diagnosed if body-image concerns are better accounted for by another disorder, such as anorexia nervosa. But might the eating disorders actually be a form of BDD? Some eating disorder researchers consider disturbed body image, not disturbed eating behavior, to be the core abnormality in eating disorders. After all, people with these disorders eat abnormally because they don't like how they look. Perhaps the hierarchy should be reversed, and the eating disorders considered a form of BDD!

It's also helpful to keep in mind that a given person may have both BDD *and* an eating disorder, in which case both disorders should be diagnosed and focused on in treatment. In women with an eating disorder who also have BDD, the BDD concerns are usually typical ones; most often, they focus on the nose, skin, or hair. If a person has both an eating disorder and BDD, it shouldn't be assumed that the eating disorder is the more severe problem or that BDD is unimportant. One study found that more than 80% of women with both anorexia and BDD said that BDD was their biggest problem or a major problem for them. This same study found that women with both BDD and anorexia are more severely ill than those with anorexia but not BDD. Compared to women with anorexia alone, those who also had BDD had significantly poorer functioning and had been psychiatrically hospitalized more often (an average of 6.3 times versus 3.8). An alarmingly higher percentage of women with BDD (63%) had attempted suicide compared to those without BDD (20%). So people with both BDD and an eating disorder may be especially ill, and it's very important for them to receive psychiatric treatment.

Depression

Because so many people with BDD are also depressed, it's reasonable to consider whether BDD is a symptom of depression, rather than a separate disorder (hypothesis 2). However, this doesn't appear to be the case. Although BDD and depression share same features, they have some very important differences that must be kept in mind when BDD is treated.

Similarities Between BDD and Depression: BDD and depression share some features: poor self-esteem, rejection sensitivity, and feelings of unworthiness and defectiveness. And like many people with depression, some BDD sufferers have

---

*If a person's only concern is with body weight and being or becoming fat, and they also meet other required criteria for an eating disorder, the eating disorder, rather than BDD, should be diagnosed. Diagnosis becomes more complicated if abnormal eating behavior is present but criteria for full-fledged anorexia or bulimia aren't met.

prominent feelings of guilt; this is usually because they feel they shouldn't be so obsessed with something as "trivial" as how they look, or because they feel responsible for ruining their appearance (for example, from skin picking, sun exposure, or cosmetic surgery).

BDD and major depression also commonly co-occur, suggesting that they may be related conditions. In fact, major depression is the disorder that's most often present in people with BDD. I've found that three quarters of people with BDD have past or present major depression (see Appendix D). Other researchers have also generally found that most people with BDD have major depression at some time in their life. Conversely, BDD also appears fairly common in people with depression (see Appendix D). In fact, BDD is more common than many other psychiatric disorders in people with the atypical form of depression (see Chapter 4).

Differences Between BDD and Depression: However, BDD and depression also have some important differences. One difference is that people with BDD have prominent obsessional preoccupations and repetitive compulsive behaviors. Depressed people often focus less, not more, on their appearance, even neglecting it, rather than obsessionally overfocusing on it. And even depressed people who dislike their appearance are unlikely to selectively and obsessionally focus on it or spend hours a day performing compulsive BDD rituals, such as mirror checking and reassurance seeking. In addition, BDD typically begins earlier in life than depression and, when untreated, appears to often be more chronic. And the results of the MRI study discussed in Chapter 10 differed from MRI results typically found in depression (in particular, the brain's hippocampal area was normal in the BDD study).

BDD also responds to treatment differently than depression. First, BDD appears to respond poorly to antidepressants other than the serotonin-reuptake inhibitors, to which depression responds very well. And available evidence, while limited, indicates that BDD only rarely responds to electroconvulsive therapy (ECT, or shock therapy), the most effective treatment for depression. If BDD were simply a symptom of depression, it would be expected to respond to all effective treatments for depression, which it doesn't seem to. In addition, BDD usually takes longer to respond to an SRI than depression does (often as long as 8–12 weeks). Also, BDD appears to require higher SRI doses than depression typically does (see Chapter 13). Furthermore, BDD and depression do not always respond to treatment concurrently. Some patients report that ECT or an antidepressant other than a serotonin-reuptake inhibitor alleviates their depression but not their BDD, which wouldn't be expected if BDD were a symptom of the depression. And occasionally, a particular SRI will diminish BDD but not depressive symptoms, or vice versa, in a person with both disorders (although usually it will work for both).

In addition, in medication studies, BDD responded to an SRI regardless of whether depression responded. In other words, depression didn't have to improve in order for BDD to improve. This, too, suggests that BDD isn't simply a symptom of depression. And when depression in a person with BDD does respond to an SRI, it usually takes longer to improve than "classic" depression usually does. Often, depression in people with BDD improves at about the same time as, or even after, BDD improves, suggesting that it's often largely due to BDD. Of interest, Dr. Hollander found in his BDD clomipramine/desipramine study (see Chapter 13) that the non-SRI antidepressant desipramine wasn't very effective for depressive symptoms; because desipramine is actually an excellent antidepressant, it may not have worked well for depression because the depression was generally due to BDD, which the desipramine didn't help much.

Conclusions: On balance, there are some similarities but many important differences between BDD and depression. It seems fairly clear that BDD isn't simply a symptom of depression or caused by depression. In fact, the depressive symptoms of people with BDD often appear to be caused by BDD. Many people say that BDD is what makes them depressed, demoralized, unable to enjoy life, and even suicidal. In fact, some BDD sufferers can't believe that someone could have BDD and not be depressed, because their BDD symptoms are so distressing and impairing. On the other hand, for some people depression begins before BDD and appears at least somewhat distinct from BDD—that is, not largely due to BDD. For yet others, the situation is even more complicated: the depression appears partly due to BDD and partly not due to BDD.

As I concluded for OCD, social phobia, and eating disorders, BDD doesn't seem to simply be a symptom of depression, but it may nonetheless be *related to* it. Consistent with this hypothesis, Drs. Harrison Pope and James Hudson have proposed that BDD is an "affective spectrum disorder"—that is, a member of a family of disorders that are postulated to be related to one another and to depression. According to this model, BDD and depression share a common underlying abnormality that causes (or at least predisposes to) both BDD and depression.

Practical Implications: It's very important to realize that people with BDD are often depressed and that, conversely, BDD appears relatively common in people with major depression. It's also important to realize that BDD is not simply a symptom of depression. For this reason, BDD should be specifically targeted in treatment and not simply treated as if it were just depression. Otherwise, the BDD and the depression may not get better.

Specifically, all the evidence that we have so far indicates that BDD should be treated with an SRI rather than a non-SRI antidepressant. Venlafaxine (Effexor) may also be effective. You should wait a longer time to see if an SRI will work (12 or even 16 weeks) than you typically would if you were simply treating depression. Also, you may need a higher SRI dose than you'd usually use for depression (see Chapter 13).

If a high dose of an SRI isn't adequately effective for BDD and any co-occurring depressive symptoms, it can be helpful to try to figure out to what extent the depression appears due to BDD. There's no way to determine this with certainty, but BDD sufferer's impression of this is very useful. You can also consider which disorder began first, and whether the severity of BDD and depression always fluctuate together or whether they can fluctuate separately. If the depression began first, and the disorders fluctuate separately, this is some evidence for their distinctiveness. When depression appears largely or entirely due to BDD, I'm more likely to focus on treatment strategies effective for BDD. When depression appears at least somewhat "distinct" from BDD, I'll still use and SRI but am more likely to add a non-SRI antidepressant (e.g., bupropion [Wellbutrin]) to an SRI and more likely to consider ECT if the depression is extremely severe (see Chapter 13).

Psychotherapy also differs in some ways for BDD and depression. BDD appears to respond best to CBT (see Chapter 14), whereas depression may respond to CBT as well as a variety of other psychotherapies. In addition, CBT for BDD and depression differs in some important ways. CBT for BDD, unlike for depression, includes exposure and response (ritual) prevention, and it heavily emphasizes behavioral experiments.

Hypochondriasis:
Bodily Preoccupation and Illness Fears

In the ICD-10 Classification of Mental and Behavioural Disorders (the international classification manual of disorders), BDD is classified as a type of hypochondriasis. People with hypochondriasis are preoccupied with fears of having, or the idea that they have, a serious disease. The preoccupation is based on a misinterpretation of bodily symptoms and persists despite appropriate medical evaluation and reassurance.

Comparing BDD and hypochondriasis is complicated by the likelihood that hypochondriasis has different subtypes—one that's more similar to OCD, one that's more similar to somatization disorder (see Appendix B for a description), and one that's more similar to depression. The subtype that's more similar to OCD also appears more similar to BDD.

Similarities Between BDD and Hypochondriasis: One similarity is that BDD and hypochondriasis both involve bodily fears and preoccupations, and sufferers frequently seek medical treatment. Repetitive body checking and reassurance seeking are also common to both. Moreover, the two disorders are similar in terms of male-to-female ratio, and they have a similar early age of onset and chronic course with waxing and waning symptoms.

Differences Between BDD and Hypochondriasis: However, the focus in BDD is on appearance rather than illness. In several studies, I've found that people with BDD have high levels of somatic concern (worry about their physical well being and health). However, their somatic concern was no higher than that of people with depression or other psychiatric disorders, suggesting that they don't have unusually high levels of somatic concern. This differs from people with hypochondriasis, who have unusually high levels of these concerns. In addition, these disorders do not seem to commonly co-occur (see Appendix D).

A comparison of the treatment response of BDD and hypochondriasis is limited by a paucity of studies. However, available data indicate that while hypochondriasis often responds to SRIs, it may also respond to non-SRI antidepressants, unlike BDD. Also unlike BDD, it may respond to non-CBT psychotherapy (as well as CBT).

Conclusions: Overall, it appears that BDD is not identical to, or a variant of, hypochondriasis. However, it's possible that BDD is *related to* the OCD-like variant of hypochondriasis, which is, like BDD, currently considered one of the OCD-spectrum disorders.

Practical Implications: Because BDD and hypochondriasis appear to have some differences, including their treatment response, it's important to differentiate them and target both of them in treatment.

Schizophrenia

Several decades ago, some authors considered BDD to be closely related to, or a form of, schizophrenia. Schizophrenia is characterized by a constellation of symptoms, including delusional thinking, hallucinations, disorganized speech (e.g., incoherence), grossly disorganized behavior, and "negative" symptoms, which include such things as lack of emotion and motivation.

Several authors, including M. V. Korkina and E. W. Anderson, considered patients with BDD to be schizophrenic. Others viewed BDD as an early sign of schizophrenia. Hay, for example, wrote in 1970 that BDD was "an ominous symptom" that was a precursor of schizophrenia. This theory was given some support by a 1978 retrospective study and which found that patients with likely BDD who received cosmetic nose surgery were more likely to develop subsequent schizophrenia than patients who had nose surgery to correct a deformity caused by injury or disease. But definitions of schizophrenia used in past decades in the United States were broader than that currently used. Thus, it's likely that BDD was mistakenly diagnosed as schizophrenia in many of these cases.

Similarities Between BDD and Schizophrenia: There are few similarities between BDD and schizophrenia. The main one is that about half of people with BDD are delusional—that is, they're completely convinced that their appearance-related beliefs are correct even though other people don't share them. In addition, a high percentage have referential thinking, mistakenly believing that other people take special notice of them and that events in their environment have special relevance to them (e.g., that people are laughing at them). Delusions and referential thinking may both occur in schizophrenia.

Differences Between BDD and Schizophrenia: Importantly, the delusional thinking that occurs in BDD usually isn't bizarre, as it is in schizophrenia. In addition, other symptoms of schizophrenia (prominent hallucinations, disorganized speech, grossly disorganized behavior, and negative symptoms) are absent in BDD. Data on the co-occurrence of these disorders strongly refute a close relationship between them: in my series of patients with BDD, none were diagnosed with schizophrenia (see Appendix D), nor have other researchers found coexisting schizophrenia in people with BDD. Similarly, schizophrenia hasn't been found in first-degree relatives of people with BDD.

Treatment response also differs. Antipsychotic medications (neuroleptics) are the mainstay of treatment for schizophrenia and are often effective. In contrast, SRIs seem most efficacious for BDD, whereas antipsychotics alone appear ineffective (see Chapter 13).

Conclusions: Overall, BDD doesn't appear to be a symptom of schizophrenia. Nor does BDD appear closely related to schizophrenia.

Practical Implications: Even though BDD is misdiagnosed as schizophrenia less often than in the past, it still happens. It's important to differentiate these disorders from each other, especially because effective treatments differ. If a person has both disorders, each disorder should each be diagnosed and targeted in treatment.

Olfactory Reference Syndrome: The Distress of Perceived Body Odor

Nikki's life centered on her body odor, which no one else could smell. Since she was 18, she'd believed that she smelled bad. At first, she thought she smelled like sweat; later she also worried about her supposedly bad breath. "I think I smell *really* bad," she said. "It's hard to describe it—it's a horrible smell sort of like an enchilada that everyone notices."

Nikki showered and changed her clothes five times a day. She used massive quantities of soap, perfume, deodorant, and mouthwash, and she constantly chewed gum and ate mints. She repeatedly checked her breath by blowing into her cupped hand. To get rid of the supposed smell she ate a special diet and scraped her tongue and mouth until they bled. She also thought that other people took special notice of the odor. "I know everyone can smell it from at least 20 to 30 feet away. Why else would they frown at me the way they do and make comments like 'It's stuffy in here?' Or why would they open the window or make a comment about soap when I'm with them?"

Nikki's preoccupation and referential thinking prevented her from working. She'd tried many jobs but quickly quit them when she thought people were talking about how bad she smelled. She became very socially isolated. She also saw numerous doctors and dentists without relief. Eventually, as a result of her preoccupation, Nikki went on disability, became depressed, and even considered suicide.

People with olfactory reference syndrome (ORS) believe they emit a body odor that smells like flatulence, bad breath, sweat, an anal or genital odor, or even nonbodily odors such as ammonia or enchiladas. Usually, they think it comes from the anus, mouth, skin, feet, armpits, or genitals. Just as other people can't perceive, or can barely perceive, the physical defects of BDD, they can't smell the body odor of ORS.

ORS hasn't been studied much, making it difficult to assess similarities and differences with BDD. One similarity, however, is that both disorders are characterized by referential thinking. When other people do such things as turn away, look disgusted, open a window, say the word "smell," sit at a distance, or hold a newspaper in front of their face, the behaviors are assumed to be a response to the repulsive odor. In addition, people with ORS engage in many BDD-like behaviors—frequently checking for the presence of the odor, repeatedly asking others whether they can smell it, and camouflaging with excessive amounts of deodorant, perfume, or mouthwash. Showering and washing or changing clothes may also be done to excess. Believing that they suffer from a medical problem, they often seek help from nonpsychiatric medical specialists—dentists for supposed bad breath, gynecologists for supposed vaginal odor, proctologists for supposed anal odor or flatulence, or surgeons for the removal of "smelly tonsils." As in BDD, such treatment tends to be ineffective.

Because they seem so similar, some authors consider ORS a form of BDD. Alternatively, BDD and ORS have both been considered a type of social phobia, reflecting the shared feature of social anxiety and avoidance.

Although ORS's treatment has barely been studied, a small number of reported cases suggest that ORS may respond to an SRI, a combination of an antidepressant and an antipsychotic medication, to a variety of antidepressants (including non-SRIs), or to the antipsychotic pimozide alone. This differs from BDD.

In summary, because relatively little research has been done on ORS, it's difficult to determine its relationship to BDD. However, this underrecognized and impairing disorder appears to have much in common with BDD as well as some differences.

Koro: Panic over Penile Shrinkage

When koro strikes, men panic and rush to emergency rooms in droves. They fear that they'll imminently die from penile shrinkage, and they implore family members and doctors to save them by pulling on their penis.

Koro, a Malay word for "the head of the turtle," consists of the erroneous belief that one's penis is shrinking and acutely retracting into the abdomen, which will kill the person when the disappearance is complete. Intense distress and panic spur the use of various mechanical means to prevent penile retraction: tying, grasping, or clamping the penis with plier-like devices. Koro occasionally occurs in women, who fear their breasts or labia will shrink. Koro usually occurs in certain parts of Southeast Asia, primarily southern coastal China and among Chinese living overseas in Southeast Asia. However, similar symptoms have also been reported in other parts of the world, such as Indonesia, India, Thailand, and England.

BDD and koro share an intense, anxiety-provoking preoccupation with a perceived defect in appearance, and some men with BDD worry about their genitals. However, Southeast Asian cases of koro differ from BDD in several ways. Men with koro believe that their body is acutely and dramatically changing, which I've seen only occasionally in BDD. In addition, men with koro fear that the disappearance of their penis will kill them, which doesn't occur in BDD.

Furthermore, unlike BDD, koro usually begins suddenly, lasts only briefly, occurs as an epidemic, and often resolves with reassurance.

However, many cases of koro from the Western world lack these characteristic features and are more similar to BDD. In these cases, men worry that their penis is too small or shrinking, but generally don't believe that it will actually disappear into their abdomen, and few believe that penile shrinkage will kill them. The belief is sometimes more chronic (lasting as long as several decades) and doesn't occur in epidemics. Some of these cases are so similar to BDD that the diagnosis of BDD is probably more accurate than koro. While the epidemic form of koro that occurs in Southeast Asia differs in many ways from BDD, it's unclear whether it's truly a different disorder than BDD or a cultural variant of BDD. This is one of the many BDD mysteries that remains to be solved.

The Delusional Variant of BDD

The relationship between BDD and its delusional variant is controversial and important. DSM-IV classifies the nondelusional form of BDD (in which people have some insight) as a somatoform disorder (i.e., a disorder involving physical complaints). However, its delusional form (in which people are convinced their appearance beliefs are correct) is classified as a type of delusional disorder. Yet when I and my colleagues compared these forms of BDD, we found that they were similar in terms of nearly all the characteristics we examined. This led us to conclude that they may actually be the same disorder, although the delusional variant seems to be more severe. People with delusional BDD tend to have more severe BDD symptoms, more impairment in functioning, and poorer quality of life.

These findings, which requiring confirmation, suggest that BDD and its delusional disorder variant should probably be classified as the same disorder. In fact, a step in that direction was taken in DSM-IV: although they remain separately classified, they may also be double-coded. In other words, a person with delusional BDD may receive a diagnosis of both BDD and delusional disorder. While this is a somewhat awkward compromise, it underscores the likelihood that BDD and its delusional variant may indeed be the same disorder.

BDD spans a spectrum of insight—from good insight, to poor insight, to absent insight (delusional thinking). This entire continuum appears to constitute a single disorder. Thinking in BDD may fluctuate along this continuum, with nondelusional thinking sometimes becoming delusional, and vice versa. In addition, insight may improve with treatment. Observations such as these further support the hypothesis that the delusional and nondelusional forms of BDD are the same disorder, as it's unlikely that people whose thinking changes in this way have two different disorders. In addition, it's sometimes difficult to distinguish delusional from nondelusional preoccupations, which gives some support to this continuum model.

The delusional-nondelusional issue is relevant to other disorders, such as OCD, anorexia nervosa, hypochondriasis, and social phobia. Like BDD, these disorders appear to span a spectrum of insight, with insight sometimes fluctuating along a continuum. This interesting issue needs to be further studied and has important implications for the classification and treatment of a number of psychiatric disorders.

From a clinical perspective, I'd consider delusional and nondelusional BDD to be the same disorder and would generally treat them the same way. In particular, as I discussed in Chapter 13, I'd recommend treating delusional BDD with an SRI, even though this isn't how other disorders characterized by delusions are usually treated. I'd also recommend that delusional BDD (and nondelusional BDD) not be treated with a neuroleptic (antipsychotic) alone. CBT treatment for these forms of BDD is generally similar, although people with delusional BDD might benefit from a heavier emphasis on cognitive restructuring and behavioral experiments (although this issue hasn't been studied). Despite similarities between BDD's delusional and nondelusional forms, it's important to keep in mind that delusional people with BDD are typically more severely ill and suicidal, and may be less likely to accept psychiatric treatment.

BDD and Personality

People with BDD can have virtually any type of personality. Some are quiet and withdrawn, whereas others are outgoing, colorful, and adventurous. Some tend to be suspicious, whereas others are trusting. Some are constrained and careful, whereas others are impulsive, craving excitement and novelty. This list could go on.

Despite this variety, however, people with BDD often do seem to have a particular constellation of personality traits. They often describe themselves as shy, quiet, self-conscious, unassertive, having low self-esteem, and sensitive to rejection. In published cases reports, shyness and an obsessional personality style have been noted. I assessed personality traits in 100 people with BDD using the NEO-Five Factor Inventory, a questionnaire that assesses five aspects of normal personality: neuroticism, extroversion, conscientiousness, openness to experience, and agreeableness. Neuroticism measures a variety of negative emotions and cognitions—in particular, anxiety, self-consciousness, anger, depression, and feelings of vulnerability. People with BDD as a group scored in the very high range on this scale, which isn't surprising, given that so many say that they often experience unpleasant emotions such as these.

On extroversion—a measure of gregariousness, warmth, assertiveness, activity/energy, and excitement seeking—the average score was in the low range. Thus, people with BDD tend to be introverted, quiet, and reserved. People with BDD scored in the low range on conscientiousness, which measures disciplined striving after goals and will to achieve. They scored in the average range on openness to experience (aesthetic sensitivity, intellectual curiosity, creativity, and willingness to try new things) and in the low-average range on agreeableness (altruistic, trusting, good natured, and agreeable, as opposed to antagonistic, irritable, stingy, and critical). In other studies, I found that people with BDD tend to be rejection sensitive and unassertive (women scored below the 15th percentile and men below the 10th percentile on assertiveness).

It's worth emphasizing that these scores are average scores, and that scores of some individuals with BDD are quite different from these averages. Also, these scores tell us, for example, that low extroversion *is associated with* BDD but not whether one causes the other.

I and several other researchers have also assessed personality disorders (see Appendix B) in individuals with BDD. These studies found that from 40% to 100% had a personality disorder, with avoidant personality disorder most common (avoidant personality disorder is characterized by social inhibition, feelings of inadequacy, and hypersensitivity to negative evaluation). Rates of narcissistic personality disorder were quite low. These findings fit with my clinical observations that most people with BDD aren't vain or self-centered; instead, they're more likely to be self-conscious, anxious, and shy.

It seems clear that BDD isn't simply a symptom or reflection of a personality problem. Many people with BDD don't have a personality disorder. And after BDD is successfully treated, what appeared to be a personality problem sometimes disappears, suggesting that what looked like personality traits were actually symptoms of, or due to, BDD. Nonetheless, as discussed in Chapter 10, it's possible that certain personality traits may contribute to the development of BDD.

Like many aspects of BDD, the relationship between BDD and personality traits—both normal and problematic—has been little studied and needs further research. Additional research will help answer such questions as whether certain personality traits predispose a person to BDD, or whether BDD changes personality.

Concluding Thoughts

On balance, it appears that BDD isn't identical to, or simply a symptom of, any other psychiatric disorder. However, it has many similarities to, and is probably related to, several disorders, most notably OCD, social phobia, depression, eating disorders, and olfactory reference syndrome. However, BDD is likely to be a heterogeneous disorder, with several different forms. Thus, it's possible that some forms of BDD are more closely related to certain disorders, such as OCD, and other forms are more closely related to other disorders, such as the eating disorders.

One way to think about BDD's relationship to other psychiatric disorders is to consider it a member of a "family" of related disorders. I mentioned that BDD is widely considered one of the "OCD-spectrum disorders," a hypothesized family of disorders that appear closely related to OCD. BDD is also a candidate for the "affective spectrum disorders," a broader grouping of disorders that may be related and which includes OCD and many of the OCD-spectrum disorders.

The practical implications of these conclusions is that BDD should be identified and diagnosed when it's present, rather than assuming it's just a symptom of another disorder. As best we know, effective treatment for BDD differs in some ways from treatments for other psychiatric disorders. If BDD isn't identified and targeted separately in treatment—if it's mistakenly diagnosed as another disorder or is ignored altogether—treatment may be ineffective. However, as detailed in Chapters 12–14, if BDD itself is treated, it's likely to improve.

In the coming years, as we better understand the cause of BDD and other disorders, we'll have a clearer understanding of their relationship to one another. This understanding will lead to their more accurate classification, better diagnosis, and more effective treatment.

· · *seventeen* · ·

For Family Members and Friends

"At least one can be patient, understanding, and loving, and pre-vent them from feeling isolated."   **A mother**

What You Can Do: An Overview

BDD has far-reaching effects. Family members and friends usually suffer, too. It's very painful to watch a loved one struggle with such a distressing and impairing disorder. You may feel helpless, because no matter how hard you try to help, it doesn't work. You may feel frustrated—even angry—because you can't get the BDD sufferer to stop worrying about their looks, stop their rituals, leave the house and do things with you, or get the right treatment. You may feel rejected, because they can get so wrapped up in the BDD that they seem to ignore you. You may feel isolated and alone, thinking that no one else in the world is struggling with a similar problem. BDD can be so stressful for family and friends that it causes intense conflict, hostility, and anger—even the break-up of relationships, loss of friendships, and divorce.

In this chapter I'll discuss ways in which spouses, family members, and friends can help the person with BDD and themselves cope better with this difficult illness. Here's a summary of some approaches that may help, which I'll discuss in more detail below.

Coping with BDD:
What Family Members and Friends Can Do

---

1) Recognize BDD symptoms, take them seriously, and talk openly about BDD

2) Encourage and support psychiatric treatment

3) If the person with BDD is reluctant to get psychiatric treatment, fo-cus on their suffering and problems with functioning

4) Don't discuss the "defect" at length or try to talk the person out of their beliefs about their looks

5) Create a supportive home environment

6) Limit your involvement in BDD rituals

7) Don't give reassurance

8) Encourage better functioning but also recognize the person's limitations

9) Encourage participation in family events

10) Give praise for even small gains

11) When assessing progress, look at the big picture

12) During times of stress, you may need to modify your expectations

13) Be patient

14) Try to limit angry outbursts

15) If the person with BDD is suicidal, get immediate psychiatric care

16) Keep your family routine as normal as possible

17) Take time for yourself

18) Don't blame yourself

19) Remember that you aren't alone

20) Maintain hope!

"The Selfish Disease":
A Husband's Perspective

"There aren't enough days on a calendar to tell you how many times I've wanted to leave my wife," Sam told me. "I'm a very loyal person, and I love her. But at times it gets to be too much. She's late when we go out, and sometimes she won't go at all. She can get so wrapped up in her obsessions that she ignores me completely. She doesn't give the children the attention they need. BDD is the selfish disease."

Sam sometimes accompanied his wife, Beth, to her sessions with me and told me about how he tried to cope with her illness. "My wife has had this problem for decades," he said. "No one knew what it was." I heard about Beth's fixation on her nose and the many unsuccessful surgeries she'd had. Her preoccupation had made it difficult for her to raise her children. Later, after they'd grown, she had a hard time focusing on a job; she wanted to work, but had been largely unemployed.

"This is a problem that affects family members, too," Sam told me. "I know how much pain this problem has caused my wife—I don't want to downplay how hard it's been for her. But it's also had a major impact on me. I hope this doesn't sound too selfish, but sometimes I think I've suffered as much as my wife!"

Sam and Beth had been married for ten years. Beth's previous husband had left her because of her symptoms. "You might be skeptical that that was the reason, that it was because of my nose obsession," she told me. "Some people think it's an excuse—that he really left me for some other reason. But it was mostly because of the BDD. I hounded him all day long. I'd plead with him to help me find another surgeon, and I'd constantly talk about how surgery would solve my appearance problem. We hardly had a social life. When we went out, I'd be late a lot of the time. I'd be in the mirror putting on makeup and styling and restyling my hair to make my nose look smaller. Sometimes I wouldn't go to social events at all because I thought I looked so bad. That really drove him crazy.

"I did manage to raise my children and actually did a pretty good job, I think, but it was very hard. I don't know how I did it. I was so focused on my nose. I couldn't stop thinking about it. It was really hard for my husband, because he ended up working two jobs and doing a lot of the child care too. I don't want you to think I was a *total* basket case—I wasn't—but life was a lot harder with my problem. My husband finally got fed up, and he left me."

Like Beth's first husband, Sam had gotten very involved in her disorder. At her insistence, Sam held magnifying mirrors and bright lights so she could get a better look at her nose, a ritual that could take more than an hour a day. Beth talked to him incessantly about her nose, saying she wanted surgery and asking if her nose looked okay. "The questioning is especially hard," Sam told me. "No matter what I say, she doesn't really believe me. She just asks me again and again! I don't know what to say." They'd missed family get-togethers and had few friends because his wife felt too ugly to be around other people. A few times Sam even drove her to an emergency room because she'd looked in the mirror and considered suicide.

"There's no worse illness on earth than BDD," Sam told me many times. "People who haven't lived with it probably wouldn't understand, but this is the most devastating thing in the world. I've seen death. I've seen murder. This is as bad. . . . Maybe it's harder for me than my wife because I'm more helpless than her. I can't do anything about it."

One of the most difficult things for Sam was the isolation. "I've felt very alone because friends and family don't understand. I've mostly dealt with this on my own. I took a risk and told a few relatives, but they don't understand it; they think it's strange. But it's the most devastating illness there is."

Like Beth's first husband, Sam had thoughts of leaving his wife. Nonetheless, he resolved to stand by her. Beth eventually got much better with sertraline (Zoloft), and the strain on their marriage diminished.

Sam's story isn't unusual. I've met countless husbands, wives, girlfriends, boyfriends, parents, and friends who've lived with BDD. They've been deeply affected by the disorder and have struggled to find ways to cope.

I never met Craig's wife because she'd left him years ago. "She left me because of my skin obsession," he told me. "I was totally obsessed. Sometimes it wasn't so bad, but when it got really bad, I'd miss work and I wouldn't go out. I'd even spend entire weekends in bed. I'd feel that life wasn't worth living and I totally ignored my wife. I was completely wrapped up in the obsession.

"We couldn't agree about whether to have children. My wife wanted to, but I was afraid that with my symptoms I wouldn't be able to take responsibility for a child. I had a hard enough time taking care of myself. My wife stuck it out with me for a couple of years. But eventually she couldn't take it anymore, and she left me. If I didn't have the disorder, I think we'd still be together today."

It isn't rare for BDD to lead to divorce. It's an extreme and striking indication of how painful this disorder can be for those who are close to BDD sufferers. I've heard similar stories from many people. Every story reflects the myriad ways in which BDD can disrupt lives and cause needless suffering. Husbands, wives, girlfriends, boyfriends, sons, daughters, close friends, and acquaintances may all experience the disorder. Sometimes they don't know the cause of the difficulties they experience—they don't know that BDD is the root of their loved one's problems because the symptoms are kept secret—but they experience its effects nonetheless.

You may recall family members and friends I described earlier in the book who were affected by BDD. Dwayne's girlfriend pulled a knife on him and threatened to harm him if he didn't stop talking about surgery. Jonathan's symptoms were so severe that his wife left him. I've heard many stories about missing important ceremonies and events—not showing up for graduations, weddings, or funerals, or not seeing a close friend before death.

Other examples are less dramatic but no less painful. Ted's wife pleaded with her husband to try medication that might decrease his symptoms; he preferred to try "natural remedies" instead, even though they hadn't worked for 15 years. As a result, their marriage suffered. Ivan's girlfriend tried to get him to go to parties with her, telling him that he looked fine—that he was very handsome— and that no one would be focusing on his hair except him. She often ended up going alone. Teachers may experience the frustration of trying to get a student with BDD to work harder, not understanding why their grades are dropping or they miss class. A boss may try to understand why his employee is late for work and takes too many sick days. They are all affected by BDD.

The "selfish disease"—Sam's description of BDD—reflects many family members' experience. The person with BDD can be so wrapped up in their obsession that family members are ignored. The BDD sufferer seems to put his or her needs first—missing the social engagement, forgoing a wedding, spending too much money on beauty products, talking about their appearance rather than showing interest in others. Even if BDD sufferers do none of these things, they may seem distant, preoccupied, and self-absorbed, rather than concerned about the people around them. But as I've emphasized throughout this book, people with BDD have little control over their obsessions. If they could take their mind off their appearance, they would. BDD may seem selfish to other people, but it isn't a selfishness problem. Effective treatment often puts an end to the "selfishness"—what appeared to be selfish behavior turns out to have been symptoms of BDD.

"I Knew Something Was Wrong with My Daughter": A Parent's Perspective

"I knew something was wrong with my daughter when she'd be in the bathroom for an hour and was upset when she came out." This mother had tried very hard to help her daughter cope with BDD. Although some of the approaches she tried—such as reassuring her—weren't successful, others were. Her daughter finally agreed to see a psychiatrist and responded well to paroxetine (Paxil).

Parents may suffer greatly. They may have to cope with their 14-year-old daughter's dropping grades and avoidance of friends and activities. They may care for a 35-year-old son who is unable to support himself or live on his own. They may finally, in desperation, take their handsome adolescent son for a chin implant because they can no longer tolerate his relentless pleas for cosmetic surgery, only to find that he's even more desperate after surgery.

Jennifer's mother worried endlessly about her daughter—how to get her back into school, how to help her find a job, how to get her to *stop worrying* so much about how she looked. Other parents do too. "We tell our daughter that she looks fine and to stop worrying so much," Molly's parents told me. "We hate seeing her so unhappy." "I know I drive them crazy, asking them if I look okay and telling them I'm ugly," Molly replied. "But it makes me mad when they say I'm attractive. They love me and want to reassure me, so they tell me I look fine. But I don't."

Coping with BDD may be particularly difficult for parents because you may feel responsible for your child's difficulties. Did you cause the problem? Did you overemphasize the importance of appearance? Should you have raised you child differently? Blaming yourself only compounds the suffering.

One mother felt helpless when it came to helping her son cope with his hair, and she blamed herself. "He's so upset over his hair that he can't function because of it. We try not to reassure him, but he's so desperate, we have to. He's having temper tantrums because he thinks his hair is getting worse. We don't know what to do!"

Her son, too, told me how his appearance concern caused his family to suffer. "I can't enjoy being with them, because I'm so upset over how I look," he said. "I can't even have a good Christmas with them. I have to ask them 'Does my hair look okay? Does it look thin?' And they say to me, 'Don't ruin the day.' But I do. And I feel bad about how much unhappiness I've caused them. I've put them through hell."

I heard from the mother of a boy who had killed himself because of his supposed ugliness. He'd seen many doctors, but BDD hadn't been diagnosed. "For many years I lost patience with my son for always staring in the mirror and saying he was ugly when he was a quite handsome boy," she wrote. "He used to say to me, 'What's this thing that's taking me over, mom?' The night before he died, he said I didn't understand him, which was true, and that there was no hope for him.

"I know that it's almost impossible to sway the mind of someone with body dysmorphic disorder, but at least one can be patient, understanding, and loving, and prevent them from feeling isolated. . . . My tragedy will always be that I didn't know and couldn't tell him that it wasn't his fault."

Suggested Guidelines for Family Members and Friends

In this section I'll describe some of the problems that family members and friends commonly encounter, as well as some approaches to dealing with them. Because of the varied ways in which BDD expresses itself—because each individual's and each family member's experience with BDD differs in some ways— this advice may not address certain problems that you encounter. But I hope it will cover many of them and that the the suggested coping strategies are helpful.

The guidelines below are easier to describe than implement. It can in fact be frustrating and difficult to do some of them. Yet all are worth trying. It can be helpful to keep in mind that they're more likely to be effective when the person with BDD has had at least a partial response to medication and/or cognitive-behavioral therapy.

Most of the approaches discussed here won't actually treat the disorder. That's the role of serotonin-reuptake inhibitors and cognitive-behavioral therapy. The coping strategies I'll discuss are additional approaches that may enhance effective treatments for BDD and make the disorder easier to live with. At the very least, they should prevent worsening of symptoms, which sometimes results from well-intentioned responses and interventions by family members and friends. They may also help counteract feelings of helplessness, anger, frustration, and isolation. Although you might feel powerless in dealing with BDD, there are many things you can do.

1) Recognize BDD symptoms, take them seriously, and talk openly about BDD

This is the first critical step. As I've emphasized throughout this book, it's easy to mistake BDD symptoms for normal appearance concerns or even vanity. It's easy to ignore the warning signs, thinking your loved one is simply self-centered or self-absorbed. You may assume that an adolescent with BDD is simply going through a "phase." BDD can also be mistakenly diagnosed as another psychiatric disorder (see Chapter 4).

Don't ignore BDD warning signs. Try not to get angry or critical, tease the person because they're so focused on their looks, or reassure them that they look okay. Instead, learn about BDD. If they have any of the signs of BDD discussed in Chapter 4, ask them about their worries and listen to their concerns in a supportive way, without criticizing or blaming them. Tell them about BDD. The sooner you can help your loved one recognize the problem, the sooner the recovery process can begin. You might worry that the BDD sufferer will react negatively to hearing that they may have a psychiatric problem. They may respond this way, but many people don't. Many are in fact enormously relieved to learn that they may have a known and treatable condition and that they aren't alone. Identifying BDD is the first step to helping both you and the BDD sufferer cope with the illness.

2) Encourage and Support Psychiatric Treatment

Getting the right treatment is essential. Don't tell BDD sufferers to just "snap out of it," try harder," or "just stop worrying." You wouldn't take this approach if they had heart disease. Saying such things will just alienate them and make them feel you don't understand. Of course, it's important to make an effort to get the right treatment (an SRI and/or CBT) and to fully participate in the treatment. But trying hard by itself isn't sufficient. Encourage the person to try an SRI and/or CBT and to stick with the treatment. Offer to make an appointment with a qualified professional and accompany them to an evaluation. Your encouragement and support can make a big difference.

You can be extremely helpful by encouraging compliance with psychiatric treatment. While many people with BDD welcome this treatment because it offers them hope of relief, others are reluctant. Your support can make a crucial difference. It can help to remind the person taking medication that side effects may not occur; if they do, they may be relatively mild and transient. Waiting it out for a while may allow side effects to pass and the medication to begin working. If they're really problematic, another medication can be tried. Don't let them stop their medication without talking with their doctor. Cognitive-behavioral therapy is challenging and difficult at times. Encourage the sufferer to remember that this is to be expected—that treatment is more likely to work if it's challenging. In addition, you can participate in exposure activities, behavioral experiments, and response prevention once the therapist shows you how to do this. You can move the avoidant person further along with your encouragement and support.

Supporting psychiatric rather than surgical treatment is sometimes difficult. People with BDD may be desperate to get surgery, and may beg and plead with you to give them financial or emotional support for it. While more scientifically rigorous studies are needed, the evidence we have indicates that it doesn't effectively treat BDD and that people with BDD are often unhappy with the results. Many say they wish that someone—including their family members—had talked them out of having it done.

Based on what we now know, the best advice is to encourage people with BDD to avoid surgery. I recommend this especially if they've already had multiple surgeries, without alleviation of their appearance-related concerns. At the very least, it's prudent to first give psychiatric treatment a good try. Encourage your loved one to try this approach first. There's no significant downside to trying it. It's more likely to be effective and is less risky than surgery.

3) If the Person with BDD is Reluctant to Get Psychiatric Treatment, Focus on Their Suffering and Problems with Functioning

It's especially distressing when someone with BDD won't accept the diagnosis or get help. Because most people with BDD have little or no insight, this difficult situation is unfortunately fairly common. Although there's no easy solution, the following approaches may be helpful:

- Without haranguing them, continue to gently *provide information about BDD and support psychiatric treatment.*
- *Emphasize how much the appearance concerns are ruining their life.* Rather than arguing with the person about how they look, convey to them that they're *overly* preoccupied, that they worry *too much,* and that they're *suffering too much* as a result of their appearance concerns. Their preoccupation has too much power over them. It's interfering with their functioning and their relationships. It's depriving them of what they want and deserve in life. It has far too strong a hold. They may not like how they look, but this shouldn't control their life or cause them so much anguish. Treatment can change all of this.
- *Emphasize that treatment can greatly diminish their suffering and improve their functioning and quality of life. Effective treatment is worth trying.* Giving it a try doesn't necessarily lead to treatment for life. In addition, the medications that work are generally well tolerated. Consulting a mental health professional about how to get the person to try psychiatric treatment is sometimes helpful as well. Periodically remind the sufferer that you are willing to help and that people with BDD can get better.

Effective treatment is the means to regaining control. *They,* not the appearance preoccupation, should be in charge. They should be able to think about whatever they want to think about. They should be able to interact with other people, free of gnawing, painful thoughts that keep them a prisoner. Tell them what some of my patients have said after they've responded to psychiatric treatment. Cassandra described herself as a caged animal—her obsessional thinking had locked her in a place where she had no freedom or pleasure. Effective treatment freed her; it allowed her to regain control of her life.

Another patient said, "The treatment I got was very freeing—it's lifted an amazing burden. I regret that I put it off for so many years." This patient hadn't been interested in psychiatric treatment. He preferred holistic approaches, which he'd tried for 20 years. He finally got tired of trying to treat himself; his approaches weren't working, and he was worn out and not living the life he'd hoped for. He decided he had nothing left to lose.

4) Don't Discuss the "Defect" or Try to Talk the Person with BDD Out of Their Beliefs about Their Looks

Some family members and friends try to talk the person with BDD out of their belief. This approach is understandable. They look fine, so why not just explain this to them? Why not just reason with them? After all, they're reasonable in other ways. Maybe all that's needed is a compelling argument or a heartfelt attempt to convince them of this.

This approach is highly unlikely to effectively treat BDD. It can also consume endless amounts of your time. Usually, everyone ends up feeling frustrated. This approach is especially likely to fail with someone with delusional BDD—that is, someone who is completely convinced that their view of the defect is accurate. You may recall Steven's statement: "I'm as convinced of what I see as you are that the box on this table is rectangular, not round." Try arguing with conviction of this strength! Following the suggestions under #3 above are more likely to help.

Nonetheless, an occasional reality check may be helpful for certain individuals with BDD. People with some insight—who realize that their view of the defect is distorted or that their belief is due to a psychiatric disorder—may benefit from an occasional reminder that their view is exaggerated and is due to BDD. Reminding them that others don't see them the way they do can help put things in perspective. But don't try to argue the point or convince someone who can't acknowledge their faulty thinking.

As medication or cognitive-behavioral treatment start to work, insight may improve; that is, the person's view of their appearance may become more realistic. At this point, it may be helpful to remind them that their view isn't accurate—that they have "foggy glasses on their brain" that prevent them from seeing themselves as others do.

In general, the less you discuss appearance at all, the better. For example, if someone is obsessed with their nose, don't tell them their nose is fine but they might want to change their hairstyle. Such benign comments generally aren't helpful. They can trigger severe distress and even new appearance obsessions.

5) Create a Supportive Home Environment

Because BDD can be so hard to cope with, it's easy to criticize and express anger toward someone who has it. It's best to avoid this. Instead, do your best to create a supportive home environment. Help them talk about their feelings of anxiety, depression, shame, and isolation. Show your support, and help them fight BDD. Without being judgmental, critical, or hostile, explain that if you participate in their rituals or help them avoid things like social situations, this will only strengthen the BDD. Let them know that you care and that you'll try to understand and support them through the recovery process.

6) Limit Your Involvement in BDD Rituals

This is one of the major pitfalls for family members and friends. You may be drawn into rituals and behaviors that seem senseless and even strange. You may be asked to participate in these behaviors, making it easier or possible for them to be done. While many BDD behaviors are done silently, in private, without involving other people, virtually any of them can involve others. You may be asked to hold mirrors to allow multiple views of the defect or to shine lights on it while it's inspected. Or the bathroom may be unavailable for hours each morning while checking and grooming rituals are performed.

You may be asked to measure a body part or to confirm that a certain measurement is normal. You may be asked to cut, groom, or style hair. You may be begged to confirm that a certain outfit is flattering or pay for expensive items, such as wigs, clothing, beauty products, or surgery. You may be implored to vacation in a cold location, where concealing clothes can be worn. Some people with BDD compulsively pick the skin of family members and friends. When family members try to prevent this, the BDD sufferer can get very upset. As one woman with BDD said, "Usually they just give in and let me do it," she said. "It's the easiest thing for them to do."

It's best for both you and the BDD sufferer to not participate in rituals. Participation helps keep them going and just feeds the BDD. Assisting with rituals also drains your time and energy. You might be tempted to participate because you hope you'll help the BDD sufferer. After all, you're responding to a plea from someone you care about, who is extremely distressed. You participate in the hope that something good will result—that once the view in the mirror is obtained, the worry will finally end. But participating in BDD-related behaviors never has and never will cure the disorder. It can even make it worse by reinforcing those behaviors.

Don't hold special lights to allow a better view. Don't groom or style hair. Don't give reassurance about the "defect" or clothing. Don't pay for yet another outfit, or for surgery after surgery. Don't allow your skin to be picked. Limit the time you spend waiting for the person while they're checking. Be consistent, and kind, in your resolve! Consistency is crucial so the person with BDD learns that the behaviors aren't acceptable or helpful. Help them develop alternative activities that they can do instead when they get the urge to do rituals.

Not participating in rituals isn't easy, and it may help to consult with a CBT therapist on the best approach. The BDD sufferer may insist that you participate and may become very distraught or even angry if you don't. It's important to first discuss that you'll no longer participate in their rituals because it isn't good for them. Explain that you know they're in pain but that participating in the behaviors can actually even increase their preoccupations and fears. It won't defeat the BDD and, ultimately, keeps it going. Even if anxiety improves by doing a ritual, the relief is only temporary. Resisting the behaviors is better in the long run. It's often difficult to hold the line, but it's best to explain that you understand their distress and are helping them control the disorder by not participating. All family members need to agree on this. The challenge is to avoid conveying anger and hostility. Try to convey understanding and support. Fortunately, treatment with medication or CBT often diminishes the rituals as well as requests that other people participate in them.

7) Don't Give Reassurance
Reassurance seeking is the BDD ritual that most often involves other people. It's also one of the most frustrating for family members. If the questioning is infrequent, it may not be particularly problematic. Some people refrain from

reassurance seeking because they realize how bothersome it can be. But others simply can't—the urge is irresistible. Parents of a 20-year-old woman with BDD told me, "We don't know how to cope. No matter what we say, the questioning persists. We love our daughter and want to reassure her that she looks fine. She thinks we're lying but we're not. We don't know what to do."

The best response to this ritual—as to all others—is to not participate. In other words, don't reassure the sufferer that they look okay. Even though they look fine, telling them this just feeds the BDD and keeps it going.

The typical—and understandable—response is to provide the reassurance the BDD sufferer seeks. After all, the person with BDD looks fine, so the natural tendency is to say so. Common responses include "You look fine!" "I can't see it at all," "It's hardly visible," or "It's not as bad as you think—it's hardly noticeable!" The problem with these responses is that although they're true, they don't stop the questioning for long, if at all. Furthermore, reassurance doesn't put an end to the appearance concerns.

Paradoxically, responding to questioning with a reassuring reply can actually perpetuate the reassurance-seeking behavior. If the response does temporarily decrease the BDD sufferer's anxiety, this transient relief fuels their attempt to obtain more relief by asking the question again. While it might seem cruel to refuse to respond to requests for reassurance, it isn't. Refraining from providing reassurance may actually stop this time-and energy-consuming behavior.

I often meet with family members, along with the person with BDD, to discuss BDD more generally and this behavior in particular. We all agree that providing reassurance isn't helpful and benefits no one. The person with BDD can generally acknowledge that they aren't reassured very much by the responses they get, and family members can readily acknowledge that no matter what they say, it really doesn't help. We then agree that, for the benefit of the BDD sufferer, family members will no longer respond to requests for reassurance. Instead, if necessary, they will remind the questioner that the behavior is a ritual—part of their disorder—and that it isn't helpful for them to respond. They may also remind the questioner that they agreed as a group not to respond.

Different families come up with their own response. Responses that may work are "I'm sorry; I know you're suffering, but I'm not going to respond to your question," "We agreed it isn't helpful for me to reassure you," "Your need for reassurance is a symptom of BDD, and it won't help if I give it to you," or "I know you're anxious, but reassuring you won't help." The main point is to avoid commenting on the person's appearance as part of the response. After giving this response it may help to do something with the person—for example go for a walk, play a game, or watch a movie. If possible, always avoid giving reassurance. Providing reassurance only occasionally—for example, only 20% of the time—may seem like very little, but it may be frequent enough to re-inforce and maintain the behavior. It's also best not to take the BDD sufferer to the surgeon, dermatologist, or other medical professional to obtain reassurance about the defect's appearance or after receiving surgical or other medical treatment they're dissatisfied with.

Occasionally, in great frustration, family members may say that the defect really looks terrible. They don't actually believe this, but they say it in anger, or because giving reassurance has been fruitless. I also recommend avoiding this response because it can cause the BDD sufferer great pain and may worsen BDD symptoms.

8) Encourage Better Functioning but Also Recognize the Person's Limitations

You may be in the position of urging the BDD sufferer to be on time for work or school, get a job or go to school, go out with friends, or leave the house. In some cases, the person with BDD lives with and is supported by family members long after the time has come to live independently.

In my experience, family members often give this kind of support quite willingly, yet providing it may be a significant strain. And you may question whether it's the right thing to do. Are you doing the BDD sufferer a disservice by having them live with you or be financially dependent on you? Should you instead require independent functioning? Are you "enabling" the disorder in some way?

Alexandra's parents expressed this dilemma. "Our daughter is 33 years old. She should be on her own by now. But we're afraid that if we ask her to leave she won't be able to support herself. We've tried it before, and it didn't work. But we wonder if we're doing the right thing by having her continue to live with us."

It's best to encourage better functioning but recognize the person's limitations. Encourage the person with BDD to get out of the house and socialize. Encourage him or her to attend family events, see friends, get a job, or go to school.

You can also help by encouraging the BDD sufferer to keep busy. This won't cure the disorder, but idleness can worsen preoccupations by leaving too much time for obsessions and rituals. You can suggest activities or help create lists of activities that the person can engage in when idle or preoccupied. A job or going to school can help decrease BDD symptoms because it fills one's time with meaningful activity, leaving less time for BDD.

Encourage your loved one to push themselves as much as possible so they function at their highest level. But don't apply too much pressure. This may only create more stress and anxiety. This process can be a delicate balancing act and will require some judgment on your part. Just how hard should you encourage and push? Try following the general approach that's used in exposure therapy and response prevention, as described in Chapter 14. Encourage them to try things step-by-step—from easier to harder to hardest—and to do these things often. Encourage them to do things they've successfully done before but which are still challenging. Also encourage them to do something a little harder than something they've already successfully done. For someone who hasn't been able to work, moving to a volunteer job and then to part-time and then full-time work can be an effective strategy. Your support and encouragement can be extremely helpful as the person with BDD negotiates these changes and challenges.

Many people with BDD can improve their functioning with adequate treatment as well as family encouragement and support. But this isn't always possible. Their symptoms may be too severe for meaningful progress to be made. In such cases, insistence that the person function better is likely to be fruitless. But it's crucial that such a person be in psychiatric treatment. This can take place in an outpatient setting, a partial hospital setting (or day hospital, in which patients attend treatment for part of the day but go home at night), or a residential setting, where the patient lives while they receive treatment. Someone who is functioning very poorly should also be taking medication and be receiving CBT. I think it's a mistake for family members to observe and care for someone who is very impaired without insisting that they obtain adequate treatment. When patients do respond to such treatment, their functioning may markedly improve; they may be able to go to school or work, and support themselves. It can be helpful for the family to meet with professionals who are providing treatment to discuss ways in which they can facilitate this transition. If the BDD sufferer is an adult, the goal is eventual self-support. Adequate psychiatric treatment with medication and behavior therapy can be critical to success.

9) Encourage Participation in Family Events

It isn't uncommon for people with BDD to avoid family get-togethers or important events such as graduations, weddings, or funerals. They may anticipate these events with great trepidation and avoid them because of having to face others, fearing they'll be judged negatively because of how they look. "I'm petrified about my brother's wedding," one man told me. "If my hair doesn't start growing back by then, I'm not going. My family will be incredibly upset, but I refuse to go."

It's best to encourage the person with BDD to participate in family events. Remind them that the focus won't be on them; at a wedding, it will be on the bride and bridegroom. Encourage them to face their fears by being around other people. If they do this enough, their fears will eventually diminish. They may even feel better afterward because they didn't miss the event. Avoiding social situations only reinforces BDD symptoms.

Because it can be so difficult for BDD sufferers to be around others, a cognitive-behavioral therapist can be very helpful in facilitating exposure to social situations and can help patients tolerate the specific social events they would like to avoid.

10) Give Praise for Even Small Gains

Resisting the urge to comb your hair in the mirror for an hour, not asking for reassurance for a day, or going to the supermarket may not seem like big feats, but they can be major accomplishments for someone with BDD. Recognize this, and praise your loved one for even small gains. Praise works better then criticism.

Recognize and support each step the BDD sufferer takes toward resisting BDD rituals, participating in activities, leaving the house, socializing more, and improving functioning at work or school. Don't expect BDD symptoms to disappear overnight. Support any improvement, no matter how limited it may seem. Just as you can't master learning to drive a car in a day, a person with BDD won't be able to return to normal functioning in a day. It takes practice and time. Encourage the BDD sufferer to keep going and not give up, even if they're having a bad day or a bad week.

Don't compare the BDD sufferer to other people who are functioning well. Most people with BDD would like to function as well as other people—if only they could. This kind of comparing only makes them feel worse. It's important to judge progress according to their current level of functioning. If a person is housebound, they probably won't be able to go to a baseball game the first time they leave the house. Going to the mailbox to get the mail may be the most they can initially do.

11) When Assessing Progress, Look at the Big Picture

When someone is working to overcome BDD and function better, look at the big picture. Are they *generally* moving in the right direction? Are they gradually doing their rituals less and going out and doing more things? Try not to judge progress on a day-to-day basis; instead, look at the big picture. It's common to have setbacks along the way. Don't be too discouraged by this. BDD symptoms typically wax and wane, and a period of improvement can be followed by some bad days. Don't fall into the trap of assuming that a bad day means all gains have been lost.

Rather than asking if the person is better today than yesterday, ask if on average the past few weeks have been better than 6 months ago or when they were at their worst. Progress isn't a straight line that moves steadily in the right direction. Instead, it's a wiggly line that has ups and downs while overall moving toward improvement. It can help to remind the BDD sufferer of this and that a setback doesn't mean they've lost all their gains. However, if a setback persists or is severe, it's wise to let the treating clinician know, as a change in treatment may be needed.

12) During Times of Stress, You May Need to Modify Your Expectations

BDD symptoms can increase at times of stress. Virtually any type of change can be stressful—positive events as well as negative ones. Don't be discouraged if the BDD sufferer has a temporary setback during stressful times. At these times, you may need to lower your expectations a little bit. Keep implementing the suggestions in this chapter (e.g., encouraging progress, praising small gains) while also keeping in mind that progress may be slower, or may even stop, during stressful times. At times like these, your encouragement, support, and understanding may be especially helpful.

13) Be Patient

Patience is enormously helpful! It's needed when waiting for a response to medication. While some people respond relatively quickly—within a few weeks—it often takes longer. A medication may take up to three months—and occasionally even longer—to work. If the first medicine doesn't work, another should be tried. Occasionally, it takes many tries to find the right one. Persistence and patience are needed in such cases.

Similarly, CBT can take time to work. It can take creativity and a good understanding of the person and their symptoms to come up with the cognitive and behavioral strategies that will work for them. As with medications, more than one try may be needed.

You'll also need to be patient when implementing the suggestions in this chapter and while waiting for symptoms and functioning to improve. Some people improve fairly quickly, whereas others need more time. Patience is also needed if symptoms flare during stressful times.

For people who are reluctant to get adequate treatment, keep in mind that time and your continued support can make a big difference. I've treated many people with BDD who finally, after many years—even many decades—of suffering, decided to give psychiatric treatment a try. In many of these cases, the continued support and patience of family members made all the difference.

14) Try to Limit Angry Outbursts

Angry outbursts, or what some of my patients refer to as temper tantrums, can seriously disrupt the family. They're a particularly difficult aspect of BDD. The outbursts usually reflect frustration and anger over the psychological pain, isolation, and disruption of life that BDD can cause.

Sometimes the outbursts are precipitated by a painful event, such as the perception of being mocked. Some of my patients routinely become very angry after receiving a "bad" haircut. Unfortunately, you may bear the brunt of this frustration and anger.

Try to understand that this behavior is related to BDD. In many cases, people with BDD don't intend to express their anger toward you; you may just happen to be present when they're feeling frustrated. Identifying precipitants of outbursts and trying to avoid them in the future may be useful. If getting into discussions or arguments about whether the defect is real—or looks really bad—triggers angry outbursts, then do everything possible to avoid these discussions. To accomplish this, try the approaches I recommended in the section on reassurance seeking. Setting limits on destructive behavior and urging the person to talk about how they feel, rather than expressing their feelings in angry behavior or attacking words, is also recommended. As BDD symptoms respond to treatment, the frustration and anger usually diminish as well.

It may be helpful to all meet together with the treating psychiatrist or therapist to discuss the outbursts and their effect on the family. Family discussions or family therapy may yield helpful strategies for dealing with anger that are tailored to your family and may make this problem easier to cope with.

15) If the Person with BDD is Considering Suicide, Get Immediate Psychiatric Care

Nothing is more likely to precipitate a family crisis than suicidal thinking or behavior, which isn't uncommon. When this occurs, you may be able to help. The most important thing you can do is to get psychiatric treatment. Contact the treating psychiatrist or therapist, a local psychiatric hospital, a community mental health center, or a hospital emergency room. You shouldn't deal with suicidal thinking or behavior on your own. Suicidal thinking and behavior are serious warning signs that the person is suffering greatly; furthermore, they may culminate in actual suicide.

A common response is to deny or minimize suicidal thinking in a loved one. It's a very difficult situation to face, and you may be tempted to ignore it in the hope that it will simply go away. But it's a serious mistake to ignore these warning signs or assume they will pass. They may not, and they may worsen if untreated. If a person with BDD appears severely depressed, it's advisable for you to ask if they've had thoughts that life isn't worth living, thoughts of harming themselves, or a plan to end their life. Asking such questions won't put the thought of suicide in their head and may even be life saving.

Usually, suicidal thinking is associated with an underlying psychiatric disorder, such as BDD or depression, which is amenable to psychiatric treatment. Insist that your loved one obtain psychiatric treatment, including medication, which often effectively treats BDD symptoms as well as associated depression, anxiety, and suicidal thoughts.

16) Keep Your Family Routine as Normal as Possible

If BDD upsets your family routine, try to get it back to normal. This may take some time. If the symptoms don't upset your routine, try to prevent this from happening. No one benefits when BDD takes over and disrupts your life. It's best for both you and the BDD sufferer to live as normal a life as possible. For example, if you're planning on having relatives over for Thanksgiving even though your daughter is going through a bad spell and doesn't want to see anyone, go ahead with the dinner and encourage her to participate. Do this without expressing anger or criticism, and don't feel guilty about it. It's best for everyone to keep your life on track so you don't feed the BDD. You'll also feel less resentful, have more energy to help the BDD sufferer, and enjoy your own life more. Consider getting professional help for yourself if you need more support and help with coping.

17) Take Time for Yourself

It's important to have some time for yourself—for your responsibilities and the things you enjoy. Don't use this time to participate in BDD rituals or provide excessive care for the person with BDD. Some family members feel they need to provide this care all the time. But by overprotecting the BDD sufferer and being overly involved in their life—without paying enough attention to your own—you can inadvertently communicate to them that they're incapable of better functioning and can't do things themselves. This can undermine their sense of confidence and self-worth. You may actually boost their feelings of self-confidence by encouraging them to do more on their own. You'll also probably feel better yourself by taking a break from the BDD, which may make your support more effective. So don't feel guilty about taking some time for yourself. If someone with BDD really does require intensive care and very close monitoring—for example, because they're so impaired, depressed, or suicidal—you probably need to get them more intensive psychiatric care. At the same time, don't avoid or give up on the BDD sufferer. Let them know that you care, support them, and want to help them overcome BDD.

18) Don't Blame Yourself

Some family members—parents in particular—wonder if they're responsible for BDD. We don't know its cause, but it's unlikely to result largely—if at all—from something you've done wrong. Instead of looking back and blaming yourself, focus on the present and future—do what you can now to help the BDD sufferer overcome their symptoms.

19) Remember that You Aren't Alone

Family members and friends may feel isolated in dealing with BDD. It's still an under-recognized problem, and some people feel a sense of stigma because a loved one has a psychiatric problem. If you do confide in other people, you may be met with disbelief. Others may find the concerns hard to understand. Reactions like these may intensify your feelings of isolation.

Realize that you're not alone. Remember that BDD isn't a rare disorder. Millions of family members are trying to make sense of it and cope with it. Consider sharing your struggles with someone you trust; support from other people can be quite helpful. Educating supportive people about BDD may help them better understand the problem.

I hope that BDD will continue to be increasingly recognized and that local and national support groups will develop. This has occurred for other psychiatric disorders, such as depression, manic depressive illness, and OCD. Many family members and friends find these groups helpful sources of information and support. Until such groups are developed for BDD, some of the existing groups for other mental illnesses may be helpful to you.

In the meantime, remember that you're not alone—you may *think* you don't know anyone else who is coping with BDD, but you probably do. BDD affects millions.

20) Maintain Hope!

Never give up hope. Most people with BDD respond to psychiatric treatment. Symptoms may not entirely disappear, but they often get much better. Sometimes the first treatment tried is helpful; sometimes it's the third, fourth, or fifth. Keep in mind that time and patience may be needed to find the treatment that works best for a particular person. Although some people with BDD don't respond to available treatments, our knowledge of BDD's treatment response is still in its very early stages. I have no doubt that we'll learn much more about BDD and effective treatments in the coming years.

·· *eighteen* ··

Getting Help for BDD

Finding Treatment

If you have BDD, it's important to get treatment from a licensed professional who is knowledgeable about BDD and can provide the treatments recommended in this book. I'd recommend that you not try to treat yourself. Professionals who may have training and experience in treating BDD include psychiatrists (medical doctors who have specialized training in psychiatric disorders and can prescribe medication), licensed psychologists, primary care physicians, licensed social workers, and nurses with advanced degrees.

It's ideal if you can be evaluated by a psychiatrist to determine whether you have BDD and so you can consider the option of taking medication. People who haven't responded to several medications may benefit from seeing a psychiatrist with particular expertise in psychopharmacology, since experience and creativity in prescribing psychiatric medicines may be beneficial. If you can't find a psychiatrist with expertise in BDD, you may want to see one with expertise in OCD because of these disorders' similarities.

If you decide to try cognitive-behavioral therapy, seek out a therapist who is not only familiar with BDD but who has training in and experience with cognitive-behavioral therapy. Most therapists aren't trained in CBT. Although there are few CBT therapists with expertise in BDD, their number is increasing. If you can't find a therapist with expertise in BDD, seeing a cognitive-behavioral therapist with expertise in treating OCD or social phobia is a good approach.

Here some sources from which you may be able to find a licensed professional with experience treating BDD:

- *www.BodyImageProgram.com.* This is the address for my website at Butler Hospital and Brown University in Providence, Rhode Island. My website can also be reached at *www.butler.org/body.cfm?id=123,* through the Butler Hospital website, and through the Care New England website. In addition to providing general information about BDD and my ongoing research studies, this website includes a referral list of professionals around the world who have experience treating

BDD. I frequently update this list. It isn't comprehensive, because there are many professionals who are qualified to treat BDD who I don't know. The important thing to keep in mind is that you should see a licensed professional who is familiar with BDD and its treatment. My website also includes descriptions of my ongoing studies, which usually include treatment studies in which qualifying individuals receive free study treatment.

- The *Obsessive Compulsive Foundation* keeps a referral list of psychiatrists and other clinicians who treat OCD (obsessive compulsive disorder). Since BDD and OCD have some features in common, consider consulting a professional experienced in treating OCD if you can't find one experienced with BDD. To obtain their referral list, call or write the OC Foundation at: OC Foundation, Inc., 337 Notch Hill Road, North Branford, CT 06471; telephone: 203-315-2190; www.ocfoundation.org.
- To find a therapist with CBT experience, you may want to contact the American Association for Advancement of Behavior Therapy, 305 7th Avenue, New York, NY 10001; telephone: 212-647-1890; www.aabt.org.
- To find a psychiatrist with expertise in BDD or OCD, you can also try calling your state psychiatric society for a referral.
- If you live near a medical school, you can call the department of psychiatry to see if they have any faculty or staff with experience treating BDD or OCD.
- The Neysa Jane Body Dysmorphic Disorder Fund is a charitable, nonprofit organization dedicated to promoting education, treatment, and research for BDD. Email: neysabdd@comcast.net; telephone: 239-594-5421.

Another consideration is whether it's best to receive treatment as an outpatient, in a partial hospital setting (day hospital), a residential setting, or as an inpatient. Outpatient visits usually occur once a week for cognitive-behavioral therapy and from once a week to a few times a year for medication visits (the frequency will depend on how you're doing, whether your medicine is being changed, and other factors). Partial hospital programs (day hospitals) usually take place 5 or 7 days a week and last for much of the day, but you return home in the evening. With inpatient treatment, you stay overnight and receive more intensive treatment. With residential treatment, you live in the treatment setting for a longer period of time.

Most psychiatric treatment these days is received on an outpatient basis, and this is often appropriate for BDD. The other levels of treatment provide more intensive treatment. Usually, inpatient treatment is reserved for people who are strongly considering suicide. To the best of my knowledge, inpatient treatment programs for BDD no longer exist in the U.S., largely because of reimbursement issues. So it would be unusual to receive BDD-specific treatment on an inpatient unit, although inpatient hospitalization does provide an opportunity to change or adjust medication. The main purpose of an inpatient stay for BDD in the United States is to keep a person safe who's at risk of harming themselves. Partial hospital programs generally don't provide specialty treatment for BDD, but they may provide useful support and structure for someone who's very distressed and having a lot of difficulty functioning. Medication treatment can also be monitored more closely than as an outpatient.

The University of California, Los Angeles (UCLA) has a residential program that specializes in OCD and BDD (http://mentalhealth.ucla.edu/projects/anxiety/ocdintensivetreatment.htm) as does the OCD Institute at McLean Hospital in Belmont, Massachusetts.

Some Things to Keep in Mind When Seeking Treatment for BDD

- See a licensed professional who is knowledgeable BDD and its treatment.

- Don't try to treat yourself.

- Tell the professional that you've read this book and think you may have BDD; tell them about your body image obsessions, not just your depression, anxiety, or other symptoms or problems.

- Based on current knowledge, serotonin-reuptake inhibitors (SRIs) and cognitive-behavioral therapy are the treatments of choice for BDD.

- Keep this book's treatment guidelines in mind while also recognizing that your treatment will need to be individually tailored to you.

- While some internet websites provide useful and accurate information on BDD, others don't. As a consumer, it can be hard to tell these apart. Some sites recommend treatment approaches that have no scientific basis and are unlikely to be helpful.

- Be persistent in getting and trying the treatments recommended in this book. Most people with BDD get better!

Additional Reading on BDD

This section offers some additional suggested reading on BDD. This includes books written for the public, which you may find particularly helpful. The listed articles are written for professionals (e.g., psychiatrists and psychologists) and are published in professional journals. You may also find some of these publications helpful.

Research on BDD is dramatically increasing, and our knowledge will no doubt substantially grow in coming years. As more research is done on BDD, more articles will be published in professional journal reporting research results.

Reading these articles is a good way to stay abreast of recent developments in the field, including treatment recommendations. You can get a list of these articles as they're published in journals by going online and searching various databases (although book chapters and some published papers and research reports aren't included in all of these databases). I'd recommend PubMed. PubMed is a service of the National Library of Medicine. It provides access to over 12 million MEDLINE citations back to the mid-1960s and additional life science journals. PubMed includes links to many sites that provide full text articles and other related resources. The address is www4.ncbi.nlm.nih.gov/PubMed/. Once you get to the site, if you type in "body dysmorphic disorder" in quotation marks, you'll find citations for many published articles reporting research findings on BDD.

Here are several books on BDD that may be helpful. They are all written for the public. You should be able to obtain them from a bookstore; if the book isn't on the shelf, you can ask the bookstore to order it for you. You can also get them online through a vendor such as amazon.com.

- *The Adonis Complex: How to Identify, Treat, and Prevent Body Obsession in Men and Boys,* by Harrison G. Pope, Jr., M.D., Katharine A. Phillips, M.D., and Roberto Olivardia, Ph.D., The Free Press, 2002: This book reveals the many types of body image obsessions that affect boys and men. These include muscle dysmorphia, other forms of BDD, and eating disorders. It offers practical approaches to overcoming these often-secret, common, and problematic concerns.

- *Cruel Reflections: Self-Help for Body Image Disturbance,* by Sabine Wilhelm, Ph.D.: This book will be published by Guilford Press in 2005. It is written by a leading expert researcher/clinician in BDD and CBT. It describes a detailed self-help approach to BDD based on cognitive and behavioral principles. It should be very helpful to both patients and therapists.

- *The BDD Workbook,* by James Claiborn, Ph.D., and Cherry Pedrick, R.N., New Harbinger Publications, 2002: This book also describes a self-help approach to BDD based on cognitive and behavioral principles.

- *The Body Image Workbook: An 8-Step Program for Learning to Like Your Looks* by Thomas F. Cash, Ph.D., New Harbinger Publications, 1997: This book and *The Body Image Workbook* (see below) describe a self-help approach based on cognitive/behavioral principles that may be helpful for milder BDD and more normal appearance concerns.

- *The Body Image Workbook,* by Thomas F. Cash, Ph.D, Fine Communications, 1998: See description above.

- *Feeling Good: The New Mood Therapy,* by David D. Burns, M.D., Avon Books, 1980. This is an excellent self-help book that explains the basics of cognitive therapy. Even though it focuses on depression, it can be very helpful in understanding cognitive therapy and in coping with BDD and related depressive symptoms.

Below are references for articles written for professionals and published in professional journals. I've included a representative sample of journal articles from PubMed published or in press by mid-2004 that may be particularly informative (the list is not exhaustive). I've tended to include only more recent review articles, because they're more up-to-date (although the information that's in them is included in this book). I've also included research-based articles. The findings from these articles are also included in this book, but you may want to consult them for more detailed information about studies that have been done. I periodically update this listing on my website at *www.BodyImageProgram. com* (http://www.butler.org/body.cfm?id=123).

General Overviews and Reviews

Phillips KA. Body dysmorphic disorder: recognizing and treating imagined ugliness. World Psychiatry 2004;3:12–17

Phillips KA. "I'm as ugly as the elephant man": How to recognize and treat body dysmorphic disorder. Current Psychiatry 2002;1:58–65

Veale D. Body dysmorphic disorder. Postgraduate Medical Journal 2004;80:67–71

Phillips KA. Body dysmorphic disorder. In: Somatoform and Factitious Disorders. Edited by Phillips KA. (Review of Psychiatry Series, Volume 20, Number 3; Oldham JM and Riba MB, series editors). Washington DC: American Psychiatric Publishing, 2001

Phillips KA, Castle DJ. Body dysmorphic disorder. In: Disorders of Body Image. Edited by Castle DJ, Phillips KA. Hampshire, England: Wrightson Biomedical, 2002

Phillips KA, Dufresne RG Jr. Body dysmorphic disorder: a guide for primary care physicians. Primary Care 2002;29:99–111

Phillips KA, Dufresne RG Jr. Body dysmorphic disorder: a guide for dermatologists and cosmetic surgeons. American Journal of Clinical Dermatology 2000;1:235–243

Hadley SJ, Greenberg J, Hollander E. Diagnosis and treatment of body dysmorphic disorder in adolescents. Current Psychiatry Reports 2002;4:108–113

Phillips KA, Castle DJ. Body dysmorphic disorder in men. British Medical Journal 2001;323:1015–1016

Olivardia R, Phillips KA. Body dysmorphic disorder in men: facing the man in the mirror. Primary Psychiatry 2001;8:32–36

Grant JE, Phillips KA. Captive of the Mirror: "I pick at my face all day, every day." Current Psychiatry 2003;2:45–52

Arnold LM, Auchenbach MB, McElroy SL. Psychogenic excoriation. Clinical features, proposed diagnostic criteria, epidemiology and approaches to treatment. CNS Drugs 2001;15:351–359

Phillips KA. Body dysmorphic disorder and depression: theoretical considerations and treatment strategies. Psychiatric Quarterly 1999;70:313–331

Phillips KA. Body dysmorphic disorder: the distress of imagined ugliness. American Journal of Psychiatry 1991;148:1138–1149

Symptoms and Clinical Features of BDD

Phillips KA, McElroy SL, Keck PE, Pope HG, Hudson JI. Body dysmorphic disorder: 30 cases of imagined ugliness. American Journal of Psychiatry 1993; 150:302–308

Hollander E, Cohen LJ, Simeon D. Body dysmorphic disorder. Psychiatric Annals 1993;23:359–364

Phillips KA, McElroy SL, Keck PE Jr, Hudson JI, Pope HG Jr. A comparison of delusional and nondelusional body dysmorphic disorder in 100 cases. Psychopharmacology Bulletin 1994;30:179–186

Veale D, Boocock A, Gournay K, Dryden W, Shah F, Wilson R, Walburn J. Body dysmorphic disorder. A survey of fifty cases. British Journal of Psychiatry 1996;169:196–201

Phillips KA, Menard W, Fay C, Weisberg R. Demographic characteristics, phenomenology, comorbidity, and family history in 200 individuals with BDD. Psychosomatics, 2005

Phillips KA. Quality of life for patients with body dysmorphic disorder. Journal of Nervous and Mental Disease 2000;188:170–175

Phillips KA, Menard W, Fay C, Pagano ME. Psychosocial functioning and quality of life in body dysmorphic disorder. Comprehensive Psychiatry, 2005

Cansever A, Uzun O, Donmez E, Ozsahin A. The prevalence and clinical features of body dysmorphic disorder in college students: a study in a Turkish sample. Comprehensive Psychiatry 2003;44:60–64

Phillips KA, Diaz S. Gender differences in body dysmorphic disorder. Journal of Nervous and Mental Disease 1997;185:570–577

Perugi G, Akiskal HS, Giannotti D, Frare F, Di Vaio S, Cassano GB. Gender-related differences in body dysmorphic disorder (dysmorphophobia). Journal of Nervous and Mental Disease 1997;185:578–582

DeMarco LM, Li LC, Phillips KA, McElroy SL. Perceived stress in body dysmorphic disorder. Journal of Nervous and Mental Disease 1998;186:724–726

Phillips KA, McElroy SL. Insight, overvalued ideation, and delusional thinking in body dysmorphic disorder: theoretical and treatment implications. Journal of Nervous and Mental Disease 1993; 181:699–702

Albertini RS, Phillips KA. 33 cases of body dysmorphic disorder in children and adolescents. Journal of the American Academy of Child and Adolescent Psychiatry 1999;38:453–459

Horowitz K, Gorfinkle K, Lewis O, Phillips KA. Body dysmorphic disorder in an adolescent girl. Journal of the American Academy of Child and Adolescent Psychiatry 2002;41:1503–1509

Pope HG Jr, Gruber AJ, Choi P, Olivardia R, Phillips KA. Muscle dysmorphia:

an underrecognized form of body dysmorphic disorder. Psychosomatics 1997;38:548–557

Olivardia R, Pope HG Jr, Hudson JI. Muscle dysmorphia in male weightlifters: a case-control study. American Journal of Psychiatry 2000;157:1291–1296

Hitzeroth V, Wessels C, Zungu-Dirwayi N, Oosthuizen P, Stein DJ. Muscle dysmorphia: a South African sample. Psychiatry and Clinical Neuroscience 2001;55:521–523

Ung EK, Fones CS, Ang AW. Muscle dysmorphia in a young Chinese male. Annals of the Academy of Medicine, Singapore 2000;29:135–137

Phillips KA, Taub SL. Skin picking as a symptom of body dysmorphic disorder. Psychopharmacology Bulletin 1995;31:279–288

Wilhelm S, Keuthen NJ, Deckersbach T, Engelhard IM, Forker AE, Baer L, O'Sullivan RL, Jenike MA: Self-injurious skin picking: clinical characteristics and comorbidity. Journal of Clinical Psychiatry 1999;60:454–459

Cotterill JA, Cunliffe WJ: Suicide in dermatological patients. Br J Dermatol 137: 246–250, 1997

Phillips KA, Coles ME, Menard W, Yen S, Fay C, Weisberg RB. Suicidal ideation and suicide attempts in body dysmorphic disorder. Journal of Clinical Psychiatry, 2005

Gunstad J, Phillips KA. Axis I comorbidity in body dysmorphic disorder. Comprehensive Psychiatry 2003;44:270–276

Phillips KA, McElroy SL. Personality disorders and traits in patients with body dysmorphic disorder. Comprehensive Psychiatry 2000;41:229–236

Zimmerman M, Mattia JI. Body dysmorphic disorder in psychiatric outpatients: recognition, prevalence, comorbidity, demographic, and clinical correlates. Comprehensive Psychiatry 1998;39:265–270

McKay D, Neziroglu F, Yaryura-Tobias JA. Comparison of clinical characteristics in obsessive-compulsive disorder and body dysmorphic disorder. Journal of Anxiety Disorders 1997;11:447–454

Phillips KA, Gunderson CG, Mallya G, McElroy SL, Carter W. A comparison study of body dysmorphic disorder and obsessive-compulsive disorder. Journal of Clinical Psychiatry 1998;59:568 575

Saxena S, Winograd A, Dunkin JJ, Maidment K, Rosen R, Vapnik T, Tarlow G, Bystritsky A. A retrospective review of clinical characteristics and treatment response in body dysmorphic disorder versus obsessive-compulsive disorder. Journal of Clinical Psychiatry 2001;62:67–72

Eisen JL, Phillips KA, Coles ME, Rasmussen SA. Insight in obsessive compulsive disorder and body dysmorphic disorder. Comprehensive Psychiatry, 2004;45: 10–15

Rosen JC, Ramirez E. A comparison of eating disorders and body dysmorphic disorder on body image and psychological adjustment. Journal of Psychosomatic Research 1998;44:441–449

Veale D, Riley S. Mirror, mirror on the wall, who is the ugliest of them all? The psychopathology of mirror gazing in body dysmorphic disorder. Behavior Research and Therapy 2001;39:1381–1393 al-Adawi S, Martin R, al-Naamani A, Obeid Y, al-Hussaini A. Body dysmorphic disorder in Oman: cultural and neuropsychological findings. East Mediterranean Health Journal 2001;7:562–567

Turkson SN, Asamoah V. Body dysmorphic disorder in a Ghanaian male: case report. East African Medical Journal 1999;76:111–114

Phillips KA, Pinto A, Jain S. Self-esteem in body dysmorphic disorder. Body Image 2004;1:385–390

Soriano JL, O'Sullivan RL, Baer L, Phillips KA, McNally RJ, Jenike MA. Trichotillomania and self-esteem: a survey of 62 female hair pullers. Journal of Clinical Psychiatry 1996;57:77–82

Phillips KA, Siniscalchi JM, McElroy SL. Depression, anxiety, anger, and somatic symptoms in patients with body dysmorphic disorder. Psychiatric Quarterly, 2004;75:309–320

Medication Treatment for BDD

Phillips KA, Albertini RS, Rasmussen SA. A randomized placebo-controlled trial of fluoxetine in body dysmorphic disorder. Archives of General Psychiatry 2002;59:381–388

Hollander E, Allen A, Kwon J, Aronowitz B, Schmeidler J, Wong C, Simeon D. Clomipramine vs desipramine crossover trial in body dysmorphic disorder: selective efficacy of a serotonin reuptake inhibitor in imagined ugliness. Archives of General Psychiatry 1999;56:1033–1039

Phillips KA, Rasmussen SA. Change in psychosocial functioning and quality of life in body dysmorphic disorder with fluoxetine versus placebo. Psychosomatics 2004;45:438–444

Phillips KA. A placebo-controlled study of pimozide augmentation of fluoxetine in body dysmorphic disorder. American Journal of Psychiatry, 2005

Phillips KA, Albertini RS, Siniscalchi JM, Khan A, Robinson M. Effectiveness of pharmacotherapy for body dysmorphic disorder: a chart-review study. Journal of Clinical Psychiatry 2001;62:721–727

Phillips KA, Najar F. An open-label study of citalopram in body dysmorphic disorder. Journal of Clinical Psychiatry 2003;64:715–720

Phillips KA, Dwight MM, McElroy SL. Efficacy and safety of fluvoxamine in body dysmorphic disorder. Journal of Clinical Psychiatry 1998;59:165–171

Phillips KA, McElroy SL, Dwight MM, Eisen JL, Rasmussen SA. Delusionality and response to open-label fluvoxamine in body dysmorphic disorder. Journal of Clinical Psychiatry 2001;62:87–91

Perugi G, Giannotti D, Di Vaio S, Frare F, Saettoni M, Cassano GB. Fluvoxamine in the treatment of body dysmorphic disorder (dysmorphophobia). International Clinics of Psychopharmacology 1997;11:247–254

Hollander E, Cohen L, Simeon D, Rosen J, DeCaria C, Stein DJ. Fluvoxamine treatment of body dysmorphic disorder (letter). Journal of Clinical Psychopharmacology 1994;14:75–77

Phillips KA. An open study of buspirone augmentation of serotonin-reuptake inhibitors in body dysmorphic disorder. Psychopharmacology Bulletin 1996; 32:175–180

Hollander E, Liebowitz MR, Winchel R, Klumker A, Klein DF. Treatment of body-dysmorphic disorder with serotonin reuptake blockers. American Journal of Psychiatry 1989;146:768–770

O'Sullivan RL, Phillips KA, Keuthen NJ, Wilhelm S. Near-fatal skin picking from delusional body dysmorphic disorder responsive to fluvoxamine. Psychosomatics 1999;40:79–81

Grant JE. Successful treatment of nondelusional body dysmorphic disorder with olanzapine: a case report. Journal of Clinical Psychiatry 2001;62:297–298

Cognitive-Behavioral Therapy for BDD

Veale D. Cognitive behaviour therapy for body dysmorphic disorder. In: Disorders of Body Image. Edited by Castle DJ, Phillips KA. Hampshire, England: Wrightson Biomedical 2002

Neziroglu F, Khemlani-Patel S. A review of cognitive and behavioral treatment for body dysmorphic disorder. CNS Spectrums 2002;7:464–471

Neziroglu FA, Yaryura-Tobias JA. Exposure, response prevention, and cognitive therapy in the treatment of body dysmorphic disorder. Behavior Therapy 1993;24:431–438

Veale D, Gournay K, Dryden W, Boocock A, Shah F, Willson R, Walburn J. Body dysmorphic disorder: a cognitive behavioural model and pilot randomized controlled trial. Behavior Research and Therapy 1996;34:717–729

Rosen JC, Reiter J, Orosan P. Cognitive-behavioral body image therapy for body dysmorphic disorder. Journal of Consulting and Clinical Psychology 1995; 63:263–269

Wilhelm S, Otto MW, Lohr B, Deckersbach T. Cognitive behavior group therapy for body dysmorphic disorder: a case series. Behaviour Research and Therapy 1999;37:71–75

McKay D. Two-year follow-up of behavioral treatment and maintenance for body dysmorphic disorder. Behavior Modification 1999;23:620–629

McKay D, Todaro J, Neziroglu F, Campisi T, Moritz EK, Yaryura-Tobias JA. Body dysmorphic disorder: a preliminary evaluation of treatment and maintenance using exposure with response prevention. Behavior Research and Therapy 1997;35:67–70

Rosen JC. The nature of body dysmorphic disorder and treatment with cognitive behavior therapy. Cognitive and Behavioral Practice 1995;2:143–166

Treatments That Appear Ineffective for BDD

Phillips KA, Grant J, Siniscalchi J, Albertini RS. Surgical and non-psychiatric medical treatment of patients with body dysmorphic disorder. Psychosomatics 2001;42:504–510

Cotterill JA. Body dysmorphic disorder. Dermatology Clinics 1996;14:457–463

Veale D. Outcome of cosmetic surgery and "DIY" surgery in patients with body dysmorphic disorder. Psychiatric Bulletin 2000;24:218–221

Dufresne RG, Phillips KA, Vittorio CC, Wilkel CS. A screening questionnaire for body dysmorphic disorder in a cosmetic dermatologic surgery practice. Dermatologic Surgery 2001;27:457–462

Harth W, Linse R. Body dysmorphic disorder and life-style drugs. Overview and case report with finasteride. International Journal of Clinical Pharmacological Therapy 2001;39:284–287

Sarwer DB, Crerand CE, Didie ER. Body dysmorphic disorder in cosmetic surgery patients. Facial and Plastic Surgery 2003;19:7–18

Veale D, DeHaro L, Lambrou C. Cosmetic rhinoplasty in body dysmorphic disorder. British Journal of Plastic Surgery 2003;546–551

Castle DJ, Honigman RJ, Phillips KA. Does cosmetic surgery improve psychosocial wellbeing? Medical Journal of Australia 2002;176:601–604

Sarwer DB, Crerand CE. Psychological issues in patient outcomes. Facial and Plastic Surgery 2002;18:125–133

Sarwer DB. Awareness and identification of body dysmorphic disorder by aesthetic surgeons: results of a survey of American Society for Aesthetic Plastic Surgery members. Aesthetic Surgery Journal November/December, 2002

Honigman RJ, Phillips KA, Castle DJ. A review of psychosocial outcomes for patients seeking cosmetic surgery. Plastic and Reconstructive Surgery 2004; 113:1229–1137

Koot VCM, Peeters PHM, Granath F, Grobbee DE, Nyren O. Total and cause specific mortality among Swedish women with cosmetic breast implants: prospective study. British Medical Journal 2003;326:527–528

Castle DJ, Molton M, Hoffman K, Preston NJ, Phillips KA. Correlates of dysmorphic concern in people seeking cosmetic enhancement. Australian and New Zealand Journal of Psychiatry 2004;38:439–444

Prevalence of BDD

Bienvenu OJ, Samuels JF, Riddle MA, Hoehn-Saric R, Liang KY, Cullen BA, Grados MA, Nestadt G. The relationship of obsessive-compulsive disorder to possible spectrum disorders: results from a family study. Biological Psychiatry 2000;48;287–293

Faravelli C, Salvatori S, Galassi F, Aiazzi L, Drei C, Cabras P. Epidemiology of somatoform disorders: a community survey in Florence. Social Psychiatry and Psychiatric Epidemiology 1997;32:24–29

Otto MW, Wilhelm S, Cohen LS, Harlow BL. Prevalence of body dysmorphic disorder in a community sample of women. American Journal of Psychiatry 2001;158:2061–2063

Bohne A, Wilhelm S, Keuthen NJ, Florin I, Baer L, Jenike MA. Prevalence of body dysmorphic disorder in a German college student sample. Psychiatry Research 2002;109:101–104

Bohne A, Keuthen NJ, Wilhelm S, Deckersbach T, Jenike MA. Prevalence of symptoms of body dysmorphic disorder and its correlates: a cross-cultural comparison. Psychosomatics 2002;43:486–490

Mayville S, Katz RC, Gipson MT, et al. Assessing the prevalence of body dysmorphic disorder in an ethnically diverse group of adolescents. Journal of Child and Family Studies 1999;8:357–362

Biby EL. The relationship between body dysmorphic disorder and depression, self-esteem, somatization, and obsessive-compulsive disorder. Journal of Clinical Psychology 1998;54:489–499

Phillips KA, Dufresne RG Jr, Wilkel C, Vittorio C. Rate of body dysmorphic disorder in dermatology patients. Journal of the American Academy of Dermatology 2000;42:436–441

Uzun O, Basoglu C, Akan A, Cansever A, Ozsahin A, Cetin M, Ebrinc S. Body dysmorphic disorder in patients with acne. Comprehensive Psychiatry 2003; 44:415–419

Sarwer DB, Wadden TA, Pertschuk MJ, Whiataker LA. Body image dissatisfaction and body dysmorphic disorder in 100 cosmetic surgery patients. Plastic and Reconstructive Surgery 1998;101:1644–1649

Grant JE, Kim SW, Crow SJ. Prevalence and clinical features of body dysmorphic disorder in adolescent and adult psychiatric inpatients. Journal of Clinical Psychiatry 2001;62:517–522

Nierenberg AA, Phillips KA, Petersen TJ, Kelly KE, Alpert JE, Worthington JJ, Tedlow JR, Rosenbaum JF, Fava M. Body dysmorphic disorder in outpatients with major depression. Journal of Affective Disorders 2002;69:141–148

Phillips KA, Nierenberg AA, Brendel G, Fava M. Prevalence and clinical features of body dysmorphic disorder in atypical major depression. Journal of Nervous and Mental Disease 1996;184:125–129

Perugi G, Akiskal HS, Lattanzi L, Cecconi D, Mastrocinque C, Patronelli A, Vignoli S, Bemi E. The high prevalence of "soft" bipolar (II) features in atypical depression. Comprehensive Psychiatry 1998;39:63–71

Brawman-Mintzer O, Lydiard RB, Phillips KA, Morton A, Czepowicz V, Emmanuel N, Villareal G, Johnson M, Ballenger JC. Body dysmorphic disorder in patients with anxiety disorders and major depression: a comorbidity study. American Journal of Psychiatry 1995;152:1665–1667

Wilhelm S, Otto MW, Zucker BG, Pollack MH. Prevalence of body dysmorphic disorder in patients with anxiety disorders. Journal of Anxiety Disorders 1997;11:499–502

Simeon D, Hollander E, Stein DJ, Cohen L, Aronowitz B. Body dysmorphic disorder in the DSM-IV field trial for obsessive-compulsive disorder. American Journal of Psychiatry 1995;152:1207–1209

Grant JE, Kim SW, Eckert ED. Body dysmorphic disorder in patients with anorexia nervosa: prevalence, clinical features, and delusionality of body image. International Journal of Eating Disorders 2002;32:291–300

Other Topics

Rauch SL, Phillips KA, Segal E, Makris N, Shin LM, Whalen PJ, Jenike MA, Caviness VS Jr, Kennedy DN. A preliminary morphometric magnetic resonance imaging study of regional brain volumes in body dysmorphic disorder. Psychiatry Research 2003;20;122:13–19

Hanes KR. Neuropsychological performance in body dysmorphic disorder. Journal of the International Neuropsychological Society 1998;4:167–71

Deckersbach T, Savage CR, Phillips KA, Wilhelm S, Buhlmann U, Rauch SL, Baer L, Jenike MA. Characteristics of memory dysfunction in body dysmorphic disorder. Journal of the International Neuropsychological Society 2000;6:673–681

Veale D, Kinderman P, Riley S, Lambrou C. Self-discrepancy in body dysmorphic disorder. British Journal of Clinical Psychology 2003;42:157–169

Buhlman U, McNally RJ, Wilhelm S, Florin I. Selective processing of emotional information in body dysmorphic disorder. Journal of Anxiety Disorders 2002; 16:289–298

Buhlmann U, Wilhelm S, McNally RJ, Tuschen-Caffier B, Baer L, Jenike MA. Interpretive biases for ambiguous information in body dysmorphic disorder. CNS Spectrums 2002;7:435–443

Veale D, Ennis M, Lambrou C. Possible association of body dysmorphic disorder with an occupation or education in art and design. American Journal of Psychiatry 2002;159:1788–1790

Phillips KA, Menard W. Body dysmorphic disorder and art background (letter). American Journal of Psychiatry 2004;161:927–928

Klesmer J. Mortality in Swedish women with cosmetic breast implants: body dysmorphic disorder should be considered. British Medical Journal 2003;7; 326:1266–1267

Barr LC, Goodman WK, Price LH. Acute exacerbation of body dysmorphic disorder during tryptophan depletion. American Journal of Psychiatry 1992; 149:1406–1407

Buhlmann U, McNally RJ, Etcoff NL, Tuschen-Caffier B, Wilhelm S. Emotion recognition deficits in body dysmorphic disorder. Journal of Psychiatric Research 2004;38:201–206

Hanes KR. Serotonin, psilocybin, and body dysmorphic disorder: a case report. Journal of Clinical Psychopharmacology 1996;16:188–189

Phillips KA, Hollander E, Rasmussen SA, Aronowitz BR, DeCaria C, Goodman WK. A severity rating scale for body dysmorphic disorder: development, reliability, and validity of a modified version of the Yale-Brown Obsessive Compulsive Scale. Psychopharmacology Bulletin 1997;33:17–22

Eisen JL, Phillips KA, Baer L, Beer DA, Atala KD, Rasmussen SA. The Brown Assessment of Beliefs Scale: reliability and validity. American Journal of Psychiatry 1998;155:102–108

Concluding Thoughts

I hope I've conveyed what my patients would want you to know about body dysmorphic disorder. BDD affects many lives, it causes great suffering, and certain psychiatric treatments are very helpful and hold out much hope for BDD sufferers.

BDD is a common but underdiagnosed disorder. Sufferers often keep their pain a secret, even from their loved ones. Courage is often needed to tell others about it. Despite the suffering it causes, it's easily trivialized. Many people with this disorder feel isolated and alone.

A woman with BDD contributed this poem to this book. It conveys how many people with BDD feel.

BEAUTY DISEASE

Absorbed solemn silence, she's locked at the glass
Every morning same again
Morning is now after one p.m.
Eyes cropped puffy, hue of spilled dirtied kerosene reflect so hunted
There's no use telling her that eyes closed never shine
Long thin oranged burnt threads of hair hanging lower each day
Tugging her hair tangled, brushing till all tangles, each one is hidden
Turning with disgust, her many other tangles sting
She draws up to make up her face again, resisting to spit in each tin-
    gling bright Wild Fuschia false promise
Lips so trivial peeling away each day more wasted Romance Rose Sun
    Kissed Sienna, Perfect Plum wears transparent
In her mouth now the taste of metal shavings, her fillings are eroding
She never knows when she has finished dressing, it never hides scars or
    shame, ashtray tints or the palette of a tired carpet
Could the doctor really remove them? Don't try to speak of pulling
    them out through her tearducts
Enough tears are already fallen

                                                            —AEP

I hope the voices in this book have spoken as strongly and as clearly as the facts. I hope that readers with BDD and their family members will take comfort in knowing they aren't alone.

Have hope! Although we still have a great deal to learn about BDD and how to heal it, the psychiatric treatments I've discussed can make a tremendous difference—in some cases, a lifesaving difference—in the lives of people with BDD.

I have no doubt that in the coming years we'll learn a great deal more about BDD. I and other researchers are rapidly learning about it, and more and more researchers are starting to study it. In five, ten, and twenty years, we'll have many more clues about its causes, and we'll certainly know much more about treatment. New treatments should become available as more medications are developed and as we learn more about cognitive-behavioral therapy and perhaps other treatments. In the future, the pain and suffering that BDD causes will diminish as the disorder becomes better known and is more accurately diagnosed, and as more people try psychiatric treatment.

Never give up! The odds are that most people with BDD who try psychiatric treatment will benefit. Remember the words of some of my patients, some of whom were very hesitant to try and who responded very well.

> *Nathaniel:* "I can talk to people without feeling they're staring at me. I'm better able to resist mirror checking. I spend less time obsessing. It comes into my mind less and it's easier to get rid of the thoughts. I can argue with myself that my obsession is irrational—I tell myself, 'just shrug it off!' I'm not so self-conscious around people anymore. It's not a life or death problem for me now."
>
> *Christina:* "I just wasn't seeing myself clearly before. I feel calmer, happier, and more confident. It's hard to believe the medication has made this much of a change, but it has. I feel the way I used to feel, before the BDD ever started. I feel great!"
>
> *Sandy:* "The medication definitely curbs the obsession. It released a log-jam. My life felt like a stream that had thousands of huge boulders and logs in it—the water couldn't flow through smoothly. Now it flows with ease. I feel full of energy and creativity."
>
> *Jason:* "I really feel better after the CBT. The BDD isn't controlling me anymore! Tell people, 'don't be afraid to get help!' "
>
> *Luke:* "Suicide is the furthest thing from my mind now. I have a great life. Thank God I got treatment. I owe my life to it."
>
> *Pat:* "Tell everyone you know with BDD never to give up! I almost did. Thank God I didn't. Finally, after all these years, I feel *really* good! Tell them there's hope."

Appendix A

Demographic Characteristics of People with BDD

In the table below, I summarize demographic findings from my two large BDD studies (see the chapter "Why I'm Updating This Book" for a description of these studies). Except for age, gender, and ethnicity, all numbers are for adults only*:

	Table 20	
Demographic Characteristic	First BDD Series (307 people)	Second BDD Series (200 people)
Age	• Average age: 31 • Two thirds were between 20 and 42 • The youngest was 6 and oldest was 80	• Average age: 32 • Two thirds were between 20 and 45 • The youngest was 14 and the oldest was 64
Gender	• 56% female • 44% male	• 69% female • 33% male
Ethnicity and Race	• 87% white • 7% African American • 7% Hispanic • 1% American Indian/ Alaska native • 1% Asian	• 86% white • 7% African American • 7% Hispanic • 6% American Indian/ Alaska native • 1% Asian • 1% Native Hawaiian/Pacific islander
Marital status	• 68% single • 20% married • 12% divorced	• 64% single • 25% married • 12% divorced

Table 20   (continued)

Demographic Characteristic	First BDD Series (307 people)	Second BDD Series (200 people)
Education (highest level reached)	• 5% part high school • 15% high school • 34% part college • 7% 2-year college • 23% 4-year college • 7% part grad school • 10% grad school	• 13% part high school • 16% high school • 30% part college • 6% 2-year college • 22% 4-year college • 5% part grad school • 9% grad school
Employment	• 34% employed full time • 12% employed part time • 16% student • 38% unemployed	• 39% employed full time • 23% employed part time • 22% student • 36% unemployed
Economic support	• 36% self-supporting • 22% partially self-supporting • 30% supported by someone else • 9% on disability for BDD • 2% on disability for other another reason	• 26% self-supporting • 35% partially self-supporting • 40% supported by someone else • 8% on disability for BDD • 10% on disability for other another reason • 7% unemployment compensation or welfare
Living situation	• 43% with spouse, partner, roommate, etc. • 33% with parents • 20% alone • 4% in a supervised setting for people with mental disorders	• 50% with spouse, partner, roommate, etc. • 27% with parents • 23% alone • 1% in a supervised setting for people with mental disorders

*90% of both series were adults (18 and older), and 10% were adolescents; totals for some categories do not equal 100% because of a small category of miscellaneous "other" or because some people endorsed more than one category (e.g., race).

Appendix B

Brief Descriptions of Selected Psychiatric Disorders

What follows are brief descriptions of the psychiatric disorders I've referred to in this book. They are based on, and are briefer versions of, definitions in DSM-IV, the official manual of definitions and descriptions of psychiatric disorders.

Mood Disorders

Major Depression   A depressive disorder characterized by depressed mood or loss of interest or pleasure, as well as other symptoms. These include abnormal sleep or appetite (too much or too little), fatigue, low self-esteem or feelings of worthlessness, guilt, difficulty concentrating, and thoughts that life isn't worth living.

Atypical Subtype   A type of major depression in which mood is reactive (that is, it brightens in response to actual or potential positive events) as well as two or more of the following features: significant weight gain or increase in appetite, an increase in sleep, "leaden paralysis" (heavy, leaden feelings in the arms or legs), and sensitivity to rejection by others leading to difficulties in social or occupational functioning.

Bipolar Disorder (Manic Depressive Illness)   A type of mood disorder characterized by episodes of depression as well as mania or hypomania (a milder form of mania). Mania consists of a distinct period of abnormal and persistent elation, euphoria, or irritability and is accompanied by some of the following symptoms: decreased need for sleep, excessive talkativeness, increased energy, inflated self-esteem or grandiosity, racing thoughts, distractibility, increased activity or physical agitation, and excessive involvement in pleasurable activities with a high potential for painful consequences (e.g., unrestrained buying sprees or sexual indiscretions).

Dysthymic Disorder   A type of depressive disorder characterized by less severe depressive symptoms that have been present for at least half of the time during the past two years. While depressed, two or more of the following symptoms must be present: poor appetite or overeating, difficulty sleeping or sleeping too much, low energy or fatigue, low self-esteem, poor concentration or difficulty making decisions, and feelings of hopelessness.

Anxiety Disorders

Panic Disorder   Panic disorder consists of recurrent panic attacks that come out of the blue; at least one of the attacks has been followed by one month or more of one (or more) of the following: concern about having more attacks, worry about the consequences of the attacks, or a significant change in behavior related to the attacks. **Panic attacks** consist of a discrete period of intense fear or discomfort that peaks within 10 minutes of onset and is accompanied by a number of physical symptoms, such as heart palpitations, sweating, trembling or shaking, shortness of breath, chest pain or discomfort, feeling dizzy, and fear of dying.

Agoraphobia   Anxiety about being in places or situations from which escape might be difficult or embarrassing, or in which help might not be available, in the event of having a panic attack or panic-like symptoms. Typically, people with agoraphobia feel anxious in or avoid being outside of their home alone, in a crowd, or on a bridge, or traveling in buses, cars, or trains.

Social Phobia (Social Anxiety Disorder)   A marked and persistent fear of one or more social or performance situations in which the person is exposed to unfamiliar people or to possible scrutiny by others. The person fears appearing anxious or doing something humiliating or embarrassing in front of others. The fears may occur in most social situations (generalized type) or in a specific situation (e.g., fear of public speaking).

Specific Phobia   This disorder consists of marked and persistent fear due to the presence or anticipation of a specific object or situation—for example, flying, heights, or spiders.

Obsessive Compulsive Disorder (OCD)   OCD is characterized by obsessions or compulsions (usually both) that cause marked distress, are time consuming (take more than one hour a day), or significantly interfere with functioning. Obsessions are recurrent, persistent, and intrusive thoughts, impulses, or images. Compulsions are repetitive behaviors (e.g., hand washing or checking) or mental acts (e.g., counting) that are performed in response to an obsession and are aimed at preventing or reducing distress or a dreaded event.

Post-Traumatic Stress Disorder (PTSD)   PTSD develops following exposure to a traumatic event. The disorder is characterized by persistent reexperiencing of the traumatic event (e.g., recurrent distressing dreams), persistent avoidance of stimuli associated with the trauma and numbing of general responsiveness, and persistent symptoms of increased arousal (e.g., difficulty falling or staying asleep or an exaggerated startle response).

Generalized Anxiety Disorder   Excessive anxiety and worry about a number of events or activities (such as school or work performance). The worry is difficult to control and is associated with a number of symptoms, such as muscle tension or feeling on edge. The symptoms cause clinically significant distress or impairment in functioning.

Substance-Related Disorders

Substance-related disorders consist of drug abuse or dependence. This includes alcohol and other drugs, such as cocaine, marijuana, opioids (e.g., heroin), and hallucinogens (e.g., LSD).

Somatoform Disorders

Somatization Disorder   This disorder consists of many physical complaints that aren't fully explained by a medical condition. They begin before the age of 30, occur over several years, and result in seeking treatment or significant impairment in functioning. Symptoms consist of pain, gastrointestinal (stomach or intestinal) symptoms, sexual symptoms, and neurological symptoms.

Pain Disorder   This disorder is characterized by pain that is the primary reason for seeking treatment and that causes significant distress or impairment in functioning. Psychological factors are judged to play an important role in the onset, severity, exacerbation, or maintenance of the pain.

Hypochondriasis   Preoccupation with fears of having, or the idea that one has, a serious disease based on a misinterpretation of bodily symptoms. The preoccupation persists despite appropriate medical evaluation and reassurance, and it causes clinically significant distress or impairment in functioning.

Eating Disorders

Anorexia Nervosa   Anorexia nervosa consists of a refusal to maintain body weight in the normal range and an intense fear of gaining weight or becoming fat despite being underweight. It also involves body-image disturbance—a disturbance in the way one's body weight or shape is experienced, undue influence of body weight or shape on self-evaluation, or denial of the seriousness of the low body weight. Amenorrhea (the absence of at least three consecutive menstrual cycles) also occurs.

Bulimia Nervosa   This disorder is characterized by recurrent episodes of binge eating, recurrent compensatory behaviors to prevent weight gain (e.g., self-induced vomiting), and a disturbance in body image (self-evaluation is unduly influenced by body weight and shape).

Binge Eating Disorder   Recurrent episodes of binge eating, which are associated with such behaviors as eating much more rapidly than normal, eating large amounts of food when not feeling hungry, and eating until feeling uncomfortably full. Marked distress over the behavior is also present. (This disorder has been proposed for inclusion in DSM and is being researched but isn't yet an official diagnosis.)

Psychotic Disorders

Delusional Disorder   This disorder consists of nonbizarre delusions (i.e., involving situations that occur in real life) of at least one month's duration. The criteria for schizophrenia have never been met.

Olfactory Reference Syndrome (ORS)   The erroneous belief that one emits a foul or unpleasant body odor (a type of delusional disorder).

Schizophrenia   Schizophrenia consists of symptoms such as delusions, hallucinations, disorganized speech, behavior that is grossly disorganized or abnormal (e.g., purposeless agitation), and symptoms such as lack of emotion or motivation. The symptoms cause impairment in functioning.

Other Psychotic Disorders   These include other disorders characterized by symptoms such as hallucinations or delusions. They include schizoaffective disorder.

Other Disorders

Koro   Koro occurs primarily in Southeast Asia and consists of a preoccupation that one's penis is shrinking and will disappear into the abdomen, resulting in death.

Trichotillomania   Recurrent pulling out of one's hair, resulting in noticeable hair loss as well as clinically significant distress or impairment in functioning.

Compulsive Shopping   A preoccupation with shopping and inability to resist buying unneeded items, with resulting marked distress, social or occupational impairment, and financial and/or family problems. (This is not an official DSM-IV disorder but is widely considered an example of an impulse-control disorder.)

Tourette's Disorder   A disorder characterized by the persistent presence of motor (movement) and vocal tics. A *tic* is a sudden, rapid, recurrent, non-rhythmic, stereotyped movement (e.g., blinking or shrugging) or vocalization (e.g., shouting or coughing).

Personality Disorders   A personality disorder is an enduring pattern of inner experience and behavior that deviates markedly from the expectations of the individual's culture, is pervasive and inflexible, and leads to distress or impairment. Personality disorders usually begin in adolescence or early adulthood and are stable over time.

Appendix C

Instruments (Scales) for Assessing BDD

The BDD Diagnostic Module:
A Clinician-Administered Instrument
to Diagnose BDD

When making a psychiatric diagnosis, clinical judgment, based on years of professional training and experience, is indispensable. However, tools that aid in making a diagnosis can be very helpful. Such tools—generally referred to as diagnostic instruments or scales—ascertain that the diagnosis is being made according to accepted guidelines and criteria. Such instruments usually consist of questions that the clinician asks the patient or self-report forms (questionnaires) that the patient fills out. These instruments specify that certain questions are asked when determining whether a psychiatric disorder is present. They are useful to clinicians because they help ascertain that the diagnosis is correct, and they're useful to researchers since they assure that different researchers ask similar questions to make the diagnosis.

The most widely used instrument for the diagnosis of a broad range of psychiatric disorders is the Structured Clinical Interview for DSM-IV, or SCID. Its predecessor, the Structured Clinical Interview for DSM-III-R, was used prior to the DSM-IV version. These instruments were developed by Drs. Robert Spitzer, Janet Williams, Miriam Gibbon, and Michael First of Columbia University. The SCID is intended for use by a clinician, who asks specified questions to determine whether diagnostic criteria for a particular disorder are met.

Because the SCID is the standard diagnostic instrument in psychiatry, yet the DSM-III-R SCID didn't include BDD, I developed a SCID-like diagnostic instrument for BDD. The version for adults is shown below and the version for adolescents follows the adult version. This instrument follows the SCID format, which provides DSM criteria for the disorder on the right-hand side; the questions the clinician asks to ascertain the presence or absence of each criterion are on the left-hand side, opposite each criterion. If the person answers "yes" to the questions on the left, which in turn indicates that they meet that criterion for the disorder, the next question is asked. More "yes" answers leads to progression through the subsequent questions. If one of the disorder's criteria aren't

Body Dysmorphic Disorder Diagnostic Module For Adults

Have you ever been very worried about your appearance in any way?

If yes: What was your concern? Did you think (body part) was especially unattractive?

What about the appearance of your face, skin, hair, nose, or the shape/size/other aspect of any other part of your body?

Did this concern preoccupy you? That is, you thought about it a lot and wished you could worry about it less? (Did others say that you were more concerned about _____ than you should have been?)

What effect has this preoccupation had on your life? Has it caused you a lot of distress?

Has your concern had any effect on your family or friends?

(If concern is completely attributable to an eating disorder, do not diagnose BDD)

A. Preoccupation with an imagined defect in appearance. If a slight physical anomaly is present, the person's concern is markedly excessive

Note: *Give some examples even if person answers no to these questions.*
Examples include: skin concerns (e.g., acne, scars, wrinkles, paleness), hair concerns (e.g., thinning), or the shape or size of the nose, jaw, lips, etc. Also consider perceived defects of hands, genitals, or any other body part.

B. Preoccupation causes clinically significant distress or impairment in social, occupational, or other important areas of functioning.

Note: *If slight physical defect is present, concern is clearly excessive*

C. The preoccupation is not better accounted for by another mental disorder (e.g., dissatisfaction with body shape and size in Anorexia Nervosa).

met, the subsequent questions aren't asked. A disorder is diagnosed if all the diagnostic criteria for that disorder are met (all the questions are answered "yes").

The questions, or probes, on the left must be asked as written, but further questions can be asked to clarify whether the criterion is met. Examples of impairment, for example, should be asked for to ascertain whether impairment is present and how severe it is. The additional questions that may be asked are determined by the interviewer and based on clinical judgment.

Body Dysmorphic Disorder Diagnostic Module for Adolescents

1. Are you very worried about how you look?
IF YES: What don't you like?
Do you think (body part) looks really bad?

    Is there anything else you don't like about how you look?
What about your face, skin, hair, nose, or the shape, size or other things about any other part of your body?

    Do you think about (body part) a lot?
Do you wish you could worry about it less? (Do others say you worry about it too much?)

    A. Preoccupation with an imagined defect in appearance. If a slight physical anomaly is present, the person's concern is markedly excessive.

    Note: *Give some examples even if patient answers no to these questions* Examples include: skin concerns (e.g., acne, scars, wrinkles, paleness), hair concerns (e.g. thinning), or the shape or size of the nose, jaw, lips, etc. Also consider perceived "defects" of hands, genitals or any other body part.

    Note: *List all body parts of concern*

2. How does this problem with how you look affect your life? Does it upset you a lot?

    Has your worry affected your family or friends?

    B. Preoccupation causes clinically significant distress or impairment in social, occupational, or other important areas of functioning.

    Note: *If slight physical defect is present, concern is clearly excessive*

3. (If concern is secondary to an eating disorder, score "1")

    C. The preoccupation is not better accounted for by another mental disorder (e.g., dissatisfaction with body shape and size in Anorexia Nervosa).

(R. Albertini, M.D., K. Phillips, M.D., Butler Hospital, Brown University, 7/30/97)

To briefly review the Diagnostic Module's questions, those opposite criterion A are straightforward ways of asking about preoccupation with appearance. An alternative question is "Some people are very bothered by the way they look. Is this a problem for you? Tell me about it." This can then be followed by "How often do you think about it? (For example, at least an hour a day?)"

The concern must relate to appearance and a worry that the body part is unattractive, defective, or "not right" in terms of how it looks. As the module indicates, it's worth giving some examples of commonly disliked body parts by asking "What about the appearance of your face, skin, hair, nose, or the shape or size or other aspect of any other part of your body," because some people are too shy or embarrassed about their concerns to volunteer all of them. If the person can't identify a particular part, but indicates dislike of their entire face, or their overall appearance, this response is also compatible with the diagnosis of BDD.

Finally, to meet criterion A, the questions about preoccupation should be asked. The question in parentheses about whether others have said the person is too concerned is optional. Some people with BDD will answer no to this question because they've never told anyone about their concern. Such a response should not be counted against the diagnosis.

The questions used to determine whether distress or impairment are present (criterion B) usually need to be followed up by additional questions created by the questioner. Asking the person to describe their distress, to get a better sense of how severe it is, and asking for examples of impairment, are useful.

Criterion C doesn't have any questions accompanying it, because the interviewer is expected to be familiar with eating disorders and their diagnostic criteria, which are provided in DSM-IV. A brief description of them is given in Appendix B. Criterion C ascertains that people who have an eating disorder, without any other body image concerns, are not diagnosed with BDD. However, it's possible for a person to have both BDD and an eating disorder such as anorexia nervosa—for example, a significantly underweight person who thinks she's too fat (as a symptom of anorexia) can also have BDD preoccupations, such as thinking she has a huge and ugly mole. While criterion C is usually easy to assess, it's occasionally difficult. As discussed in Chapter 16, differentiating BDD from anorexia nervosa and bulimia nervosa is occasionally a complicated clinical judgment.

A person who—on the basis of the questions in the Diagnostic Module, as well as additional related questions determined by the interviewer—meets BDD criteria A, B, and C is considered to have BDD.

Available data indicate that the BDD Diagnostic Module has excellent interrater reliability (kappa = .96). That is, two clinicians who assess individuals in separate interviews with the Diagnostic Module are able agree on whether BDD is present in a high percentage of cases.

In most cases, diagnosing BDD is fairly straightforward. Occasionally, however, a fair amount of clinical judgment may be necessary to determine whether the criteria for BDD are met. In particular, determining whether distress or impairment are severe enough to qualify for a psychiatric diagnosis requires clinical judgment. Indeed, criterion B specifies that distress or impairment must be "clinically significant." Such judgment may also be needed to ascertain whether particular body-image concerns are a feature of an eating disorder or BDD. The more severe and classic the BDD symptoms are, the more obvious it is that BDD is the correct diagnosis. But clinical judgment is particularly important when assessing less classic cases, cases with features of both BDD and an eating disorder, and milder BDD, which must be differentiated from normal concern. Thus, in general, the ratings should depend on the patient's report, but the final rating is based on the interviewer's clinical judgment.

The BDDQ:
A Self-Report Screening Instrument
for BDD

The BDDQ, or Body Dysmorphic Disorder Questionnaire, is a self-report screening instrument for BDD that the patient fills out. This questionnaire was shown in Chapter 4. A version for adolescents is shown on the next page. A person who appears to have BDD according to this instrument should ideally be seen by a clinician to confirm the diagnosis—to determine that the defect is actually nonexistent or minimal, whether distress or impairment are clinically significant, and to differentiate BDD from an eating disorder if this is unclear.

Available data suggest that there is excellent agreement between the BDDQ and a clinician's judgment of whether BDD is present (as assessed with the BDD Diagnostic Module). I and my colleagues, Drs. Katherine Atala and Harrison Pope of Harvard Medical School, found that the BDDQ had a sensitivity of 100% and a specificity of 89% among 66 outpatients in a psychiatric setting. This means that in a group of individuals who are judged by a clinician to really have BDD, the BDDQ will accurately ascertain that BDD is present in 100% of the cases. And in a group of individuals whom a clinician judges really don't have BDD, the BDDQ will accurately determine that BDD is *not* present in 89% of the cases.

Dr. Jon Grant similarly found, in a study of 122 patients hospitalized on a psychiatric inpatient unit, that the BDDQ had a sensitivity of 100% and a specificity of 93%. And Dr. Ray Dufresne of Brown Medical School and I obtained very similar results in a dermatology setting. We used a slightly modified version of the BDDQ. The main difference between this version and the one in Chapter 4 is that some yes/no questions were replaced by a 5-point scale, on which an answer of 3, 4, or 5 is equivalent to a "yes" answer on the BDDQ's earlier version. Using the newer version in 46 patients who were seen in a dermatology setting, we found that the BDDQ had a sensitivity of 100% and a specificity of 93%.

So in summary, the BDDQ can be successfully used in a dermatology setting and in psychiatric inpatient and outpatient settings to screen for the presence

BDDQ for Adolescents

This questionnaire asks about concerns with physical appearance. Please read each question carefully and circle the answer that is true for you. Also please write out your answers where asked.

1) Are you very worried about how you look?   Yes   No
   - If yes: Do you think about your appearance problems   Yes   No
     a lot and wish you could think about them less?

   - If yes: Please list the body areas you don't like: _____

   _____

   _____

Examples of disliked body areas include: your skin (for example, acne, scars, wrinkles, paleness, redness); hair; the shape or size of your nose, mouth, jaw, lips, stomach, hips, etc.; or defects of your hands, genitals, breasts, or any other body part.

(NOTE: If you answered "No" to either of the above questions, you are finished with this questionnaire.)

2) Is your **main** concern with how you look that you aren't   Yes   No
thin enough or that you might get too fat?

3) How has this problem with how you look affected your
life?   Yes   No
   - Has it often upset you a lot?
   - Has it often gotten in the way of doing things with
     friends or dating?   Yes   No
     - If yes: Describe how: _____

   _____

   - Has it caused you any problems with school or work?   Yes   No
     - If yes: What are they? _____

   _____

   - Are there things you avoid because of how you look?   Yes   No
     - If yes: What are they? _____

   _____

4) How much time a day do you usually spend thinking about how you look? (Add up all the time you spend, then circle one)

a) Less than 1 hour a day b) 1–3 hours a day c) More than 3 hours a day of BDD. The data above suggest that the BDDQ may slightly overdiagnose BDD, which screening measures usually do. Ideally, someone who appears to have BDD on the basis of the BDDQ would then be interviewed by a clinician to confirm the diagnosis.

An advantage of the BDDQ over the clinician-administered BDD Diagnostic Module is that the possible presence of BDD can be assessed when a clinician isn't available to use the Diagnostic Module. Because the BDDQ is a brief self-report instrument, larger numbers of people can be easily assessed. In addition, some people might feel less self-conscious when filling out a self-report form and more willing to reveal their concerns.

The BDD-YBOCS:
A Measure of BDD Severity

There are several methods for assessing BDD severity: the Yale-Brown Obsessive Compulsive Scale Modified for BDD (BDD-YBOCS), the Clinical Global Impression Scale, and the Body Dysmorphic Disorder Examination.

The BDD-YBOCS is particularly useful for assessing the severity of BDD. It has been used as the primary outcome measure in most BDD treatment studies. The BDD-YBOCS is based on the Y-BOCS, which was developed in the 1980s to assess the severity of obsessive compulsive disorder (OCD). Because of the many similarities between BDD and OCD, Dr. Eric Hollander and I slightly modified it to access current severity of BDD.

The BDD-YBOCS rates the severity of BDD symptoms during the past week. The first five items rate BDD-related *thoughts,* and the second five items rate BDD-related *behaviors.* The BDD-YBOCS also includes an insight item and an avoidance item.

This rating scale, like the BDD Diagnostic Module, is a semi-structured interview, meaning that the interviewer should assess the items in the listed order and ask the questions provided. However, the rater can ask additional questions to clarify responses. In general, the ratings should depend on the patient's report, but the final rating is based on the interviewer's clinical judgment.

If the person being assessed volunteers information at any time during the interview, that information should be considered. Ratings should be based primarily on reports and observations gained during the interview. Each item is rated for the time period *during the past week* up until and including the time of the interview. Scores should reflect the average occurrence of each item for the entire week. For questions 1 through 5 (which rate BDD-related thoughts), the *total* (composite) effect of *all* body parts of concern are rated. For items 6 through 10 (which rate BDD-related behaviors), the *total* (composite) effect of *all* behaviors is rated.

Before proceeding with questions 1 to 5, the rater must first determine that the person has BDD and must identify the body parts the person is excessively concerned with. The previously described BDD Diagnostic Module can be used for this purpose. BDD behaviors, which are assessed with questions 6 through

Body Dysmorphic Disorder Modification of the Y-BOCS (BDD-YBOCS)

For each item, circle the number identifying the response that best characterizes the person the **past week**.

1. **Time** occupied by thoughts about body defect

   How much of your time is occupied by THOUGHTS about a defect or flaw in your appearance (list body parts of concern)

   - 0 = None
   - 1 = Mild (less than 1 hr/day)
   - 2 = Moderate (1–3 hrs/day)
   - 3 = Severe (greater than 3 and up to 8 hrs/day)
   - 4 = Extreme (greater than 8 hrs/day)

2. **Interference** due to thoughts about body defect

   How much do your THOUGHTS about your body defect(s) interfere with your social or work (role) functioning? Is there anything you aren't doing or can't do because of them?

   - 0 = None
   - 1 = Mild, slight interference with social or occupational activities, but overall performance not impaired
   - 2 = Moderate, definite interference with social or occupational performance, but still manageable
   - 3 = Severe, causes substantial impairment in social or occupational performance
   - 4 = Extreme, incapacitating

3. **Distress** associated with thoughts about body defect

   How much distress do your THOUGHTS about your body defect(s) cause you?

   - 0 = None
   - 1 = Mild, and not too disturbing
   - 2 = Moderate and disturbing
   - 3 = Severe and very disturbing
   - 4 = Extreme and disabling distress

4. **Resistance** against thoughts of body defect

   How much of an effort do you make to resist these THOUGHTS? How often do you try to disregard them or turn your attention away from these thoughts as they enter your mind? (Only rate effort made to resist. NOT success or failure in actually controlling the thoughts)

   - 0 = Makes an effort to always resist, or symptoms so minimal doesn't need to actively resist
   - 1 = Tries to resist most of time
   - 2 = Makes some effort to resist
   - 3 = Yields to all such thoughts without attempting to control them but yields with some reluctance
   - 4 = Completely and willingly yields to all such thoughts

5. *Degree of control* over thoughts about body defect

How much control do you have over your THOUGHTS about your body defect(s)? How successful are you in stopping or diverting these thoughts?

0 = Complete control, or no need for control because thoughts are so minimal

1 = Much control, usually able to stop or divert these thoughts with some effort and concentration

2 = Moderate control, sometimes able to stop or divert these thoughts

3 = Little control, rarely successful in stopping thoughts, can only divert attention with difficulty

4 = No control, experienced as completely involuntary, rarely able to even momentarily divert attention

6. *Time* spent in activities related to body defect

How much time do you spend in ACTIVITIES related to your concern over your appearance (*read list of BDD rituals the person performs; see below*)

0 = None

1 = Mild (spends less than 1 hr/day)

2 = Moderate (1–3 hrs/day)

3 = Severe (spends more than 3 and up to 8 hrs/day)

4 = Extreme (spends more than 8 hrs/day in these activities)

Read list of activities (check all that apply)

_____ Checking mirrors/other surfaces
_____ Changing/selecting clothing
_____ Grooming activities
_____ Applying makeup
_____ Scrutinizing others' appearance/comparing
_____ Questioning others about your appearance/discussing your appearance
_____ Skin picking
_____ Touching the body areas
_____ Excessive exercise
_____ Other

7. *Interference* **due to activities related to the body defect**

   How much do these ACTIVITIES interfere with your social or work (role) functioning? Is there anything you don't do because of them?

   0 = None
   1 = Mild, slight interference with social, occupational, or role activities, but overall performance not impaired
   2 = Moderate, definite interference with social, occupational, or role performance, but still manageable
   3 = Severe, causes substantial impairment in social, occupational, or role performance
   4 = Extreme, incapacitating

8. *Distress* **associated with behaviors related to body defect**

   How would you feel if prevented from performing these ACTIVITIES? How anxious would you become? (*Rate degree of distress/frustration the person would feel if the behaviors were suddenly interrupted*)

   0 = None
   1 = Mild, only slightly anxious if behaviors were prevented
   2 = Moderate, reports that anxiety would mount but remain manageable if behaviors were prevented
   3 = Severe, prominent and very disturbing increase in anxiety if behaviors were interrupted
   4 = Extreme, incapacitating anxiety from any intervention aimed at modifying activities

9. **Resistance against compulsions**

   How much of an effort do you make to resist these ACTIVITIES? (*only rate effort made to resist, not success or failure in actually controlling the activities.*)

   0 = Makes an effort to always resist, or symptoms so minimal doesn't need to actively resist
   1 = Tries to resist most of the time
   2 = Makes some effort to resist
   3 = Yields to almost all of these behaviors without attempting to control them, but does so with some reluctance
   4. = Completely and willingly yields to all behaviors related to body defect

---

10. **Degree of control over compulsive behaviors**

    How strong is the drive to perform the BEHAVIORS? How much control do you have over them?

    0 = Complete control, or control is unnecessary because symptoms are mild
    1 = Much control, experiences pressure to perform the behaviors, but usually able to exercise voluntary control over them
    2 = Moderate control, strong pressure to perform behaviors, can control them only with difficulty
    3 = Little control, very strong drive to perform behaviors, must be carried to completion, can delay only with difficulty
    4 = No control, drive to perform behaviors experienced as completely involuntary and overpowering, rarely able to even momentarily delay activity

11. **Insight**

    It is possible that your defect might be less noticeable or less ugly than you think it is?

    How convinced are you that (name body part) is as unattractive as you think it is?

    Can anyone convince you that it doesn't look so bad?

    0 = Excellent insight, fully rational
    1 = Good insight. Readily acknowledges absurdity or unreasonableness of thoughts or behaviors but does not seem completely convinced that there isn't something besides anxiety to be concerned about
    2 = Fair insight. Reluctantly admits that thoughts or behaviors seem unreasonable but wavers
    3 = Poor insight. Maintains that thoughts or behaviors are not unreasonable
    4 = Lacks insight, delusional. Definitely convinced that concerns are reasonable, unresponsive to contrary evidence

Body Dysmorphic Disorder Modification of the Y-BOCS
(BDD-YBOCS) (continued)

12. **Avoidance**	0 = No deliberate avoidance
Have you been avoiding doing anything, going any place, or being with anyone because of your thoughts or behaviors related to your body defect? (*If YES, then ask:* How much do you avoid? *Rate degree to which patient deliberately tries to avoid things. Do not include avoidance of mirrors or rituals.*)	1 = Mild, minimal avoidance 2 = Moderate, some avoidance clearly present 3 = Severe, much avoidance; avoidance prominant 4 = Extreme, very extensive avoidance; patient avoids almost all activities

10, must also be identified before proceeding with the BDD-YBOCS. They can be identified by asking the person whether they engage in any behaviors in association with the appearance concern. Behaviors such as the following should be specifically asked about to determine whether they are present.

- Checking mirrors or other reflecting surfaces (or checking the body areas directly without a mirror)
- Seeking reassurance about the appearance of the body part or discussing it with others
- Asking others to look at or verify the existence of the "deformity"
- Requesting surgery, dermatologic treatment, or other treatment
- Comparing with others
- Touching the body part
- Grooming behaviors (e.g., hair combing, hair styling, or shaving)
- Skin picking
- Face washing and other cleansing routines
- Applying makeup
- Camouflaging (time spent applying it)
- Rearranging or selecting clothing to hide the "defect"
- Changing clothes
- Any other BDD-related behaviors (e.g., measuring, reading, dieting, excessive exercise, weight lifting or seeking information about how to fix the perceived flaw)

On repeated assessment, the body parts of concern and associated behaviors should be reviewed. The BDD-YBOCS can be used over time to assess improvement or worsening in the individual's symptoms.

This instrument has acceptable psychometric properties, with adequate interrater and test-retest reliability, frequency of item endorsement, internal consistency, and validity. It is also sensitive to improvement in symptoms with treatment.

More than 500 people with BDD who have participated in my studies (and who have met full criteria for BDD at the time they were assessed—which most have) have had an average BDD-YBOCS score of 31. Two thirds of people scored between 25 and 37. Although the BDD-YBOCS doesn't have an empirically derived cutpoint that designates the presence of clinically significant BDD, a reasonable guide is that a total score of 20 or higher would generally indicate the presence of current BDD. A total score of 24 or higher would generally indicate the presence of current BDD of at least moderate severity. Scores in the 20s generally designate milder-moderate BDD, scores in the 30s generally designate moderate to severe BDD, and scores in the 40s designate very severe BDD.

Other Severity Measures

The CGI differs from the BDD-YBOCS in that it rates severity of the disorder globally, with a single rating—for example, "moderately ill." It doesn't have separate items, nor does it provide questions to be asked by a clinician. The Clinical Global Impressions Scale (CGI) is a 7-point scale that is used in research of many psychiatric disorders; it measures current global severity of the disorder and can also be used to rate improvement or worsening of symptoms with treatment.

The Body Dysmorphic Disorder Examination (BDDE) is a semi-structured clinician-administered instrument developed by Dr. James Rosen to both diagnose BDD and assess its severity. This scale has the advantages of including various clinical features of BDD that the BDD Diagnostic Module doesn't include, and it assesses severity of individual BDD behaviors. The main disadvantages are that it is more suitable for patients with milder BDD, and it is fairly time consuming to administer.

Appendix D

Co-occurrence of BDD and Other Disorders

Table 21 on the next page shows the prevalence of BDD among individuals with other psychiatric disorders. These rates were obtained by the researchers indicated in the table's footnotes. Most of the studies from which the rates were obtained are referenced in Chapter 18.

Table 22 shows the converse: the rates of other psychiatric disorders among individuals with BDD whom I and my research team have assessed. The presence of these coexisting disorders was determined with the Structured Clinical Interview for DSM-III-R or DSM-IV (the SCID), which was discussed in Appendix C. A disorder is considered to be current if criteria have been fulfilled during the past month. The lifetime percentage indicates whether the disorder has *ever* been present, either currently or in the past.

Table 22 has two different sets of numbers. The first column, labeled "Clinical Sample," includes 307 people with BDD (175 who saw me for a clinical consultation and 132 who participated in my medication treatment studies). The second column of numbers, labeled "Interview Sample," consists of 200 individuals with BDD who are participating in my study of the course of BDD (how people with BDD do over time). This sample is broader than the one in the first column, as only two thirds of the interview study participants were seeking or receiving psychiatric treatment at the time of the interview and so may be more similar to people with BDD in the community. Other researchers have assessed rates of co-occurring disorders in much smaller samples; the findings are generally similar to those in Table 21, although they do vary somewhat from study to study. (Some of the journal articles that report these results are listed in Chapter 18).

Table 21. Percentage of Individuals with Other Disorders Who Have BDD

Psychiatric Disorder	Percent
MAJOR DEPRESSION	8% (28 of 350)[a]
Atypical major depression	14% (11 of 80)[b]
	42% (36 of 86)[c]
SOCIAL PHOBIA	11% (6 of 53)[d]
	12% (3 of 25)[e]
OBSESSIVE COMPULSIVE DISORDER	37% (25 of 68)[f]
	24% (158 of 646)[g]
	19% (30 of 161)[h]
	15% (9 of 62)[i]
	12% (51 of 442)[j]
	8% (3 of 40)[e]
	8% (4 of 53)[d]
	3% (6 of 231)[k]
TRICHOTILLOMANIA	26% (6 of 23)[l]
PANIC DISORDER	2% (1 of 47)[d]
GENERALIZED ANXIETY DISORDER	0% (0 of 32)[d]
POST-TRAUMATIC STRESS DISORDER	20% (11 of 55)[m]
ANOREXIA NERVOSA	39% (16 of 41)[n]
SCHIZOPHRENIA	4% (4 of 110)[o]
PSYCHIATRIC INPATIENTS WITH VARIOUS DISORDERS	13% (16 of 122)[p]
Major depression	21% (12 of 57)[p]
Substance use disorder	26% (16 of 61)[p]

[a]Nierenberg AA, Phillips KA, Peterson, et al., 2002; the rate of BDD in people with atypical depression (14 %) was higher than in those with non-atypical depression (5%)
[b]Phillips KA, Nierenberg AA, Brendel G. et al., 1996
[c]Perugi G, Akiskal HS, Latanzi L, et al., 1998
[d]Brawman-Mintzer O, Lydiard RB, Phillips KA, et al., 1995
[e]Wilhelm S, Otto MW, Zucker BG, et al., 1997
[f]Hollander E, Cohen LJ, Simeon D, 1993
[g]Hantouche EG, Bourgeois ML, Bouhassira M, et al. (the 646 subjects had definite or probable OCD or an OCD-spectrum disorder [e.g., trichotillomania])
[h]Diniz JB, Rosario-Campos MC, Shavitt RG, et al., 2004
[i]Phillips KA, Gunderson CG, McElroy SL, et al., 1998
[j]Simeon D, Hollander E, Stein DJ, et al., 1995
[k]Jaisoorya TS, Reddy J, Srinath S, 2003
[l]Soriano JL, O'Sullivan RL, Baer L, et al., 1996
[m]Zlotnick C, Phillips KA, Pearistein T
[n]Grant JE, Kim SW, Eckert ED, 2002
[o]Poyurovsky M, Kriss V, Weisman G, et al., 2003
[p]Grant JE, Kim SW, Crow SJ, 2001

Table 22. **Percentage of Adults with BDD Who Have Another Disorder**[a]

Psychiatric Disorder	Clinical Sample[a]		Interview Sample[a]	
	Current[b]	Lifetime[b]	Current[b]	Lifetime[b]
MOOD DISORDERS				
Major depression	58%	76%	35%	75%
Bipolar disorder	8%[c]	9%[c]	16%	8%
Dysthymic disorder[d]	6%		8%	
Total[e]	69%	87%	46%	84%
ANXIETY DISORDERS				
Panic disorder	7%	13%	9%	20%
Agoraphobia	3%	3%	1%	2%
Social phobia[f]	32%	37%	32%	39%
Specific phobia	8%	10%	16%	20%
Obsessive compulsive disorder	25%	32%	24%	33%
Post-traumatic stress disorder[g]			4%	9%
Generalized anxiety disorder[d]	0%		4%	
Total[e]	55%	64%	56%	70%
PSYCHOTIC DISORDERS[d,h]				
Schizophrenia	0%	0%		
Schizoaffective disorder	.01%	.01%		
Total	.01%	.01%		3%
SUBSTANCE-RELATED DISORDERS				
Alcohol	7%[c]	20%	8%	43%
Other drug	7%[c]	17%	11%	34%
Total[e]	13%[c]	28%	16%	48%
SOMATOFORM DISORDERS[d]				
Somatization disorder	1%		0%	
Pain disorder	3%		0%	
Hypochondriasis	5%		2%	
Total[a,e]	7%		2%	
EATING DISORDERS				
Anorexia nervosa	1%	3%	1%	9%
Bulimia nervosa	3%	8%	3%	7%
Total[e]	4%	10%	4%	15%

(continued)

Table 22.   *Percentage of Adults with BDD Who Have*
Another Disorder[a]   (continued)

Psychiatric Disorder	Clinical Sample[a]		Interview Sample[a]	
	Current[b]	Lifetime[b]	Current[b]	Lifetime[b]
TRICHOTILLOMANIA	2%	2%	1%	3%
TOURETTE'S SYNDROME[i]	0%	0%		3%
OLFACTORY REFERENCE SYNDROME[d]				4%

[a]These results are from my two BDD series. For the Clinical Sample, DSM-III-R criteria were used; for the interview sample DSM-IV criteria were used. For detailed results for the clinical sample see Gunstad and Phillips, 2003
[b]Current = past month. Lifetime = ever, including past month
[c]Results are reported only for individuals who sought a clinical consultation, not those who participated in a treatment study, because the treatment studies excluded people with these disorders, which would skew the results. The mood disorders' total is also for the clinical consultation group only, because the treatment studies excluded people with bipolar disorder.
[d]Columns are blank because we assessed only the current or lifetime presence of these disorders or the disorder was not assessed at all in one of the studies.
[e]Because some individuals had more than one disorder in a given category, the total for that category may be smaller than the sum of the individual disorders in the category. For example, 3% of individuals had lifetime anorexia nervosa, 8% had lifetime bulimia, but 1% had both anorexia and bulimia, so the total lifetime percent for the eating disorder category is 10%, not 11%.
[f]This rate applies only to "primary" social phobia—that is, social phobia that doesn't appear to be largely due to BDD. If social anxiety due to BDD were included, the percentages would be much higher.
[g]PTSD was assessed only in the interview sample.
[h]Excluding delusional BDD; in the interview study, individual psychotic disorders were not diagnosed.
[i]In the interview study, any tic disorder was assessed (rather than Tourette's Syndrome).

GLOSSARY

Amygdala   A small almond-shaped structure deep in the brain. It is important for processing stimuli that communicate emotional significance in social situations, such as emotional facial expressions. It also evaluates the environment for possible threat and evokes fear and a behavioral response (e.g., escape).

Anafranil   See clomipramine.

Antidepressant   A class of medications effective for treating depression as well as a variety of disorders, such as dysthymia, panic disorder, social phobia, eating disorders, obsessive compulsive disorder, hypochondriasis, and others. Certain antidepressants are also used to treat nonpsychiatric disorders, such as headache and pain syndromes. There are many different types of antidepressant medications.

Augmentation   The addition of a medication to a "primary" medication to boost its effect. This approach is commonly used for depression and other disorders. In BDD, the augmenting medication is usually added to an SRI.

BDD-YBOCS   A scale that assesses severity of BDD symptoms during the past week. See Appendix C.

Behavioral experiment   This is an experiment that a person designs and carries out to collect evidence for and against a particular hypothesis. The purpose is to objectively determine whether or not the hypothesis is true. This technique is used in cognitive-behavioral therapy.

Benzodiazepine   A type of medication used primarily to treat anxiety and insomnia.

Buspirone (Buspar)   A type of antianxiety medication with effects on serotonin. It is sometimes used to augment an SRI when treating BDD.

Caudate   The caudate is a C-shaped structure deep in the brain's core, which is involved in regulating voluntary movements, habits, and cognitions (e.g., memory). It is probably involved in BDD.

CBT   See cognitive-behavioral therapy.

Celexa   See escitalopram.

Citalopram (Celexa)   A type of serotonin-reuptake inhibitor (a class of medications with antiobsessional and anticompulsive properties).

Clomipramine (Anafranil)   A type of serotonin-reuptake inhibitor (a class of antidepressant medications with antiobsessional and anticompulsive properties).

Cognitive-behavioral therapy (CBT)   A broad term that encompasses a number of specific therapeutic approaches. The *cognitive* aspect focuses on cognitions—that is, thoughts and beliefs. The goal of cognitive therapy is to identify, evaluate, and change distorted, unrealistic, and unhelpful ways of thinking. The *behavioral* aspect focuses on problematic behaviors, such as excessive checking and social avoidance. The aim is to stop performing such behaviors and substitute healthier behaviors. Often, cognitive and behavioral approaches are combined—hence, the commonly used term "cognitive-behavioral therapy," or CBT. CBT is used to treat disorders such as depression, phobias, panic disorder, obsessive-compulsive disorder, eating disorders, among others. It is currently the therapy of choice for BDD.

Cognitive errors   Also known as thinking errors. These are ways of distorted thinking that fuel negative automatic thoughts. Examples of cognitive errors are mind reading, fortunetelling, and catastrophizing. During cognitive restructuring, cognitive errors are identified, and more rational and helpful alternative beliefs are generated.

Cognitive restructuring: A component of cognitive therapy and, more broadly, cognitive-behavioral therapy. Cognitive restructuring involves learning to identify and evaluate negative thoughts and beliefs as well as cognitive errors. This process generates more accurate and helpful beliefs.

Cognitive therapy   Cognitive therapy is a very practical, here-and-now treatment that teaches specific skills and uses cognitive approaches to learning. It is used to treat a host of psychiatric disorders, including BDD. It includes cognitive restructuring. In BDD and many other disorders, cognitive therapy is combined with behavioral techniques—hence, the term cognitive-behavioral therapy.

Compulsion   A repetitive behavior (e.g., hand washing or checking) or mental act (e.g., counting) performed in response to an obsession and aimed at preventing or reducing distress or a dreaded event. May also be referred to as a "ritual." Compulsions are usually difficult to resist or control. They are characteristic of obsessive compulsive disorder and BDD (e.g., mirror checking and reassurance seeking).

Controlled study   A type of study in which the treatment being investigated is compared to another type of treatment received by a "control group." The control group may receive a standard and proven treatment, a competing experimental treatment, no treatment (e.g., they may be on a treatment waiting list), or a placebo. A placebo in a medication trial is an inert substance (e.g., a "sugar pill") that physically resembles the treatment under investigation. If treatment is shown in a controlled study to be as effective as a proven treatment, or more effective than placebo, this is strong evidence that the treatment is effective.

Delusion (delusional thinking) A false belief based on incorrect inference about external reality that is firmly sustained despite what almost everyone else believes.

Delusional BDD A form of BDD in which the belief about the appearance defect is held with absolute conviction and certainty. This form of BDD is probably the same disorder as the nondelusional form of BDD, in which the person can acknowledge that their view of the defect may be distorted or inaccurate.

Diagnostic instrument A questionnaire filled out by patients, or a set of questions asked by clinicians, that is used to make psychiatric diagnoses. Usually, the instrument asks questions that determine whether DSM criteria for a disorder are met. Diagnostic instruments for BDD are included in Chapter 4 and Appendix C.

Dopamine One of the brain's many neurotransmitters (chemical messengers transmitted between nerve cells). Dopamine plays an important role in certain movement disorders and in many psychiatric disorders, especially those characterized by delusional thinking and hallucinations.

DSM DSM stands for Diagnostic and Statistical Manual of Mental Disorders. It contains the official classification and nomenclature system for psychiatric disorders used in the U.S. Disorders in DSM are defined by diagnostic criteria that describe their essential features.

> **DSM-III-R** The version of DSM in use from 1987 to 1993.

> **DSM-IV** The current version of DSM, published in 1994.

> **DSM-IV-TR** This version has the same diagnostic criteria as DSM-IV, but the descriptive text has been updated.

Dysmorphophobia A previous term for BDD. It is sometimes used in a broader sense than BDD, to refer not only to the specific disorder BDD but to any excessive preoccupation with a minimal or nonexistent defect in appearance.

Electroconvulsive therapy (ECT) Also known as shock therapy, this is a very effective treatment for depression. It is usually reserved for more severe depression that hasn't responded to antidepressant medication.

Escitalopram (Lexapro) A type of serotonin-reuptake inhibitor (a class of antidepressant medications with antiobsessional and anticompulsive properties).

Exposure   A component of cognitive-behavioral therapy effective for obsessive compulsive disorder and other disorders. *Exposure* consists of facing feared and avoided situations—for example, social situations or work. Exposure is combined with response prevention, which consists of not engaging in compulsive behaviors. When treating BDD, exposure is often also combined with a behavioral experiment.

Exposure hierarchy   A method used in exposure therapy consisting of a list of situations that cause anxiety. The situations are rated according to how much anxiety they produce and how much they're avoided.

Fluoxetine (Prozac)   A type of serotonin-reuptake inhibitor (a class of antidepressant medications with antiobsessional and anticompulsive properties).

Fluvoxamine (Luvox)   A type of serotonin-reuptake inhibitor (a class of antidepressant medications with antiobsessional and anticompulsive properties).

GABA (γ-amino-butyric acid)   One of the many new neurotransmitters (chemical messengers) in the brain. GABA is ubiquitous in the brain and is the primary inhibitory neurotransmitter.

Habit Reversal   This is an established treatment for trichotillomania (hair pulling) that's increasing being used for other problematic habits, such as skin picking. It consists of awareness training, learning a competing response, relaxation, rewarding yourself for not picking, and learning to use habit reversal in a wide range of situations.

Hallucination   A sensory perception that seems real but occurs without external stimulation of sensory organs. Hallucinations may be visual (involving sight), auditory (involving hearing), somatic (involving a bodily sensation), tactile (involving the skin), olfactory (involving smell), or gustatory (involving taste).

ICD-10   The current international classification and nomenclature system for medical and psychiatric disorders published by the World Health Organization. Its psychiatric classification system is very similar to that of DSM-IV.

Ideas of reference   The belief that casual incidents and events have a special meaning that is specific to the person. This is a type of **referential thinking.**

Illusion   A misperception or misinterpretation of a real external stimulus, such as hearing running water as the sound of whispering.

Insight-oriented psychotherapy   Also known as psychodynamic or exploratory psychotherapy, this is a type of "talking therapy." It focuses on increasing self-awareness and bringing about behavioral change (e.g., improving relationship with others) through exploration of one's perceptions and interactions with others.

Insomnia   A subjective complaint of difficulty sleeping.

Lexapro   See escitalopram.

Luvox   See fluvoxamine.

Magical thinking   The erroneous belief that one's thoughts, words, or actions will cause or prevent a specific outcome in a way that defies commonly understood laws of cause and effect.

MAOI (MAO inhibitor)   A class of antidepressant medication.

Minoxidil   A medication taken to promote hair growth.

Mindfulness   Mindfulness skills are psychological and behavioral versions of meditation practices from Eastern spiritual training. They involve a particular way of observing and being aware of your thoughts and emotions by focusing on them "in the moment" in a nonjudgmental way. Mindfulness is used in the treatment of certain psychiatric disorders and is a potentially useful addition to the core CBT approaches for BDD.

Mirror retraining   A technique used in cognitive-behavioral therapy that focuses on 1) learning to look at your *entire* face or body (not just the disliked areas) while looking in the mirror, and 2) learning to *objectively* (rather than negatively) describe your body while looking in the mirror.

Morphometric magnetic resonance imaging (MRI)   This is a brain imaging technique used commonly in medicine. It provides a picture of the brain's structure. Functional MRI provides a picture of the brain's activity.

Muscle dysmorphia   A form of BDD in which people—usually boys and men—think they're too small, thin, or inadequately muscular, even though they look normal or even unusually muscular.

Neuroleptic   A type of medication used to treat Tourette's disorder, delusional disorder, schizophrenia, bipolar disorder (manic depressive illness) and other disorders. Neuroleptics may also be used in combination with other medication to treat obsessive compulsive disorder and major depression. They are sometimes used to treat nausea. They are also known as an antipsychotic, even though they are commonly used to treat symptoms other than psychosis.

Neuropsychological studies   Studies that use neuropsychological tests to assess brain function. These tests often consist of cognitive (e.g., language, memory, or attention) or sensorimotor (e.g., perception, ability to draw a line, finger tapping) tasks.

Neurotransmitter   A type of chemical messenger in the brain that transmits messages between neurons (nerve cells). There are many types of neurotransmitters, which include serotonin, norepinephrine, GABA, and dopamine. Abnormal functioning of brain neurotransmitters is implicated in many neurological and psychiatric disorders.

Obsession   A recurrent, persistent, and intrusive thought, impulse, or image that is difficult to dismiss despite its disturbing nature. Obsessional thinking is characteristic of obsessive compulsive disorder as well as BDD.

Obsessive compulsive spectrum disorders (OCD–spectrum disorders)   A grouping of disorders postulated to be related to obsessive compulsive disorder on the basis of similarities in symptoms and other characteristics. BDD is widely considered an OCD–spectrum disorder because of its many similarities to OCD.

Occipitotemporal cortex   A region towards the back of the brain between the occipital and temporal lobes. It contains the fusiform face area, which responds selectively to visual images of human faces. It also contains the extrastriate body area, which responds to visual images of human bodies and non-face body parts. These areas may be important in BDD.

OCD   See obsessive compulsive disorder.

Open study   An uncontrolled study in which both the patient and the doctor know what treatment the patient is receiving.

Orbitofrontal cortex   An area on the bottom of the front part of the brain that's involved in memory and social functioning. This area plays an important role in OCD and may also be important in BDD.

Orbitofrontal-striatal-thalamic circuit ("worry loop")   This brain circuit connects the orbitofrontal cortex, striatum (which includes the caudate), thalamus, and other nearby brain structures. It plays an important role in OCD and may also be involved in BDD.

Overvalued idea   An unreasonable and sustained belief that is held with less than delusional intensity (i.e., the person is able to acknowledge the possibility that the belief may not be true). Synonymous with poor insight.

Parietal lobe   An area on the upper sides of the brain towards its back that has many functions. It plays a role in body image and may be important in BDD.

Paroxetine (Paxil)   A type of serotonin-reuptake inhibitor (a class of antidepressant medications with antiobsessional and anticompulsive properties.)

Paxil   See paroxetine.

Pimozide (Orap)   A type of neuroleptic medication.

Placebo   In a medication study, an inert substance, sometimes called a "sugar pill," that physically resembles the treatment being studied. The patient is unable to discriminate between the placebo pill and active treatment and is unaware of which treatment he or she is receiving. In a "double-blind" trial, the physician is also unaware of whether the patient is receiving placebo or active treatment. This study design guards against bias in assessing treatment outcome. If the treatment being studied is more effective than placebo, this is strong evidence that it is effective.

Prospective study   A study that is done "forward over time." In other words, such studies measure characteristics or events as they occur after the study has started. In contrast, retrospective studies are done "backward over time," in that they collect data about events that have already occurred.

Prozac   See fluoxetine.

Referential thinking   The belief that casual incidents and events have a special meaning that is specific to the person. Includes ideas of reference and delusions of reference.

Refocusing   This technique involves gently focusing your attention and thoughts on what's going on around you rather than on BDD thoughts. It can be a useful addition to the core CBT treatments for BDD.

Response (ritual) prevention   An aspect of behavioral therapy in which repetitive behaviors, such as excessive mirror checking, are resisted. Also known as **ritual prevention.**

Retrospective study   A study done "backward over time"; in other words, data are collected about events that have already occurred. This is in contrast to a prospective study, in which data are collected about events or characteristics at the time they actually occur.

Ritual   Another term for a compulsion—that is, a repetitive behavior (e.g., hand washing and checking) or mental act (e.g., counting) performed in response to an obsession and aimed at preventing or reducing distress or a dreaded event.

Selective serotonin-reuptake inhibitor (SSRI)   A type of serotonin-reuptake inhibitor (SRI) that has prominent effects on serotonin but little direct effect on other neurotransmitters. The SSRIs are fluoxetine (Prozac), fluvoxamine (Luvox), paroxetine (Paxil), sertraline (Zoloft), escitalopram (Lexapro), and citalopram(Celexa).(Clomipramine [Anafranil], an SRI, has fairly prominent effects on the neurotransmitter norepinephrine in addition to serotonin.)

Serotonin   One of the many neurotransmitters (chemical messengers) in the brain. Serotonin plays an important role in mood, sleep, appetite, pain, and other bodily functions. Abnormal functioning of serotonin is involved in a wide variety of psychiatric disorders, including depression, obsessive compulsive disorder, and eating disorders. It probably plays an important role in BDD.

Serotonin-reuptake inhibitor (SRI)   A class of antidepressant medication with prominent effects on serotonin. This is a broader term that encompasses the narrower term SSRI. Unlike other antidepressants, SRIs have anti-obsessional and anti-compulsive properties, and they effectively treat obsessive compulsive disorder. The SRIs currently marketed in the U.S. are clomipramine

(Anafranil), fluoxetine (Prozac), fluvoxamine (Luvox), paroxetine (Paxil), sertraline (Zoloft), citalopram (Celexa), and escitalopram (Lexapro).

Serotonin transporter gene   This gene codes for a protein (the serotonin transporter) that's like a molecular "vacuum cleaner" which sucks up serotonin from the spaces (synapses) between brain nerve cells. The serotonin transporter is also the main target of the SRIs. Very preliminary evidence suggests that this gene may play a role in causing BDD.

Sertraline (Zoloft)   A type of serotonin-reuptake inhibitor (a class of antidepressant medications with antiobsessional and anticompulsive properties).

SRI   See serotonin reuptake inhibitor.

SSRI   See selective serotonin reuptake inhibitor.

Striatum   A part of the brain that consists of the caudate and an area called the putamen. This area is involved in regulating voluntary movements, habits, and cognitions (e.g., memory). It's important in OCD and other disorders, and may be important in BDD.

Supportive psychotherapy   A type of talking therapy that focuses on the creation of emotional support and a stable, caring relationship with patients. The therapist focuses more on providing support than on increasing patients' understanding of themselves. Advice, learning new social skills, and assistance in problem solving are often components of this approach.

Thought record   A form used in cognitive restructuring (see Chapter 15 for examples).

Zoloft   See sertraline.

INDEX

Lightning Source UK Ltd.
Milton Keynes UK
22 November 2010

163274UK00002B/21/P